FOR DUMMIES™

BUSINESS AND
GENERAL
REFERENCE
BOOK SERIES
FROM IDG

Successful Presentations For Dummies

Cheat Sheet

W9-CDJ-712

Preparation

1. Don't get talked into making a presentation that you don't want to make.
2. Organize your information in a simple pattern that the audience can easily recognize.
3. Use various types of material — examples, stories, statistics, quotes — to maintain audience interest.
4. Use your introduction to set the audience's expectations.
5. Have a special conclusion ready that you can go right into if you run out of time. Never omit a conclusion.
6. Anticipate the questions you'll be asked and have answers ready.
7. Practice out loud.

The Room

1. Get to the room early so that you have time to make changes if it's set up improperly.
2. Close the curtains so that the audience can't stare out the windows.
3. Control audience seating. Make sure that chairs and tables are arranged in the configuration that you want. Remove extra chairs.
4. Check the microphone and sound system while standing exactly where you'll be using them.
5. Make sure that the room isn't too cold or too stuffy.
6. Find out exactly where the room is located and how long it will take you to get there.

Delivery

1. If standing behind a podium makes you feel more comfortable, do it.
2. Try to establish eye contact with your entire audience.
3. Vary the rate, pitch, and volume of your voice, as well as its tone.
4. Don't stand with your hands clasped in front of your crotch.
5. Look at the audience more than your notes.
6. Don't pace back and forth, jingle change in your pocket, or play with your hair.
7. Convey enthusiasm for your subject. It's contagious.

Successful Presentations For Dummies™

Cheat Sheet

BUSINESS AND GENERAL REFERENCE BOOK SERIES FROM IDG

Using Humor

1. Make sure that your humor relates to a point in your presentation.

2. Avoid sexist, ethnic, racist, and off-color humor.

3. Make offensive jokes acceptable by changing their targets from ethnic groups to rival organizations.

4. If you can't tell a joke well, use humor that doesn't require comic delivery: a personal anecdote, funny quotation, or amusing analogy.

5. Build rapport by poking fun at yourself — appropriately.

Visual Aids

1. Don't make slides and overheads that are difficult to read. Avoid too many words per line, too many colors, and designs that are too busy or too small.

2. Check text for spelling errors.

3. Take advantage of computer software templates that help you design visual aids.

4. You know you need time to design slides and overheads. Don't forget to leave time to *produce* them.

5. Number all your slides and overheads.

6. You can't check the working condition of the slide or overhead projector too many times.

7. Bring an extension cord and adapter.

Managing Stage Fright

1. Alcohol and pills don't work. If they wear off before you speak, you'll be even more nervous. If they don't, you'll be incoherent.

2. Channel nervous tension into your performance.

3. Work off nervous energy by taking a few deep breaths.

4. Leave time to go to the bathroom shortly before you speak.

5. Remember that the audience wants you to succeed.

...For Dummies: The Best-Selling Book Series

Praise for Malcolm Kushner

The Author

"In an hour's time, he taught me practical techniques for dramatically improving my communications with humor, while bringing my audience and me great fun."
> — Richard Weise, Senior Vice President, General Counsel and Secretary, Motorola

"Our audience of over 500 was delightfully entertained while gaining valuable ideas for effective communication in the workplace."
> — Curtis Malone, AT&T Network Systems

"I have managed the dinner program for several years and have never had a dinner speaker earn such high praises."
> — Marcia McCann, Program Manager (UNIX Symposium), Digital Equipment Corp.

"He was dynamic. He was exciting. He successfully combined humor and information, making each point memorable."
> — James E. Harris III, General Manager, Integrated Storage Products Division, Sony Electronics

"Members were delighted with your entertaining, absorbing and very useful advice on dealing with the many stressful and humorless situations we encounter each day."
> — Nancy Klossner, Executive Director, Minnesota Trial Lawyers Association

"Your seminars broke all our past attendance records. Moreover, the evaluations were the highest we have received over the past twenty years."
> — John Dunn, Education Chair, Law Practice Management Section

Kushner's *The Light Touch*

"Highly recommended."
> — *Library Journal*

"A light, amusing and practical book that should be on every executive's desk. . . ."
> — United Press International

"Kushner's book offers insightful techniques that anyone can use to anticipate awkward or tense situations and prepare humorous responses that will seem spontaneous. . . ."
— *San Francisco Chronicle*

"His anecdotal, how-to approach is at least as much fun as a night at the local comedy club. . . ."
— *The Dallas Morning News*

"More than just a book about incorporating jokes into public speaking, *The Light Touch* concerns itself with management and its problems, including motivating others, improving productivity, and getting out of awkward business situations."
— *Publishers Weekly*

"If there are two books you should read this year, this book is both of them."
— *Communication World*

". . . an entertaining, as well as useful, read."
— *Seattle Times*

BUSINESS AND GENERAL REFERENCE BOOK SERIES FROM IDG

References for the Rest of Us!™

Do you find that traditional reference books are overloaded with technical details and advice you'll never use? Do you postpone important life decisions because you just don't want to deal with them? Then our *...For Dummies*™ business and general reference book series is for you.

...For Dummies business and general reference books are written for those frustrated and hard-working souls who know they aren't dumb, but find that the myriad of personal and business issues and the accompanying horror stories make them feel helpless. *...For Dummies* books use a lighthearted approach, a down-to-earth style, and even cartoons and humorous icons to diffuse fears and build confidence. Lighthearted but not lightweight, these books are perfect survival guides to solve your everyday personal and business problems.

> *"More than a publishing phenomenon, 'Dummies' is a sign of the times."*
> — The New York Times

> *"... you won't go wrong buying them."*
> — Walter Mossberg, Wall Street Journal, on IDG's ...For Dummies™ books

> *"A world of detailed and authoritative information is packed into them..."*
> — U.S. News and World Report

Already, hundreds of thousands of satisfied readers agree. They have made *...For Dummies* the #1 introductory level computer book series and a best-selling business book series. They have written asking for more. So, if you're looking for the best and easiest way to learn about business and other general reference topics, look to *...For Dummies* to give you a helping hand.

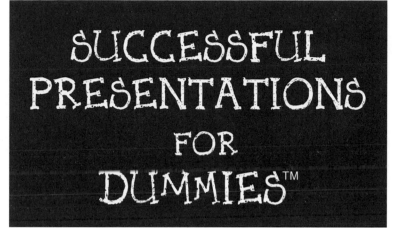

SUCCESSFUL PRESENTATIONS FOR DUMMIES™

by Malcolm Kushner

Foreword by Norman R. Augustine
President and CEO, Lockheed Martin

IDG Books Worldwide, Inc.
An International Data Group Company

Foster City, CA ♦ Chicago, IL ♦ Indianapolis, IN ♦ Braintree, MA ♦ Dallas, TX

Successful Presentations For Dummies™

Published by
IDG Books Worldwide, Inc.
An International Data Group Company
919 E. Hillsdale Blvd.
Suite 400
Foster City, CA 94404

Library of Congress Catalog Card No.: 95-81964

ISBN: 1-56884-392-5

Printed in the United States of America

10 9 8 7 6 5 4 3 2 1

1A/RX/QR/ZW

Distributed in the United States by IDG Books Worldwide, Inc.

Distributed by Macmillan Canada for Canada; by Computer and Technical Books for the Caribbean Basin; by Contemporanea de Ediciones for Venezuela; by Distribuidora Cuspide for Argentina; by CITEC for Brazil; by Ediciones ZETA S.C.R. Ltda. for Peru; by Editorial Limusa SA for Mexico; by Transworld Publishers Limited in the United Kingdom and Europe; by Al-Maiman Publishers & Distributors for Saudi Arabia; by Simron Pty. Ltd. for South Africa; by IDG Communications (HK) Ltd. for Hong Kong; by Toppan Company Ltd. for Japan; by Addison Wesley Publishing Company for Korea; by Longman Singapore Publishers Ltd. for Singapore, Malaysia, Thailand, and Indonesia; by Unalis Corporation for Taiwan; by WS Computer Publishing Company, Inc. for the Philippines; by WoodsLane Pty. Ltd. for Australia; by WoodsLane Enterprises Ltd. for New Zealand.

For general information on IDG Books Worldwide's books in the U.S., please call our Consumer Customer Service department at 800-762-2974. For reseller information, including discounts and premium sales, please call our Reseller Customer Service department at 800-434-3422.

For information on where to purchase IDG Books Worldwide's books outside the U.S., contact IDG Books Worldwide at 415-655-3021 or fax 415-655-3295.

For information on translations, contact Marc Jeffrey Mikulich, Director, Foreign & Subsidiary Rights, at IDG Books Worldwide, 415-655-3018 or fax 415-655-3295.

For sales inquiries and special prices for bulk quantities, write to the address above or call IDG Books Worldwide at 415-655-3200.

For information on using IDG Books Worldwide's books in the classroom, or ordering examination copies, contact Jim Kelly, Director of Corporate, Education and Government sales, at IDG Books Worldwide, 800-434-2086.

For authorization to photocopy items for corporate, personal, or educational use, please contact Copyright Clearance Center, 222 Rosewood Drive, Danvers, MA 01923, or fax 508-750-4470.

is a trademark under exclusive license to IDG Books Worldwide, Inc., from International Data Group, Inc.

About the Author

Photograph taken by
Paula Court.

Malcolm Kushner, "America's Favorite Humor Consultant," is an internationally acclaimed expert on humor and communication and a professional speaker. Since 1982, he has trained thousands of managers, executives, and professionals on how to gain a competitive edge with humor. His clients include IBM, Hewlett-Packard, AT&T, Chevron, Aetna, Motorola, Sony, and Digital Equipment Corporation.

A popular speaker at corporate and association meetings, Kushner was a keynote speaker at the 1994 Inc. 500 Conference and a featured speaker at the 1994 APICS Top Management Summit. His five-city lecture tour sponsored by the State Bar of California Law Practice Management Section in 1992 received the highest evaluations over the last 20 years and broke all past attendance records.

Kushner has also written speeches for some of the nation's leading corporate executives. His work has included everything from employee pep talks and commencement speeches to Congressional testimony.

A Phi Beta Kappa graduate of the University of Buffalo, Kushner holds a B.A. in Speech-Communication. His M.A. in Speech-Communication is from the University of Southern California, where he taught freshman speech. He also has a J.D. from the University of California Hastings College of the Law. Prior to becoming a humor consultant, he practiced law with a major San Francisco law firm.

Kushner is the author of *The Light Touch: How to Use Humor for Business Success* (Simon & Schuster). Widely praised, it has been translated into five languages. He is also co-creator of *Well...There You Go Again: The Humor That Shaped America (Volume I)* — the first multimedia product devoted to Ronald Reagan's speeches and humor. It is now on display at the Ronald Reagan Presidential Library.

Frequently interviewed by the media, Kushner has been profiled in *Time* Magazine, *USA Today*, *The New York Times,* and numerous other publications. His television and radio appearances include CNN, National Public Radio, CNBC, "Voice of America," and "The Larry King Show."

Kushner is also the creator of the widely quoted "Cost of Laughing Index" — a price index of the 16 leading humor indicators in America. This annual index has been featured on *Good Morning America*, *The Tonight Show,* and the front page of *The Wall Street Journal.*

Need a great speaker for your next meeting or convention? Contact Malcolm at P.O. Box 7509, Santa Cruz, CA 95061 or call 408-425-4839.

Dedication

This book is dedicated to my parents — Pauline, Hank, and Helen. Thank you for all your love and support.

Acknowledgments

"You love me. You really love me." (Oops, I thought this was my Academy Awards speech.) This is actually the speech about people I love. Let's start with the people at IDG books. My thanks go to Marc Mikulich for talking me into writing this book and to Kathy Welton for making it happen; to Stephanie Britt for being a superb managing editor; to Stacy Collins for extraordinary promotional efforts; and to Mary Bednarek for permissions wizardry. And very special thanks and kudos go to Tim Gallan who had to actually edit the book in between taking all my phone calls and listening to me kvetch. Thanks also to editors Michael Simsic and Diana Conover.

Speaking of special thanks, I must shower praise upon my wife, Christine Griger, who edited my work as it came out of the printer. (Tim, if you think *your* job was tough, you should have seen what the stuff looked like *before* Chris's edits!) And I must also thank my five-year-old son, Sam, who occasionally stopped asking me to play with him and allowed me to write.

Special editorial thanks also go to San Francisco comedy coach John Cantu who went above and beyond the call of friendship by providing a continuous sounding board to bounce around ideas. His unerring instinct in going for the comic jugular helped sharpen many of the jokes in the book. Loyd Auerbach, Allatia Harris, and N.R. Mitgang also received repeated calls to tap into their expertise — and came through every time.

I also want to thank all the other people who were interviewed for the book. They gave generously of their time and expertise, selflessly sharing the secrets of their success. They include John Austin, Neil Baron, Donna Bedford, J.E. Aeliot Boswell, Rachael Brune, Joe DiNucci, Steve Fraticelli, James Harris III, Barbara Howard, Joyce Lekas, Marcia Lemmons, Jim Lukaszweski, Chuck McCann, Jeff Raleigh, Steve Resnick, Jackie Roach, Zack Russ, David Schmidt, Ken Sereno, Alan Weiner, and Bill Zachmeier. (I've probably forgotten someone, and if I did, I apologize.)

Thanks for support and encouragement go to Rich Herzfeld, Bob Reed, Jack Burkett, Stu Silverstein, Linda Mead, Debra DeCuir, Karen Kushner, Barabra Nash, and Arthur, Karen, Heather, and Amy Tamarkin. Thanks for fabulous research assistance goes to the reference librarians at the main branch of the Santa Cruz Public Library. Extra special thanks go to Tom Daly IV at *Vital Speeches* for granting permission to use so many of the quotes contained in the book. And thanks to Norman Augustine for taking time out from running one of the nation's largest companies to write the foreword.

I love you. I really love you all.

(The Publisher would like to give special thanks to Patrick J. McGovern and Bill Murphy, without whom this book would not have been possible.)

Credits

Contents at a Glance

Cartoons at a Glance

By Rich Tennant

Table of Contents

Foreword

My hands trembled as I held the letter asking me to write a foreword for an upcoming book and wondered what I should do. The message had come unsolicited from someone I did not know. Being an author myself, I knew full well the mental turmoil that writing such a foreword would entail. My schedule was booked solid for months to come. I had every justification to respond with a polite "No thank you."

And yet, the anguished appeal intrigued me. "Twelve years ago, I was an attorney with an international corporate law firm. Today, I'm a humor consultant. Whether or not you think the world needs a humor consultant, I'm sure you'll agree we can use one less attorney." The logic was unassailable, the candor refreshingly frank. I was reminded of a similarly mournful letter I received some years ago from Laurence Peter of *Peter Principle* fame. After reading my book, *Augustine's Laws*, he despondently wrote to inform me, "You have undermined my entire life's work. You have risen not one but two levels above your level of competence."

After that tragic turn of events, I knew I could not turn my back on Malcolm Kushner. He was a lawyer — it's true — but a *recovering* lawyer. The only risk I faced was that if my daughter, a practicing lawyer, were to see this, she would undoubtedly carry out her earlier threat relating to some other matter to sue me — that is, to sue me as soon as I finished paying her way through law school. Nonetheless, it was my duty to help Mr. Kushner with this small gesture. Hence, this foreword.

Malcolm Kushner categorizes himself as a business humor consultant — one of a truly rare breed. Some years ago, the first management guru decreed that business and humor do not mix. From that moment, it has been axiomatic that executives have favored bottom lines over punch lines. Except for the odd — and usually lame — opening joke of a speech, no executive would risk the opprobrium of one's colleagues by actually trying to entertain an audience with humor. The potential for danger was reinforced in my own mind recently when I asked my closest advisor — my wife Meg — what I should say in an upcoming graduation speech. She thought for a moment, then offered some very sage advice. "Whatever you do," she said, "don't try to sound witty, intellectual, or charming. Just be yourself."

That is what I have in my own career tried to be — and surprisingly, it is not difficult. Thus, I am the quintessentially humorless engineer who has descended into management. Many years ago, I wrote what I considered to be a brilliant paper on some management topic. The paper was apparently so brilliant no one ever felt the need to comment on it. Or, perhaps it was so boring no one could ever get through it. In any case, I decided with my next effort to slip in a little humor and see if anyone noticed. I was truly shocked at the outpouring of positive comments — about the humor! But the pivotal fact was that I had merely wrapped my serious points in humor — and they had not been missed at all by my readers. Sort of a case of a wolf in sheep's clothing — if sheep, in fact, wear clothes.

Some would say that my book of *Laws* aspired to humor with such observations as: "Executives who do not produce successful results hold on to their jobs only about five years; those who produce effective results hang on about half a decade." And: "If a sufficient number of management layers are superimposed on top of each other, it can be assured that disaster is not left to chance." Or: "Most projects start out slowly and then sort of taper off." However, I would simply point out that all such observations were based on empirical data and were in no way attempts at humor.

It is true that humor can be an extremely effective tool when used properly. One recalls the nearly tragic circumstances in March 1981, when President Reagan was shot by a very disturbed young man. While the president was still in surgery, word got around of his own comment to his wife as he was being admitted to the hospital: "Honey, I forgot to duck." On the operating table, he said to the doctors, "Please assure me that you are all Republicans." Those one-liners helped calm a frightened nation.

Over the course of my own career, during which I served for several years as a senior government official and later in private business on a number of large business transactions, I have found that humor frugally employed at a key moment can help "disarm" otherwise emotion-packed confrontations.

Perhaps the best example of an occupation that most ably employs humor in serious, life-and-death situations is professional athletics. I have often felt that we in business could learn a great deal from the utterances of those on the playing field. For example, regarding the challenge of dealing with criticism, what better illustration than the comment of hockey great Jacques Plante, who once said of his profession of goaltending, "How would you like it in your job if every time you made a small mistake, a red light went on over your desk and fifteen thousand people stood up and yelled at you?"

In the same vein, management theory was illustrated by the late Yankee skipper Casey Stengel, who said, "Management is the art of getting credit for the home runs your players hit." A similarly accurate description was offered by Orlando Magic General Manager, Pat Williams, who said coaching is "like a nervous breakdown with a weekly paycheck." That just about sums up a CEO's life, too.

And of course, the eminent philosopher, Yogi Berra — who is known for such pithy sayings as "No one goes there anymore because it's too crowded" — demonstrates the capabilities of humor better than just about anyone else. I am happy to report that Malcolm Kushner follows closely in the Berra tradition. He uses humor effectively in illustrating how businesspeople can make more successful presentations. His book is educational, understandable, and enlightening. And it is funny. I commend it to the reader with the observation Woody Allen once made, "Eighty percent of success is showing up." To which, I'm sure Mr. Kushner would add, "And the other 20 percent is having your transparencies in order."

My hope is that the book becomes a best-seller, assuring that Mr. Kushner will never have to return to the profession he abandoned. Everyone knows we have enough lawyers in business, but we are woefully short in the humor consultants department. So I welcome his effort and wish him all good fortune. Truly, he has followed Mr. Berra's timeless advice: "When you come to a fork in the road, take it."

Norman R. Augustine
President and CEO
Lockheed Martin Corporation

Introduction

Welcome to *Successful Presentations For Dummies*, the book that gives a new meaning to the term "influence peddling." No, you won't learn anything illegal, but you will learn how to use basic presentation skills to influence your boss, coworkers, relatives, loved ones, butcher, baker, candle-stick maker, and anyone else who matters in your life. You can even influence people who don't matter — like your senator.

This book provides all the tools you need to make successful presentations. And that doesn't mean just formal speeches. Some of the most important presentations you will ever give may not involve a microphone or a podium: an impromptu talk about your strategy to some customers; an answer that defuses a hostile question at a business meeting; an impassioned plea to a police officer not to issue the ticket. Success or failure in all of these situations, as well as in formal speeches, depends on how you present yourself.

That's why this book covers the full range of presentation skills. You will learn everything from how to develop and deliver a good speech to how to think on your feet. An old philosopher once said, "Every time you open your mouth, your mind is on parade." This book will ensure that your parade looks sharp, sounds smart, and dazzles your audience.

Why You Need This Book

Whether you're dealing with one person or one thousand, the ability to transmit ideas in a coherent and compelling fashion is one of the most important skills you can ever develop. It's a basic survival skill, and it always has been. From the earliest caveman who yelled "Fire!" to the latest web surfer who flamed someone on the Internet, people have made presentations to motivate, persuade, and influence each other.

Want to get a good job? Want to get promoted? Want to command the respect of your peers? Want to get a date? The key to success is your presentation. To get what you want in life, you have to present yourself forcefully, credibly, and convincingly. Sure, you can speak softly and carry a big stick, but the real winner is the person who talks you out of the stick.

In the information age, presentation skills are even more important than ever before. We live in a society of sound bites. Communication is the currency of the realm. In survey after survey, presentation skills are cited as a key factor in hiring and promotion decisions. The days when you could rise to the top just by being good at your job are over. Boards of directors, executive committees, and customers want more. You've got to know how to get your message across.

Now let's admit it. Many people get nervous about giving presentations, particularly in a public speaking setting. My goal in writing this book is to rid you of those fears forever. If you simply apply the techniques described in *Successful Presentations For Dummies*, you will be able to give a talk more competently than many Oscar-winning performers. (You don't believe me? Just watch the Academy Awards and listen to the acceptance speeches.) I'm not saying you'll be the next Cicero, but you will learn to deliver a speech in an organized and engaging manner.

And don't fall for the big myth that you have to be "a born speaker." Nothing could be further from the truth. Some of the greatest orators in history were anything but "naturals." Demosthenes — the famous speaker of ancient Greece — was a shy, stammering introvert when he decided to become a successful presenter. He taught himself to speak by rehearsing with rocks in his mouth. If all you have in your mouth is your foot, then you're way ahead of the game.

If you've already got the "gift of gab," there are still many tips and tricks you can pick up from *Successful Presentations For Dummies*. For example, you wouldn't believe how often experienced speakers completely undermine their entire presentation with poorly designed slides and overheads. If you learn nothing more than how to correct this common mistake, this book will be well worth what you paid for it.

Let's talk straight. There are lots of books about presentation skills, and they're written by people who have various credentials. But how many of them taught speech at the University of Southern California, practiced law with an international law firm, ghost-wrote speeches for leading business executives, traveled the lecture circuit as a keynote speaker at major corporate and association meetings, and appeared on *The Gong Show* — without being gonged?

I've done all that stuff and more, and that's what's unique about this book. It contains a treasure trove of nuts-and-bolts information based on real-life experience. You will learn what really works and what doesn't. Because if there's a mistake to be made, I've already made it. Now you won't have to repeat them.

How to Use This Book

If you want to improve the full range of your presentation skills, then read the entire book. You will become an expert communicator.

Too busy to read a whole book? Don't worry. *Successful Presentations For Dummies* is designed with your time constraints in mind. The book is divided into easy-to-read segments that cover very specific topics. Choose an area of interest, such as how to fake charisma, and turn directly to it.

You can also use the book to accent the design of your home or office. Just put it on a bookshelf in full view. The bold yellow and black of the cover contrast nicely with the muted brown tones of many bookcases. (And anyone seeing the book on your shelf will assume you've read it and will think you're smart.)

How This Book Is Organized

Successful Presentations For Dummies has five major parts, each of which is divided into chapters covering specific topics. The chapters are self-contained units of brilliant insight. So you don't have to plow through them in sequence. You can read them separately or together in any order you wish. Don't worry about missing any gems of wisdom. The book is thoroughly cross-referenced and guides you to related items of information.

Each part covers a major area of presentation skills. Here is a brief tour of what you will find:

Part I: A Crash Course in Influencing People

In every old war movie, there comes a point when the bad guys tell the hero, "We have ways of making you talk." What are those ways? Do they work? Can you apply them to your advantage? These are some of the questions that I will address in this section. You will learn what makes people respond and why; how to establish credibility; how to become extremely confident; and how to use this knowledge to shape powerful presentations.

Part II: Preparing Your Presentation

In today's fast-paced, competitive environment, fortunes can rise or fall on the basis of a single presentation. So it better be good. That means informative, to the point, attention grabbing, and memorable. And it doesn't get that way by luck or accident. Careful preparation — from topic selection to outline structure to choice of material — is the key. In this section, I will show you how to develop a speech that will command an audience's attention, influence its thinking, and achieve your goals.

Part III: Delivering Your Presentation

Should you use a podium? Does it matter what you wear? Should you make a lot of gestures? What if you get stage fright? How fast should you speak? How do you handle a tough audience? These are just a few of the issues involved in transforming your written message into a masterful oral performance. And there are lots more. In this section, I'll help you to deliver a presentation that wows an audience. Simple, proven techniques guarantee your success even if you're nervous, shy, or disorganized. But don't worry; you'll be great.

Part IV: Scoring Points with Humor

Humor is a powerful communication tool. It gains attention, creates rapport, and makes your message more memorable. It can also relieve tension, enhance relationships, and motivate people. Anyone can learn to use humor effectively. You don't have to be "naturally funny" or know how to tell jokes. All you need is a sense of humor. In this section, you will learn how to transform your sense of humor into a powerful business asset.

Part V: The Part of Tens

You've heard of the seven deadly sins? In this section, I talk about the ten fatal flaws — surefire ways to screw up any presentation. But you'll also find lists to help you literally add magic to your presentations, as well as keep you focused on your goals. You'll even learn how to find great material on the World Wide Web.

Icons Used in This Book

Technical Stuff

This nerdy guy appears beside discussions that aren't essential to your understanding of basic presentation skills concepts — stuff like the physics of microphone feedback or the use of survey research tools in measuring attitude change. Of course, some people *can* be impressed by this information at cocktail parties. (And if you meet any of them, then you're attending the wrong parties.)

Tip

This icon signals important advice about how to maximize the effectiveness of your presentation.

Remember

An elephant never forgets, but people do. This icon alerts you to information you'll want to remember (unless you're subpoenaed by a Senate subcommittee).

Anecdote

When I feel like telling a story, I let you know with this icon.

Common Knowledge

This icon marks the prevailing opinion about a specific aspect of developing or delivering a presentation. You'll learn what the gurus and authorities — the usual suspects — think about an issue.

Uncommon Knowledge

This icon points to information that will justify your purchase of this book — brilliant advice that you won't readily find anywhere else. Most of it's based on my personal experience, knowledge, and insight (not to mention modesty).

Warning

To indicate potential problems, I use this icon.

Where Do I Go from Here?

You hold in your hands a powerful tool — a guide to increasing your influence through the sheer force of your presentations. This tool can be used for good or evil. That's up to you. Consider yourself warned. To begin your journey, turn to the table of contents or index, pick a topic of interest, and turn to the page indicated. Good luck in your travels. You're now ready to dive into this book, unless you plan to wait for the movie version.

Part I
A Crash Course in Influencing People

In this part . . .

Presentations are designed to influence an audience, and certain basic rules apply. In these chapters, I discuss what makes people respond and why. I show you how to establish credibility, how to extend your influence, and how to use this knowledge to shape powerful presentations.

Chapter 1

How to Talk Someone into Something

In This Chapter

▶ Key factors controlling the persuasion process

▶ Eighteen persuasive techniques that work (without brass knuckles)

▶ How to become your own spin doctor

*E*ver since cavemen developed language to accompany the club, we've been able to change people's minds without changing their faces. (Except in certain parts of my old neighborhood.) In fact, talking someone into something is probably the second oldest profession. (It also has a lot to do with the oldest one.) No matter what you're talking about or who you're talking to, the ability to use words to influence others is at the heart of any successful presentation.

What Is Persuasion?

Aristotle defined persuasion as the faculty of discovering all the available means of influence. (My definition is discovering all the available means of peddling influence.) There are other definitions, but all of them have the same idea at their core — making the audience members do something. If you want them to perform some mental or physical action (change their minds, change their voter registration, change their underwear — whatever), you need to persuade them.

Why everything you say involves persuasion

The common knowledge divides presentations by various purposes. Traditionally, the big three are speeches to inform, speeches to entertain, and speeches to persuade. Here's the uncommon knowledge — everything you say involves persuasion.

It's obvious that a traditional speech to persuade involves persuasion. You want the audience to do something: Buy your product. Support your candidate. Accept your ideas. Whatever. It's less obvious that you want the audience to do something no matter what type of presentation you deliver. Are you giving a speech to entertain? You want to persuade the audience that you're entertaining. If you don't, your speech will be a failure. Are you giving a speech to inform? You want to persuade the audience that you know what you're talking about. If persuasion is defined as attempting to influence people, then there's a persuasive component to all communication.

Key factors in the persuasion process

There are four key factors in the persuasion process, according to Kenneth K. Sereno, Associate Professor of Communications at the University of Southern California. (He's also a prominent consultant to individuals and corporations regarding a wide variety of interpersonal communication problems.) These factors determine the outcome of all our attempts to persuade.

Attitudes

Attitudes refer to positive or negative feelings you have toward people, things, and ideas. "They play a major role in how you interpret information and how you behave," says Ken.

Values

Values refer to important guidelines for living your life. Examples include treating other people fairly, achieving wealth, and getting a good education. "Values are very important because they guide your entire belief system," explains Ken. "If you can change someone's values, then you can change all the attitudes related to those values." (By the way, here's one of Ken's favorite values: Do unto others before they do unto you.)

Ego involvement

Ego involvement refers to the importance that a person attaches to a particular issue or topic. For example, members of both the National Rifle Association and handgun control groups would be highly ego involved regarding any effort to ban the sale of hand guns. People who don't care one way or the other would exhibit low ego involvement.

Here's why ego involvement is significant. The more highly involved people are in a particular topic (the more they care about it), the more difficult it is to change their attitude about the topic. The lower their involvement, the easier it is to persuade them.

Credibility

Credibility refers to how believable you are. If you have high credibility, then you're very believable. If you have low credibility, then what you say will be doubted or disregarded. Now here's an important point: A person's credibility will vary depending on the topic under discussion and who the audience is. For example, a biologist might be highly credible talking about evolution. But if the biologist talks about stock market tips, he or she might have no credibility. (Especially the biologists I know.) If the audience members are fundamentalists who believe in creationism, the biologist wouldn't even have any credibility talking about evolution. (For a full discussion, see Chapter 2.)

How to Be Persuasive

Want the audience to see things your way? Most speakers do. (It sure beats getting tomatoes thrown at you.) Whether you're speaking to entertain, inform, or persuade, here are 18 powerful techniques that will help the audience see things as you do. Some are more applicable to traditional speeches to persuade. Some apply to any type of presentation. All of them will be useful to you as a presenter. (They all work individually, but for an extra punch, you should try using them in combinations.)

Know when to use one-sided and two-sided messages

We've all heard that there are two sides to every story. The question is when do you tell both sides? Here's the answer: If the audience knows both sides of the story, then you must address both sides. Because the audience already knows the opposing arguments, you have to show why those arguments are wrong. Otherwise, you won't be persuasive. Also, the audience may think that you don't know the other side — which will make you look dumb. So you support your side and argue against the other side. That's a two-sided message.

If the audience doesn't know both sides, then you only present your side. (There's no point educating the audience about the opposing arguments.) That's a one-sided message. But be very careful with a one-sided message. Don't use it if there's any possibility that the audience may learn about the other side of the story. You want to be the one to tell the audience about it — so you can show why it's wrong.

Know when to use an inductive or deductive approach

In a deductive approach, the speaker starts by telling the audience what it is he or she wants them to do. (Buy my product. Vote for my candidate. Etc.) Then for the rest of the presentation, the speaker gives reasons and arguments for taking that action. In an inductive approach, the speaker gives reasons and arguments first that lead to an inevitable conclusion — what the speaker wants the audience to do. (The speaker reveals his or her purpose at the end, after he or she has supported the purpose with plenty of reasons.)

In most circumstances, a deductive approach is more effective. It's an easier argument for audiences to follow. You tell them what you want, and then you tell them why. They can then understand each of your arguments. They know what points you're trying to make. With an inductive approach, audiences don't know what you want until the end. So they may misinterpret the arguments and evidence you present in support of your position.

But there are exceptions. If you know that the audience will be hostile to your purpose, then use an inductive approach. That way your arguments and evidence will at least be heard and may decrease the audience's resistance to your position. Teenagers know this instinctively. They'd never use a deductive approach when asking their parents to use the car. "Mom and Dad, I want you to let me use the car." (Already the parents are shaking their heads "No.") "It will show that I can assume more responsibility. And I'll even use it to do the grocery shopping and some of your other errands." Instead they'd use an inductive approach. "Mom and Dad, I want to show you that I can assume more responsibility." (The parents are shocked — and interested.) "I'd like to do some of your errands, like the grocery shopping." (The parents are thinking "Great.") "Of course, I'll need the car." The parents may still refuse, but you can see that the inductive approach has a much better chance of succeeding here.

Distinguish features from benefits

A basic rule of sales presentations is to sell benefits, not features. It's the difference between saying, "This car has a turbocharged engine that can go up to 150 miles per hour" (feature), and "This car is so fast you'll be able to outrun the police" (benefit — depending on your line of work). Benefits are much more persuasive. The distinction is important for any type of message, not just sales presentations. ("If we each bicycle to work one day a week, the carbon monoxide content of the air will decrease 20 percent." "If we each bicycle to work one day a week, the air we breathe will be healthier. It will smell better. And it will put us in a better mood by taking the form of a clear blue sky, rather than a smoggy gray cloud.") How do the audience members benefit if they do whatever it is that you advocate? Tell them.

Provide a clear alternative

Have you ever reached a point in an argument where you screamed at your opponent, "So what do you want me to do?" (It's a very big line in intra-family squabbles.) Suddenly, this person who has been busting your chops for an hour falls silent. After all his or her screaming about why you shouldn't do such-and-such, it becomes clear this person has no alternative course of action to offer. Your opponent just lost.

Simply arguing against something is not persuasive. If you want your audience members to stop driving cars because they're polluting, then tell them what alternate source of transportation they can use. Always provide a clear alternative.

Threaten a third party

Have you ever seen a movie where the bad guys tell the good guy, "We have ways of making you talk"? Remember what happens next? They threaten him. "We'll leave you in this cell for a few months to think about things." "We'll give you a few lessons with this electric cattle prod." "We'll make you watch movies that featured Roseanne." Typically, these threats prove worthless. Our hero won't crack. "There's nothing you can do to get me to talk," he'll say. That's when the bad guys smile knowingly. They wheel in a cage containing our hero's wife and children. "Now you'll talk," say the bad guys. Before they can finish that sentence, our hero is telling them everything they ever wanted to know.

Want your threats to be persuasive? Don't threaten harm to the person you're trying to persuade. (Talk or we'll shoot.) Threaten harm to a significant third party. (Talk or we'll shoot your kid.) By the way, this doesn't just apply to spies and torture. A common, everyday example is the argument to stop smoking or drinking. You can tell the smokers or drinkers that if they don't stop, they'll kill themselves. Or you can tell them that if they don't stop, their children will lose a parent and perhaps become destitute. The second argument is much more influential.

Put values into conflict

Want to guarantee that you'll produce an attitude change? Put two of your listeners' values into conflict with each other. One of the values will have to yield. Let's look at an example. I had a friend who always complained that he needed more exercise, but he never did anything about it. That's because one of his core values was laziness. This guy hated to exercise. It just so happened that another one of his values was cheapness. He always had to get his money's worth out of anything he bought. (He'd sit through a movie he hated because he'd calculate how much it cost to view each minute based on the price of admission. If he left early, the price per minute would increase.) Anyway, I convinced him that his only hope of exercising was to spend several hundred dollars to join a gym. That would put two of his values into conflict — cheapness and laziness. If cheapness prevailed, he'd become physically fit. (And that's just what happened. Just like with the movie, he realized that the more he used the gym, the more he was getting for his money.) Anytime you can show your audience that two of their values are in conflict, you will produce an attitude change. It's up to you to structure the situation so that it turns to your advantage.

Present new information

"We've been over this a million times." Have you ever heard that from someone who refuses to see things your way? But you try yet again to show this person why you're right and he's wrong. Don't bother. You're the one who's wrong — in how you're attempting to persuade. You're just repeating the same old arguments. They won't work. Your opponent has already evaluated them and rejected them. You need to offer *new* information. Is there a new study, new data, a new statistic that supports your view? That's where your chances for persuasion lie.

Tell them what you want

Are you trying to persuade your audience members to do something? Buy your product. Agree with your position. Vote for your candidate. Well, tell them. This advice sounds obvious, but it's amazing how often this crucial step is omitted. In sales presentations, it's called asking for the order. Ask your audience members for the order. Don't assume that they know what you want them to do. Tell them clearly and precisely.

Anticipate counterarguments

Anticipate counterarguments and dispose of them during your talk. Then if someone raises an objection after you've spoken, it's not that big a deal. You've already indicated you were aware of the argument and diminished its importance. In contrast, if you haven't anticipated and acknowledged the argument, then the objector's words will carry much more force. (See the section on using two-sided messages earlier in this chapter.)

Show how your position is consistent with theirs

People resist change. (Except certain panhandlers.) That's why persuasion is so difficult. People don't like to give up their views for your views. Your efforts in that direction can even have a boomerang effect — the more you try to make them accept your position, the more stubbornly they cling to their own. That's why you should show them why your position is consistent with theirs. It's a much smaller leap. Then accepting your ideas doesn't mean changing their own. "Audiences look for a connection between what they want and believe, and what the speaker advocates," explains Ken Sereno. "You want them to perceive what you want them to do as consistent with their own ideas, values, and goals. Then they won't fight it."

Start with points of agreement

If you want to talk people into your point of view, start by showing where you agree with them. By showing that you have some points of agreement, you establish a positive relationship with the audience members and decrease resistance to your message. If you go right to the areas of disagreement, then you antagonize people immediately. That's why politicians always find an opening point of agreement, even if the crowd is completely hostile to their positions. ("I think all of us here can agree that we want a bright future for our country.") If you can't find anything to agree with your audience about, you can always use this classic: "I think all of us here today can agree that dialogue is very important." (I've been hearing that line more and more in public discourse for the past few years. It's a sad commentary on our times.)

Use a variety of devices

To paraphrase an old saying, don't put all your arguments in one basket. Use a variety of devices. Make threats. Use guilt. Offer new information. Put values in conflict. Support your arguments with different types of evidence. You never know what's going to work. (For a model of this approach, listen to the next on-air fundraiser held by your local National Public Radio station. They'll just keep throwing persuasive devices up against the wall until something sticks.)

Suggest small, specific steps

Be realistic about what you can talk someone into. You have a far greater chance of success if you advocate a small change rather than a large one. For example, say you're trying to persuade teenagers to improve their health through better eating habits. If you tell them to stop eating junk food and give them a bunch of great reasons for doing so, they probably won't stop eating junk food. Instead, you can give them the reasons for not eating junk food and then tell them to *eat less junk food — in a very specific amount.* ("When you go to a fast food place and order a burger and fries, don't eat all the fries. Eat only three quarters of them.") Some of them might actually take your advice.

Cut through complex arguments with a simple demonstration

After the Space Shuttle Challenger exploded, a distinguished panel of scientists, government officials, and aerospace executives was asked to determine the cause of the accident. Although mounting evidence indicated a problem with the shuttle's O-rings, numerous hearings proved inconclusive. The inquiry was changed forever after physicist Richard Feynman performed a little experiment while the panel was in session. He dropped a piece of rubber from an O-ring into a glass of ice water, simulating the conditions during the shuttle launch. (Feynman suspected that the freezing temperature at the time of the launch had prevented the rubber on the O-ring from functioning properly.) As Feynman expected, the rubber failed to perform properly in the glass of ice water. His simple demonstration was broadcast on television news programs throughout America, and it ended the debate about what caused the shuttle disaster.

Cut through complex arguments with a simple statement

During my third week of law school, my class took a field trip to the State Court of Appeals. We observed one appeal that I'll never forget. The case involved food stamps. Some governmental body (I think it was the City of San Francisco) wanted to decrease the number of people eligible for the stamps. So it claimed that a certain group of poor people didn't qualify for them. The government's attorney supported this claim with a bunch of legal jargon that I didn't understand. The attorney for the poor people counterargued with some of his own jargon. Then the government's attorney said something I finally understood. He said that all the mumbo jumbo he had just argued had been upheld in a previous case in which the poor people were deprived of welfare benefits, so it should also apply to this case involving food stamps. Before he could continue, one of the justices said, "So counselor, first you got them off welfare and now you want to starve them." The judge's simple comment cut through a lot of . . . stuff. (*Stuff* is a legal term meaning "crap.") It put the argument in perspective and basically ended the argument.

Here's another example as described in a speech given by Sue Suter, former United States Commissioner of Rehabilitative Services:

> A few years ago, there was a bill in our state legislature to increase wages for personal attendants so that high turnover rates could be reduced. Many prominent rehabilitation organizations came to the legislative hearings in support of the bill. But it was one consumer, named Terry Gutterman, who made the issue understandable to legislators by simply asking them to "Imagine giving the keys to your house to 14 different people in a single year." That message got through — I believe — in large part because of one small action by one person. The bill passed.

Have a topper ready

The persuasion process is like a chess game. Success often depends on the ability to think several moves ahead. What does that mean in practical terms? You have to anticipate the rhetorical moves of your opponent and be ready to neutralize them. Have a *topper* ready — a line that squelches your opponent's momentum. (Who is your opponent? An audience member who asks a hostile question. A co-panelist who argues against your ideas. Anyone opposed to your position.)

Prominent New York business lawyer Richard Herzfeld uses this technique in contract negotiations. Inevitably someone will object to a clause by saying, "You don't need it because you already have it." (In other words, the provision is already somehow covered in the contract.) Rich's reply: "If you think it's already there, then you shouldn't mind putting it in again."

It's no fun being the victim of a topper. Here's how Vice President Al Gore described the experience in a speech about the national information infrastructure:

> Speaking of clichés, I often use the analogy to autos, saying that if cars had advanced as rapidly as computer chips in recent years, a Rolls Royce would go a million miles an hour and cost twenty-five cents.
>
> The last time I used it was at a meeting of computer experts and one of them said, "Yeah — but that Rolls Royce would be one millimeter long."

That shows the classic use of a topper. It completely undermined the Vice

President's snappy analogy. The computer expert was prepared to top the analogy because the analogy was a cliché. (The computer expert knew a topper for the analogy would eventually come in handy.)

Harness the power of guilt

You should never forget the power of guilt. (Several major religions have done very well with this persuasive device.) Want a televised lesson in how to use guilt effectively? The next time there's a fundraiser for any nonprofit organization, just turn on the tube. The telethons for various diseases will make you feel guilty that you're healthy. The infomercial about forgotten children overseas will make you feel guilty that you're not starving, and the fundraiser for the local PBS station will make you feel guilty for watching the station without being a member. (Freeloader.) TV can provide you with plenty of great ideas for how to effectively harness the power of guilt.

Give them an out

Have you ever had to admit you were wrong? It's never fun. (Some people may say that you were "eating crow.") Even if you're only admitting it to yourself, no one likes to be wrong. That's another reason why persuasion is so difficult. When you get people to see things your way, on some level they're admitting that their way was wrong. "Give them an out," advises Ken Sereno. "Let them save face. Tell them you'd have seen things their way too, given the information they had." (But don't be condescending.) It's like giving them a bridge to cross over to your side rather than making them leap the chasm.

Prescriptions from the Spin Doctor

There's an old inspirational story about three workers carrying bricks from a truck and placing them in a pile at a construction site. A bystander asks the workers what they're doing. The first says, "I'm carrying bricks." The second says, "I'm making a wall." The third says, "I'm building a cathedral."

The third worker should have been a spin doctor. He instinctively knew that the common knowledge — you see what you want to see — is wrong. He exemplified the uncommon knowledge: you see what someone else can convince you to see.

The term *spin doctor* originally applied to the public relations types who tell us how to perceive political events. (You see them on the tube after every presidential debate. No matter what actually occurred, their candidate "won.") Now it refers to a growing army of people who want to influence public opinion — lobbyists, public affairs officers, corporate communications personnel, cab drivers.

The next two sections describe what you need to know to function as your own spin doctor.

Control the definition

Psychotherapist Thomas Szasz has said, "In the animal kingdom, the rule is eat or be eaten; in the human kingdom, it's define or be defined." That's a very apt description of the prime rule of spin doctoring — you want to control the definition of things and events. From who "won" a debate to what is a "gang" to who is in a "bad mood," this process of defining occurs constantly at every level of our lives.

At the macro level, a good example comes from the Census Bureau. The Bureau is currently battling with several ethnic groups over definitions of ethnic identity. One of the big issues is who is Hispanic? Should the definition be based on ancestry, language, surname, or other factors? The outcome of this definitional battle concerns millions of Americans.

At the micro level, a good example comes from a speech given by former First Lady of the U.S., Barbara Bush, in 1990.

> We are in a transitional period right now, fascinating and exhilarating times, learning to adjust to the changes and the choices we, men and women, are facing. I remember what a friend said, on hearing her husband lament to his buddies that he had to babysit. Quickly setting him straight, my friend told her husband that when it's your own kids, it's not called babysitting!

All of us engage in these micro level disputes every day. Has anyone ever asked you why you're depressed and you replied that you're not depressed, you're just tired? That's a battle over definition. But you probably knew that, right? What you really want to know is how to win the battle.

Watch your language

The main weapon in this battle over definition is language. The outcome of a war of words can be just as significant as the outcome of a war with guns and soldiers. You don't have to look further than our legal system for numerous examples. Is a 16-year-old a child or an adult? (It makes a big difference if you're being tried for murder.) Is telling a joke about a woman's anatomy sexual harassment or kidding around? Is a tool shed with someone living in it a rental dwelling or an out building? Is your Congressional representative animal, mineral, or vegetable? The person who prevails in these definitional battles is the person who uses language most skillfully.

Ambrose Bierce, famed author of *The Devil's Dictionary*, defined language as "the music with which we charm the serpents guarding another's treasure." He may have been cynical, but he was right. That's why politicians go to great lengths to stamp their wording of events on the public's mind. A recent headline in *The New York Times* says it all — "Shifting Public Opinion by the Turn of a Phrase." The article described the battle between Democrats and Republicans regarding the portrayal of changes to Medicare. It was suggested that Democrats would benefit by portraying the changes as "cuts." Republicans would benefit by saying the changes were designed to "increase spending at a slower rate."

The struggle to define a situation through language is most evident in the widespread use of euphemisms. An attorney will strut before a jury claiming, "My client is not a member of a gang. It's a youth organization." The doctor won't tell you that your aunt died. He'll say there's been some "negative patient care outcome." Congress won't raise taxes. They'll ask for "revenue enhancers." The message is clear. (Sort of.) If you want to influence your audience, create some euphemisms. They may not make the world go round, but they'll definitely help you doctor the spin.

The most famous formula for persuasion is probably Teddy Roosevelt's advice to "speak softly and carry a big stick." (It just goes to show how little has changed since our cave-dwelling ancestors invented language.) Fortunately, social science's insights into the nature of the persuasion process have given us less and less reason to carry sticks. The basic rules and techniques of persuasion described in this chapter really do work. Keep them in mind as you explore the rest of this book. They play a role in almost any type of presentation you might have to deliver. If they don't work, don't worry. It won't be a failure. It'll just be a "success deficiency."

Chapter 2
Establishing Credibility

• •

In This Chapter

▶ Removing barriers to believability

▶ Strengthening your credibility

▶ Faking charisma

• •

*Q*uestion: How can you tell when Senators are lying?

Answer: Their lips are moving.

Now that's a credibility problem. (OK, let's be fair. The joke could also apply to Congressional representatives.) It shows what you're up against when no one is inclined to believe what you say.

Credibility equals believability. It's one of the most important qualities that you can bring to a presentation, and it can make up for a multitude of sins. When you have very high credibility, people don't care if your presentation isn't perfect. So your opening joke wasn't that funny. So your message could be better organized. So what? We believe what you say. But when you have very low credibility, a perfect presentation doesn't matter — no one believes you anyway. Want to learn how to raise your credibility? Keep reading.

The Biggest Myth

The biggest myth about credibility is that it comes from the speaker. It doesn't. "A speaker's credibility comes from the audience," explains Ken Sereno, Associate Professor of Communications at the University of Southern California. "Only the audience can decide if it wants to believe the speaker." Does that mean you have no control over your credibility? No. There are many things you can do to shape an audience's opinion of your credibility. Think of it like the process of getting a grade in school. Only the teacher (or audience) can assign the grade to the student (or speaker), but the student can do all sorts of things — turn in homework, prepare for class, obey the rules — to influence what grade is assigned.

Key Variables Affecting Credibility

There are five key variables that affect the perception of your credibility. The two most important are character and competence. The other three — composure, likeability, and extroversion — have a lesser effect, but none of the five variables operate in isolation. A lesser factor can sometimes neutralize one of the important factors. For example, a chemistry professor is usually perceived as highly competent to talk about molecular structure. That competence generates a lot of credibility, but audience perceptions would change if the professor exhibited extreme anxiety when asked a question. The lack of composure would erode his credibility.

Character

Character is the most important factor in how an audience judges your credibility. It refers to your honesty, fairness, and trustworthiness. If you're not perceived as honest, fair, and trustworthy, the other factors don't really matter. Does that mean you have to be a pillar of the community? No. (Lot's wife became a pillar of the community because she *lacked* character.) It means you have to convey the fact that you're reasonably honorable and ethical. As an old philosopher once said, you should have character, not be one.

Competence

Competence is the second most important factor affecting credibility. It refers to your expertise in a particular subject or topic. The more education, training, and experience that the audience knows you possess in a given area, the more competent the audience will perceive you to be. For example, a medical doctor would ordinarily be perceived as competent to discuss the treatment of sickness and disease, whereas a carpenter would not be. If the topic of the presentation was construction of wood frame houses, the audience's perception of the competence of each speaker would, of course, reverse.

Composure

Speakers who appear nervous are perceived as less credible than speakers who appear at ease with themselves and their audience. Have you ever watched witnesses testify at a trial? Their body language says a lot. If their eyes dart back and forth and they squirm in their seats, their behavior raises a lot of doubts. And when those beads of perspiration form on their foreheads and upper lips, their credibility goes out the window. Something about sweat just breeds distrust. (Think of it as the Nixon effect.)

Likeability

Speakers who are more likeable are perceived to be more credible. (I guess there's a natural tendency to distrust people you don't like.)

Extroversion

Speakers who are moderately extroverted come across as more credible than highly extroverted speakers or introverts. Here's why. Speakers who are very outgoing come on too strong. (Picture a high-pressure salesperson.) It makes people suspicious. They start thinking, "What's the catch?" On the other end of the spectrum, introverts cause suspicion because they can't overcome their shyness. They stay in their shell, and people wonder what's going on in there.

Barriers to Believability

On the old TV sit-com *Get Smart*, secret agent Maxwell Smart would inevitably make some outrageous claim that would be greeted with complete skepticism by his boss or partner. (Something like "I was captain of the Queen Elizabeth.") After a long silence, Smart would alter the claim. And he'd preface the new one by saying, "Would you believe . . .?" ("Would you believe I once owned a leaky rowboat?") No one ever did. His claims were too absurd to be credible. There are other reasons why people have trouble believing what someone says. Here are a few of the reasons that you may encounter:

Stereotypes

Depending on who you are and what you do, there may be a stereotype blocking your path to high credibility. Are you a used car salesperson, real estate agent, auto mechanic, politician, journalist, or attorney? Then you know what I mean. Dishonesty is the stereotypical trait associated with these trades and professions. (In fact, a recent survey reported in *The Wall Street Journal* found that while blacks and whites disagree widely over the honesty of judges and police, both races have low opinions of lawyers.) Are you a blonde woman? Then your audience may assume that you're dumb. If you know that you'll be the victim of a stereotype, be prepared to address the issue. Acknowledge the stereotype and distance yourself from it.

 A friend of mine who is a real estate broker uses humor to break the stereotype. He begins a presentation by saying that he has a great split-level home for sale. Then he shows a slide of a house with a tree crashed through it. When the audience stops laughing, he says, "Not all real estate brokers are liars. We may exaggerate a little, but we tell the truth a lot more than you think."

Conflicts of interest

Are you a doctor touting a new wonder drug developed by a company owned by your brother? Maybe it is a great drug, but it will be easier to make your audience members believe that fact if they hear it from someone else — because you have an obvious conflict of interest. What can you do? Acknowledge the conflict. If you don't and the audience later becomes aware of it, then you'll have *no* credibility. If you do acknowledge the conflict, at least you'll score some points for honesty.

Not-so-hidden agendas

Are you making a presentation arguing against using a marketing strategy recommended by a coworker with whom you've had a long history of antagonism? If people know about the antagonistic relationship, then they'll have difficulty accepting your words at face value. They'll have to wonder how much of your argument is motivated by dislike of your coworker. Closely related to the conflict of interest, the not-so-hidden agenda makes your audience question your motivations. What can you do? Acknowledge the problem, ask the audience to give you a fair hearing, and argue the merits of your position.

Mistakes

The perception of competence is a very fragile thing. One mistake can cause an audience to totally reevaluate its opinion of a speaker's competence. Suppose that a law professor is reviewing the history of the O.J. Simpson trial at the Rotary Club. The professor gives what seems to be a very thorough and informative talk. During the question and answer period, an audience member says, "The professor said that the killing occurred on a weekend. But everyone knows it occurred on a weekday." Suddenly the audience is wondering what other mistakes the professor may have made. Maybe he's not so competent after all. The reevaluation will be based on three factors: how basic the mistakes were, how many mistakes were made, and how the speaker explained the mistakes. ("Oh, did I say weekend?" asks the professor. "I thought I said weekday." "Well," replies the audience member, "here are ten other facts you got wrong. . . .")

Flip-flops

By *flip-flops,* I don't mean those cheap shoes that are so popular with beachgoers. You flip-flop when you say one thing, and later say the exact opposite. Politicians do this all the time. ("I won't vote for increased taxes." Six months later: "I've decided to vote for a tax increase.") But here's an important distinction.

A flip-flop isn't lying. It just means that the speaker has changed his or her mind. (For a politician, that occurs every time a new poll comes out.) Even though this change of mind may be sincerely felt, it still makes it tough for an audience to believe what the speaker says. Tomorrow, the speaker may flip-flop again.

If you have to flip-flop, what can you do to salvage your credibility? The classic strategy is twofold. First, you portray yourself as having the courage and open-mindedness to change your position. ("I know I said that I wouldn't vote to increase taxes. But I've listened to the arguments that many of you have made in favor of a tax increase — the need for more schools, libraries, and police. You've persuaded me that you're right.") Second, you argue that conditions have changed since your original statement. ("Six months ago when I said I wouldn't vote for a tax increase, the revenues projected by the Office of Management and Budget were far greater than today's estimates. So I have to vote for a tax increase just to save the programs to which we're already committed.")

Truth or consequences

Are you lying? It's a major barrier to believability — especially when you're caught. If that happens frequently, you'll develop a reputation as a liar. Then no one will believe you even when you do tell the truth. (Remember the boy who cried wolf?) Lying isn't limited to telling outright falsehoods. It also includes shading the truth through omissions, distortions, and gross exaggerations. Any of those activities will brand your words suspect in the eyes of your audience. I've known several sales executives who suffer from this problem. They have a reputation for bending the truth more often than Uri Geller bends spoons. "Our new software release will be fully compatible with your old hardware and very simple to upgrade." Uh-huh.

How to Improve Your Credibility

Just because your audience decides how much credibility you possess doesn't mean that you should leave things up to chance or fate. This section discusses a few ways to influence your audience's decision.

Display your credentials

If competence is the second most important factor in establishing credibility, then you want to let the audience members know that you're competent. They need to be made aware of your education, experience, and overall expertise. Here are some of the things that they may find impressive:

- **Degrees, certificates, and licenses.** Remember the Scarecrow in the Wizard of Oz? He wasn't officially smart until he had a diploma. Do you have a degree from an institution of higher learning or trade school? Or a certificate that you completed some type of specialized training? Or a license to practice a particular occupation? These types of credentials convey an official certification of your expertise.

- **Honors and awards.** You don't have to be a Nobel prize winner to impress people with awards. If you received an award for selling the most cookies in your girl scout troop twenty years ago, that can still be relevant to a sales training presentation today. Have you received any honors or awards from employers or trade and professional associations? They can help validate your expertise. And here's some uncommon knowledge. *Honors and awards can also be used to establish your character — the most important factor in credibility.* Have you been honored for your community service? Have you received an award from a service club, charity, church, or synagogue? These types of honors show that you're a good person.

- **Publications.** Even in this age of electronic communication, there's still something about the printed word that impresses people — if you wrote the words. I know lawyers who wrote one article for a law journal thirty years ago and are still talking about it. Why? Because it impresses their clients. Have you written an article for a trade or professional journal, an opinion piece for your local newspaper, a column for the PTA newsletter? Even just writing a letter to the editor can be impressive — if it's in a prestigious publication. (And remember, what's prestigious is determined by your audience.)

- **Experience.** Presumably you're speaking about something because you have some experience related to the topic. What is it? You've been in the industry for twenty years. You've coached a winning Little League team twice before. You've handled emergency operations during a natural disaster. Sometimes just your job title is enough to communicate your experience. (Manager of Obfuscation at XYZ Corporation.)

So how do you inform the audience about your impressive credentials? After all, it's a bit unseemly to stand up and launch into an extended discussion of how great you are. (I've seen plenty of speakers do that, and it usually backfires. It makes them seem desperate. It's like listening to a name dropper. You want to say, "Enough already. Here's a phone book. Throw it on the floor so you can drop a few thousand names all at once and get it over with.")

The best way to communicate your credentials is to let the person introducing you handle the bulk of that chore. (See Chapter 3.) You should also mention your credentials yourself — when appropriate. Don't force them into your presentation; use them as logical supports for your points. ("In my 20 years in the computer industry, this is the first time that I've seen a product receive these kinds of reviews. . . ." "In my freshman year at Harvard, I had an experience that I'll never forget. . . .")

Associate yourself with high-credibility organizations

Are you a member of a prestigious organization? Make sure the audience knows about it. What if you're not a member? Don't worry. You can link yourself to groups that have high credibility in other ways. ("In preparing for this talk, I spent several days talking with scientists at the Mayo Clinic.")

Admit shortcomings

You can build credibility by admitting a mistake or a failure. It's relatively easy to do, and it's something that everyone will believe. Doing so will help you to be perceived as honest.

Display similar values

People have a natural tendency to believe those who share their values and to distrust those who don't. If your values, beliefs, and attitudes match those of the people in your audience, let them know — as early in your talk as possible.

Remember that actions speak louder than words

Are you recommending that your audience take a certain action? Then take that action yourself. Lead by example. Are you talking about the need for people to contribute more to charity? Make a big donation. Are you telling people that too much television viewing is destroying their lives? Bring your TV to the presentation and give it away. Any time you can find an action that supports what you'll be saying — do it. Your credibility will flourish.

Obtain testimonials

You can talk about yourself all day, but it's much more convincing if someone else sings your praises. (It's called third-party credibility.) So collect some testimonials about your character and competence. Get quotes from customers, colleagues, and people held in high regard by your audience. Make sure the person introducing you works some of the quotes into his or her remarks, and use some yourself when appropriate.

Dress the part

You can't judge a book by its cover — but people do it all the time. You're going to be judged by the way you look. So dress the part. Good grooming will improve your credibility. There are lots of studies where two people are sent into a store to buy something. One person is dressed like a bum. The other person is dressed in impeccable business attire. The well-dressed person always receives much better service.

Remember that credibility is dynamic

There's some good news and some bad news. Credibility is what social scientists call a *dynamic variable,* which means nothing more than it's a variable that constantly changes. That's both the good and bad news. If you start your talk with low credibility, the audience may give you high credibility by the time you're through. But the converse is also true — you can start high and end low. So even if you're very believable going into your talk, you have to work at maintaining that status. An old philosopher once said that if you're resting on your laurels, then you're wearing them in the wrong place. That's especially true when it comes to credibility.

When silence is golden

Unless you're claiming your rights under the Fifth Amendment, one way to increase your credibility is to remain silent. It creates an aura of knowledge. You appear to be cerebral — listening and pondering. Many positive character traits are associated with silence. It means you're *not* a squealer or stool pigeon, and it may even mean that you *are* the strong, silent type. But most important, by remaining silent, you ensure that you won't diminish your credibility by saying something dumb. There's a lot of fortune-cookie wisdom that recommends the prudence of suppressing your urge to speak.

✔ If there is a substitute for brains, it has to be silence.

✔ Most of us know how to say nothing, but few of us know when.

✔ Wise men think without talking; fools reverse the process.

✔ Half of wisdom is being silent when you have nothing to say.

✔ If a thing will go without saying — let it.

And let's not forget the one that you hear from every motivational speaker on the professional lecture circuit:

✔ We were given two ears and one mouth, so we ought to listen twice as much as we talk.

(I always wonder what this means for the nose. We were given one nose, but it has two nostrils. Does that mean we're supposed to stick it in other people's business twice as much or just blow it off?)

How to Fake Charisma

The dictionary defines *charisma* as a special magnetic charm or appeal that allows someone to attain the devotion of large numbers of people. When it comes to presentations, we associate the term with spellbinding speakers such as John F. Kennedy, Franklin D. Roosevelt, Martin Luther King, and Amy Semple McPherson. What was it about these speakers that was so attractive to their listeners? Can we learn and apply the secret of their charisma?

The common knowledge regarding charisma is that you either have it or you don't.

Here's the uncommon knowledge. Anyone can learn to fake a moment of charisma. No, you may not be history's next silver-tongued orator. You may not even keep your audience awake for the entire length of your talk, but you can provide at least one moment of inspiration. The ability to inspire people lies at the heart of charisma.

For an extreme example of the problems speakers face, suppose that you're an accountant — a profession that's stereotyped as actively noncharismatic. Isn't there one inspirational moment you can share with your audience? (The company that would have gone bankrupt if you hadn't come to the rescue. How your careful review of the ledger saved your employer thousands of dollars.) It doesn't even have to be work related. Think about all your life experiences. Did you help an ailing relative recover from an often-fatal disease? Did you face down the school bully? Did you ace a test without studying? Think of one thing you've done that will inspire people. If you insist that you don't have even one example (which I don't believe for a minute), then use an inspiring story from someone else. People don't really care who it happened to anyway. They just want to be inspired.

Here's one more tip for faking charisma. Be enthusiastic. Enthusiasm is contagious, and there's no known cure for it. You can be talking about the world's most boring topic that's of no interest to anyone in the audience, but if you're enthusiastic, people will respond to you. When you're enthusiastic, you become more animated and excited. You generate more energy. You become . . . well, charismatic.

The 5th Wave By Rich Tennant

"THESE TWO SEEM A LITTLE SLOW TO CATCH ON. MAYBE IF WE JUST LEFT THEM ALONE WITH THE SNAKE A WHILE."

Chapter 3

Increasing the Influence of Your Presentation (Without Thugs or Drugs)

Controlling How You're Introduced

The master of ceremonies arrived at the podium. He called the meeting to order. After reviewing a few logistical details, he introduced the featured speaker — me. Here's what he said:

> Our speaker today has an interesting background. He is an attorney who created his own profession. He trains managers, professionals, and executives how to use humor in their work. His clients include AT&T, Baxter Healthcare, Hewlett-Packard, Aetna, Digital Equipment Corporation, and the IRS.
>
> He has a masters degree from the University of Southern California and a law degree from Hastings College of the Law. He has been featured in *Time* magazine, *The Wall Street Journal,* and *The New York Times*. He's appeared on *The Larry King Show,* and his book, *The Light Touch: How to Use Humor for Business Success,* has been translated into five languages. But he says his most important accomplishment is that he was on *The Gong Show* — without being gonged.
>
> He also said I'd get at least two laughs if I read this introduction word for word, exactly the way he wrote it.

Please give a warm welcome to Malcolm Kushner, America's Favorite Humor Consultant.

I wanted to die of embarrassment. Yes, I'd written the introduction, but he didn't read it exactly the way I wrote it. He *added* the line saying that I'd written the introduction and asked him to read it word for word. So instead of making the audience feel that it would hear an exciting, well-credentialed speaker, the introduction made them anticipate a raging egomaniac. (Fortunately I thought of a quip to handle the situation — "I also wrote that line about telling him to read it the way I wrote it.")

The way you're introduced is extremely important. It's the first opportunity to set audience expectations, and it can affect your entire presentation. A good introduction prepares the audience to be receptive to you and your message. You start with the deck stacked in your favor. The game is yours to lose. A bad introduction does nothing for you, and a really bad one — well, you can spend your whole speaking time just trying to recover from it.

That's why you want to control your introduction as much as possible. Here are some suggestions for asserting your influence.

Write your own introduction

The best way to control your introduction is to write it yourself. No, it's not foolproof (as the example that opens this chapter illustrates). But it's still your best hope for getting it exactly the way you want it. Once in a while, people really will read it just the way you wrote it, and even if they don't, they may still incorporate a lot of what you've written into their own version.

What to include and exclude

What should you put in your intro? Whatever makes the audience most receptive to you and your message. This usually means telling them what you'll be discussing, why it's of interest, and why you're of interest. Let them know something about your background. Why are you talking about the topic? What makes you an expert?

But don't go overboard. The most common mistake with these intros is making them into a laundry list of positions and achievements. Boring. (I know, I know. It's hard to omit that gold star you received in kindergarten, but take my word for it — the audience won't mind.) Exclude the stuff that doesn't really matter. Be objective about it. Make believe you're in the audience. What gets you interested? Or puts you to sleep?

How long should it be?

One to two minutes should be enough time to say anything that needs to be said about you. If you need more time, take a hard look at what you're including. Think highlights.

Carry an extra copy

If you're lucky enough to persuade the person introducing you to read the introduction you've written, don't press your luck. Don't assume that he or she will have a copy of it when the time to introduce you arrives.

"I could have sworn it was in here with my other papers." "My secretary must have forgotten to give it to me." "I never got a chance to read that intro you sent me. Do you have another copy?" These lines will sound all too familiar if you give more than one or two presentations per year. There must be some major scientific phenomenon lurking here. Introducers can never seem to keep their hands on your introduction. It's like their hands are gateways to another dimension. Send them an introduction and it disappears into a black hole.

Fortunately, there's a simple solution. Always bring along at least one extra copy of your introduction. (Hey, I never said this was rocket science.)

Contact the person introducing you

Speak with the people introducing you well in advance of your presentations. Find out how they plan to handle your introduction. And help them out. If you'd like them to read an introduction that you've written, now is the time to ask — not after they've already written one themselves. You'll have a much better chance of yours being used if it's offered *before* they've invested a lot of time and effort.

Even if you don't offer to write the intro, offer information that will be useful for it. Give the people introducing you a sense of who you are. Tell them what message you want to get across — what image you want to convey. Show them how the intro can support your speaking goals, and tell them what *not* to include. If your name is Samuel and you're known as Samuel, tell them not to refer to you as Sam. Or if you don't want references to personal information — age, marital status, number of children — make your wishes known.

The dumbest thing you can do is to just send a packet of information — a resume, a bio, stuff like that. Do you really expect this total stranger who is introducing you to figure out what's important? Please, give yourself and the introducer a break. At least provide some clues. Write some notes in the margins. Call up and discuss what you've sent. The introducer isn't a mind reader.

And neither are you. So if at all possible, find out exactly what the introducer plans to say. Then, even if it's less than ideal, at least you'll know what's coming and you can adjust your own remarks appropriately.

How to get them to do it your way

There's never a guarantee that the people introducing you will do it the way you want it done. You can only try your best to influence them. One technique is to tell them it's very important to do the intro as you've instructed. Why? Because otherwise your presentation will be much less effective. Or because the opening to your presentation is based on what's said in the intro. Or because you'll kill them if they don't.

Recovering from a bad introduction

Assume that anyone who introduces you won't do it the way you want. That assumption doesn't make you a pessimist or a cynic; it makes you a realist. And hopefully it will make you vigilant. It doesn't mean that you'll never receive a terrific introduction or that you won't receive good ones frequently. It just means that you must always be ready to recover from a bad one.

Here are a few ideas for your recovery program. (And they *don't* involve twelve steps.)

Don't attack the introducer

The person introducing you breaks his promise and doesn't read the intro you've written. He pronounces your name incorrectly. He gets your title wrong. And he references the drunk-driving arrest you begged him not to mention. Now it's your turn. You'd love to tell the audience that this guy is the world's biggest jerk. Don't. The audience doesn't want to be dragged into your dispute. It will just make everyone uncomfortable. It's like being forced to listen to people talk about their impending divorce: no one wants to hear it. Even more important, the audience may side with the introducer — particularly if they're members of the same group (like the organization sponsoring your presentation). Just suppress your anger and focus on damage control.

Have some bridge lines ready

A lousy introduction is like a train wreck. You're waiting in the station for the audience to arrive, but the person introducing you has driven the train off the tracks somewhere up the line. When this disaster occurs, you have to lead the audience out of the wilderness and back to the station. That's where bridge lines come in.

A bridge line is a transition from the introduction you've received to the introduction you're now going to give yourself. It leads the audience smoothly away from the wreckage and into the station where they belong. You should always have a bridge line ready in case you get a bad introduction.

Here are a few bridge lines to keep in mind:

> "What he really meant to say was . . ."
>
> "The notes that I forgot to give her said . . ."
>
> "Let me add a little bit to that . . ."
>
> "One of the things I didn't get a chance to tell him was . . ."

After you use the bridge line, just reintroduce yourself. But don't forget that you still have to tie in your self-introduction with the rest of your presentation.

Refer to a previous introduction

Want to be diplomatic? Compliment the person introducing you for the "great" introduction. Then contrast it with an introduction you've received in the past.

"Thanks for that great introduction. I'm always glad when I get a good introduction. It reminds me of an introduction I got last year when the person introducing me said. . . ." Then do the introduction you wished you'd gotten. (By the way, it doesn't matter if you really spoke at some event last year or not. Just make something up.)

Prepare two openings for your presentation

If you get a bad intro, then you just have to reintroduce yourself. Simple enough in theory, but then there's practice. Getting a bad intro is a stress-producing event. You're standing in the wings, psyched up, ready to go on, when all of a sudden you hear this incredibly horrible introduction. Key information is missing or mangled; your topic isn't announced; whatever. And you're freaking out — not the best state of mind for instantly constructing a self-introduction that will save the day.

That's why you should prepare two openings for your presentation. You use one if you receive the introduction you desire. You use the alternate opening if you receive an inadequate introduction. Think about how the introducer can screw up your intro. Then write an opening that compensates for those deficiencies. What information is absolutely essential for the audience to have? That's what you want to be prepared to give them.

Using Your Presentation as Personal PR

When you make a presentation, you usually invest a lot of time and effort putting it together. Then you hope someone will show up to hear it. You give it. And it's over so quickly. Maybe you've influenced a few people, but wouldn't you like a larger return on your investment?

Don't worry. It's easy to maximize the pay-off for your time and effort. The secret is surrounding your presentation with a public relations blitz. Spread the word that you'll be saying a few words. Why? Reputation and prestige.

Neil Baron was a marketing manager for Digital Equipment Corporation when he gave a presentation at a major event for customers. He included slides that amusingly depicted various parts of the customers' brains. The slides were a major hit, and so was the presentation. It became known within Digital as "the brain speech," and Neil became known as "the brain guy" — not a bad reputation to achieve in a Fortune 500 company. Did Neil achieve household name status with his speech? No. Did he become famous within his company? You better believe it. (See Chapter 11 for a full discussion of the brain speech and illustrations of the slides.)

Making a presentation is a prestigious event. The amount of prestige can vary wildly depending on the audience and occasion, but there's always some prestige. It's not just anyone who has been asked to stand up and speak. It's *you*.

Just the fact that you've been asked to make a particular presentation can enhance your reputation — regardless of how you actually perform. I'll give you an example from personal experience. I was a keynote speaker at the 1994 *Inc.* 500 Conference. People are always impressed with this fact, even though they weren't at the conference and they don't know how I performed. I could have bombed. (I didn't. In fact, I was even quoted in *Inc.* magazine for telling the best joke at the conference.) Just the fact that I was asked to speak at that conference enhanced my reputation. Just the fact that you're asked to speak at a meeting of *your* company, club, or association will build your reputation.

Pop artist Andy Warhol once said that everyone would be famous for fifteen minutes. If you're making a presentation, you can be famous a lot longer than that — if you want to be.

Part II
Preparing Your Presentation

The 5th Wave   By Rich Tennant

"What do you mean the Poultry Association is tomorrow, and the Investors Forum is today?"

In this part . . .

Great presentations don't happen by accident. Careful preparation is the key. In this part, I help you prepare a great presentation. I cover picking a topic, developing an outline, selecting and organizing material, writing an attention-grabbing introduction and a memorable conclusion, and preparing eye-catching visual aids. You'll also learn the best ways to rehearse.

Chapter 4

Getting Started: On Your Mark, Get Set, Now What?

* *

* *

Why Are You Making a Presentation?

There are three types of speakers in the world: those who make things happen, those who watch things happen, and those who wonder what happened.

If you want to avoid wondering what happened, then you better know why you're speaking in the first place. How do you achieve such wisdom? The traditional approach tells you to look at the function of your talk. Are you trying to inform, persuade, inspire, or entertain? I don't find these distinctions particularly useful. Any good speech should accomplish all of those functions, and every good speech is ultimately a form of persuasion (see Chapter 2).

A more useful analysis can be made in terms of motivation — your motivation for speaking and the audience's motivation for listening. Have you been asked to speak? Have you been ordered to speak? Do you want to speak? Does the audience want to hear you? Has it been forced to hear you? Will it listen to you?

However you slice the analysis, the purpose remains the same — you want to know why you're speaking. You don't want to end up wondering what happened.

Should you speak?

First and most important, you should decide whether you even want to give the speech. Unfortunately, most people give little, if any, thought to this question. So here's some uncommon knowledge — *just because you're asked to speak doesn't mean you have to.* (Yes, I know there are exceptions. If your boss tells you to give a presentation, you'd better do it. I'm talking about truly voluntary situations.)

Imagine that someone from the local chapter of an association or service club calls and suggests that you give a speech. While extending this invitation, the caller sings your praises. You're a genius. You'd be great. The audience would hang on your every word. You'd be following in the footsteps of other luminaries who've addressed the organization. And of course, you wouldn't have to talk long — only about ten or twenty minutes. So really, it would be easy for you to do.

Easy? Listen to some reality from John Austin, speechwriter extraordinaire, who fields these requests for his clients all the time. "Program chairmen and women are desperate people, and they desperately have to fill time," he observes. "They will go to any length to flatter someone and cajole them against their better judgment to speak. Never let someone tell you it's just ten or twenty minutes. That's a very long time to fill profitably." You don't believe it? Try John's proof. Stand facing a spouse, friend, or family member and continue to look at one another for five minutes. You'll see just how long it seems — and that's only *five* minutes.

As John rightfully points out, *the key time factor isn't how long you'll speak, it's how long it will take you to prepare.* "Do you have the time to commit to doing a job that won't embarrass you?" asks John. "That's the question you have to answer honestly before agreeing to speak." In answering that question, don't be deceived by the fact that you have to speak for only "ten or twenty minutes." Here's some more uncommon knowledge: It's harder to write a short speech than a long speech. Or as John observes, "Someone once said, 'I would have given a shorter speech, but I didn't have time to prepare it.'"

So what's the bottom line? Don't be bamboozled into giving a speech if you don't want to give one, you have nothing to say, or you don't have time to prepare one. Remember, silence is golden — especially in contrast to a bad speech.

Set specific goals

What do you want to accomplish? Your answer to that question is central to every decision you make about your talk. Yet most people answer it in the vaguest terms. "I want to be a hit." "I want to impress my boss." "I want to get it over with."

That's why management communications counselor Jim Lukaszewski suggests creating a set of specific message goals. "Do you want to build your credibility?" he asks. "Do you want to get the audience members to agree with your position on an issue? Do you want them to learn something? Do you want to make them laugh? What do you want them to do?"

Write down your goals and refer to them as you develop your presentation. It's a good way to make decisions about what to include. Anything that doesn't further a goal should be rejected.

Essential information (occasion, audience, setting, and stuff like that)

No matter what type of presentation you've been invited to deliver, certain information is basic and essential. You must first know the name of your contact person. Armed with that knowledge, you can ask your contact to provide the rest of the information that you need. Here are some of the questions you want answered:

The event

- ✔ What's the purpose of the meeting?
- ✔ Is it a regularly scheduled meeting or a special event?
- ✔ Is it a formal or informal event?
- ✔ What's the atmosphere — very serious or light?
- ✔ Is your talk the main attraction?

The format

- ✔ What's the agenda for the day?
- ✔ What's the format for your speech:
    - a general session?
    - a breakout session?
    - a panel discussion?
    - before, during, or after a meal?
- ✔ What time do you begin speaking?
- ✔ How long are you expected to speak?
- ✔ Will there be other speakers?

✓ When will they be speaking?

✓ What will they be speaking about?

✓ Will any of them be speaking in opposition to your views?

✓ What occurs before your speech?

✓ What occurs after your speech?

The location

✓ Where will you speak?

- inside or outside?

- what type of room: banquet, meeting, auditorium, and so on?

✓ How will the room be set up?

✓ What equipment is available for you?

The audience

✓ What's the size of the audience?

✓ Has it been required to attend?

✓ Are the people there to hear you or for some other reason?

✓ How much do they know about your topic?

✓ Will they be in a rush to leave?

✓ Will they be drinking?

✓ Will they be drifting in and out as you speak?

✓ How have they responded to other speakers?

✓ What other speakers have they heard?

✓ What do they expect from you?

See Chapter 2 for a detailed discussion of audience analysis.

Selecting a Topic (or Shaping the One You've Been Assigned)

What are you going to talk about? And who gets to decide? The answers to these questions play a large role in determining the success or failure of your presentation, so think about them carefully. Don't *assume* you're locked into a particular topic. You have options.

You're in control

You have a lot more control over your topic than you might suspect. When you're asked to speak about a certain subject, that's not the end of the discussion. It's just the beginning. If you don't like the topic, ask to change it. You'd be surprised how many organizations will quickly accommodate your request. If you can't completely change it, then try to slant it in a way that suits your needs.

Let's see how this works in real life. My local Rotary Club invited me to give a talk about humor in business. That's not what I wanted to talk about. I could have asked to change the topic to brain surgery, but the club wouldn't have agreed. Who wants to hear me talk about brain surgery? I'm not a brain surgeon. I haven't had brain surgery, and I don't know anything about it. (Well, I know a few people who could use brain surgery, but that's another story.) Instead, I asked to speak about humor in education — specifically an experimental program that I was running at the local high school. The club readily agreed. Why? It had a slot in its program for someone to speak about humor. It didn't really matter to the club whether it was humor in business or humor in education. It did matter to me, however.

Even when you're locked into a particular topic, you still have a lot of leeway in how to proceed. Suppose that you're a computer guru and you've been asked to speak about the new Windows software from Microsoft. Will you give a broad overview? Will you give a list of specific tips for using it most effectively? Will you give a history of how it was developed? *You can still essentially pick your topic even though it's been assigned.*

Sometimes you may have free reign over the topic because the sponsoring organization doesn't care what you speak about. You may be given only the vaguest of guidelines — speak about business. The organization may just want you to show up and talk. The topic is up to you. You're in control.

Analyzing your speaking situation

So how do you decide what to talk about? Let me answer that with an academic concept called the "rhetorical situation." Developed by Professor Lloyd Bitzer, it focuses on the *constraints* placed on you by the situation in which you find yourself speaking. For example, if you're eulogizing a slain hero, you're expected to praise, not disparage, the person. If you're speaking at a sales meeting, you're expected to motivate "the troops." Every speaking situation creates certain expectations.

An interesting example of this concept comes from a commencement address given by Robert Leestamper, Deputy President of Richmond College in London. In his speech, he refers to the traditional constraints faced by commencement speakers and how he handles them:

I know you'll share my pleasure in learning that I have solved a problem that has puzzled higher education for generations. I refer to the problem of devising a commencement speech that is timely, memorable, brief, and inspiring. This problem, which recurs every Spring, has frustrated the best efforts of scholars, scientists, scribes and statesmen. I discussed this problem with a friend of mine. . . . With his advice in mind, and help from Shakespeare, Jefferson, Lincoln, Kipling, Churchill, and various unnamed contributors, I offer the following: A timely, memorable, brief, and inspiring commencement speech of which not one word is mine, but I do claim authorship of structure.

"Members of the graduating class, lend me your ears: these are the times that try men's souls, but tell me not in mournful words that life is but an empty dream for when in the course of human events it becomes necessary to strive, to seek, to find, and not to yield, then we must summon up remembrance of things past, recalling that our forefathers brought forth new nations, and asked not what they could do for them, but said instead, 'we have nothing to fear, but fear itself.'"

That's about half of it, but you get the idea. (And he did give a "real" address after reciting his generic one.)

While Mr. Leestamper's generic speech was intended as humor, the problem it was intended to "solve" was quite real — meeting the expectations of the speaking situation. So how do you decide what to speak about? Start by analyzing your speaking situation in terms of expectations:

✔ What does the organization sponsoring your talk expect?

✔ What does the audience expect?

✔ What do you expect from the audience?

Then identify any other constraints:

✔ What can you cover in the amount of time you've been given?

✔ How will the time of day affect what you can say? (Audiences are more alert mid-morning than mid-afternoon, for example.)

✔ Does the physical setting place any limits on what you can say or do?

✔ Is there anything that might offend the audience if you referred to it? (Find out from your contact.)

And last, but not least:

✔ What do *you* want to talk about?

Picking a Powerful Title

"What's in a name?" asked Shakespeare. "A rose by any other name would smell as sweet." But would it sound like something that you'd want to smell? That's the issue. The title of your talk is what attracts an audience. If the title doesn't sound interesting, no one will come to "smell" your speech — no matter how sweet it may be.

Here's a perfect example. I gave a talk at a conference for computer professionals. The meeting planner needed a title for the program guide and suggested "Using Humor in a High Technology Environment." Yawn. My suggestion was "High Tech Doesn't Have to be Dry Tech." Which program would you rather attend? Which title suggests the speaker might be more fun and creative? The first title sounds boring and unimaginative. The second title has some snap to it.

Some of you may be thinking that the second title, while snappy, doesn't precisely indicate the topic of the speech — how to use humor. The first title, while stodgy, clearly identifies the topic. I don't think it's a problem. But if you do, it's easy to fix. Just add a subtitle: "High Tech Doesn't Have to be Dry Tech: Using Humor in a High Technology Environment."

The title is particularly important if you speak at a breakout session. That's when you're at a conference where the audience can choose from among several sessions held simultaneously. Jack Burkett, President of the Paradigm Group, faces this problem all the time. He sells software and model documents that help companies keep track of their internal business practices. He's often asked to speak about this topic at breakout sessions. Well, let's face it, how to create, maintain, and distribute documentation of your business practices is not the world's most exciting subject. Yet his talk gets standing room only crowds. Why? Perhaps it's the title — "Discipline Without Bondage."

A powerful title ensures that someone will show up for your session. So how do you come up with a powerful title? Here are a few ideas:

- **Use an exciting verb:** "Astounding Your Clients With Service."
- **Adapt a song title:** "Take this Job and Love It" (Dennis Jaffe).
- **Adapt a book title:** "The Unbearable Darkness of Seeing" (Thomas Frentz).
- **Adapt a movie title:** "The Good, The Bad, and The Ugly: A Timeless Tale for Implementation or Reimplementation Projects."
- **Use a pun:** "Product Pricing: Now Makes Cents!"
- **Ask a question:** "Now That I've Got a Computer, What Do I Do With It?"

- ✔ **Be surprising:** "Say Yes to Stress" (Scott Hunter).

- ✔ **Be provocative:** "Let Thomas Jefferson Rest in Peace: Taking Back Control of Our State Budgets" (Kay Bailey Hutchison).

- ✔ **Use how to:** "How to Get Breakthrough Ideas" (Michael Michalko).

- ✔ **Show an attitude:** "Uninvoiced Receipts Can Be Reconciled? You Bet!"

- ✔ **Use an analogy:** "Truth, Like Roses, Often Comes With Thorns: The Immigration Issue in the United States" (Richard D. Lamm).

- ✔ **Adapt a well-known concept:** "The 90s MIS Holy Grail: Connecting the Desktop to Corporate Databases" (Gene Cort).

- ✔ **Use a number:** "Eight Myths about Drugs: There Are No Simple Solutions" (Lee Brown).

Research Tips and Tricks

The traditional way to approach research is to look at primary and secondary sources.

Primary sources are the original sources. Secondary sources are everything else. For example, if you were talking about what's in the Declaration of Independence, the primary source would be the original copy of the Declaration. Secondary sources would be books and articles about what's in it or a professor talking about what's in it.

Do-it-yourself titles

Having trouble devising a catchy title for your talk? Don't sweat it. Here are some ready-made names that you can complete by filling in your specific topic:

The ABCs of _____

A Nuts-and-Bolts Guide to _____

Doing _____ by the Numbers

_____ 101

The Myth of _____

Beyond _____

Do It Yourself _____

The Ten Commandments of _____

Those are the traditional definitions. Now let me explain how I use the terms. By *primary sources,* I mean any information that comes from people — yourself or people you've interviewed. I use *secondary sources* to refer to all non-people sources — books, articles, movies, and so on. I find it more convenient to classify research in this manner.

Primary sources

An old philosopher once said it's more interesting to hear a speaker who met an old philosopher than a speaker who read about one. That's true. People like to hear first-hand accounts of events and experiences, and it's really not that difficult to come up with them.

Mining yourself for material

If you're old enough to give a speech, you're old enough to have life experiences that you can use in your speech — personal anecdotes, war stories, insights, and observations. But that's the common knowledge. Everyone knows you're supposed to try to include personal material. It makes any presentation more interesting. The uncommon knowledge involves how you obtain and use that material.

Creating new personal material

Suppose that you have to talk about trends in the economy and you don't have any personal anecdotes that directly relate to the topic. Get some. It's very easy. Will you mention new housing starts as a trend indicator? Drive around and count the number of housing developments you see under construction. Now you've got a personal experience that you can fit to your data. "One of the most important indicators of our economic future is housing starts. As I drove to work the other day, I counted fifteen houses under construction. Each one was swarming with workers sawing, hammering, and nailing. Piles of wood and bags of cement covered each site. Dump trucks pulled in and out hauling earth away. Architects studied plans. Little sandwich trucks stopped by to sell lunch to the construction workers. It's amazing how much economic activity is generated by building a house. So it's good news that housing starts nationally have increased x percent during the past year."

Will you be speaking about television? Watch some. Is your topic politics? Attend a city council meeting. No matter what you discuss, you can always find an easy way to develop personal material.

Using what you already have

Now let's talk about the material you already possess. Here's the obvious way to use it. Imagine that you're a teacher and that you have an anecdote about the dumb excuses your students make when they're late for school. You can use the story to illustrate your point about about the need to take responsibility and not make excuses. That's OK, especially if you're talking to teachers.

But there's another, more powerful way to use the anecdote. *You can unleash its emotions.* You can emphasize the *frustration* you felt when the students made their excuses. Then, even if your audience isn't teachers, they'll understand what you mean because everyone can relate to frustration.

"Emotions are universal," explains comedy coach John Cantu. "That's what any audience can connect with. If I'm an accountant and you're a teacher, I don't really connect with the physical facts of your story — the students making excuses. But I do connect with the emotion — the frustration."

So here's what he suggests. After you've picked a topic, take a sheet of paper and list some basic emotions — love, anger, fear, hate, embarrassment, and so on. Then think of experiences that you've had that caused each emotion. For example, what has made you angry? If you get stuck, narrow it down to specific situations. What about your work makes you angry? What about your family makes you angry? What about your school? What about your softball team? Mechanically go through a variety of situations. After you find a good anecdote based on anger, write it down and edit it into its best form. Go through your talk and find a place where you can talk about anger and then tie in the anger with the anecdote.

"Find the emotion first," John advises. "Then find the story. That way the audience will always connect with it."

Interview people

One of the best, and most neglected, sources of primary material is other people. They have stories. They have experiences. They have insights. You just have to interview people to get ahold of this vast source of information. Writers and journalists do it. Police do it. Even game show hosts do it. Speakers, however, tend to ignore interviews as a source of information, and that's a mistake.

It's really no big deal to arrange and conduct an interview. People love to talk about their work and hobbies. If you have to speak about cars, you can call an auto dealer, tell him or her that you will be giving a speech about cars, and ask if he or she could spend five minutes talking with you. Most people won't refuse that request. They'll be delighted to give you information. Whatever your topic happens to be, interview a few people in that profession or industry.

Now let's talk about the interview. The common knowledge is that the last two questions should be: "Is there anything you thought I should have asked that I didn't ask?" and "Do you want to add anything?"

Here's some uncommon knowledge from comedy coach John Cantu. The single best question you can ask is *"What do you know now about (the topic) that you wish you knew when you were starting out?"* (It's especially useful in situations when you may have less than a minute to conduct the interview — talking to

---

Personal anecdote checklist

Personal anecdotes are among your most valuable assets as a speaker. They gain a lot of attention because they're real. So you should stockpile as many as you can remember. Need some help recalling an anecdote based on a real life experience? The following list will help jog your memory.

Your most embarrassing experience

The angriest you've ever been

The most inappropriate letter you've ever received

Your first date

The strangest habit of a friend, relative, or coworker

The dumbest thing you've ever heard

Your first day on the job

The worst boss you've ever had

The saddest thing that ever happened to a friend

The biggest mistake you ever made

A strange dream

The most bizarre thing you've ever seen or heard

Your wildest vacation story

The weirdest thing that ever happened at a business meeting

Eating out: strange restaurants, waiters, food, poor service

Relatives

Learning to drive

High school: prom, teachers, classes

College: dorm, professors, exams

Anecdotes your parents told you

Your first job interview

Something that seems funny now but didn't when it happened

The strangest gift you've ever received

---

someone in an elevator, buttonholing someone at a business function, meeting a celebrity on a plane.) "You'll be amazed at the information this question produces," says John. "Not only do you get information about your topic, you get insight into the people you interview. Their answers reveal what they think is important and give you a sense of their values." If you can only ask one question, ask this one.

Secondary sources

Once again, my definition of *secondary sources* is any source that isn't a person. Here are a few secondary sources that you should find particularly useful.

Library

Everyone knows that the library is packed full of research and reference tools. So here's some uncommon knowledge from comedy coach John Cantu:

Make the children's section your first stop at the library. "If you can find a children's book about your subject, it will cover most of the key points," John explains. "It's a good way to begin an outline."

The Wall Street Journal

Speechwriter John Austin likes *The Wall Street Journal* as a source of statistics, anecdotes, and examples. "Look at the three main stories on the front page," he advises. "They always use the same formula. They start with a very specific anecdote and use it as a springboard to discuss a general theme." For example, "The lead paragraph might give a detailed description of a car accident caused by brake failure," he says. "Then the rest of the article becomes a discussion of brake safety." So if you're talking about cars, safety, insurance, brakes, or any other related topic, you can use that opening anecdote somewhere in your presentation. You'll probably find some relevant statistics elsewhere in the article.

Day and Date Book

John Austin also likes the *Day and Date Book* as a research tool. "It lets you go back and find out what was happening at a particular time," he explains. "It's great for setting a mood or context for the subject of a talk." For example, John writes a lot of speeches about the energy business. His clients often want to speak about business changes in the context of societal or global changes. How does John write about that topic? "I look in the *Day and Date Book* and see what caused the changes that made the economy more global or focused more attention on the environment," he says. "That information then gets woven into the speech."

Chase's Annual Events

This book provides an easy way to write the opening to a talk. Just look up the events for the day you're speaking. Then pick one (or more) and use it to lead into your talk. "Today is the Fourth of July — the birthday of the United States, but also the birthday of Abigail Van Buren who you know as Dear Abby. So in honor of the occasion, I'm going to spend our time together today by giving you some advice." (The opening is only the most obvious place to refer to an event of the day. You can drop this type of reference into any section of a presentation. The line about advice could be used as a transition to a major point or to lead into the conclusion.)

Videos

Do you need to get up to speed quickly on the topic of your talk? Watch a video about it. Your local library and video rental store have lots of documentaries and "how to" videos on every conceivable subject. No, you won't get all your information from a video, but it's a good starting point. Videos also provide lots of good ideas for visual aids that you might want to use in your speech.

Chapter 5

Relating to Your Audience (Without a Paternity Test)

A sports announcer came to dinner at the home of a young baseball player and talked sports with the ballplayer while the ballplayer's wife bustled about the kitchen preparing the meal. Suddenly the couple's baby started to cry. Over her shoulder, the wife yelled, "Change the baby." The ballplayer was embarrassed. He said, "What do you mean, change the baby? That's not my line of work." His wife turned around, put her hands on her hips, and said, "Look buster, you lay the diaper out like a diamond, you put second base on home plate, put the baby's bottom underneath, and if it starts to rain, the game ain't called, you start all over again."

The wife got her message across very effectively. Why? Because she knew how to relate to her audience.

Audience Analysis

How do you relate to an audience? You start by learning as much about the people in the audience as possible. Who are they? What do they believe in? Why are they listening to you? This process is known as *audience analysis*.

The more information you possess, the more you can target your remarks to reflect an audience's interests. By targeting your audience's interest, you increase the likelihood that members of the audience will listen to you. Displaying your knowledge about an audience usually scores some points with them. It compliments the audience. It shows that you bothered to learn about them.

Audience analysis also helps you shape your message. What types of arguments should you make? What will be the most effective examples? How complex can you make your explanations? What authorities should you quote? The answers to these and similar questions should determine much of the structure and content of your presentation.

Demographic information: age, sex, and stuff like that

The first thing I always want to know about an audience is its size. Will it be 10 people, 100 people, or 1,000 people? The size of the audience determines a lot of aspects of the presentation. For example, a large audience eliminates the use of certain types of visual aids and requires the use of a microphone. A smaller audience is often less formal. Certain gimmicks that work with a large group will seem silly with a small one. ("Turn around and shake hands with the person behind you" just doesn't cut it when the entire audience is seated in one row.)

The second thing I want to know is the general nature of the audience. What's the relationship of the audience members to each other? Do they all come from the same organization? Do they share a common interest? I use this information to shape my message at a very basic level.

The next thing I want to find out is specific demographic data about audience members. What's their age range? What kind of schooling have they had? Here's a list of standard demographic items.

- ✔ Age
- ✔ Sex
- ✔ Education level
- ✔ Economic status
- ✔ Religion
- ✔ Occupation
- ✔ Racial/ethnic makeup
- ✔ Politics
- ✔ Cultural influences

The common knowledge is that you should gather as much demographic information about your audience as possible. Here's the uncommon knowledge. You can collect a lot more of this stuff than you'll ever use. Yes, theoretically you may want to tailor your speech to reflect every last characteristic of your audience, but in reality, you may not have the time or inclination to do that.

For example, suppose that you work for a drug company. You've been asked to present an overview of the company to a group of prospective investors. Is their age, sex, or religion going to affect what you say? Certainly you could think of ways to take advantage of your knowledge of these characteristics, but the shape of your presentation will probably be a lot more heavily influenced by your knowledge of the audience's occupations and educational background. Are some of the prospective investors doctors? (They may know more about drugs than you do.) Are they professional investment advisors? Or are they wealthy individuals without a clue about corporate finance? (How sophisticated should you make your analysis of the "numbers?") You get the idea. Instead of wasting a lot of time impersonating a census taker, zero in on the audience characteristics that will make a real difference to your presentation.

Audience attitudes, values, and beliefs

While speakers tend to focus on audience census data, they tend to overlook audience beliefs, attitudes, and values. The reason is simple. It's difficult to develop this information. It's easy to learn how many audience members are male or female, but it's tough to learn what they're thinking. Yet their beliefs, attitudes, and values will color their interpretation of every aspect of your presentation.

What exactly do you need to know? In essence, you want to compose a mental profile of your audience. You want to know "where they're coming from." Here are some of the questions you'll want answered.

- What is the audience's attitude about the subject of your talk?
- What is the audience's attitude toward you as the speaker?
- What stereotypes will the audience apply to you?
- Will anyone have a hidden agenda?
- What values does the audience find important?
- Does the audience share a common value system?
- How strongly held are their beliefs and attitudes?

The answers to these questions will help determine your approach to the subject.

What do they know and when did they know it?

Legendary football coach Vince Lombardi was giving his team a lecture on the basics. "We're going to start from the beginning," he said. "This is a football." That's when one of his players responded, "Hold on, coach, you're going too fast."

Want to start at the beginning with your audience? Then you'd better find out how much they already know. Two of the biggest mistakes speakers make are talking over the heads of their audiences and talking at a level that's too elementary.

Here are some questions to ponder before you make your presentation:

- ✔ How sophisticated are the audience members about your topic?
- ✔ Will there be experts in the audience?
- ✔ Have they heard other speakers talk about your topic?
- ✔ Why are they interested in your topic?
- ✔ Will they understand jargon related to your topic?
- ✔ Do they already know the basic concepts of your topic?
- ✔ Do they think they know a lot about your topic?
- ✔ How did they get the information they already have about your topic?
- ✔ Are they already familiar with your approach and attitude toward the topic?

Once again, the answers to these questions will play a major role in how you construct your presentation. What your audience knows will determine how much background you need to provide, the sophistication of the language you can use, and the examples you include.

How to Find Out

The more information you can obtain about your audience, the better. How do you get information on your audience? Your prime source should be your contact at the organization sponsoring your presentation. "The first thing I ask for is a list of people and their titles," says Jim Lukaszewski. "That immediately tells you a lot about how sophisticated your audience will be." Your contact should also be able to answer many of your questions about the audience's demographic makeup, its attitudes, and its responses to past speakers.

But don't put all your eggs in one basket. The following are some other sources of information that you should investigate:

- ✔ Officers and officials of the organization
- ✔ Public relations people (Does the organization have a PR department or PR agency?)
- ✔ Publications from the organization (Does it issue annual reports, newsletters, brochures?)
- ✔ Personal acquaintances who are members of the organization

And here's some uncommon knowledge from Jim Lukaszewski. If you really want to get good information, interview members of your audience. "I ask the sponsor to send me the names of a dozen audience members," says Jim. "I also ask the sponsor to call these people to let them know I'll be calling." Then he calls them, introduces himself, and briefly describes his presentation. He also asks them three questions: What's important about this to you? If you could decide what I'd talk about, what would you have me talk about? What questions would you have me answer for a lot of people? "The more important the speech, the more audience members I call," he says. "I once gave a speech to twenty executives in a company, and I called every one of them."

John Cantu also says that it's important to interview your audience members. He likes to ask them about past speakers. Who was the audience's favorite speaker? Least favorite? Why? John says that one of your best sources of information about an audience will be a previous speaker. "Try to determine whether someone has spoken who was really a big hit," he advises. If there is such a person, try to speak with him or her. Find out what that person said. What worked? What didn't? What would the speaker do differently if given another chance?"

And last but not least — want to get a really good sense of how your audience relates to speakers? If you're going to speak at a regularly scheduled meeting, attend one of the meetings beforehand. (Many clubs and associations have monthly meetings built around a lunch or dinner speaker. They'll be delighted to let you come to one — especially if you pay for your own lunch or dinner.)

What's in It for Them?

No matter how diplomatically you phrase it, there's only one question that an audience member ever really wants answered: what's in it for me? Why should an audience listen to you? Successfully answering that question can go a long way toward establishing a positive relationship. In order to answer successfully, you need to learn what the audience members expect and tell them how you'll provide it.

What do they expect?

"I saw a world-famous economist speak to a group of 3000 people, and he made time go backward," says high-tech marketing manager Neil Baron. "He used arcane language from the semiconductor industry, but no one was from the semiconductor industry. And no one cared about it. After the first hour, people started breaking out magazines. And because it was a dark room, they used cigarette lighters and flashlights to read. It looked like a candlelight vigil in memory of the guy's speech."

Why would anyone talk about semiconductors to people who had no interest in them? What did the speaker think the audience expected? Sometimes you've just got to wonder.

But you shouldn't wonder about what *your* audience members expect. Find out why they're attending your presentation. Are they interested in your topic? Were they ordered to attend? What do they expect to learn or see or hear? What do they expect you to say or do?

Highlight the benefits

Make sure the audience knows what it's going to get out of your presentation. Identify and emphasize the benefits early in your talk and issue frequent reminders.

Communication expert Alan Weiner says all audience members subconsciously ask themselves a benefits question: Will they hear anything to help them save or make money, save time, or reduce stress, anxiety, ambiguity, and confusion? So a smart speaker will address as many of these issues as possible. Alan uses an example of a CEO who has to tell his company's employees about an impending reduction in force. Here's how Alan would advise him to begin: "I hope as a result of my appearance today, you'll have less stress over what the next couple of months of your life are going to be like, you'll be able to plan better and sleep better." Despite discussing bad news, the CEO is putting the message in terms of audience benefits.

"Using those key topics of saving money, saving time, and reducing stress is at the heart of audience analysis," explains Alan. "They should always be included in your introduction in some form or another. The secret to audience analysis is the perception that you've done an audience analysis."

I'd add sex and health to Alan's list of key topics. Sex and health are topics of universal interest. They span age, gender, culture and geographic boundaries. (And if you don't believe me, just turn on your TV and watch some infomercials.)

Putting Your Audience in the Picture

If you really want to relate to your audience members, you have to see the world from their point of view and let them know that you can see it their way. How do you do this? One of my favorite examples comes from management communications advisor Jim Lukaszewski. He was scheduled to make a presentation to the executives of a large waste removal company. Prior to his presentation, he arranged to spend three days working on a garbage truck. "The whole hierarchy of the company was run by people who had started as garbagemen," he explains. So as soon as he got up to speak, he let them know that he'd just spent three days hauling garbage. "They were eating out of my hand," he recalls. (So to speak.) Jim's point is well taken. His audience could relate to him because he demonstrated an understanding of their experience. He had thrown garbage into the back of the truck.

What if you don't have the experience? You can still communicate that you understand the world of your audience. "Sometimes acknowledging your *dissimilarity* shows that you understand your audience," says Joe DiNucci, Vice President of Manufacturing Industries at Silicon Graphics. "I had to give a speech to a group of our telesales people. These are young kids who wear headsets all day. Well, I've never sold over the phone." (It's probably the only way Joe hasn't sold. He's a legendary sales executive in the computer industry.)

So how did he relate to his audience? He told them, "I've been selling since 1965, but I've never sold on the phone. So in preparing for this meeting, I had to ask myself what do you people do to sell over the phone. How in the world would you do that? That is really hard." Then to show he understood how hard it is, Joe cited a study about lying. And he asked his audience to guess the results of the study. "Which way is it easiest to detect when someone is lying?" Joe asked. "Choice one is a face-to-face conversation. Choice two is a telephone call. Choice three is a videotaped conversation. Choice four is a letter." After revealing that the correct answer was a telephone conversation, he drew some positive inferences for his audience. "I guess it means that successful telephone sales people must have substantially higher integrity," he said. "So I'd like them for in-laws and neighbors." Then he talked about the sales implications — the differences between selling over the phone versus face-to-face selling, as well as the similarities.

If you don't have the specific experience, you can substitute a study. "I call it a data bridge," Joe explains. "People love studies and data if it's related to what they do." (You're not going to find a study of greater interest to salespeople than a study about lying.) But remember, first you have to acknowledge that you don't have the experience — otherwise you'll lose credibility.

The next sections show two more ways to put your audience in the picture.

Making personal experience universal

Philosophers have said that no man is an island, but many speakers remain unaware of that fact — every other word out of their mouths is "I." I this. I that. I the other. They live in the land of I. (An I-land, get it?) Unfortunately for them, that's not where audiences live.

"Audiences don't want to hear a speaker say 'I' a lot," says San Francisco comedy coach John Cantu. "They want to hear the word 'you.'" He favors a three-to-one ratio. "Everytime a speaker says 'I,' there should also be at least three 'yous.'"

But don't audiences want to hear about a speaker's personal experience? Isn't that what you bring to the table as a speaker? Yes. It's how you go about describing that experience that's key. *You've got to find and emphasize the universal aspects of your personal experience.*

Contrast these two examples of a retired plumber speaking:

Example 1:

"You know I used to be a plumber. Let me tell you about the time I flushed an alligator down the toilet and it got stopped up."

Example 2:

"Did you ever have a job that you really hated but you couldn't quit because you needed the money? I used to be a plumber. And I couldn't quit because I needed the money. And let me tell you about what happened when an alligator got flushed down a toilet and stopped it up."

"In the second example, the plumber can tell the same story, but I relate to him in a completely different way," explains John. "I'm not relating to him on the basis of a plumber telling me about plumbing. I'm relating to the fact that he had a humorous experience with a lousy job."

Localizing and customizing your remarks

Big time politicians and big time comedians have something in common (besides the fact that people laugh at them). Both use "advance men" to gather information about local news, business, and people at the places where they'll be performing. Why? So they can work local references into their presentations. Customizing your talk to your audience is one of the most powerful and effective ways of relating to your audience. Customizing grabs the audience's attention and gets the audience involved in your presentation. It makes the speaker a bit of an insider and lets the audience know that the speaker went to the trouble of learning about the audience.

Here's the really good news: A little, and I mean very little, customization goes a long, long way. I've given speeches where I made five or six references geared specifically to a particular audience, and afterwards I was showered with praise for the research I did to learn about the group. The references don't even have to be all that specific. I often use a joke about three business establishments located adjacent to each other on the main street in town. Depending on who I'm addressing, those businesses have been software companies, real estate agencies, law firms, computer manufacturers, phone companies . . . well, you get the idea. (I always make sure to get at least one very specific reference that clearly shows I did some research.)

What kind of information should you use for these specific references? The names of key members of the audience are always good — especially if you can use them in a way that reflects their personalities. For example, during a speech about using humor in the workplace at an insurance company's management retreat, I suggested that the audience start every memo with a funny, relevant quote. "Everyone will pay attention to it," I said, "except Mr. Executive. Never send him anything in writing. Memos disappear on contact with his desk. In fact, the Clinton Whitewater team is interested in buying that desk." The audience of managers who had been frustrated for years with Mr. Executive's lack of response to memos roared with laughter. (By the way, Mr. Executive isn't his real name. But you already knew that, right?)

How did I know about Mr. Executive? I worked closely with the company's communications director as I prepared my talk. He told me about the key players and what I could or couldn't say about them. That's an important point. You don't want to offend anyone. When I'm going to use a name, I always clear it with a high-ranking member of the group.

What else can you refer to? Local news events if you're speaking out of town. Customs or rituals associated with the organization you're addressing. The organization's history. Use your imagination. If you were a member of the audience, what would impress *you* if an outsider referred to it?

Pushing their hot buttons

You can use a specialized form of customizing your remarks that immediately establishes you as an insider and connects with your audience. It's called pushing their hot buttons. You purposely work in a reference to a *buzz issue* — something that's a source of minor controversy with the audience. The key word is *minor*. You want to get a rise out of them, not have them rise up against you.

One of my favorite examples is the time I suggested an audience ease up on memo and report writing. "You're wasting too much Xerox paper," I explained. The room burst into laughter and applause. Why? The people in the audience, employees of a Fortune 500 company, had been ordered to reduce their use of copier paper as a cost savings measure. They thought it was ridiculous.

When digging for buzz issues, you need to keep a couple of things in mind. First, you have to find one that will cut across the *entire* audience. (Very often when I ask my contact for a buzz issue, I'll get something that would be hilarious to a handful of key players, but that no one else would comprehend. Use your judgment. Make sure that the "issue" is an issue for everyone.) Second, you've got to make sure that the issue isn't too controversial to mention. Again, this is a judgment call. (But your contact will usually be reliable here because it's his or her butt on the line if you stir up a hornet's nest and start a riot.)

One of the simplest ways to find a buzz issue is to ask your contact if any recent or pending legislation will negatively affect the audience. When the answer is yes, you have your issue.

Cross-Cultural Audiences

A mother mouse was trying to teach her offspring the ways of the world when she found herself, and her family, face-to-face with a great big cat. Her children were terrified. But the mother remained calm and started barking like a dog. The cat heard the barking, turned tail, and took off. The mother mouse turned to her little ones and said, "Now you see that's the importance of a second language."

When the mother mouse spoke to the cat, she faced a challenge that's becoming more prevalent with each passing day. She had to communicate with an audience from a different culture, but at least she had one advantage — she could speak a language her audience understood.

With today's global economy and the spread of multinational corporations, more and more presentations involve a speaker of one culture addressing an audience of another. That situation creates a whole special set of communication problems. If you think relating to an audience of your peers is tough, try speaking to an audience from another culture — especially when you *don't* speak its language.

In order to understand the special problems involved, I spoke with my friend J. E. Aeliot Boswell. Aeliot is one of the most prominent family law attorneys in Beverly Hills, California and an expert in cross-cultural communication. She's had to become one by virtue of her practice. She specializes in international family law and child abduction. An authority on the Hague Convention and international jurisdiction, she frequently makes presentations at conferences held around the globe. She also teaches seminars in cross-cultural communication for attorneys. Here are her basic tips to keep in mind when you address an audience from a different culture:

Don't fall for stereotypes

Don't assume you know about a culture because you know the popular stereotypes. Find out what the culture is really like. You'll spare yourself a lot of embarrassment.

Don't assume your humor will work

What makes something funny? While one could write a dissertation on this subject (and many have), the short answer is that much humor is rooted in cultural values. So something that's funny in one culture may not be in another. "Unless you're very familiar with the culture, using humor is usually a mistake," says Aeliot. "No one may get your joke, or even worse, they may find it offensive."

Do project humility

"The best way to win over audiences from any culture is to project the fact that you care for them and are really interested in them," says Aeliot. "You're really happy and honored to be there with them. That's a cultural universal." In contrast, the opposite approach — arrogantly communicating that the audience has lucked out by being in your presence — is a big turnoff (and a common mistake).

Don't greet the audience in their language if you don't speak it

It's almost a cliché for a speaker addressing an audience that speaks a different language to start by saying a few words or a sentence in that language. (Typically, it's something like "I'm happy to be here today" in whatever language is native to the audience.) The common knowledge is that this gesture shows that the speaker tried to learn a little of the audience's language.

In my opinion, if you're only going to learn one line, save it for the end. "If you've established a connection with the audience, ending with a line in their language really cements the relationship," says Aeliot. Her recommendation: End by saying, "Thank you for being here with me today" in their language.

If you want to open with a line in the audience's language, Aeliot suggests that you learn how to say, "I'm sorry for not knowing how to speak your language." It's much more effective than a greeting like, "I'm happy to be here today." (See the preceding rule regarding humility.)

Tips and Tricks for Creating Rapport

The major goal when relating to your audience is to establish rapport with them — a feeling of mutual warmth and a sense that you're on the same wavelength. The following sections present a few ways to achieve that goal.

Acknowledge what the audience is feeling

If you're speaking under any special circumstances, acknowledge it. Is the audience sweltering in a hot, stuffy room? Would the audience prefer to be anywhere but listening to you? Has the audience made certain assumptions about you? Get it out in the open. Otherwise, it will remain a barrier between you and your audience.

Assuage their fears

"Most audiences carry a few basic fears to any presentation," says Jim Lukaszewski. "They fear the speaker will be dull, have nothing of value to say, speak too fast, avoid eye contact, and fail to connect with the audience." That's why a strong opening is essential. You have to take command immediately and show the audience that it has nothing to worry about.

Share something that helps the audience know you

Jim Lukaszewski believes that one of the quickest ways to bridge the gulf between speaker and audience members is to share something personal. Tell them something that lets them get to know you. What can you share?

- **An unusual experience.** It helps the audience relate to you in a concrete way. "I talk about when I was 14 in Minneapolis and I was involved in a fire rescue program," says Jim. "Talking about it helps the audience see me as a real person, not just as an expert in management communications."

- **Your personal principles or beliefs.** This will help the audience understand where you're coming from. They'll be able to better evaluate your remarks and put them in a context — two things that we routinely do with people we already know.

- **Your avocations and hobbies.** What are your interests outside of work? How you entertain yourself says a lot about you. Providing that information will help the audience feel like they know you.

Don't whine about your problems

Nobody wants to hear how you got a flat tire on the way to the meeting and then couldn't find a parking space. Nobody cares about your problems unless they're directly related to your topic. No one wants to hear you whine. As Jim Lukaszewski says, "Fifty percent of your audience won't care. Twenty-five percent will have troubles worse than yours. And twenty-five percent will be glad you have problems."

Identify and address audience subgroups

Keep in mind that an audience may be made up of numerous subgroups — each with its own special needs and agendas. You need to include something for each of them if you want to create rapport with your entire audience. (A common example of this situation is the convention dinner attended by spouses. Half the audience is made up of people with the same occupation — engineers, doctors, whatever. The other half — the spouses — fall into two major categories. Those who have careers outside the home and those who are homemakers. So you immediately have three subgroups. The spouses with careers can probably be even further subdivided.)

Identify influential audience members

Sometimes an entire audience's response hinges on the reaction of a few key audience members. You may run into this situation if the audience comes from a single organization. They look to their leaders for cues about how to respond. I've spoken at corporate meetings where every time I told a joke, all eyes turned to the CEO. If he smiled, everyone would laugh. If he didn't smile, there was dead silence. (Well, not complete silence. You could hear me sweating.) Identify the audience leaders and get them on your side. Play to them and you'll be playing to everyone.

Express your emotions

If you want the audience members to express their emotions (heap praise upon your performance, shower you with an outpouring of love, hurt their hands applauding), then you have to express yours. "Let them know you care about them," says Jim Lukaszewski. "Tell them you're glad they came, you hope they learn something and that you're there for them."

President Ronald Reagan relates to his audience

During his presidency, Ronald Reagan was known as "The Great Communicator" because of his ability to speak persuasively to the American people. One of his secrets was establishing a positive relationship with the audience within the first few moments of his speeches. He would find a common bond, show his knowledge of the audience, or empathize with their concerns. One way or another, he always established a connection. Here are a few examples:

The International Association of Chiefs of Police: "You and I have a few things in common. Harry Truman once said about the job I have that being President is like riding a tiger: A man has to keep on riding or he'll get swallowed. Well, that's a pretty good description of what you do for a living."

The American Medical Association: "I'm delighted to address this annual meeting of the AMA House of Delegates, and I want to congratulate Dr. Jirka and Dr. Boyle on their new positions. I can't help but think what a great place this would be and what a great moment to have a low back pain."

Presidential Awards for Excellence in Science and Mathematics Teaching: "Well, it's wonderful to have all of you here today at the White House. We want you to enjoy our little get-together today. So please lean back, relax, and stop worrying about what the students are doing to the substitute teachers back home."

The Indiana State Legislature: "You know, the late Herb Shriner, who was from Fort Wayne, said he was born in Ohio, but he moved to Indiana as soon as he heard about it."

Focus on their needs not yours

You have to focus on what will interest your audience, not what will interest you. "I see speaker after speaker violate this basic rule," says Neil Baron. "If people have been sitting on their butts for ten hours, they don't care that you prepared a 60-minute talk. Cut it down to 20 minutes and they'll think you are a genius." How often does that happen? Not often enough — and that's Neil's point. Put the audience's needs ahead of your own. You don't have to ignore your own needs, but your needs won't be served if no one is listening.

A cynical old philosopher once said that an audience is a group of people waiting to be bored. Prove him wrong. Tailor your remarks to your audience. Think about their needs. Put them in the picture. Create some rapport. They won't be bored. And even if they are, they'll like you too much to admit it.

Chapter 6
Organizing Your Presentation

・・

・・

Here's the standard advice for organizing a speech: Tell the audience what you're going to say, then tell them, and tell them what you've told them. I've heard many consultants offer this bromide and then wait to be hailed as geniuses. (They look meaningfully into their clients' eyes like they've just delivered some great insight.) But here's the problem with the tell, tell, tell formula — it doesn't really tell you anything. (How's that for irony?) It's like telling someone that you build a ship by assembling a bunch of material so that it will float while you're in it. OK, great. But how do you do that?

This chapter provides a detailed look at how to organize a presentation. You'll learn everything from how to decide what to tell an audience, to how to arrange what you tell an audience, to how much to tell an audience. It's a tell-all chapter. (Hey, at least it's not a kiss and tell.)

Selecting Material

Before you can organize your presentation, you must first choose the material for your presentation. Your real task is deciding what *not* to use. Here's why. No matter what your topic, you'll always be able to find a lot more material than you'll have time to discuss. And more important, there's a limit to how much material that audiences can absorb. If you give them too much, it can actually reduce the amount that they ultimately comprehend and remember. (Someone should have told that to my high school French teacher.)

Here are a few guidelines to keep in mind when choosing material:

- ✔ **Select a variety of material.** You know the expression "different strokes for different folks"? Applied to presentations, it means using different types of material — anecdotes, statistics, examples, quotes, and so on. A variety of material makes your presentation more interesting. It also increases the chance that each member of your audience will find something appealing in your speech.

- ✔ **Keep your audience in mind.** Choose material that your audience will understand and find interesting. The question isn't what you know about the topic. It's what does the audience need to know in order to make your presentation a success.

- ✔ **Always carry a spare.** Keep some material in reserve — an extra example, statistic, or anecdote. You never know when you'll need it.

Patterns of Organization

Imagine that someone hands you a piece of paper that says "m," "d," "u," "y," "m." It doesn't seem to mean much. (Unless it's supposed to be an eye test.) Now assume that the person hands you the paper with the letters arranged as "d," "u," "m," "m," "y." Is your reaction a little different? Congratulations, you've recognized a pattern.

Patterns play a critical role in how we assign meaning and how we interpret messages. You could read a lot of perceptual psychology theory to figure out this stuff, but I'll give you a break and skip it. Suffice it to say that human beings have a natural tendency to organize phenomena into patterns. The way we shape those patterns determines much of the outcome of our communications with each other.

Information arranged in a pattern is also easier to process and retain. Try a little experiment. Here are two columns of words. Which one is easier to memorize?

be	to
question	be
to	or
that	not
not	to
the	be
be	that
is	is
to	the
or	question

I think you see my point; it applies to every presentation you give. The more order and structure you provide for your audience, the more effective your message will be.

Two key rules

Want the pattern to strengthen your presentation as much as possible? Just follow these next two rules:

Make the pattern obvious

Have you ever seen those pictures that are all little dots? You know, the ones that you can't tell what the picture is supposed to be until you hold it close to your face? And then you're supposed to be able to see an image? (It's some kind of "new age" art thing.) Yes, the dots form a pattern because some people see the image, but the pattern sure isn't obvious — at least to me and many other people who have never perceived the image. (I've flattened my nose trying to see the image, but it still looks like dots.)

Keep this in mind when you put together a presentation. You don't want a "little dot" pattern that won't be recognized by everybody. You want a pattern that your whole audience can perceive. Your speech isn't an intelligence test. You don't want to find out whether your audience is smart enough to discover your hidden structure. You want to make sure that your pattern is obvious so that your audience can perceive it — easily. You *can't* make it too obvious.

Choose an appropriate pattern

Consider your topic and audience when choosing a pattern. What pattern will best help get your message across? For example, if you're talking about the history of a land use dispute in your neighborhood, a chronological pattern probably makes more sense than a theory/practice pattern.

Commonly used patterns

While patterns are infinite in variety, certain ones appear over and over again. Here are a few of the most common patterns for presentations:

- **Problem/solution:** State a problem and offer a solution. What you emphasize will depend on what the audience members already know. Do you need to make them aware of the problem or do they already know about it? Are there competing solutions? And so on.

- **Chronological:** Will you be speaking about a series of events? (The history of accidents at that corner where you want a stop sign.) Organizing your talk in a past/present/future pattern will make it easy to follow.

- **Physical location:** You might want to use this one if you're talking about things that occur at various locations. Are you giving the company orientation presentation to new employees? You can divide the talk by floors (first floor, second floor, third floor), buildings (Building A, B and C), or other physical areas (North American operations, European operations, Asian operations).

- **Extended metaphor or analogy:** "Today I'll talk about how giving a presentation is like the flight of an airplane. We'll talk about the takeoff, the landing, the flight, the passengers, and the control tower. The takeoff is the introduction. . . ."

- **Cause/effect:** Everyone knows that this pattern is useful for scientific discussions. It also works great for assigning blame. "The southern region decided to listen to some management guru this quarter. So it instituted new procedures, bought new expense reporting software, and made a commitment to innovative sales methods. As a result, its gross sales declined by 50 percent, and its margins shrank 10 percent." (But the guru had record profits).

- **Divide a quote:** Clergymen often use this device in sermons. "The Bible says, 'Wisdom is better than rubies.' What does this really mean? Let's start with wisdom. Is it just your IQ? No. Most of us know people who have a high IQ who aren't very wise."

- **Divide a word:** "Today, I'm going to talk about 'LOVE.' 'L' stands for laughter. Laughter is very important in our lives because. . . ."

- **Catch phrase:** "What you see is what you get. What I see today is broken homes, increased poverty, and more school dropouts. What we're getting is an unraveling social fabric, more people in need of assistance, and an uneducated work force. Let's take a look at these problems."

- **Theory/practice:** You can use this one for talking about something that didn't turn out as planned. (The big gap between theory and practice.)

- **Topic Pattern:** This is a free-form pattern. You divide your topic into logical segments based on your own instinct, judgment, and common sense. (I often use this pattern in my presentations about humor. The segments are: why humor is a powerful communication tool, how to make a point with humor, and simple types of non-joke humor anyone can use. It's an easy-to-follow pattern that makes sense for the material.)

Packaging and bundling

According to management communication advisor Jim Lukaszewski, *one of the most powerful ways to organize information is in the form of a numericalized list.* For example, you can say, "I have some good ideas." Or you can say, "I have four good ideas." The number makes the statement much stronger. "When you numericalize the answers, you grab peoples' brains," Jim explains. "They'll count them. Mention that you have four good ideas and just talk about three. Sooner or later, someone will ask about the fourth idea."

You can use this technique to organize your entire presentation ("Ten Ways To Stop Crime"). Or you can use it for individual segments. ("We've talked about the importance of humor, how to write a joke, and how to tell a joke. Now let's talk about six simple types of humor that don't require comic delivery.") "When you package and bundle the elements of your talk, the audience members know exactly where you're going," says Jim. "It helps them follow and understand your message."

But don't go overboard. If you make the list too long, you can actually lose the audience. "A politician running for higher office designed a program of 101 reasons to vote for him," Jim recalls. "The opening line of his speech was always 'First. . . .' But by the time he got to 'Fifteen . . . ,' the audience realized that he was going to discuss every one of those 101 reasons. Have you ever seen facial expressions of panic mixed with boredom?"

So use your common sense. "It's like the press conference that Moses held after receiving the ten commandments," says Jim. "That night on the TV news, this is how the story was reported: 'Today, Moses went up Mt. Sinai and received the ten commandments. The top two are. . . .'" Keep the lists short.

Outlining

An outline is a blueprint for your talk. It lets you see what points you're making, how they're related to each other, and if they're arranged in a proper order. A good outline shows you how to construct a good speech. And like a blueprint for a building, an outline for a talk can take many shapes and forms.

Most people associate outlines with the traditional method emphasized in high school — the Roman numeral outline. (Each Roman numeral represents a major point. Each uppercase letter represents a subpoint, and each Arabic numeral represents a support for the subpoints.) But here's the uncommon knowledge: You can create outlines in many different ways. The key is to choose a method that works for you. As long as your method lets you break the talk into parts and see the relationship between the parts, you'll do fine.

When should you make an outline?

There are two basic choices regarding when to make an outline — before you've written your talk or after you've written it. The experts disagree on which way is best. (But I can resolve that issue. The best way is the one that works for you.) What follows are some considerations:

Before you write the presentation

With this approach, you focus on your purpose and identify the ideas that will achieve that purpose. Then you turn the ideas into major and minor points and fit them into an outline structure. Only then, when you can see exactly what you'll say, do you begin to flesh it out. This is an absolutely logical way to proceed. If the outline makes sense, it helps ensure that the presentation will make sense. (In fact, it's the way I was taught to answer exam questions in law school — always outline first.)

After you write the presentation

Alternatively, you may just plunge right into developing the presentation word for word. "What would you tell a close friend about the topic?" asks Allatia Harris, Dean of the Communications Division at Mountain View College. "You'll do a better job just talking it through off the cuff to a friend than starting with an outline." She advises that you think about the order in which you'd tell it to your friend, as well as what examples you'd use. "If you care about the person you're talking to and you care about the topic, everything else falls into place," she says. Write the outline after the speech is written. That will enable you to discover any flaws in your speech's structure so that you can rewrite where appropriate.

How many points should you have?

The number of points in an outline should reflect the number of points in your presentation. So the real question is how many points should you have in your presentation? There's no pat answer, but here are a few guidelines:

- **Decide what the audience needs to know.** What points are absolutely essential for you to include in your message. (And I mean *absolutely* essential. If one of these points were omitted, your presentation couldn't succeed.)

- **Don't put in too much information.** Many people try to pack too much information into a single presentation. "You can talk for an hour," notes John Cantu, "but you can't give an hour's worth of information. The audience can't absorb it at that rate."

- **Rule of thumb: no more than seven main points.** Experts disagree over the maximum number of points that you should have in a talk, but the highest number I've come across is seven. Less is usually better. (Some experts believe that an audience can't recall more than five main points. Or as Allatia Harris puts it, "When you have to count them on more than one hand, they get tough to remember.") The amount of time you have to speak is also a critical factor. Many experts suggest three major points for a half-hour talk. "You can roughly cover one major idea per eight minutes of time," says John Cantu. "That leaves three minutes for an introduction and three minutes to conclude."

> ✔ **Reorganize to reduce the number of points.** You've gone through your material and found fifteen main points that are absolutely essential. Don't even think about doing your presentation that way. First, make sure that you really can't lose a few of them. Second, reorganize the points so that they're included under fewer headings. Think of five to seven major points under which your fifteen points can be subcategorized.

Timing

Most people associate "*timing*" with how to tell a joke. That's *not* how I'm using the term here. By *timing,* I mean how much time it takes to deliver a presentation and how to make it fit the time you've been given. This section presents some thoughts on the subject.

How long should a talk be?

William Gladstone once observed that a speech need not be eternal to be immortal. His point is well taken. The tendency to speak longer than necessary is a stereotypical trait long associated with public speaking.

Perhaps the most famous example (often held up as a warning) is President William Henry Harrison's Inaugural Address — the longest one ever given. He spoke outdoors for one hour and 45 minutes on a cold, rainy day in Washington D.C. As a result, he caught a cold and died a few weeks later. In contrast, Lincoln's Gettysburg Address — one of the most eloquent speeches of all time — can be recited in about two minutes.

So how long should a speech be? Abraham Lincoln's response was "Like a man's pants — long enough to cover the subject." Here are a few additional guidelines:

> ✔ **Don't feel obligated to fill your entire time slot.** "Just because you've been given 45 minutes to speak doesn't mean you must speak for 45 minutes," says John Cantu. "If you can do it in 30 or 35 minutes, by all means do so." (But use your common sense. I recently spoke at a conference where another speaker, who was slotted for a one-hour presentation, completed his talk in ten minutes. The conference organizers were less than thrilled.)

> ✔ **It's better to be a little too short than a little too long.** If you conclude five minutes early, people in the audience will be thrilled. If you conclude five minutes late, they'll be impatient and possibly angry. Your audience members are busy. They have people to see and places to go. They expect you to be done on time. Don't disappoint them.

> ✔ **Twenty minutes is a good length.** If you can choose how long you'll speak, pick twenty minutes. It's long enough to cover a lot of information thoroughly, let the audience get to know you, and make a good impression. And it's short enough to do all that before the audience's attention span reaches its outer limit.

Timing tips and tricks

Einstein's theory of relativity may say that time and distance are identical, but many public speakers apparently disagree. They just can't go the distance in the time they've been allotted. Want to avoid that problem in your next presentation? Here are a few tips and tricks to ensure that you and your audience finish at the same time:

Estimate the time from the length of the script

Here's John Cantu's script-to-speech ratio: one double-spaced page of 10-point type equals two minutes of speaking time. So preparing a standard 20-minute talk is like writing a 10-page essay. (Keep that in mind when the person inviting you to speak says it will be easy to do.)

Convert practice time into a realistic estimate

Many speakers practice their talks aloud to get an idea of how long it will take to deliver. Here's a warning from John Cantu: For every minute that you practice your speech alone, there will be a time increase of about 33 percent when you speak in front of people. "There's an automatic slowing down when you talk to an audience because you're waiting for feedback," explains John. "So a five-minute talk to yourself at home might run 6^1/$_2$ or 7 minutes in front of an audience. A 10-minute talk could run 13 or 14 minutes." The time increase may range as high as 50 percent when you speak to an audience of several hundred people. "It's one of the reasons that meetings often run over time," notes John.

Make an adjustment for humor

If you use humor in your talk and it's effective, then part of your speaking time will be consumed by audience laughter and applause. That's good. Forgetting to account for that time when estimating how long your talk will last is bad. The diminished time effect is particularly pronounced for audiences of more than 300 people. "Large groups laugh in three waves," observes John Cantu. "The first group gets the joke right away. The second group gets it a little later. And the third group laughs after they hear everyone else laughing." So in a large audience, you have to allot even more time for audience response to humor. His rule of thumb: 10 to 15 seconds per wave of laughter in a large crowd. "So figure 45 seconds per joke," he says. "And if it's only 30 or 35 seconds, don't worry. The time you'd be short at the end will be eaten up by the longer applause you get because people think you're finishing early." (John says his calculations are based on the assumption that your jokes are funny. If they're not, give him a call.)

Be prepared to cut

You were told that you'd have 30 minutes to speak. But the meeting doesn't go as planned, and the schedule is thrown off. It's time for your talk. The meeting organizer says you've only got 15 minutes. (And believe me, this happens all the time.) What do you do? "The biggest mistake you can make is trying to give your 30-minute talk in 15 minutes," says John Cantu. "Speakers think that if they talk louder and faster, then some of what they're saying will sink in." Wrong! Here's what really happens. The speaker comes across as hyperactive and the audience comes away with nothing — except a bad impression of the speaker. You need to plan in advance. "Decide on your five most important slides or two most important points," John advises. "So when someone tells you to cut your time, you're prepared."

Don't cut the conclusion

When you need to cut part of your talk, don't cut the conclusion. Your presentation is like the flight of a plane, and the passengers are your audience. When you forgo the conclusion, it's like a crash landing. If you've been told in advance that your time will be shortened, cut from the body of your talk. Eliminate some examples or even a main point if necessary. What if you need to cut while you're speaking and you're rapidly running out of time? Find a logical place to stop and sum up what you've already said. Even better, have a conclusion that you can go into from any point in your talk. That way, no matter what happens, you'll always have a smooth landing for your audience.

Communicate your awareness of time

Audiences have been burned over and over again by speakers who went way past their time limit, and they worry about it happening again. You can ease their fears by making occasional references to indicate that you know how much time has passed (and how much *more* time will pass until you're done). It's as simple as saying things like: "I can't teach you everything there is to know about clown noses in twenty minutes, but in our time together today. . . ." "For the next five minutes I'd like to discuss. . . ." "Now we've arrived at the second half of my talk and I'd like to shift gears to. . . ." "And in conclusion, I'd like to spend the next three minutes summarizing what we've just discussed. . . ."

Short takes on long speeches

The long-winded speaker has inspired a plethora of folk wit regarding the subject of public speaking. Here's a small sample:

- Many a public speaker who rises to the occasion stands too long.

- No speech is all bad if it's short.

- The longest word in the English language is "And now a word from our guest of honor."

- If the speaker won't boil it down, the audience must sweat it out.

- An after-dinner speech is like a headache — always too long, never too short.

- It's all right to have a train of thought if you also have a terminal.

- Second wind: what a speaker acquires when he says, "In conclusion."

- A speech is like a love affair — any fool can start one, but it takes a lot of skill to end one.

Chapter 7

Material: Building the Body
of Your Speech

*L*egend has it that, after attending a church service, Mark Twain told the minister that he had a book at home containing every word of the sermon. The minister was outraged and said it was impossible, but Twain reasserted his claim. The minister challenged Twain to send the book to him, and Twain agreed. The next day Twain sent the minister an unabridged dictionary.

Every word of *your* presentations will appear in that book, too. Unfortunately, that's not much help when you're putting your talk together. After you have a topic and an outline, you still have to figure out exactly what you're going to say. What approach will you take? How will you support your ideas and arguments? How will you get the audience to understand what you mean and agree with you? That's what this chapter is all about.

How to Make Your Speech More Appealing

Traditional speech educators make all kinds of distinctions among speeches to inform, persuade, inspire, and entertain. They usually talk about logical and emotional appeals solely in the context of speeches to persuade. (Heck, I taught the topic that way, too, when I taught freshman speech at the University of Southern California.)

But I'm going to tell you a secret. Although those distinctions are great for making up exam questions, they're not particularly useful in real life. The bottom line is that all speeches attempt to be persuasive in one form or another. (See Chapter 1.) So here's some uncommon knowledge: analyzing any presentation you make in terms of logical and emotional appeals is worthwhile.

Logical appeals

A logical appeal is based on rational evidence and arguments. Logical appeals are supposed to appeal to the audience's "head." For example, say you're giving a talk about the need for a traffic light at a busy intersection. You could point out that there have been a large number of accidents at the intersection, that the city has spent a lot of money defending the resulting lawsuits, and that the city's insurance premiums would decrease if a traffic light was erected. That's a logical appeal.

Logical appeals are typified by scientific debates. A scientist asserting a particular position goes through a long chain of reasoning that's subject to strict empirical procedures. The conclusions are carefully measured against the experimental evidence. Anything that doesn't follow logically is rejected. Think of Mr. Spock from *Star Trek* or Sherlock Holmes. They are the ultimate practitioners of the logical appeal.

Emotional appeals

An emotional appeal is based on feelings and passions. Emotional appeals are supposed to speak to the audience's "heart." Again, say you're giving a talk about the need for a traffic light at a busy intersection. You could point out that helpless toddlers have been among the accident victims there or that recovery time for an injured adult caused his family great financial hardship. You might even argue that anyone who supports family values would want a traffic light. Those points constitute an emotional appeal.

Emotional appeals tie your topic to an issue that arouses great passion in your audience. Politicians use this appeal every time they talk about patriotism, the American way, and the American dream. Here's a classic example from a speech that Ross Perot gave when he re-entered the presidential campaign of 1992:

> When I think of all the sacrifices my parents and all the generations who came before them made in the earlier times for us so that we could live the American dream, certainly we all dedicate ourselves to seeing that you, the young people in our country, will have the American dream passed on to you.

Even the very young ones write to me. This little girl, a beautiful little girl, Adrian Cagiano. I'll leave this picture for you. Here are a few excerpts from her letter:

"My name is Adrian Cagiano. I am 9 years old, almost 10. I wish you would really run for President and I wish I could vote. I think everyone should get to say how they would like to see things done. I just don't think a small group of people should decide all these things for a whole bunch of people."

This is signed Adrian, Rural Route 2, Augusta, Kansas.

Now when you're hot and you're tired, and you're worn out some day, take a look at this little girl and her sisters, and you'll say whatever it takes we've got to do it, we've got to pass on the American dream to them.

Mr. Perot has asked the people in his audience to support the American dream, to feel guilty if they don't do so (because earlier generations made sacrifices), and to do it for the kids. Gets you right there, doesn't it? But that's the idea of an emotional appeal. It's *supposed* to tug at your heartstrings.

The one-two punch

Some people think with their heads. Others think with their hearts. And some of us use both. That's why the most effective way to connect with an audience is to offer a combination of logical and emotional appeals. In doing so, you cover all the bases.

The classic example is the Labor Day telethon for muscular dystrophy. The purpose of the show is to raise money to cure a horrible disease, and the show's organizers wisely intersperse logical and emotional appeals. You can see a scientist talk about exactly how the dollars that have been contributed are spent on research: Since last year, a promising theory has been pursued in the lab. Experiments have created more promising leads. Additional money can provide the staff and equipment to follow these new leads. Eventually this research will result in a cure. This appeal is entirely logical.

The logical appeal is followed by an emotional appeal: Jerry Lewis interviews the poster child. A short film shows young children afflicted with the disease enjoying activities at camps funded by contributors. Jerry Lewis tells a heart-rending tale about how one family copes with the disease.

The combination of these appeals is very powerful. Are the appeals effective? The numbers speak for themselves. Almost every year, the telethon breaks its old record for money raised.

Forms of Support

This section isn't about hosiery. Support refers to the items you use to prove and illustrate your points — the basic material that makes up your speech. Stories, statistics, and examples are forms of support.

There are three basic rules regarding supports:

- ✔ **Rule one:** Make sure that your supports really support something. Don't throw in quotes, statistics, and stories just to show off. Use them only to prove, clarify, or illustrate a point.

- ✔ **Rule two:** Use a variety of supports. Why? Different people respond to different types of information. Some people like statistics. Others like quotes and stories.

- ✔ **Rule three:** Less is more. One dramatic statistic is better than three boring statistics. One great example is better than two so-so examples.

What's the story?

An article in the *Wall Street Journal* described the hardships endured by a professor returning to Florida from a conference in Scotland. When the professor arrived in Orlando, a pound of explosives was found in his suitcase. His suitcase had been randomly selected for a security exercise when his plane had stopped in Amsterdam. Airport police had botched the exercise by leaving the explosives in the suitcase. Even after the Orlando police sorted out the details, the professor still feared for his life. He was convinced that a terrorist had planted the explosives. Commenting on the case to the *Wall Street Journal,* an Orlando police officer said, "He went through quite an ordeal, but at least he'll have some great cocktail stories."

The traveling professor will also have some great stories for his next presentation. As communication expert Jim Lukaszewski says, "A picture may be worth a thousand words, but a good story is worth 10,000 pictures."

The power of stories is deeply rooted in the human psyche. From the time that our ancestors sat around the first campfire to the most recent release of Hollywood's latest epic motion picture, stories have been major vehicles for communicating values, culture, and history. In fact, prior to the invention of writing, stories were the prime source of transferring knowledge from one generation to another. And today's stories remain powerful tools for moving ideas from one person to another. Whether you hear a child pleading, "Tell me a story," or an adult asking, "So what's the story?" we hunger for information packaged in this familiar format.

Here are some guidelines for using stories effectively. Most of them come courtesy of management-communication advisor Jim Lukaszewski. (He's founder The Lukaszewski Group, Inc., a management communications consulting company based in White Plains, New York.)

Tell stories for a purpose

A story should have a reason for being told. And the reason — a lesson, moral, objective — should be obvious to the audience. One of the fastest ways to turn off an audience is by telling pointless stories.

Tell stories about people

Let's face it, we're a narcissistic species — we like to hear stories about ourselves. So if your story involves people, it will get attention. And if you can talk about people familiar to the audience, even better. Here's the uncommon knowledge. If you can't talk about real individuals, talk about hypothetical people. Use names. Personify your stories. Jim Lukaszewski guarantees that this will get your audience involved.

Tell success stories

Nothing succeeds like success, and that includes success stories. Think of the stories that you liked as a child. Most of them ended with the words "happily ever after." Those words are the sign of a success story. People like to hear stories about how an idea or action worked out successfully.

Tell personal stories

Anytime you can add a personal story, you can get people's attention. People are much more interested in personal stories than they are in just plain facts.

What if you don't have many personal stories? Here's some uncommon knowledge: interview other people and tell *their* stories. (I'm *not* saying you should act as if their story happened to you. Identify the story as someone else's and tell it — for example, "A friend of mine went to a wedding where the bride had a bit too much to drink, and. . . .") Getting stories from other people is so simple to do, yet so few speakers do it. Other people's stories are a great source of material that you shouldn't overlook.

Consider telling stories in the present tense

Telling a story in the present tense gives it more immediacy and impact. "The story is happening right now, and the listener is there," says Murray Ogborn, one of the nation's leading trial attorneys. He recommends the technique to lawyers who want to engage a jury's attention. Here's his favorite example: "John was stopped at the light when he was violently struck from the rear" is less effective than "Joan is sitting in her car at the stop light, thinking of the joy she experiences when her children come racing in from school, when suddenly her body is thrown forward as the defendant strikes her motionless vehicle from behind." Quite a contrast isn't it? And you don't have to be a lawyer to use this technique — it works for anyone. (In fact, this technique works very well for complaining about attorneys. "My lawyer didn't return my phone calls" is less effective than "I'm sitting by my phone waiting for my lawyer to call like he promised, as the sheriff's deputies march in and out of my house removing my furniture, my possessions, and even my baby, who's crying as they carry her out of the house from which I'm being wrongfully evicted due to a computer error at the bank that my attorney said he'd take care of three weeks ago.")

Try stories out first

The first time to tell a story shouldn't be when you're standing at a podium addressing your audience. You need to know how the story will work. Try stories on your friends, neighbors, colleagues, and anyone who will listen. Theoretically, the story will get better every time. By the time you use the story in a presentation, you should have a polished gem.

Develop a repertoire of stories

Every story won't work with every audience, so having a selection of stories from which to choose is nice. Develop several stories that you feel comfortable telling; then you can fit them to your topic and your audience.

Collect stories

Most of us are exposed to good stories every day. You see them in the newspaper. You hear them on radio and TV. People tell them to you. Write down the stories you like. Collect them. Start a file. Then you'll have them available when you need them. Jim Lukaszewski especially likes *Readers Digest* as a source of stories. "Their stories are rarely more than 75 words, which is about 30 seconds of speech time," he observes.

Types of stories

You can use many different types of stories to liven up your presentation. Here are a few of the more common ones:

Success story

A success story documents the triumph of people, actions, or ideas. Here's how Marvin Runyon, Postmaster General of the United States, used a success story in a speech about customer satisfaction:

> Service quality is very important to our customers. Many businesses depend on us for reliable, timely, and accurate delivery of their products and information.

> One such customer is Time-Warner. Earlier this month, I met with Gerry Leven, President and Co-CEO of Time-Warner Inc., one of our biggest customers.

On November 4, the day after the election, I stood in their computer room in New York City at 12:00 noon and watched as the special "Presidential Election" edition of *Time* began its print run at 18 sites across the country.

Time employees had worked through the night — reporters, editors, photographers, computer operators. Everyone involved in the production of the magazine had been racing against the clock to get the election results and the stories behind the scenes for the special edition.

Gerry said the cover photograph and others had been shot at 12:40 a.m., when the President-elect came out to greet his supporters. And, in less than 12 hours, four million copies of Bill Clinton's face on the cover were rolling off the presses for distribution to readers around the world.

The old saying is true — *Time* flies. The magazine's success depends on it. And, for your companies, accuracy and reliability are important for your success, too.

We must meet your communication needs so that you can meet the needs of your customers.

Parable

A parable is a story with a simple moral or lesson. Here's how FBI Director William Sessions used a parable in a speech about changes in the legal system:

In May of 1990 at the Seventh Circuit Judicial Conference, Professor Michael Tigar, Professor of Law at the University of Texas, told a parable about the future of the American judicial system. His story began in the future — the day the vending machines in the courthouses all over America — the machines that dispense justice — stopped working.

The machines just wouldn't dispense justice — no matter how much money you put in or how you jiggled the knobs and handles.

The cause? The parable reports that legions of lawyers in three-piece suits, who knew how to use the machines, put in handfuls of money, got mouthfuls of goodies, and then jammed the machines with sticky paper.

Judges ignored the actions of the lawyers — or gave them a slap on the wrist. Others who didn't know how to use the machines despaired and got angry.

The system — the legal system — justice — had been shut down by the crass commercialism of the lawyers and the lack of professional responsibility on the part of the judges.

Professor Tigar's moral to this story: A profession is different than the marketplace. It's members must be proficient in their discipline — but they must do more than simply perform for money. They must work for the social good, within the discipline of the profession.

Story about a famous person

A story about a famous person always gets attention because of the celebrity factor. Here's how Patrick C. Burns, Assistant Director of the American Alliance for Rights and Responsibilities, used a story about Thomas Edison in a speech about winning the war on drugs:

> I am not here today, however, to talk about litigation, but about what works. When I think about what works, I am always reminded of the story I was told, as a boy, about Thomas Edison.
>
> It seems Edison spent nearly two years fooling around with various filaments to make the light bulb, and a local newspaper got tired of waiting for him to come up with something really useful. So the local editor challenged Edison by announcing a wager: if Edison would come up with a working lightbulb by a given date, the newspaper would reward him with $10,000. In those days, this was a monstrous sum.
>
> Twenty-four hours before D-day, a reporter from the newspaper visited Edison at his shop in Menlo Park and found the haggard scientist working frantically. He hadn't slept in 36 hours and his shop was littered with bits and pieces of flotsam and jetsam. Anxious to record the agony of defeat to be touted in the next day's headlines, the reporter asked:
>
> "Mr. Edison, you have tried a *million* things — the hair of a beard and the hair of a horse, spider webs and silk worm threads, carbon and copper — *and you have made absolutely no progress at all*."
>
> Mr. Edison is said to have turned to the reporter and replied:
>
> "*Sir*, what do you know of progress? I know *a thousand things that do not work.*"
>
> And Edison found a working filament a few hours later.
>
> And so it is with the drug problem in America. We know a thousand things that do not work. And we are on the verge, I think, of finding a working filament.

Personal story

A personal story comes out of actual experience. Here's how Ross Perot, founder of Electronic Data Systems, used a personal story about achieving the American dream in a speech given during his campaign for President of the United States:

> One of my most poignant memories is the day Mort Myerson became the president of Electronic Data Systems. His 95-year-old grandfather was there.
>
> His grandfather had had to flee Russia many years ago because he happened to be a Jew. He lived in an attic in Brooklyn for 18 months working as a tailor as a young man, so he could get enough money to buy a train ticket to Fort Worth, Texas. He reared a fine young son and that son became Mort Myerson's father.

He was there when Mort became president of E.D.S. At the beginning of the meeting Mr. Myerson came forward with tears in his eyes and hugged Mort and said, "Son, through you I have fulfilled all of the dreams I had as a young man when I came to America."

Humorous story

A humorous story amuses your audience while making a point. Here's how Clyde Prestowitz, Jr., founder and President of the Economic Strategy Institute, used a humorous story to illustrate false premises in economic policy:

> Some of the major problems underlying the U.S. economy are well illus trated by a recent story about the hiker in California who ate a condor, a protected species of bird. It seems that the hiker was apprehended and taken before a judge, who sentenced him to life at hard labor. Before leaving the courtroom, however, the defendant asked the judge to listen to his side of the story because he felt there were exonerating circumstances. The hiker explained that he had been lost in the wilderness and had been hiking for three days and three nights without food or water, and just by chance had spotted this bird sitting on a rock, had thrown a rock at it, killed it and ate it, and then walked for three more days and three more nights before getting to civilization. Said the hiker, "If I hadn't eaten that bird, I wouldn't be alive to be here today." The judge responded by saying that those certainly were unusual circumstances and in view of the fact that the hiker's life had been in danger he, the judge, would suspend the sentence. The defendant thanked him and began to leave the courtroom, but as he did the judge asked, "Oh, by the way, what did the condor taste like?" The hiker paused for a moment and responded, "Well, it was kind of between a bald eagle and a spotted owl."

> The point is, you see, that the judge was operating on the basis of a false premise. He was assuming that he and the hiker adhered to similar premises and views about protective species. In the same way, the United States has been operating on a basis of three false premises for most of the past forty-five years with regard to its economic policies.

Startling story

A startling story catches the audience by surprise. Here's how special education teacher Cynthia Ann Broad, a Michigan Teacher of the Year, used a startling story to show that society can't afford to ignore the educational needs of *any* children:

> I'd like to tell you the story of two educationally handicapped children.

> The parents of the first child were not considered successful. His father was unemployed with no formal schooling. His mother was a teacher — and there was probably tension in the family because of the mismatch.

> This child, born in Port Huron, Michigan, was estimated to have an IQ of 81. He was withdrawn from school after three months — and was considered backward by school officials.

Physically, the child enrolled two years late due to scarlet fever and respiratory infections. And he was going deaf. His emotional health was poor — stubborn, aloof, showing very little emotion.

He liked mechanics. He liked to play with fire and burned down his father's barn. He showed some manual dexterity, but used very poor grammar. But he *did* want to be a scientist or a railroad mechanic.

The second child showed not much more promise.

This child was born of an alcoholic father who worked as an itinerant — a mother who stayed at home.

As a child, she was sickly, bedridden, and often hospitalized. She was considered erratic and withdrawn. She would bite her nails, and had numerous phobias. She wore a backbrace from a spinal defect and would constantly seek attention.

She was a daydreamer with no vocational goals, although she expressed a desire to help the elderly and the poor.

Who were these children?

The boy from Port Huron became one of the world's greatest inventors — Thomas A. Edison

And the awkward and sickly young girl, became a champion of the oppressed — Eleanor Roosevelt.

Checklist for storytelling

Want to develop your storytelling skills? Jim Lukaszewski advises you to start by answering the following questions:

- What's the communications objective, moral, lesson, punch line, or purpose of the story?

- What's the plain language synopsis of what you're trying to get across?

- What's the beginning, the middle, and the end?

- Does it have a people focus? Who are the main characters in the story? Why are they interesting?

- What is the sequence of events that makes the story work? Are there some facts or data that should be put into the story? Does the story as you currently tell it have too many facts and too much data? Do they really help the story or hurt the story?

- What are the human factors in the story that make it interesting?

How to use quotations for maximum impact

"I often quote myself, it adds spice to the conversation." George Bernard Shaw said it; and if I were Shaw, I'd quote myself also. Because most speakers aren't Shaw, quoting someone other than yourself works better.

Quotes get immediate attention — especially when they're attached to a famous name. In today's sound-bite society, quotes provide a great way to gain "mindshare" with your audience.

Here are a few guidelines for using quotes effectively:

Relate the quote to a point

A quote should be used to make a point. Otherwise the quote is irrelevant — no matter how funny or insightful it is. Sometimes you may find a great quote that just doesn't fit, and you can't make it fit without reworking a great deal of your talk. Just accept the fact that the quote doesn't fit. Save the quote for your next speech.

Don't drop names

If you use quotes only to drop the names of the people you're quoting, you can come off as a jerk. An audience can tell when a speaker tries to appear smart by throwing names around. "As Albert Einstein once said. . . ." "According to Socrates. . . ." "I believe it was James Joyce who observed. . . ." The giveaway is that the quotes have nothing to do with what you're talking about. They're forced into your speech so that you can drop the famous name. Including such quotes is a dumb way to seem smart, and it doesn't work.

Use a variety of sources

Unless you're doing a tribute to a particular celebrity, no one wants to hear endless quotes from a single source. That type of repetition gets boring fast. If you're only going to quote Yogi Berra, then why didn't you just get Yogi to give your speech? Mix it up a bit. Go ahead and quote Yogi, but quote Aristotle, Confucius, and Captain Kangaroo, too.

Keep it brief

You don't want to lose the conversational quality of your presentation, and a long quote starts to sound like you're reading it, even if you're not. Shorten lengthy quotes and tell the audience that you're paraphrasing.

Don't say "quote . . . unquote"

It sounds stupid unless you're doing a dramatic reading from a trial transcript. Just say Mr. or Ms. So-And-So once said — and give the quote. Or give the quote and then say who said it.

Do use surprising quotes

One of the most effective uses of quotes is citing a surprise source. A Republican speaker supports his position by quoting a Democrat. A union leader advances her cause by quoting management. Tipper Gore quotes Snoop Doggy Dogg. This contrast always gets attention because it's so unexpected. Use of this technique is also a powerful way to support your side of an argument.

Here's how President Ronald Reagan used this technique in his 1987 State of the Union Address to defend his tough policies against the Soviet Union:

> Our commitment to a Western Hemisphere safe from aggression did not occur by spontaneous generation on the day that we took office. It began with the Monroe Doctrine in 1823 and continues our historic bipartisan American policy. Franklin Roosevelt — Franklin Roosevelt said we ". . . are determined to do everything possible to maintain peace on this hemisphere." President Truman was very blunt: "International Communism . . . seeks to crush and undermine and . . . destroy the independence of the Americans . . . we can't let that happen here."

> And John F. Kennedy made clear that ". . . Communist domination in this hemisphere can never be neglected."

> Some in Congress may choose to depart from this historic commitment, but I will not.

A variation on this technique involves the surprise generated not only by *who* said the quote, but *when* it was said. Here's an example from a speech about public opinion and conservation by Richard Lindeborg, a Market Research Analyst with the U.S. Department of Agriculture's Forest Service:

> "Is it the lumberman, then who is the friend and lover of the pine, stands nearest to it, and understands its nature best? Is it the tanner who has barked it, or he who has boxed it for turpentine, whom posterity will fable to have been changed into a pine at last? No! No! It is the poet: he it is who makes the truest use of the pine — who does not fondle it with an axe, nor tickle it with a saw, nor stroke it with a plane. . . .

> "The popular view of the moment is that environmentalism is a new movement, a movement that has grown to fundamentally alter our society, a movement that is here to stay.

> "Fundamentally altered society? We'll see how true that is. Here to stay? I'll talk a bit about that in a moment. Is it new? Hardly."

The quote I just read to you is not some bit of 1990s new-age environmentalism. It is not some bit of 1970s Earth Day rhetoric. It is Henry David Thoreau, writing in the *Atlantic Monthly* in 1858.

Don't round up the usual suspects

If you listen to enough speeches, you may notice that certain quotes tend to get used over and over again. Yes, we know that Shakespeare said, "The first thing we do, let's kill all the lawyers." Other popular favorites include certain lines by Woody Allen, Franklin D. Roosevelt, and Winston Churchill. Want your quotes to really stand out? Find some fresh ones.

Where do you look? Newspapers and magazines provide a good start. Many of them have sections that feature recent quotes from newsmakers.

And here's some uncommon knowledge. The letters to shareholders that appear in the annual reports of public companies are an excellent source of quotes from business leaders. You can find the CEOs of Fortune 500 companies saying some amazing things in these letters — particularly in years when their companies lose money. These reports can easily be obtained by contacting the companies or visiting your local library. Other off-beat quotes can come from television, movie, or comic-book characters.

Mark Twain said what?

One of the biggest media brouhahas during Dan Quayle's tenure as Vice President involved his misspelling of the word potato. While visiting a school in New Jersey, Mr. Quayle told a sixth grader that the word was spelled "potatoe." He made the mistake because he read from a flash card that had the word misspelled that way. Two days later, the national press was still hounding the Vice President about the incident. He responded: "I should have caught the mistake on that spelling bee card. But as Mark Twain once said, 'You should never trust a man who has only one way to spell a word.'"

That should have been the end of the incident. But a new controversy ignited when reporters checked the quote with Twain scholars around the country. The scholars claimed that Twain had never said it. And then the whole thing hit home — Mr. Quayle's staffers defended him by saying the quote came right out of a book that I had written.

It was true. I had written a book called *The Light Touch: How to Use Humor for Business Success,* and in it I had advised using the Twain line to defend yourself if you were ever accused of making a spelling mistake. The Vice President used it perfectly. The defense should have worked. (And it would have worked for anyone else. The fact that reporters bothered to call Twain scholars around the country to check the quote shows how much they had it in for the Vice President.)

But this is a cautionary tale, and I bring it up now to show you the dangers involved in quote attribution. My source for the Twain quote was a book called *The Dictionary of Humorous Quotations.* It was published by Doubleday in 1949. No, it wasn't *Bartlett's Familiar Quotations,* but it was a reference book from a major publisher. And it was written by Evan Esar, one of the major American humor scholars for the first half of the twentieth century. If you can't rely on that type of source, what can you rely on? And that's my point: be ready to defend your attributions because if you look in several quote books, you'll often find the same line attributed to several different people. You can quote me on that.

Be careful about attribution

If you're not sure who said the line that you're quoting, cover yourself. Say, "I believe it was Mr. Famous Name who once said. . . ." Another hedge is to say "As an old philosopher once said. . . ." After all, everyone is a philosopher of one sort or another. So if turns out that the line came from Donald Duck, you can still argue that he was being philosophical.

Doing it by the numbers: statistics and other numerical data

Benjamin Disraeli, the famous British Prime Minister, once said, "There are three kinds of lies: lies, damned lies, and statistics." He may have overstated the case, but not by much. Statistics enable you to slice up reality in a way that suits your perspective. Just consider the following statistical observations:

- Half the world is below average.
- A man heard that 90% of all accidents occur within ten miles of home — so he moved.
- An insurance agent said, "Do you know that someone dies every time I breathe?" His prospect said, "Try mouthwash."

All right, maybe I'm being a little facetious, but here's the point — no matter what your position on any issue, you can usually find a statistic to support you. And using statistics for support is important. Here's why: First, some people are numbers people. Numbers people ignore other types of support. Their faith resides entirely in numerical data. They want to see the "bottom line." (Do you know any engineers, accountants, or bankers? I rest my case.) Second, some people are words people. They're easy to spot. Blank looks descend across their faces at the mere mention of numerical data. But even words people are impressed by a dramatic statistic — if you can get them to understand it.

Statistics and numerical data can provide some of the most influential support in your entire presentation, but they commonly lose their impact because speakers use them incorrectly. Here are some suggestions for getting your numbers to register on your audience's bottom line:

Don't spew numbers

Most people can't process numbers as rapidly as they can process other types of information, so don't drown your audience in numerical data. Give your listeners time to digest each statistic. If you don't space statistics out, the audience will — space out, that is. (An exception to this rule involves *startling* statistics. A discussion of this exception appears later in this chapter.)

Round off numbers

Are you telling aerospace engineers how to build a more efficient jet engine? Are you briefing medical researchers about the results of your company's new wonder drug? Are you telling a gathering of organized crime leaders how you will split the take of your proposed scam? Then by all means, use exact numbers. But if exact numbers aren't critical to your subject matter or audience, then give everyone a break — round them off. Your listeners don't need to know that the candidate you backed won with 59.8% of the vote. Just say 60%.

Use a credible source

A statistic is only as impressive as its source. Did you get your numbers from *The Wall Street Journal* or *The National Enquirer*? A big difference lies between the two.

And here's the uncommon knowledge. Don't jump to the conclusion that *The Wall Street Journal* is the more credible source. Credibility all depends on your audience. You may be speaking to people who read *The National Enquirer* religiously and distrust *The Wall Street Journal* as a tool of the rich. Only your audience can bestow credibility upon a source. Keep that point in mind when you select your statistics.

Repeat key numbers

If you want people to hear and remember an important statistic, say it more than once.

Here's an example from a speech by Richard McGuire, New York State Commissioner of Agriculture and Markets:

> I quote from the report:
>
> "Of the more than 220,000 intentional and unintentional deaths from acute poisoning, *suicides account for approximately 91 percent,* occupational exposure for 6 percent and other causes, including food contamination, for 3 percent."
>
> Let me repeat that. Of the 220,000 deaths, 91 percent were suicides!

Put statistics into familiar terms

Numbers are abstract concepts. If you want numbers to have a real impact, you've got to discuss them in a way that people can understand. You must explain numbers in terms that have real meaning for your audience.

Here's how Richard Stegemeier, Chairman, President, and CEO of Unocal Corporation, did it in a speech about global competitiveness:

> Economist Thomas Hopkins estimates that federal regulations are costing American consumers $400 billion every year.
>
> How much is $400 billion?
>
> It's about ten times the size of our trade deficit with Japan.
>
> It is about double the annual cost of public education in America, from kindergarten through the 12th grade.
>
> It's about 33 percent larger than our entire defense budget.
>
> It's enough to give every household in America $4,000 every year.

In fact, my cousin (the teacher) used this technique to teach third-grade math in a gang-infested public school. He'd say, "If your side has six knives, and the other side has eight knives, how many more knives does your side need to make it a fair fight?" This question always got his students' attention. (Unfortunately, they always answered "Three." My cousin didn't know if that answer meant that they couldn't add correctly or meant that their idea of a fair fight was having an extra knife.)

Create a picture

One of the best ways to put statistics into familiar terms is to transform your numbers into a concrete image. Let your audience *see* the statistic. Paint a picture for them. Here's an example from a speech about evolution given by William Johnson, Associate Dean of Academic Affairs at Ambassador University:

> Brontosaurus, "thunder lizard," was 70 feet long and weighed 30 tons. It was longer than a tennis court and equaled the weight of six elephants.

Use analogies to create a picture

Want an easy way to create a picture with numbers? Analogize your abstract statistics to easy-to-visualize images. Here's an example from a speech given by Dr. Lonnie Bristow when he was President-Elect of the American Medical Association:

> Right now it requires four workers to pay for each Medicare beneficiary. But in a few years, as the whole population gets older and older, there'll be only two workers available to pick up the tab. And all the while that bill keeps swelling up just like a balloon. That means by the time most of the baby boomers are ready for Medicare, the balloon may have burst.

Use startling statistics

The big exception to the general rule that statistics are boring is the *startling* statistic. This term refers to numerical data that's so surprising that it just grabs your attention. A startling statistic is inherently interesting.

The following is an example from a speech about world population given by Jeff Davidson, Executive Director of the Breathing Space Institute:

The Lennon sisters, who appeared on the Lawrence Welk Show, had eleven children in their family. If each family member had eleven children for eleven generations, they would exceed the current population of earth — and that's just one family!

In fact, if you have a series of startling statistics, you can create a dramatic effect by stringing them together. (This is an exception to the rule against spewing numbers at your audience.) Here's an example from a speech by James Hayes, Co-Founder of "The New American Revolution" and Publisher Emeritus of *Fortune* Magazine:

Consider these few stunning facts:

Every five seconds of the school day, a child drops out of school.

Every 55 seconds a child without a high school diploma gives birth to a child.

Every seven minutes a child is arrested on a drug offense.

Every 14 hours a child the age of five or younger is murdered.

Every day one point three million latch key kids ages 5 – 14 are left to fend for themselves for much of the day.

Every day 135,000 children bring guns to school.

Every day three children die of injuries inflicted by abusive parents.

All this in the most prosperous nation in the history of mankind!

Combine statistics in interesting ways

Sometimes two statistics that are individually boring become interesting when contrasted with each other. The possibilities for this type of statistical analysis are endless. The only limit is your time and imagination.

Robert Eaton, Chairman and CEO of Chrysler, combined two statistics in a speech about the role of government interference in free enterprise:

I recently ran across two articles which I found interesting. The first, from *Newsweek*, said there are 131,803 pages of federal regulations sitting on shelves in Washington.

The other, from *U.S. News & World Report*, told me that "nearly 130,000 bureaucrats make their living devising and enforcing rules and regulations."

Now, I don't know how coincidental those numbers are, but that comes out to *one page for every single regulator!*

Can you imagine 130,000 bureaucrats standing at attention for muster every morning in Washington with somebody going up and down the ranks saying, "Here's your page, here's your page, here's your page."

Be creative

There are as many ways to slant numbers in your favor as there are to present them, so be creative. Play around with different ways to deliver numerical data. A clever example comes from a speech about engineering given by Louis Rader, Professor Emeritus of Business Administration at the Darden Graduate School of Business Administration. Here's how he used a hypothetical set of statistics to dramatize a point about product quality:

> An emphasis on product quality far beyond what we had considered acceptable. Many of our CEO's felt that 99 percent was good enough. If this figure (99 percent good) were converted into our daily non-industrial life, what would it mean?
>
> More than 30,000 newborn babies would be accidentally dropped by doctors and nurses each year.
>
> There would be 200,000 wrong drug prescriptions each year.
>
> Electricity would be off for 15 minutes each day.
>
> Ninety-nine percent good means 10,000 bad out of one million. Now world-class industry is aiming for four bad in a million, essentially zero defects.

(Additional information about hypothetical examples is available later in this chapter.)

Consider using visual aids

If you have a great deal of numerical data in your presentation, consider putting it into a visual format — slides or overheads of charts or graphs. If your audience members can see the data, it will be much easier for them to digest it. (See Chapter 11 for an extended discussion of this topic.)

More Support: Definitions, Analogies, and Examples

Humans do not live by bread alone. And speakers don't support their ideas by stories, quotes, and statistics alone — especially if no one understands their ideas. In this section, I discuss three types of support that *explain* a speaker's ideas — definitions, analogies, and examples.

Definitions

In *Through the Looking Glass*, Humpty Dumpty has the following famous exchange with Alice (of Wonderland fame) about the meaning of words:

"I don't know what you mean by 'glory,'" Alice said.

Humpty Dumpty smiled contemptuously. "Of course you don't — till I tell you. I meant 'there's a nice knock-down argument for you!'"

"But 'glory' doesn't mean 'a nice knock-down argument,'" Alice objected.

"When I use a word," Humpty Dumpty said, in a rather scornful tone, "it means just what I choose it to mean — neither more nor less."

"The question is," said Alice, "whether you *can* make words mean so many different things."

"The question is," said Humpty Dumpty, "which is to be master — that's all."

If you want to be the master of your words, make sure that you define important terms in your talk. A famous legal case involving a contract worth thousands of dollars turned on the definition of the word *chicken*. One side said that *chicken* referred to a fryer. The other side said that the same word referred to a roaster. If you don't want to be fried or roasted by *your* audience, make sure that you're all speaking the same language. Here are a few ways to use definitions in a presentation:

Use the dictionary definition

Here's an example from a speech about ethics given by Dexter Baker, Chairman, Executive Committee, Board of Directors, Air Products and Chemicals, Inc.:

> Webster says ethics is about dealing with good and bad, with moral duty and obligation. A system of moral values. Principles of conduct that help mold our judgments and guide our decisions.

Use your personal definition

Here's an example from a speech by Brent Baker, Rear Admiral, United States Navy, Chief of Information:

> How do I define *quality* in a news report or analysis. My measure is summed up in three words: *accuracy, objectivity, and responsibility*.

Explain your definition if the word is emotionally charged

When a word is emotionally charged, some members of your audience may misinterpret your remarks unless you clearly explain *your* use of the term. The following is an example from a speech that George Marotta, a Research Fellow at Stanford's Hoover Institution, gave to a local chapter of the National Association of Retired Federal Employees:

> Thank you for inviting me to speak to you today about two subjects which I believe are very much positively correlated: bureaucracy and the national debt.

Bureaucracy is a pejorative term used to refer to organizations which are large and hierarchically structured. Today I am using it to refer to the bureaucracy of the federal government. In all of this, please understand that we all were federal bureaucrats and were proud to serve our government.

Use a story to define your terms

A story provides a great way to define your terms because it can grab audience attention at the same time (if the story is interesting or entertaining). Here's an example from a speech about innovation given by Robert G. McVicker, Senior Vice President, Technology, Quality Assurance, and Scientific Relations at Kraft General Foods:

First, let's get some idea of what innovation is. Back in the late 19th and early 20th centuries, there was a great German chemist named Johann von Baeyer. He made many contributions to science, and in 1905, he was awarded a Nobel Prize. One morning, Baeyer came into his laboratory and found that his assistants had built an ingenious mechanical stirring device operated by water turbines. The professor was fascinated by the complex machine, and he summoned his wife from their apartment next door. For a while Frau Baeyer watched the apparatus in silent admiration. And then she exclaimed, "What a lovely idea for making mayonnaise!"

There's a basic distinction to be made here: the good professor's students were the inventors — but his wife was the *innovator.*

Use the derivation of a word to define it

Explaining the history of a word's meaning reinforces its definition with your audience. (Doing so also makes you sound smart.) Here's an example from a speech about the crisis in solid waste management given by William Ruckelshaus, Chairman and CEO of Browning-Ferris Industries:

Many of you have seen the famous old painting of a Victorian doctor at the bedside of a sick child. The doctor is sitting with his head bowed, not performing any medical miracles, just waiting. The title of this painting is "The Crisis," and it refers to the period in an illness when all that can be done has been done; the patient will either get better, or she will die.

This was the original meaning; but a word like "crisis," so exciting and laden with emotion, could not long be confined to medicine alone. It became our general term for any situation in which disaster is somewhere in the offing, however remote. We don't have squabbles, or problems, or difficulties; in everything from international affairs, to government budgets, to education we have crises.

And naturally, we have a crisis in solid waste disposal, too. I mentioned the original derivation of this term, and its true meaning, because I think it's important in understanding where we really are regarding solid waste in this country. . . .

. . . In the past few years we've been able to diagnose the "disease," as it were, and we've been able to apply some basic cures. Is the crisis over?

Analogies

An analogy is a comparison that highlights similarities (and differences) between two objects or concepts. An analogy provides one of the fundamental ways that we gain new knowledge. Analogies allow us to explain the unknown in terms of the known. When a toddler asks, "What's a jail?" and a cynic answers, "It's like a school, but there's no teacher," that's an analogy. Here are a few less-cynical examples of interesting analogies that speakers have used in their presentations:

Frog death

What we have suffered in America is analogous to the way you cook a live frog. If you try to put a frog in boiling water, it'll jump right out. But if you put it in cold water and gradually raise the heat to boiling, it will sit there until it's cooked. We Americans, partly because of a healthy lack of interest in government, are being gradually cooked by bureaucrats and politicians who, had they attempted to sell us the huge burden of government we now suffer under all at once, would have been run out of town on a rail.

— Edward Crane, President, Cato Institute

Electric transformer

How does a person develop a unique center of meaning? Maybe an electric transformer will help us answer the question. We know that a transformer is an instrument which modifies electrical current and voltage. The transformer reshapes the electrical current which flows into it and sends it out to do its job. Likewise, people have transformers inside of them which reshape the messages which flow into them. These transformers are one's intellectual capacity, emotional development, educational experience, cultural influences, religious commitment, and vocational or professional expertise.

— Carl Wayne Hensley, Professor of Speech Communication, Bethel College

Search for the Holy Grail

Under these [civil discovery] rules, litigants can force their opponents to open a staggering number of their files to inspection. Like a medieval king's demand that his knight ride out and find the Holy Grail, it's a task that's easy to request and hard to fulfill.

— Stephen Middlebrook, Senior Vice President and Executive Counsel, Aetna Life & Casualty

Sea turtles

MBAs are like sea turtles. MBAs, like sea turtles, are hatched by the multitudes from business schools around the world only to perish moments later. As they flop frantically from the beaches to the relative safety of the sea, many are gobbled up and picked off by predators and competitors. The few that survive seem to live long, endless lives.

— Karen Stephonson, Anthropologist

Plane guided by radar

The power of analysis means you can see things other people cannot. It's like an F-15 guided by the long-range radar of AWACS homing in on an enemy pilot who doesn't have a clue what lies ahead. It's like an A-10 crew with night vision sights facing Russian-made tanks that can't see in the dark.

— Gary Klein, Chairman and Chief Scientist, Klein Associates

Examples

Two of the most frequently used words in the world are *for example.* We use these words to illustrate what we're talking about, and that's why examples are probably the most common devices for supporting ideas and assertions.

Types of examples

There are two major types of examples: real and hypothetical. A real example is based on fact. A hypothetical example is based on imagination — it's made up.

Real

A good illustration of a real example comes from a speech about the Endangered Species Act given by Brock Evans, the National Audubon Society's Vice President for National Issues:

> We who favor strengthening the Endangered Species Act submit that the genetic codes and knowledge inside these plants, animals, and vertebrates that we are now destroying is a biological treasure of the highest order and should be protected instead.
>
> Let me give you a couple of examples of what this biological richness means to us and our own survival. Take food for example: about 15 or 20 years ago, much of the U.S. corn crop was affected by a mysterious blight that no one could alleviate. Crops failed, and with it millions of dollars of lost income, and hopes and dreams of many farming families, not to mention direct threats to our food supply if it continued. Scientists searched everywhere for a cure — and finally found it, on an obscure

hillside on the outskirts of Mexico City, where still grew a wild strain of maize, the original corn. This wild strain had the genetic code to enable us to adapt it to our corn crop and stop the ruinous blight.

But we found it just in time — because that field was scheduled for yet another housing development. The passage of a few more months would have meant we would have lost that remedy, and who knows how many future corn crops, forever.

Hypothetical

An entertaining illustration of a hypothetical example comes from a speech by Scott Rasmussen, President and CEO of RCM Communication Corporation:

> In effect, experts who believe in the power of institutions view the future in the same way that Star Trek presents the future — as an extension of today with a few new gadgets. As you know, the crew of the Enterprise has the wonderful ability to beam back and forth to any planet on a moment's notice. Despite this, social patterns on the Enterprise are unchanged from the twentieth century.
>
> Star Trek may be great television, but it is a lousy way to predict the future. In the real world, if we could suddenly beam back and forth at will, every aspect of the social order would be fundamentally changed. For a dramatic example, think of how a jealous lover would respond to a suspected affair! If you were a parent, how would you know if your child really went to his room?

Combination

The combination example is when you create a hypothetical example but emphasize that it's more than imaginary. You made the example up, but it's real. I know that sounds strange, so here's an example from a speech about workers' compensation given by Douglas Leatherdale, Chairman and CEO of The St. Paul Companies:

> Imagine yourself as — the president of an insurance company.
>
> Oh, yes, there's a catch: Your company writes only workers' compensation insurance. In fact, all of the operations in the United States that write workers' comp — insurance companies, self-insurance groups, government pools, and other entities — have been rolled into one company. *Your* company.
>
> You begin operations in 1984. You start with capital of $7 billion. You plan to charge premiums, pay claims, and invest your holdings wisely.
>
> Most important: You plan to base your rates on the losses you expect over the course of a policy. If rates are adequate, you'll at least break even — if not make money.
>
> So far, so good. Sounds pretty easy.

You track your results year by year. But instead of going *up*, your capital gradually, steadily, goes *down*. You followed the rules, and thought you did everything you were supposed to, *except* for one other catch: In many states, as your losses increased, you *weren't* allowed to charge the rates you needed to cover losses. Over time, your losses ate up your surplus.

By the end of 1991, that seven billion dollars had turned into a one billion dollar *deficit.*

So much for your insurance career.

The president in my story is imaginary, but the problem isn't. That's what *actually* happened to workers' comp insurers in the 1980s.

Tricks and tips

Want to get maximum mileage from your examples? Here are a couple of items to keep in mind:

An example has limited power

One example can *support* an idea, thesis or argument. *It can't prove it.* So don't expect a mass migration of opinion toward your position just because you offer a single good example. However, a single example can *disprove* an idea, thesis, or argument. Keep that in mind when you're arguing *against* something.

Don't ignore positive examples

Too often speakers tell you what you shouldn't do, but they never say what you should do. That's a pet peeve of communication expert Jim Lukaszewski, and I agree with him. So here's some uncommon knowledge from Jim: Use wrong way, right way examples, and make sure that you're prepared to show the right way. "You can take a specific situation and talk about how it might have been handled differently," notes Jim. "But if you're going to give just one side, talk about the right behavior and allude to the wrong one — not the other way around. You don't want to leave the audience hanging."

Say Something Memorable

You've been asked to give a presentation. You've put a lot of work into learning about your audience, slanting your topic for maximum interest, designing a well-organized structure, and selecting interesting material. After all is said and done, you want the audience to remember some of what was said. Unfortunately, you're fighting an uphill battle. Studies show that audience members recall a relatively small percent of what they hear in a speech. Here are some ideas for increasing that percentage:

Tell them something that you found memorable

If something is so moving or interesting that you've remembered it for a long time, then maybe someone else will find it memorable, too. Share memorable material with your audience — a story, an insight, or a piece of advice. The worst that can happen is that they'll forget it.

Stories

Newton Minow, Director of the Annenberg Washington Program, used this technique to share a memorable story with his audience:

> President Kennedy told a story a week before he was killed, a story I have never forgotten. The story was about French Marshal Lyautey, who walked one morning through his garden with his gardener. He stopped at a certain point and asked the gardener to plant a tree there the next morning. The gardener said, "But the tree will not bloom for one hundred years." The Marshal looked at the gardener and replied, "In that case, you had better plant it this afternoon."

Insightful observations

Carl Wayne Hensley, Professor of Speech Communication at Bethel College, used the technique in a speech about communication:

> In my first undergraduate course in psychology, my professor said something which has stayed with me: "Remember, puppy love is real to the puppy." Each person's perspective is intimately real to him, and he can communicate with us only out of who he is.

Advice

Willard Butcher, Chairman of the Chase Manhattan Bank, passed along some memorable advice in a speech to business students:

> Forty years ago, I received some simple advice that has stayed with me from a family friend named Marion Folsom, the architect of our nation's social security system and then a top executive of the Eastman Kodak Company.

> "Bill," Mr. Folsom said, "you're going to find that 95 percent of all the decisions you'll ever make in your career could be made as well by any reasonably intelligent high school sophomore.

> "But they'll *pay you* for the other 5 percent."

Tell them something practical

The technique that I favor is giving the audience a bit of information that's so useful that they can't forget it. And they can't forget you — because they associate you with the information. Whenever the audience applies the information, they think of you.

A good example concerns name badges at meetings and conventions. Such badges often come in a badge holder that must be pinned to your jacket, but the pins make a hole in your jacket. Want to avoid this problem? Here's a bit of wisdom passed on to me by a friend: Fold a business card into thirds lengthwise, put it in your jacket breast pocket so that the top of the card is sticking out of the pocket, and then pin the badge holder to the top of the business card. Voilà. You're now wearing a name badge without making a hole in your jacket. (I've been using this trick for years now, and whenever I do, I think of the friend who told me about it.)

Tell them what to remember

Want to really make sure that the audience remembers a key point? Jim Lukaszewski recommends taking the direct approach. He tells the audience what they should remember.

"People will follow instructions," he explains. "I say something like, 'I think you'll find this speech memorable. Let me tell you what you'll remember from this talk.' And then I tell them." He says if you do this two or three times during your talk, people will remember a lot of it.

In closing, let me leave you with a practical piece of advice that I think you'll find memorable: *If you really want to be remembered, make a major gaffe.* Some examples:

- ✔ Senator Edmund Muskie, upset about criticism of his wife, crying during a presidential campaign appearance in New Hampshire.
- ✔ President Gerald Ford claiming that Eastern Europe isn't dominated by Communism during a debate with Jimmy Carter.
- ✔ President George Bush declaring that September 7th is a day that will live in infamy during a speech to veterans.
- ✔ Bill Clinton talking on and on and on during the 1988 Democratic National Convention.

These screw-ups will live on forever. Because, in the words of John Kenneth Galbraith, which have stayed with me for years, "If all else fails, immortality can always be assured by spectacular error."

Chapter 8

Introductions: Getting Off on the Right Foot

- -

In This Chapter

▶ Setting audience expectations

▶ What to include in your introduction

▶ Ten common introductions to avoid at all costs

▶ Twenty-one ways to get off to a great start

▶ Introductions for special situations

- -

My model of making a presentation is the flight of an airplane (which you'll hear about ad nauseam throughout this book). In this model, the introduction is equivalent to the plane's take-off. The passengers want a smooth take-off. They want to eat peanuts, drink sodas, read magazines, and get where they're going. They don't want to sit on the runway forever, gain altitude too fast, have the plane careen wildly through the sky, or use the barf bag. If the pilot provides a rotten take-off, two things happen: The pilot loses a lot of credibility (everyone wonders if he or she can really fly the plane), and the passengers get worried about the rest of the flight — they expect more trouble.

The same considerations apply to your introduction. You're the pilot. Your audience (the passengers) want your introduction to lead smoothly into the body of your talk. How you perform the introduction will affect your credibility and determine the audience's mind-set for the rest of your presentation.

Why the Introduction Is the Most Important Part of Your Speech

The first semester that I taught freshman speech at the University of Southern California, I thought I did a pretty good job — until I saw the student evaluations. Yeah, I'd done OK. I was interesting, prepared and dynamic. I was accessible to students. I was a good teacher. But . . . and it was a big but . . . they said the class was just common sense.

I could feel their disappointment rising out of the evaluation questionnaires. Just a class in common sense. How could they have that attitude? Well, they had it. And I figured every other student I ever taught there would have it. So I needed to adapt to this reality.

The second semester, I had a new introduction to the course:

> This is a class in common sense. This is the only course you'll take in college that *is* common sense. Sure you can take calculus, and biology, and physics. But what good are those when a storekeeper gives you the wrong change? In this class, you'll learn what to say to that storekeeper. You'll learn how to speak to people and get your message across. You'll learn how to communicate. It's a class in common sense. You'll learn common sense skills that you can use for the rest of your life. It's a class in common sense.

You get the idea. I said it was a class in common sense a few hundred times. Then for the rest of the semester, I taught the class exactly the way I had during the first semester.

When the student evaluations came in, I felt like I was waiting for an envelope to be opened at the Academy Awards. Guess what? They said it was a class in common sense. And that's why they thought it was a *great* class. My introduction had totally changed the perception of the course.

Setting expectations

Basic psychology tells us that the way we perceive things is highly affected by what we've been led to expect. The classic example is Tom Sawyer and the fence from Mark Twain's novel *Tom Sawyer*. When Tom asks his friends to help him paint the fence, they turn him down flat. Why should they do his work for him? When Tom makes like it's a big deal to paint the fence — it has to be done just right and not just anyone can do it — they beg him for an opportunity. By the end of that scene, Tom's friends are paying him for the privilege of painting the fence. It was all in the setup — how the fence-painting was introduced.

That's why the introduction is the most important part of your presentation — *it sets the audience's expectations.* It determines how the audience will interpret and react to everything else you say. And it's your best chance to shape their reaction in your favor.

Yes, the introduction has to gain attention, lead into the rest of your talk, and perform all those other traditional functions you always hear about. That's the common knowledge. But all of those functions are encompassed in setting expectations.

Your goal is to set the audience's expectations and *surpass* them. That guarantees your presentation will be a success.

Traditional functions

Now don't get me wrong. I'm not saying that the traditional functions of the introduction aren't important. They are. But it's more productive to view them in the context of setting expectations.

What are the traditional functions? That's subject to debate. In the Kushner system, there are five traditional functions for the introduction. They're debatable because some of the functions overlap, and one of them can be eliminated if it's handled by the person introducing you. But here's how I see them:

Gain attention

The introduction must gain attention. This is a no-brainer. If no one is paying attention, it doesn't matter what you say — no one will hear it. That's the common knowledge, but it must be qualified a little. There are lots of ways to get attention. (Think of the class clown from high school.) What you want is *positive* attention. Keep this in mind when you're planning that socko attention-getting opening involving a whoopee cushion and seltzer bottle.

Create rapport

The introduction must also create rapport between you and your audience. Research suggests that we form opinions about others within several seconds of meeting them. First impressions are everything, so you want to make a good one. You want the audience to think highly of you. At a minimum, you want them to recognize that you've worked hard on their behalf to prepare your presentation.

Show your credentials

Who are you? Why are you giving this talk? What's so special about *you*? Inquiring minds want to know — especially your audience. Strictly speaking, providing this information does *not* have to be a function of the introduction you deliver; it can be handled by the person introducing you. And it's better that way — then it doesn't sound like you're tooting your own horn. But if it's not handled by the person introducing you or there's no one introducing you, then you have to handle it.

Provide reasons for listening

What's in it for me? That's the overriding question that the audience wants answered — fast. Why should they listen to your presentation? The introduction has to give them motivating reasons to keep listening.

Describe what you'll talk about

The introduction must give the audience some idea of what you'll be talking about. This function can range from a general idea of the topic and your approach to a preview of your specific points. For the most effective fulfillment of this function, you should also give the audience an organizational pattern for your presentation. In other words, the introduction should tell the audience how to process the information that will follow. It can be as simple as saying you're going to discuss a problem and a solution. First you'll show the three historical causes of the problem. Then you'll show how the problem affects everyone here today. Then you'll discuss possible solutions. The point is that the introduction should give the audience a conceptual framework that will help them easily understand your presentation.

The bottom line is that these traditional functions of the introduction all affect audience expectations and are effected by the audience's expectations. For example, how many reasons for listening do you need to give? It depends. If you know the audience expects to be bored, then you better give a lot. How big a deal should you make of gaining attention? It depends. If the audience already expects to be fascinated by you or your topic, then gaining attention isn't a problem — you automatically have it. How much does the audience know about you? What do you expect them to think about your message? Will they disagree with you? Will they be friendly? Do they care? You have to start with what the audience expects. Then you use the introduction to shape those expectations.

No matter how you conceptualize it, every speaker wants the introduction to accomplish the same thing: Have the audience say, "Wow. I've got to hear the rest of this talk."

How to Create the Perfect Introduction

It's been said that a journey of one thousand miles begins with the first step. That also applies to presentations — a speech of any length begins with the introduction. Here are the steps that you must take in making this first leg of your journey:

Answer audience questions

The audience has several questions it wants answered within the first few minutes of your talk. Think of the questions journalists ask to report a story: who, what, when, where, why, how. That's what your audience wants to know.

- ✔ Who are you? (Do you have any experience or credentials?)
- ✔ What are you going to talk about?
- ✔ When will you be through?
- ✔ Where is this talk going? (Is there some sort of organization?)
- ✔ Why should I listen? (Really a "what" question — what's in it for me?)
- ✔ How are you going to make this interesting?

Include necessary background

Is there information that the audience needs in order to understand what you'll be talking about? Give it to them in the introduction. If your presentation won't make sense unless they know the definition of a certain term or they're aware of a certain fact, tell them. Also, you may need to provide background about why you *won't* be covering a particular subject — especially if the audience expects you to address it.

Greetings and acknowledgments

Many speakers open presentations with endless greetings and acknowledgments to the sponsoring organization and key members of the audience. Boring. No one wants to hear you list the names of every dignitary on the dais. Alright, sometimes you have to name names, but you don't have to do it as your opening line. If you have to acknowledge a bunch of people, do it as the second item in your introduction — not the first. That's what I do when I speak at meetings where there are a lot of VIPs who must be recognized. I open by poking fun at myself for being an attorney and then I survey the audience for their attitudes about humor and communication. At that point, the audience is laughing and has bonded with me. Then I can pause and go into what an honor it is to be addressing the group and acknowledge some of its important members.

Make it the right length

The introduction should usually be about 10 to 15 percent of your presentation. Don't take forever.

Write it out

Write out your entire introduction word for word. Don't worry that you're just supposed to use key words or sentence fragments in writing your speech, and don't worry that a fully scripted speech might sound strained. The introduction is an exception. Here's why:

First, if you write out your intro, you can edit it into its best form. If you just make a note that you're going to tell a certain story in the introduction, you don't practice the story. You figure you already know it. Then when you tell it, you end up rambling; you don't economize words; and the story doesn't achieve its maximum impact. Second, the introduction is the most anxiety-producing section of your presentation in terms of delivery. This is when stage fright will be at its peak. If you get really nervous and your introduction is just a few key words, you may not even remember what they represent. Writing out the introduction word for word helps ensure that you will carry it off successfully even if you suffer from a case of the jitters.

Write the introduction last

The introduction is the first part of your presentation, but it should be written last. Why? It's an introduction. You need to know what you're introducing. After you write the body of your speech and your conclusion, then you've got something to introduce. That's when you write the introduction.

Remember the show biz formula

In planning your introduction, it never hurts to recall the show biz formula: strong opening, strong close, weak stuff in the middle. Your introduction is the strong opening. Your conclusion is the strong close. Those are the two parts of your presentation that will have the most impact on how the audience remembers your performance. So make sure your introduction *is* strong.

What not to do

Sometimes what you don't say in your introduction is even more important than what you do say. You don't want to get started on the wrong foot — especially if it's in your mouth. Here are some common mistakes to avoid:

Don't say "Before I begin. . . ." This is a patently absurd phrase. It's like airline personnel who ask if anyone needs to preboard the plane. You *can't* preboard. Once you start going on the plane, you *are* boarding. And once you say, "Before I begin," you've begun.

Don't get the names wrong. If you're acknowledging people, organizations, or geographic entities such as towns or cities, make sure that you know their names and pronounce them correctly. No one likes to be called by the wrong name. Messing up names makes you look very unprepared, lowers your credibility, and makes the audience wonder what else you're going to goof up.

Don't admit that you'd rather be anywhere else. Because if I'm in your audience, my response will be "So get out of here." Yes, you may be in a position where you're giving a presentation that you don't want to give, but don't whine to the audience. No one wants to hear it, and it doesn't help. You still have to give the speech, and you just seem like a big baby.

Don't admit that you're not prepared. It's insulting. If you're not prepared, why are you speaking? No one wants to waste time listening to someone who isn't prepared. Although this is common sense, a lot of speakers make this mistake. Why? They're really making excuses in advance. They know they're not prepared. They know their presentation will stink, and they want the audience to know that they're really not a terrible speaker — they're just not prepared. The logic seems to be that if you alert the audience in advance that you know your speech is lousy, somehow that improves your image. Wrong. You just seem like a jerk for being unprepared. If you're not prepared and you're going to speak anyway, just do it.

Don't admit that you've given the identical speech a million times for other audiences. Even if your audience knows it, don't rub their faces in it. Every group likes to feel unique. Let your audience operate under the illusion that you prepared the talk especially for them. And if you're smart, you'll throw in a couple of customized references to promote this illusion.

Don't use offensive humor. A lot of speakers still labor under the myth that you've got to open with a joke. You don't. But if you do, it better not be a racist, ethnic, sexist, or off-color joke. There's no faster way to turn off an audience.

Don't announce you had a ghostwriter. It's like a magician showing how the tricks are done. Your audience likes to think it's hearing from you. Let them think so. Remember, a "ghostwriter" is supposed to be invisible — you know, like a ghost.

Don't ask about the time. Maybe it's just a pet peeve, but I get irritated when speakers start by asking how much time they have. Don't they know? It seems a little late to be asking. Are they now going to completely change their presentation based on the answer? It also distracts the audience. Everyone starts thinking about what time it is and when they have to be somewhere else and how much work they still have to get done. It's not exactly the attention mode you want the audience in when you're speaking.

Top ten introductions to avoid

Introductions are like strangers in trench coats. Some expose you to a world of wonderful news ideas. Others just expose themselves. Here are the ones to avoid:

The apology

Unless you've accidentally activated the emergency sprinkler system, shut off the power for the room, or knocked the podium off the stage, *never begin by apologizing*. Here's why. First, it sets a horrible tone to the audience expectations. When you start by apologizing, they expect something bad. Why else would you be apologizing?

Second, an apology draws attention to something the audience might not otherwise notice. That's why you should never apologize in advance. If you don't start by apologizing for your speech, the audience might actually think it's good. And if they don't? You can always apologize later.

The cliché

You've heard the cliché introduction a million times — literally. That's why it's a cliché. "A funny thing happened to me on the way over here today." "We are at a crossroads." So what's wrong with these intros? Well, they're not horrible, but they don't exactly grab your attention. It's kind of like my grandfather used to say: "You can do better." (How's that for a guilt trip?)

The bait and switch

This introduction gives a great build-up to a speech that isn't given. The intro excites the audience. Everyone is tingling with anticipation. And then the presentation goes in a different direction. That's why it's called bait and switch — the speaker promises one thing in the intro and delivers another in the speech.

The con man (or woman)

This introduction consists of a massive pile-up of fake compliments. It reeks with insincerity. It wants you to think it's dressed in silk, but it's obviously polyester.

> It's a pleasure to be here today with such a great group. Actually, it's more than a pleasure — it's an honor. Because it's always an honor to address sophisticated people such as yourselves. And I can tell just by looking at you that you're a highly intelligent, talented group of people. You're the type of people my mother would be proud of — and she had some very exacting standards in that department. In fact, you're really role models. . . .

This introduction is the verbal equivalent of a sideshow barker in a striped jacket and checked pants. It generates negative attention and lowers credibility.

The nerd

You come to hear a presentation that is presumably in your language. But right from the start, you realize that something is wrong. The speaker is using phrases like "published API," "callable mechanisms," "Posix compliant," and "C++." You have no idea that C++ is a type of computer programming code. You think it's the grade that the speaker ought to receive for this presentation.

The rise of high-tech has caused an increase in this type of introduction. Attending one of these talks is like watching an outtake from *Attack of the Killer Pocket Protectors*. But it's not just engineers who do this. It's anyone caught up in the jargon of his or her trade or profession. It's OK to use jargon, but just don't open with such a heavy dose of it that you lose the audience. And when you use it — make sure that everyone understands it.

The space-case

This introduction creates a sense of wonder. The audience wonders what planet the speaker is from because everything is said very slowly with lots of pauses and hesitations. This sort of intro has a dreamlike quality — a sense of confusion. It's like watching someone give a speech in his or her sleep. Hello. Earth to speaker. Wake up. Snap out of it. But the speaker doesn't appear to know where the presentation is heading. And the audience wants to head for the doors.

The travelogue

This introduction is usually performed by speakers who have come from out of town. First, they have to tell you how much they love your city. And because they know the compliment is supposed to seem sincere, they go into specifics. They give you a travelogue of everything they've done since their arrival. "I love coming to San Francisco. It's one of my favorite places on earth. It's so beautiful. You've got that beautiful bay and that wonderful skyline. This afternoon, I was down at Fisherman's Wharf. What a great place — all those shops and restaurants. Then I went to Golden Gate Park. The Japanese Tea Garden and the museums were terrific. Then I went to. . . ." Enough already. Just give the speech.

The propmaster

The speaker is introduced. The audience gives a warm welcoming round of applause. The speaker ascends the stage and walks to the podium. The speaker deposits a stack of notes on the podium. The speaker shuffles the notes until they're arranged in the desired order. The speaker looks at the microphone. The speaker plays with the microphone until it's adjusted properly. The speaker puts on a pair of reading glasses. The speaker pours a glass of water. The speaker drinks the water. The speaker looks for the switch that turns on the podium light.

The audience is bored out of their minds. If the speaker is Marcel Marceau — fine. No one expects to hear anything. If the speaker is anyone else, get the props arranged ahead of time.

The ignoramus

This introduction is delivered exactly as planned in advance despite the fact that an earthquake has just shaken the meeting site or a bomb has exploded outside the meeting room or a chandelier has fallen on an audience member.

The speaker just ignores these events. The introduction proceeds as if nothing unusual has occurred. Perhaps this works for an audience of ostriches. Unfortunately, humans tend not to hide their heads in the sand. If something weird happens, it must be addressed in the introduction. By ignoring it, you lose your credibility and your audience.

The pest

Pests want to get the audience involved right away. They come out and immediately fire questions at individuals in the crowd. "You, sir, in the front row. What's your name? Do you live here in town? And what do you do for a living? Great. Great. That's terrific. You down in the back. On the aisle. Yes, you ma'am. What's your name?" This is intimidating and annoying. People like being in the audience because they can melt into a vast sea of anonymity. They don't want to be called on by the speaker. And they don't want to answer personal questions from speakers who haven't revealed anything about themselves. Sometimes it's OK to ask questions to individuals in your audience, but not right away. Warm them up first. Let them get to know you. Otherwise, you'll be a pest, and you'll just bug the crowd.

Ways to Begin

There are as many ways to begin a presentation as there are presentations. (This must be true. I read it in a fortune cookie.) Your opening can be as simple as stating your topic: "Today I will speak about elephant seal mating rituals." Or it can be as dramatic as this opening from a John Cantu speech:

> One summer day a couple of years ago, I turned the corner and an 18-year-old kid stuck a gun in my stomach and said, "Bang, bang, you're dead." He pulled the trigger. As I fell to the ground, I heard someone in the background saying, "All clear. Game is over." That was a typical weekend of training for the National Guard.

"The audience was riveted," recalls John Cantu, a renowned San Francisco comedy coach, "because they pictured me being mugged in the street." He notes that the opening is powerful because he didn't trick the audience. "I didn't say I turned a *street* corner or that a *punk* was standing there with a gun. The audience assumed those things and created its own mental image."

No matter how the introduction begins, the effect that every speaker desires is identical — you want to knock the socks off the audience. You want them to focus their full attention on you and hang on your every word. The big question is how do you do this? Well, there's no magic formula.

But there *are* lots of ways to begin. On the next several pages is a list to get you started. It's not exhaustive. It's just here to give you ideas. I've grouped the openings into three categories: openings based on material, openings that deal directly with the audience, and simple but effective openings.

Material-based introductions

One of the most popular types of introductions is the opening based on material. The speaker begins with a joke, quotation, story, or similar item. What follows are are some examples.

Quotation

Quotations make good openings for several reasons: they're easy to find; they're easy to tie into your topic; and they make you sound smart.

Here's how Warren Manshell, an investment banker with Dreyfus Corporation and a former ambassador to Denmark, opened a speech about the Constitution:

> "The Constitution is an invitation to struggle for the privilege of directing foreign policy." That is Edwin Corwin's famous description of the Constitution, and the history of executive-congressional interplay in the area is replete with examples to prove his point.

Rhetorical Question

Asking questions is an effective way of introducing a topic. A rhetorical question involves the audience as they mentally answer.

Here's how John Lewis, a managing partner with Squire, Sanders & Dempsey, used rhetorical questions to begin a speech:

> Why are 300 people with a deep interest in education gathered in Southern California to debate "school choice"? What is "school choice"? Why do some believe it is a solution to the problems that confront public education today? What are those problems?

Joke

People like to laugh. If you can tell a joke, you've got a powerful skill at your disposal. But don't blow it. If you open with a joke, make sure that it makes a point. And definitely make sure that it's not offensive — off-color, ethnic, racist, or sexist.

Here's how Winston Lord, Chairman, National Commission on America and the New World, Carnegie Endowment for International Peace, used a joke to begin a talk about what America needs to do to succeed in the new world order:

Two key principles run throughout the report, and I would like to illustrate them with a story of three astronauts sent on a major mission to uncharted territory, much like the uncharted new world we are facing. The astronauts, American, Russian, and Japanese, were told that on this long journey they could each take along 150 pounds of whatever they wished. The Japanese astronaut took along 150 pounds of English language books in order to learn the language and be competitive. The American took her husband, who weighed about 150 pounds. And the Russian took 150 pounds of Cuban cigars. They returned several years later to a huge crowd and an international television audience. The Japanese gets off and gives a speech in flawless English. The Americans get off holding babies in each arm. The Russian gets off with a scowl on his face and says, "Does anyone have a match?"

The story illustrates the principles in this report. The two things we have to do in the new world is, one, domestic renewal and discipline to restore our competitiveness at home, the type of discipline the Japanese astronaut showed. And second, reflecting what the Americans did, we need to create abroad what might be called "creative" or "fertile" coalitions, one that we and our allies can act together in all our common interests. And if we can do these two things, we believe our journey in this new world will indeed be matchless.

Story or anecdote

Everyone loves stories — especially if they're real, personal, and relevant. Here's how Alexandra York, founder and President of the American Renaissance for the Twenty-First Century, used a personal anecdote to begin a speech about American culture:

What is the *current* state of our culture? By way of a short answer, let me relate a true, personal experience.

A few years ago, while recovering from a tennis injury, I worked out regularly with a personal trainer. At that time, the new Broadway musical casually named *Les Miz* had reawakened interest in Victor Hugo's immortal book, *Les Miserables,* on which the play was based. New Yorkers were reading or rereading the book with fervor — on subways and buses, on bank lines, in doctors' offices, and even on exercise bikes. One day at my "very upscale" gym, the woman next to me warmed up on her bike reading a paperback of that great, classic novel which she had propped up on the handlebars while she cycled. A trainer wandered by — a male in his mid-thirties with a B.S. degree — and noted the reading material with visible surprise. He stopped short and asked in wonderment, "They made a book of it already?" So may we ask in wonderment, "What is the state of a culture where such a question can be asked by a college graduate?"

Statistic

There's some good news and some bad news about statistics. The bad news is they tend to put people to sleep. The good news is that dramatic, carefully chosen statistics keep people *from* going to sleep. They serve as a wake-up call. Here's an example used by C.E. Ritchie, Chairman and CEO of The Bank of Nova Scotia, in a speech about Canada's competitive position:

> In the current issue of the Harvard Business Review, there is an article entitled "The New Labour Market" that speaks volumes about globalization and competitiveness, two ideas that will be the subject of my remarks today.
>
> The article contains some striking figures showing the number of college graduates in science and engineering in 13 countries. By now, it will surprise no one that Japanese engineering graduates — 75,000 strong in 1986 — outnumbered our class of 8,400 by a ratio of almost 9 to 1. But who would have guessed that Mexico graduated more than 25,000 engineers in that same year — *four times* Canada's production. Or that the Philippines graduated 23,000 engineers, again almost four times Canada's output.

Fact

An interesting or startling fact always provides a good way to start a presentation. If you find the fact fascinating, chances are your audience will too. Douglas E. Olesen, President and Chief Executive Officer of Battelle, used an intriguing fact to begin a speech about waste minimization:

> In just a few years, the most widely viewed artwork in the world may not be the Mona Lisa, or the Statue of Liberty, or even the Mapplethorpe exhibit. No, it just might be a landfill in Kearny, New Jersey. The state recently closed the landfill, and now it's considering one artist's idea to beautify this one-hundred-foot high mountain of buried garbage. The artist wants to turn the dump into an enormous celestial calendar and call it "Sky Mound." Really. It will have steel posts, earthen mounds, a plume of burning methane, and radiating gravel paths aligned with the seasonal movements of the sun, the moon, and the stars. Why might that be the most widely viewed artwork in the world? Well, I'm not sure how many people will go out of their way to visit, but it just so happens that the site is bordered by the New Jersey Turnpike and an Amtrak commuter line. Also, Newark Airport is nearby. So we're going to have millions of commuters driving, riding, and flying by wondering if they're looking at art or at trash, or both.

Good sources for unusual facts include Paul Harvey's radio program "The Rest of the Story." (Many episodes of "The Rest of the Story" have also been collected in book form.)

Historic event

An historic event that relates to your topic is always a good way to begin. Historical references make you look smart and put your topic in perspective.

Julia Hughes Jones, Auditor of Arkansas, used this device in a speech about women and equality:

> Why is a vote important? Many times, a single vote has changed the course of history. More than a thousand years ago in Greece, an entire meeting of the Church Synod was devoted to one question: Is a woman a human being or an animal? It was finally settled by one vote, and the consensus was that we do indeed belong to the human race. It passed, however, by just one vote. Other situations where one vote has made a difference:
>
> In 1776, *one vote* gave America the English language instead of German.
>
> In 1845, *one vote* brought Texas and California into the Union.
>
> In 1868, *one vote* saved President Andrew Johnson from impeachment.
>
> In 1923, *one vote* determined the leader of a new political party in Munich. His name was Adolph Hitler.
>
> In 1960, *one vote* change in each precinct in Illinois would have defeated John F. Kennedy.

Today

Any fact about the date you're speaking can be used to open your presentation. Is it a holiday? Is it a famous person's birthday? Is it the day the lightbulb was invented? This device is closely related to the historical event opening, but it's not identical. You're not looking for an historic event related to your topic. You're looking for an event that occurred on this date. (Once you find it, then you'll relate it to your topic.)

John V.R. Bull, Assistant to the Editor, *The Philadelphia Inquirer*, used this device in a talk called "Freedom of Speech: Can It Survive?"

> Today is marked on my calendar as "Traditional Columbus Day," which seems a particularly good time to take stock of our legacy from that adventure of 500 years ago. A consequence of that journey was the creation of the United States of America, a nation that *Time* magazine last week called "a daring experiment in democracy that in turn became a symbol and a haven of individual liberty for people throughout the world." But today as we survey — and presumably celebrate — that "daring experiment," there are strong indications that we may have failed to create a lasting monument to freedom, for those very blessings of liberty that we thought were enshrined forever as inviolate constitutional guarantees — freedom of speech, press, and assembly — are under attack as seldom before in our nation's 215-year history.

A good source for devising this type of introduction is *Chase's Annual Events*. It lists significant birthdays and events — both current and historical — for every day of the year.

Definition

In this introduction, the speaker opens by defining terms that will be used in the presentation. Here's how Jukka Valtasaari, Finland's Ambassador to the U.S., defined his terms in a speech called "Changes in Europe and Russia":

> In the United States, the word *change* implies vitality and renewal. People elect leaders to implement change. In Europe, change has acquired a momentum of its own, an impetus that surpasses the decisions of national governments. Therefore, the real topic in Europe is not change itself, but rather the context in which change takes place. I am here to present the Finnish perspective on that context.

Prop

An interesting use of a prop in an introduction comes from a speech by Joan Aitken, an Associate Professor at the University of Missouri-Kansas City. Her talk, given to a parents workshop, was entitled "Light the Fire: Communicate With Your Child."

> As I light these four candles, I want to share some things I've heard my five-year-old child say:
>
> *Candle 1.* "Whoops."
>
> *Candle 2.* "Why do elephants put dirt on their backs?"
>
> *Candle 3.* "Knock, knock." ("Who's there?") "Bananas." ("Bananas who?") "Bananas are something monkeys like to eat. Ha, ha, ha, tee-he, ho."
>
> *Candle 4.* "Your lap is my favorite place, Mom."
>
> As I blow out these four candles, I want to share some things I've said to my son:
>
> *Candle 1.* "What's the matter with you?"
>
> *Candle 2.* "I don't know why elephants do things."
>
> *Candle 3.* "I don't get it. Is that joke supposed to be funny?"
>
> *Candle 4.* "Ow. You're getting so big. Get off me."

Magic Trick

Magic tricks are always crowd-pleasers and attention-getters. Here's a trick that Roy Reiman, President of Reiman Publications, used in his opening in a commencement address:

So, just to be sure you're awake and alert this morning at least before I begin, I'd like to give you a 20-second math quiz: I want all of you to think of a number from 1 to 10. Keep it to yourself. Okay, multiply that number by 9. Now forget that first number you had, and add two digits of your new number together.

Got it? Now subtract 5 from that number. Okay, we're almost done. Now think of the letter of the alphabet that coincides with that number — in other words, if you have the number 2, your letter would be "B." So think of the letter that coincides with your number.

All right, now think of a country that begins with that letter. You have a country that begins with that letter? Now, lastly, think of an animal that begins with the letter "E," as in "echo."

Have it? Gee, it's amazing how all of you think alike. You're all thinking of an *elephant* from *Denmark*, aren't you?

For more "magical ideas," see Chapter 24.

Example

An easy way to start a talk is to give the audience an example of what you're talking about. John Goodman, President of the National Center for Policy Analysis in Dallas, used this device in a speech about market incentives for health care:

> Let me give you an example of what I'm talking about. Most of you know that, if you go to your doctor and you put cash down on the table at the time you receive treatment, then the fee is likely to be lower than if you tell your doctor he's got to fill out ten or twelve different forms and try to collect from Medicare or Blue Cross or some employer's health care program. With most markets, if you pay at the time you get service, then you get a lower price than if you make the seller jump through hoops in order to get paid. You know that. I know that, and I thought until recently, everybody in the whole country knew that. However, last spring we discovered there were about 500 people scattered around the country that did not know that fact — and, lo and behold, all 500 of them ended up on Hillary Clinton's health care task force.

Title of your speech

Many speakers use the title of their speech as part of their introduction. Here's how Harry Freeman, President of The Freeman Company, began a speech entitled "Corporate Strategic Philanthropy":

> Corporate strategic philanthropy — hardly a striking phrase. In fact, it's quite a mouthful. And yet this wordy phrase describes one of the fastest changing, most exciting and challenging, and most often overlooked facets and opportunities of the modern business world.

Audiovisual aids

Audiovisual aids — slides, overheads, audiotapes, videotapes, multimedia programs — can be used very effectively in introductions. Wendy Liebmann, President of WSL Marketing, used a cartoon to begin a presentation about consumer trends:

> I was asked to speak to you today about consumer trends. That's sometimes a dangerous pursuit because the speed at which things change in this country and around the world is so great that before you know it, today's trend is yesterday's memory.
>
> This cartoon from *Advertising Age* sums it up perfectly. For those of you who can't see it . . . that's a trend we'll discuss later . . . there's a man sitting at his desk (another trend we'll talk about later) listening to his voice mail (yet another trend we'll talk about later) and the message is "While you were away from your desk the following trends have bitten the dust."

Audience-centered introductions

You can also build your introduction around the audience. In this type of opening, you involve them by making specific references to them, asking them to do things, or trying to elicit an emotional reaction from them.

Provoke them

Here's how James P. Grant, Executive Director of the United Nations Children's Fund (UNICEF), used this opening at an international development conference:

> Permit me to begin with a few friendly provocations: First, I would suggest that nobody — not the West, not the United States, nobody — "won the Cold War."

Compliment them

Here's the key. The compliment must be honest and specific. The more specific you make it, the more effective it will be. Eric Rubenstein, Board Chairman and President of the Single Room Operators Association, complimented his audience in a speech to Job Resources, Inc.:

> I am delighted to be here. Let me compliment your fine organization, Job Resources, on having counseled and job-trained more than 7,000 individuals, and having also obtained permanent employment for over 2,000 men and women since 1979. Clearly much of your success is due to the hard work and dedication of your founder and Executive Director, Ms. Michal Rooney. Job Resources' track record is especially impressive because you only assist disabled individuals, economically disadvantaged people, and displaced workers. Your nonprofit agency truly helps needy people train for and obtain jobs, and this is appreciated.

Show your knowledge of them

An audience is always complimented if you know something about them. It shows that you made an effort to learn about them. The perfect place to display this knowledge is in the introduction.

Here's how C.J. Silas, Chairman and CEO of Phillips Petroleum Company, did this at a speech to the Alabama Business Hall of Fame:

> Thank you for honoring me as your guest this evening and for inviting me to take part in the induction of four outstanding leaders into the Alabama Business Hall of Fame. Tom Moore tells me that when the Board of Visitors organized the Hall of Fame in 1973, it was the first of its kind in the nation.
>
> Since then, you've been the standard by which other such halls of fame have sprung up nationwide.
>
> In the process, you've honored dozens of Alabama business leaders — not just for their accomplishments, but for their character.

Develop a common bond with them

Anytime you can show how you have something in common with the audience, that's good. John Rindlaub, Chairman and CEO of Seafirst Bank, used this type of opening in a speech to an insurance industry conference:

> I appreciate the invitation to be here . . . since I've always had a warm spot in my heart for the insurance industry. I know that's hard to believe. But there's a reason.
>
> My father was Controller of American Re-Insurance . . . and one of the founders, and an Executive Vice President of the Municipal Bonds Insurance Association.
>
> For 20 years, around the dinner table, I heard stories about the insurance industry. So it's a pleasure to be here today with insurance professionals.

Simple but effective introductions

It's been said that nothing is more simple than greatness. If that's true, then this section contains some really great ways to begin a presentation. (They don't get any simpler than this.)

Emphasize the importance of your subject

Saying that something is important gets immediate attention. We're socially conditioned to respond to that word. Here's how Kevin J. Price, Executive Director of the Free Enterprise Education Center, used this device to begin a talk to the Rotary Club in Warsaw, Poland:

I am pleased to be here with you today and to share with you the free market discussion. This topic is important because many of the activities that are part of the free market — marketing, capitalization, etc. — cannot be done without a free enterprise system. In this session, we will examine the elements of the free market, the role of government in a free society, and other aspects of the free enterprise system.

Refer to the occasion

Here's how former U.S. Surgeon General Antonia C. Novello used this device to open a speech at the regional meeting for Universal Salt Iodization Toward the Elimination of Iodine Deficiency Disorders in the Americas held in Quito, Ecuador:

> It is a pleasure to be here. More than a pleasure, it is a thrill. If that sounds dramatic, I need remind you of why we are here. This is evolution, human history in the making. There is a palpable sense of progress in this room, at this conference, in many of the rooms and buildings I have visited while traveling throughout Latin America over the past several months. There is the power of knowledge in this room, the excitement of knowing that a momentous decision about the future of humankind is ready for the taking. We have made the slow ascent up the learning curve of Iodine Deficiency Disorders, and now we are nearing its peak: there is no more pressing need for research or investigation into the problem, and it is no longer necessary to search for solutions. We are ready to act.

Play off what the person introducing you said

Sometimes the person introducing you will make comments that you can refer to in your opening. The following is an example from a speech given by James R. Houghton, Chairman of Corning Incorporated:

> Thank you very much, Frank. At a time like this I get a little worried how to respond to an introduction like that. The only one I've heard that really works is the following: "Frank, thank you for that wonderful introduction. Of all the introductions I've ever had, yours is certainly the most recent."

> The other thing that I would say to you up front is that Frank is right, my great-grandfather did found the company, but I have to tell you unequivocally standing here that my current position has nothing at all to do with my name. It's all sheer brilliance! Now if you believe that, you'll believe anything, I guess.

Describe how your talk relates to previous talks

Here's how Shaun O'Malley, Chairman and Senior Partner of Price Waterhouse, did it in a speech about international accounting standards:

I've been listening with great interest to the preceding sessions and to what Messrs. Damant, Tweedie, and Wyatt have said this afternoon. Much of what I've heard has been remarkably similar to the comments we at Price Waterhouse hear regularly from our clients and to the kind of feedback we hear at the Financial Accounting Federation, or FAF in the U.S., hear routinely from local companies and securities analysts.

Special Situations

Sometimes the situation dictates the opening. In 1984, management guru Tom Peters was scheduled to be the keynote speaker at a meeting of federal executives in San Francisco. It was shortly after the publication of *In Search of Excellence* — a runaway best-seller that he co-authored. Both the book and Tom Peters were indelibly etched into the public consciousness. Major business magazines had done cover stories on the book and its co-author. You couldn't pick up a newspaper without finding a business columnist writing about excellence. An "excellence" movement was sweeping the nation. And Tom Peters had started it. Tom Peters was who these federal executives wanted and expected to see.

Unfortunately, Tom Peters was unable to make his scheduled appearance. Fortunately, the sponsor of the meeting was informed ahead of time. With less than 24 hours notice, I was picked as the substitute speaker. Now that was quite an honor, but it put me in kind of a ticklish situation. A bunch of federal executives expecting to see the widely acclaimed co-author of the hottest management book of the time would see me — an attorney turned humor consultant — instead. I would have to address that situation immediately in my introduction.

Here's how I opened: "How many of you have read *In Search of Excellence*?" Every hand in the room shot up. "Then you probably already know what Tom was going to talk about. I'm going to give you some *new* information." They laughed. They applauded. And they dropped their defensiveness. They gave me a chance. I followed up by connecting my topic — humor and communication — to the general topic of excellence. It was a hit.

Here are some other special situations and ideas for handling them:

The title of your talk is in the program, but you've changed your topic. John Austin, speechwriter extraordinaire, suggests this opening: "Don't believe everything you read — like your program."

You expect a large crowd but get a small one. Whatever you do, don't proceed like you got the big crowd you expected. You'll look like an idiot if you make expansive gestures and speak at the top of your lungs to a handful of people, and they'll wonder if you're a bit out of touch.

So what can you do? Take a cue from Joe DiNucci, a vice president at Silicon Graphics Computer Systems. He expected 50 people at a sales presentation. Four showed up, and two of them didn't speak English. "I started by taking my jacket off to make it more casual," he told me. "Then I thanked them for coming and emphasized that we could take advantage of the small size of the audience. The presentation could now be more interactive. They could interrupt with questions. They would actually benefit from the low turnout." His goal was to make them feel rewarded, not punished, for coming.

Your audience has more technical expertise in the subject than you have. Change the focus of the talk away from the technical details and concentrate on the big picture. Michael O'Hare, Professor of Management at UC Berkeley, used this technique to talk about waste disposal to a group of people who use radioactive isotopes in their businesses:

> I've got some notes here about the importance and the central place of radioactive waste disposal in the economy of an industrial society. I'm going to save us all a lot of time. You just talk to the people across the table about that. There's nothing I can tell this audience that you don't already know more about in the context of your own businesses than I do.
>
> But I would like to make three major points about waste disposal. They generally go toward raising this issue to a higher and more important level.

You're the last speaker at an all day conference. The audience is burned out. You know they're burned out. They know that you know they're burned out. So acknowledge it. That's what Neil Baron, a Sybase marketing manager, did when he was the eighth speaker at an all-day technical conference. His topic was the three commandments for product sales.

> I was talking to my wife and she asked, "Why don't you have ten commandments? Shouldn't there always be ten?" And I said, "It's 4:30. Who the heck wants to stick around and listen to ten commandments. And second, Moses didn't have to follow seven other speakers."

Or you can try this line used by Chuck Lamar, a vice president of U.S. West Communications:

> Thanks for sticking around for our closing session. I certainly hope we've saved the best for last.

Your audience doubts your honesty. This is a major credibility problem that must be addressed immediately. Otherwise, your presentation will be a big waste of time. After all, why bother speaking if no one will believe anything you say? Sometimes just acknowledging the audience's negative attitude toward you is a good way to start. It shows you're being "honest" about something.

Here's how CIA Director Robert Gates handled the problem in a talk called "CIA and Openness: Relations with the People of the United States." He delivered it to the Oklahoma Press Association.

An oxymoron is a figure of speech which is seemingly self-contradictory. Examples might include "bureaucratic efficiency," "government frugality," or "CIA openness." The latter oxymoron is the subject of my remarks today.

You might anticipate that a speech on openness in the CIA would be a prime candidate for the collection of the world's shortest addresses. It is a subject that rockets every outside observer's most cynical instincts into the starting blocks — prepared to disbelieve every word, beginning with "I'm glad to be here today."

Now that you know that I know that I stand here looking over a yawning chasm of credibility, like Indiana Jones in the last crusade, I will now step out into that chasm on faith, the faith that what I have to say will persuade you of our seriousness of purpose and action.

What Type of Opening Should You Use?

You've got all these ways to open. How do you choose one? Allatia Harris, Dean of the Communication Division at Mountain View College in Dallas, offers a general approach to making your selection: Make believe you're going to talk to a friend about your topic. How would you start in a way that would get his or her attention? What would cause your friend to have this discussion with you?

Alan Weiner, President of Communication Development Associates, has a specific recommendation: Go with an anecdote. He says his company's research and testing show that anecdotes make the most effective opening, followed by quotations and statistics.

Alan advises clients to make their first four words "About a year ago," "About a month ago," "About a week ago," or any other time frame. Why? "Because these are the adult equivalent to 'Once upon a time,'" he explains. "Anecdotes start back in time and move forward. They get and hold audience attention."

Following the basic rule to write the introduction last, Alan suggests thinking through the nuts-and-bolts of your talk before worrying about the opening anecdote. "You'll find it after you outline all your points and subpoints. Because each of those points will suggest stories. And one of those stories will become the opening anecdote." He likens the process to a journalist who gives an article to an editor. The editor reads the article and finds something in it to use as the headline. Your anecdote is the headline for your talk. It will leap out at you as you prepare your talk.

Tuning up your introduction

You've heard of singers introducing songs? Meet a speaker who sings introductions. Bill Zachmeier makes a lot of presentations. As a professor of school administration at San Jose State University, he speaks to students, teachers, administrators, professional associations and countless other groups of people. And he almost always begins his presentations by singing. He uses no musical accompaniment. He just tells the audience he's going to sing a song before he gives his talk.

Initially, people tense up — until he starts to sing. "It takes ten seconds before they realize it's going to work," he explains. "Then they relax. They smile. And when the song is over, I get a nice round of applause." Then he'll say, "If you behave yourself during my talk, I'll sing another song at the end. If you don't behave, I'll sing two songs."

Not until after his song does Bill tell them what he'll talk about. But by then he's built rapport, and the audience stays with him. And he keeps his promise: he sings another song at the end.

If you've got a good voice and you want to try this, here are three things to remember:

- Keep the song short — not much more than a minute. (Two minutes is way too long.)

- The song works best with a large audience of people who don't already know you.

- And if you're speaking to a group Bill has already addressed, don't sing "Danny Boy" — they've probably heard it from Bill.

So what opening should you use? Here are some factors to consider:

- **Your style:** Can't tell a joke? Then don't even try. There's something about giving a presentation that makes people feel obligated to tell jokes. You're not.

- **Your time limits:** Don't use a time-consuming opening — long story, complex magic trick, extended example — if you don't have a lot of time.

- **Your relation to the audience:** Do they know you? Do they know of you? Are you a complete stranger? Will they like or dislike your message? How much rapport do you need to establish?

- **Your rhetorical constraints:** The occasion and circumstances of your presentation may narrow your choice of openings. Is the event somber or festive? Is it formal or informal? Are certain topics off limits?

Alright, bottom line, what opening should you use? The one that works best for *you*.

Chapter 9

All's Well That Ends Well: Conclusions and Transitions

. . . .

In This Chapter

▶ The big finish

▶ Creating a powerful conclusion

▶ Ten common conclusions to avoid at all costs

▶ Eleven ways to close in style

▶ Moving smoothly from one idea to another

. . . .

*W*hen I was a kid in New York, a popular battle cry on the playground was "Don't start what you can't finish." This advice was inevitably directed at a bespectacled young scholar who, after receiving an endless dose of harassment, had finally mustered enough courage to mumble a negative remark to the source of his ill fortune — the school bully. But the advice always arrived too late. Even as it was shouted, the bully was preparing to thrash him into tomorrow. Although my young colleagues' advice referred to the fisticuffs of the moment, they could have been talking about presentations. Too many people who start presentations don't know how to finish them.

The conclusion is one of the most important parts of your presentation. If the introduction is your first impression, the conclusion is your last one — *and your last chance to make one*. It plays a key role in determining how your audience will remember you and your message.

In my model of a presentation as the smooth flight of an airplane, the conclusion is the landing. The passengers — your audience — don't want the landing to be sudden or bumpy. They don't want to land in the wrong place. And most important, they *do* want you to land.

What the Conclusion Must Do

A cynic might say the conclusion's job is to let the audience know when to wake up. Whatever. For non-cynics the conclusion has three major functions. To be successful, it must accomplish each of them. Here they are:

Summarize your speech

The conclusion must provide a summary of your major points. This quick review should also remind the audience of your attitudes toward the ideas you've expressed. It should also show how the points relate to each other and your topic.

Provide closure

The conclusion must give the audience a feeling that your presentation is complete. People have a psychological need for closure. They want a presentation to have a beginning, a middle, and an end — especially an end. They don't want to be left hanging. Your conclusion must address this need.

Make a great final impression

The conclusion is your last chance to influence audience expectations. You want to end on a high note. Go out with a bang. Leave them stamping in the aisles. (Pick your own cliché.) The conclusion should grab their attention and score a direct hit on the gut level. It should possess an emotional appeal that illuminates the compelling nature of your entire presentation.

How to Create the Perfect Conclusion

Remember the ending to every fairy tale you've ever heard? "And then they lived happily ever after." You can create perfect endings for your presentations, too. Just follow these simple rules:

Make it sound like a conclusion

People expect a conclusion to sound a certain way — like a conclusion. Audiences tend to become upset if you think you're finished but they don't. So make the wrap-up obvious. Use phrases such as "in conclusion," "to conclude" or "in closing." They're always good starting points — for ending.

Cue the audience in advance

It's common knowledge that you have to let the audience know you're concluding.

They like it even better if you let them know ahead of time. Tell them when you're getting *close* to your conclusion. "Turning now to my final point." "I'll give two more examples before I wrap up." These types of statements give the audience confidence that you'll reach your final destination. It also helps them formulate an estimated time of arrival.

Make it the right length

The conclusion should usually be about 5 percent to 10 percent of your talk. It can be too short, but a much more common mistake is making it too long. Don't go on forever. Sum up and sit down.

Write it out

There are two main reasons to write out your conclusion. First is the stage fright issue. The period when you're concluding is the second most jittery time for presenters. (The most likely time for stage fright to strike is when you begin.) If you write out the conclusion, you don't have to worry about forgetting it. Second, and more important, if you write out the conclusion, you'll know when to conclude. It's insurance against rambling.

Make the last words memorable

President Ronald Reagan once gave a speech in an unusual time slot — *before* a luncheon. Here are the last two lines of his conclusion:

> Thank you and God bless you. And now the words you've been waiting to hear from me: "Let's eat."

The last few lines of your conclusion are the most important. So make them memorable. Go for an emotional connection with the audience. Make them laugh. Make them think. Make them stand up and applaud.

Here's a simple formula for setting up your final line: Just say, "I have one final thought that I want to leave you with." (An alternative is "If you remember just one thing I've said today, remember this. . . .") Then give them a heck of a thought. Word it strongly and make it relevant — to your talk and your audience.

Always provide an opportunity for questions

Here's some uncommon knowledge. It comes from Jeff Raleigh, a senior vice president with public-relations mammoth Hill & Knowlton. Always make yourself available for questions, even if you're talking to a large group and even if there's no time for a formal question-and-answer session. Announce in your conclusion that you'll be staying around to answer any questions. "You've got to stay involved with your audience," Jeff explains. "If you don't make this offer, people may have unanswered questions and think you don't care about them. Making the offer always makes you look good."

Remember it ain't over till it's over

Have you ever done this? You're in the audience. You hear a presentation that you think is absolutely terrific. When it's finished, you go to talk with the speaker, and he or she gives you the brush off. Bummer. First, you feel stupid. Then you get angry. And then you change your opinion of the presenter and the presentation, right? Now you think the speaker is a jerk, and the speech wasn't so great after all.

So don't be a jerk. Be kind to your fans. And don't forget — the fact that you're finished speaking doesn't mean that you're done.

What not to do

Sometimes what you don't say in your conclusion is even more important than what you do say. What follows are some common mistakes to avoid.

Don't go overtime. Make the conclusion coincide with the end of your allotted time. If you want to be perceived as a genius, finish five minutes early, but don't go longer than expected. An old joke on the lecture circuit defines a "second wind" as what a speaker gets after he or she says, "In conclusion." Don't let that happen to you. It's not pretty. (The classic example is Bill Clinton's nominating speech at the 1988 Democratic convention. It clocked in at 32 minutes and became a source of national amusement.)

Don't change your delivery. If you didn't begin with a sonorous oratorical style, then there's no reason to end with one. Just keep doing what you were doing. (Unless the audience has fallen asleep.)

Don't ramble. Reviewing the points you've already made should be done in a brief and orderly manner — preferably in the order you discussed them. Make the conclusion easy to follow. Stick to your plan.

Don't add new points at the end. The conclusion is a time to review what you've already said — not make another speech. Introducing new ideas in the conclusion means that you haven't properly fit them into the overall framework of your presentation, which in turn means that these ideas will have less impact. The audience will have to figure out where they belong. And you know what? The audience wants to go home.

Don't say you forgot to mention something. It makes you look disorganized, and the audience worries that you'll make another speech. Here's one solution: If the point is really important, boil it down to a very succinct statement. Then, after you've summarized the points you've already made, say you want to leave the audience with one final thought. Then give them the point you forgot to mention. If you had already planned to leave them with a different final thought, don't worry. Just say you want to leave them with two final thoughts. First give the point you forgot and then give the final thought you had planned. (Yes, this is an exception to the rule against adding new points at the end.)

Don't be wishy-washy. It's always important to sound like you believe in whatever it is you're talking about, and this advice is especially true for the conclusion. Be decisive. Take a position. Let the audience know where you stand.

Top Ten Conclusions to Avoid

Have you ever watched a Bugs Bunny cartoon? The conclusion is always the same — "That's all folks." While that closing works for a cartoon, it would never work for a presentation. (In presentation parlance, it's called a *nonexistent conclusion.*) Here's why you should avoid the nonexistent conclusion, as well as nine other horrible yet common conclusions:

The nonexistent conclusion

A famous philosopher once said, "I think, therefore I am." Unfortunately this philosophical principle doesn't apply to conclusions. Just because you think you have one doesn't mean you do. In fact, the nonexistent conclusion is an all too common mistake. The speaker comes to the last point and just stops. No review. No wrap up. No conclusion. In my airplane flight model of public speaking, this is equivalent to flying into the Bermuda Triangle. One moment the plane is on the radar; the next it's gone. We can't even say that it crashed; it just disappeared. In fact, the most common mistake with conclusions is not having one, and it's easy to understand why. People run out of preparation time. So they never get around to writing a conclusion, and they figure they'll just wing it. (Famous last words — so to speak.)

The "tree crashed into my car, officer" conclusion

This one sneaks up on the audience. They're just cruising along listening to the presentation when all of a sudden, they've smacked right into the conclusion. Where did it come from? Nobody saw it coming. Every conclusion needs to announce itself. Don't let yours jump out at the audience.

The cloned conclusion

This one is especially frustrating for the audience. The audience listens to the speaker go into the close; the points are reviewed; and everything builds toward a big finish. They're ready to applaud and head for the exits. But the speaker doesn't stop speaking. Suddenly the speaker is doing another conclusion, and then another, and another. The conclusion is cloning itself. In my airplane model of public speaking, this is equivalent to the plane coming in for a landing, bouncing on the runway and heading back into the sky — repeatedly. Don't make this mistake. Bring your speech in for a landing — once. If the audience truly wants an encore, they'll let you know.

The tacky conclusion

This conclusion has no apparent connection with the talk that precedes it. The speaker knows a conclusion is needed and just tacks one on. (Hence the name.) Don't *jump* to a conclusion. Build a bridge to it from the body of your talk and help your audience across.

The wimpy conclusion

The speaker wimps out at the end — apologizing for a variety of presentation sins, both real and imagined; making excuses for what he or she perceives as a poor performance; and just generally whining. This kind of conclusion can really undercut an otherwise solid performance. Let the audience decide for themselves how you did. Don't lead a chorus of criticism.

The airline baggage conclusion

The body of your speech is in Spain and your conclusion is in Canada.

Here's the problem: This conclusion lets you know it's coming, and it sums up the main points, but it's not the conclusion to the speech that was given. It's the conclusion to some other speech. There's been a mix-up somewhere. The speaker has used the wrong landing pattern. Sound farfetched? Well, it's not that uncommon. It usually occurs when the speaker introduces new information in the conclusion. For example:

> And in conclusion, we need tougher drug laws to make our country great again. We can't afford to keep losing thousands of jobs a year to the underground economy. We can't afford to pay higher taxes because of the money lost to the underground economy. And we can't afford to have legitimate businesses lose the managerial talent of the dealers running the underground economy. That's why we have to crack down on drugs.

Very rousing. Very inspiring. There's just one thing — the entire speech was about the debilitating physical effects of drugs. There wasn't a single mention about economic consequences. So great conclusion, wrong speech.

The pinball machine conclusion

This one bounces all over the place. The speaker is summing up one point, then another, then back to the first point, then an inspirational closing quote, then back to that first point, and then. . . . What's the audience's reaction? TILT.

The run-out-of-gas conclusion

The speaker starts to review the various points made in the presentation. For the first point or two, this review sounds strong and confident. Then the speaker becomes more tentative and hesitant as if he or she can't remember all the points that were made. After struggling to complete the review, the speaker just sputters to a stop. It's as if the speaker had been cruising on fumes and then finally ran out of fuel.

The endless conclusion

You guessed it. This conclusion seems to go on forever. Is it really possible for a summary of the main points to take longer than the actual points? Not according to well-established laws of time and space. But the endless conclusion defies Newtonian physics. What goes up doesn't have to come down. It just keeps going, going, going . . .until the audience is gone.

The "that's it?" conclusion

This conclusion gets its name from the audience reaction it generates. When the audience hears this conclusion, they say, "That's it?" They experience a complete letdown — a deflation — because the presentation creates expectations that aren't met. (Technically, this isn't a conclusion problem — but that's when the problem shows up.) It's like attending a lecture by a prestigious diet doctor who says he'll reveal the secret of weight loss, and at the end, the big secret is "Eat less." (Or like a presentation I attended where the speaker promised to reveal the secret of harnessing the power of humor. His conclusion: "Think funny.") That's it?

Wrapping It Up in Style

It's been said that a speech is like a love affair: Anyone can start one, but it takes a lot of skill to end one well. This section contains some ways to end *your* speech that will keep the audience loving you.

Refer back to the opening

If one of the functions of the conclusion is to provide closure, then referring back is a great way to do it. You use the conclusion to return to remarks you made in your introduction. If you asked a question in the opening, you answer it in the conclusion. If you told a story, you refer to it again. This technique gives a wonderful sense of completeness to your presentation.

A good example comes from a speech by Farah M. Walters, President & CEO, University Hospitals of Cleveland. In a conference sponsored by a clearinghouse for women's support groups, she opened with an anecdote about her daughter Stephanie — a member of an intramural touch football team.

> Stephanie came home one night, and she was really upset. "You know, Mom," she said, "we've been playing this game for weeks, and the boys never pass the ball to the girls. We complained to the boys, and they didn't listen. We complained to the coach, and he talked to the boys, but they still didn't listen. So today, we were so upset that the four of us sat down in the middle of the field at the start of the game, and we sang: "I am woman, hear me roar."

At the conclusion of the speech, she returned to the opening anecdote and tied it all together with her theme — options for women.

So my friends, if I were asked to give a benediction to today's talk, it would be this: May we in this room — and our daughters and our daughters' daughters — one day sit down in the middle of a large playing field, but never again to sing "I am woman, hear me roar" out of frustration. Because by then, we will have reached our chosen destination, and such a roar will be a roar of celebration."

Use a quotation

You can never go wrong ending with an inspirational quotation related to your message. Just make sure it's inspired and related. Here's an example from a speech about the future of telecommunications given by AT&T Vice Chairman Randall Tobias:

And I hope you would agree with the philosopher John Dewey who said, "The future is *not* ominous but a promise; it surrounds the present like a halo."

Ask a question

Asking the right question can be a powerful way to end a presentation. Presumably the question implies an answer — the one you want the audience to reach. Michigan Governor John Engler used a powerful question to close an address to his state legislature about a school reform plan:

My friends, the eyes of the nation are upon us. This is Michigan's moment — a moment that will tell future generations here and across America what kind of leaders we were. Will we put our kids first? That is the ques-tion before every single person in this chamber. *Our* answer is *their* future.

Tell a story

The story can be funny, shocking, moving, dramatic, educational, personal, fictional, biblical, or allegorical. You get the idea. Here's a story that Donna Shalala, U.S. Secretary of Health and Human Services, used to conclude a presentation at a conference on family violence:

Let me conclude by telling you about a child psychologist named Sandra Graham-Berman who took responsibility for doing even more. Several years ago, she became aware of a support group for battered women. But she heard that there was no professional support for their children. On her own time and with her own money, she began a support group for the children of these battered women. She began to see the girls and boys act out, talk out, and draw out their fears and frustrations. She helped them learn they are not alone in their pain. And she taught them that when mommy is in trouble — when she is being hurt by daddy — it's possible to get help by dialing 9-1-1.

A few years later, a shy, 8-year-old girl walked in on a fight. Her father— if you can believe it, a child psychiatrist — was beating her mother on the head with a hammer.

Try to imagine that. Try to imagine what you would do.

Well, that little girl knew what to do. She remembered the lesson taught her by a caring adult. And so she went to that phone, picked it up, pressed 9-1-1, and saved her mother's life. The father is in prison now, and the family's trying their best to build a new life. If that little girl can have the courage to pick up the telephone, surely we can have the courage to prevent such stories from happening.

Recite a poem

It should be short. It can be inspirational or funny, and it must tie into your talk. Here's a verse used to conclude a speech by Albert Casey, former President and CEO of the Resolution Trust Corporation (and it ties into *any* talk):

I should like to close with the immortal words of Richard Goodwin:

I love a finished speaker.
I really truly do. I don't mean one who's polished.
I just mean one who's through.

Thank you.

Tell a joke

President Ronald Reagan used a joke to conclude an address to the nation about Labor Day:

It's like the fellow who took some land down by a creek bottom all covered with brush and rocks. And he cleared the brush, and he hauled the rocks away. And then he started cultivating, and he planted. And finally he had a beautiful garden. He was so proud that one Sunday after the church service he asked the minister if he wouldn't come by and see what he had done. So the minister came by. And when he saw the corn that had been planted there, he said he'd never seen any corn so tall, and the Lord had really blessed the land. And then he looked at the melons, and he said he'd never seen any as big as that, and thank the Lord for that. And he went on praising the Lord for everything — the squash and the beans and everything else. The farmer was getting a little fidgety. Finally, he interrupted and said, "Reverend, I wish you could have seen this place when the Lord was doing it all by himself."

Well, I've always liked that story because it makes an important point. God gave us this great and good land, but it's up to us to make it flourish, to preserve its freedom, and to see it grow to greatness. And this Labor Day, thanks to the American people, our country is growing stronger every minute. I just have one final thing to say: Keep it up, America. You're doing great.

Tell them what to do

This type of ending is very specific. The audience is told *exactly* what to do. Here's what the late J. Peter Grace, Chairman of W. R. Grace & Co, told his audience to do as he concluded a speech on government waste.

Get behind Citizens Against Government Waste and join the 535,000 Americans who care about the future of their country and are willing to stand up and be counted. Call 1-800-BE-ANGRY and find out how you can get involved.

Ask for help

Just ask for help. People really do respond. My favorite example of this technique comes from a speech that I gave to my local Rotary Club. The presentation described an experimental humor program that I was organizing in our local high school. As an incentive for students to participate, I wanted to establish a prize fund, so I needed prizes. The entire conclusion to my presentation was a plea for help.

An old philosopher once said, "There's no subject, however complex, which — if studied with patience and intelligence — will not become more complex." Well, there's nothing complex about my subject today. In fact, it's real simple. The whole program depends on having great prizes. And having great prizes requires your support. So please help in any way you can. Your generosity is the key to the program's success.

They helped.

Make a candid assessment

Don't pull any punches. The unwatered-down truth always gets attention — it's so rare to hear it. Here's an example from a speech given by FBI Director Louis Freeh:

> We have to ask the fearful questions:
>
> Will crime ever recede? Or are we doomed to live in an increasingly lawless society where criminals kill and plunder and corrupt in such growing and epidemic proportions that our freedoms are eventually destroyed?
>
> Some feel the issue is in doubt. My own view is that we can win the struggle against crime. But we should have no illusions. Success hinges on a number of things: All of law enforcement must truly redouble its efforts; government at all levels must provide the needed crime-fighting resources; we must have unprecedented determination; and those members of the public who support the law only when it suits them must instead obey it 24 hours of every day.

Match your conclusion to your mission

The traditional thinking about the conclusion is that it should reflect your purpose in making the presentation. If your goal is to entertain the audience, you can close with a joke or story that "leaves 'em laughing." If your goal is to persuade people about some idea or issue, you close with an appeal that makes them change their minds. If your goal is to motivate them, you use an inspirational closing.

The conclusion that you've probably heard about the most is the call for action. This is traditionally used in persuasive appeals — sales presentations, charity solicitations, and campaign speeches. At the conclusion of the presentation, the speaker urges the audience to take some action. Buy my product. Make a donation. Vote for me.

Here's a humdinger of a traditional call for action from a speech on biotechnology and U.S. policy given in Chicago by Richard Mahoney, Chairman and CEO of Monsanto Company:

> Ladies and gentlemen, I am not here today to depress you but to rouse you to action. Chicago — and the Midwest — have an enormous stake. Studs Terkel calls Chicago the city of "I will" — and never before have we so sorely needed people who will say "I will."
>
> I urge you to write to Jim Edgar, and Paul Simon, and Carol Mosely-Braun — and make them make sense at the state level and in Washington.

Urge improvement in capital gains tax policy to free investment in innovation.

Urge product liability reform — especially punitive damages at the state and federal levels.

Urge a national policy of scientific literacy for our young people.

Urge the media to reject fringe views of science scares masquerading as media balance.

Urge funding for regulatory agencies to reduce product approval times.

Urge a sense of national pride that we have a successful pharmaceutical industry willing to invest heavily in R&D — leaders in the world — instead of bashing it because it's profitable.

Urge Congress to follow the historic instruction given to new doctors: First, do no harm — help if possible — but first, do no harm.

Whew! If I lived in Chicago, I'd write to my Congressional representative right now.

Here's the uncommon knowledge. *Every presentation should conclude with a call to action.* It doesn't have to be a call to action in the traditional sense (buy, give, vote), but it should ask every member of the audience to take some type of action. Because that's what really involves them.

What if you're doing a speech to entertain or inform? No problem. Just follow Joe DiNucci's example. A legendary executive at Silicon Graphics Computer Systems, Joe ends every speech with a call to action. "It's not just for sales presentations," he explains. "No matter what I'm talking about, I'll find a way to close with a call to action. Even if it's just telling the audience to think about something or ask themselves a question. You've got to tell them to do something." So do that.

Transitions

Some of my first observations about public speaking occurred when I was in the Cub Scouts. I must have been seven or eight years old at the time. The Cub Scouts are organized around two major units — the pack and the den. The pack is made up of all the Cub Scouts in a given community. It's divided into dens of several boys each.

Back when I was a Cub Scout, a den meeting was held each week. We spent part of the meeting working on arts and crafts projects under the supervision of an adult known as the den mother. Once a month, there would be a pack meeting where everyone showed up. At some point, a representative from each den would come forward to address the full assemblage about their arts and crafts project.

A typical presentation would go something like this: "We made a jewelry box. First our den mother gave us some Popsicle sticks. And then our den mother gave us some glue. And then our den mother helped us glue the sticks together into a box. And then our den mother gave us some more Popsicle sticks. And then our den mother helped us glue them into a cover. And then our den mother gave us some paint. And then we painted the box and the cover. And then our den mother put the boxes aside to dry. And then we brought them here to show you." *And then* he'd hold up the box for everyone to see *and then* he'd return to his seat.

Even at that young age, I knew that something didn't sound right: the transitions were terrible. (All right, maybe I didn't realize the problem until much later — like last week. But I did know something was amiss.)

Transitions may be the most overlooked part of any presentation; yet they're one of the most important. Transitions don't call a lot of attention to themselves, so it's easy to forget about them. They don't involve dramatic rhetorical devices like the introduction or conclusion. They don't offer fascinating information or anecdotes like the body of the presentation, but they're still a big deal. Why? Because they're the glue that holds the whole thing together.

What transitions must do

Even if your presentation has the world's greatest introduction, body, and conclusion, you still have to get from one to the other. That's where transitions come in. They connect the various parts of your presentation, and they flesh out its organization. Transitions let your audience know when you're moving from one idea to another and how all your ideas fit together.

Transitions have a close working relationship with a presentation's organization. In my model of a presentation as the smooth flight of an airplane, the organization is the flight plan, a map of the plane's journey. Unfortunately, passengers never get a copy of this plan. They know their destination but they don't know how the plane will get there. That's the function of transitions. The transitions are the pilot's announcements of your location, route, speed, altitude, and time left in the trip. They highlight the structure of the presentation and get the audience smoothly from point to point in the journey.

The common knowledge about transitions is that they have two traditional functions:

✔ To lead from one section or idea to another.

✔ To provide internal summaries that let the audience know where they're at, where they've been, and where they're going in regard to the presentation.

Here's the uncommon knowledge. Transitions can also be used to gain and hold audience attention.

Transition missions

Transitions have a lot of work to do — especially for such an overlooked part of a presentation. The following are three important tasks that they can perform:

Lead from one idea to another

The primary role of the transition is to lead your listeners from one idea to another.

Perhaps the most important transition in this regard is the one between the introduction and the body of your talk. In my airplane model, this is when the plane pulls out of the takeoff pattern and settles into cruising mode. Turbulence here can make the passengers very nervous. They want to know that the plane is heading in the right direction.

Also very important are the transitions between major points. This is where speakers often screw up. You know what I'm talking about. You're sitting in the audience listening to a speech. The speaker is talking about the monetary policy of Bolivia. But the next thing you know, the speaker is discussing a labor shortage in Eastern Europe. How did we get from Bolivia to Eastern Europe? Probably without a transition.

Fortunately, there's a simple way to handle the transition between introduction and body, as well as the transitions between main points. Here's the secret: Organize your presentation around a number of points and state that number in your introduction. Then the transitions are a breeze. "Today I will be speaking about the three reasons for the coming worldwide depression. First, is the monetary policy of Bolivia. . . .The second reason we are headed for a worldwide depression is the labor shortage in Eastern Europe. . . . Third,. . . ." It's transitions by the numbers. But you know what? It's easy and it works.

Summarize

The second traditional function of transitions is to provide internal summaries — short announcements that let the audience know where they are, where they've been, and where they're going. The need for these summaries is frequently dismissed by inexperienced speakers who feel that they're too repetitive — that they're just filler. Well, yes and no. Internal summaries *are* repetitive, but they're *not* filler. They play a vital role in any presentation, especially presentations longer than a few minutes.

Here's why. When it comes to understanding a presentation, speakers have a distinct advantage over the audience — they know what they're trying to say. (All right, so maybe you can think of a few exceptions. They're in Congress, right?) Speakers know exactly what their message is, how it's structured, and all its points and subpoints. In writing the presentation, speakers have an opportunity to read their message many times. Audiences don't have that luxury. They only hear the presentation once — as it's given. They can't put it in reverse, play it again, and freeze-frame the parts they didn't catch.

It's also more difficult to follow the structure of an oral work than a written work. A book or article has headings and subheadings and paragraphs. A speech has only what the speaker tells the audience. That's why internal summaries are a necessity. And that's why you need a lot of them. They keep reminding the audience of how the presentation is organized and where you're up to. Think of the internal summary as a "You are here" sign in a large building with a confusing floor plan. Your audience wants to see one those signs every so often along the hallways.

Here are a few tips about using internal summaries:

- ✔ An internal summary should succinctly state what you just covered and announce where you're up to.
- ✔ Use an internal summary every time you move from one major point in your presentation to another major point.
- ✔ Internal summaries can also be used when moving from subpoint to subpoint.
- ✔ The longer your presentation, the more internal summaries you need.

Get attention

Transitions can also be used to gain attention. Although they're not traditionally used for this purpose, there's no reason they shouldn't be. Under the traditional view, transitions can serve as internal summaries telling your audience where they've been, where they are, and where they're going. It's this last part — *where they're going* — that raises interesting possibilities for gaining attention.

When you tell your audience where they're going, why not make it exciting? Instead of just restating the structure of your talk in a straightforward, matter-of-fact manner, employ a little pizzazz. Use a *teaser*. A teaser is the short blurb you hear on radio and television programs just before the commercial. "Coming up in the next half of our show: a man abducted by a UFO reveals recipes he learned on board." "A politician who *kept* a promise — right after these announcements." The teaser is designed specifically to get your attention and keep you from changing the channel.

If you want an example of the same principle in another medium, let's go to the movies. What do you watch before the feature presentation? Coming attractions. Why are they shown? So you'll come back to the theater after the current movie has finished its run.

You can use the teaser technique to make your internal summaries excite the audience about what lies ahead in your presentation. Give them some great coming attractions that keep them glued to their seats. How do you do that? Think about why the audience should even listen to your talk. What's in it for them? As you write your transitions about what's coming up, frame them in terms of audience benefits. I do this whenever possible in my presentations on humor and communication for managers, executives, and professionals. "In that last example, the man defused the entire problem simply by showing he had a sense of humor. And he didn't tell any jokes. In a few minutes, I'll show you several other ways to use your sense of humor to defuse hostile situations. But first I want to talk about. . . ."

Whether or not you use the teaser technique, you need to tell your audience where you're heading. So what the heck. Go the extra step and make it fascinating.

Common mistakes with transitions

Transitions are the glue that holds a presentation together. Unfortunately, many speakers become unglued trying to insert transitions properly. Here are some mistakes to avoid:

Too few

The biggest mistake with transitions is not having enough of them. It never hurts to have more because you can never make your presentation too clear to your audience. You've been living with your presentation for quite awhile. You're intimately familiar with it; your audience isn't. The more guidance you can give them about how it's structured and where it's going, the better. Not sure if you need a particular transition? Apply the Kushner rule of transitions: When in doubt, *don't* leave it out.

Too brief

If the transition is too brief, it can be easily missed by your audience. That's equivalent to having no transition at all. The most common, and overused, brief transition is "and." A close runner-up is "in addition." I've heard presentations that used "and" almost exclusively as a transition. (The Cub Scouts speech at the beginning of this section on transitions is an example.) The effect is almost comical. The presentation sounds like it's just a bunch of disjointed ideas tacked together — the tack is the "and." And. . . . And. . . . And. . . .

Too similar

Variety is the spice of life. It also works wonders with transitions. Don't use the same couple of transitional phrases over and over again. It gets boring. Use an assortment of transitions. Here are a few to get you started:

Now let's take a look at . . .

In addition . . .

Let's change direction for a moment . . .

The next point is . . .

For example . . .

By that I mean . . .

On the other hand . . .

Turning to . . .

Another area for consideration is . . .

The possibilities are endless.

So in conclusion . . . let me leave you with three final thoughts. A good conclusion is like a movie trailer — it summarizes your message and gives your audience a positive impression. A good transition is like a train — it carries your audience smoothly from one idea to another. And a good transition leading to a good conclusion is like a fanatic's doomsday sign — it says "The End is Near."

Famous last words

Every presentation must have a conclusion, including the big one we call life. And that's when our words take on a special significance. Even condemned murderers are given an opportunity to make a statement before they're executed. In fact, their final interaction with another human being is when the warden asks, "Do you have any last words?" The following are some famous "closing" remarks.

"They couldn't hit an elephant at this dist. . . ."

—General John Sedgwick, Union Army

"I don't feel well."

—Luther Burbank

"Don't let it end like this. Tell them I said something."

—Pancho Villa

"Dying is easy. Comedy is difficult."

—Edmund Gwenn

"Water."

—Ulysses S. Grant

"Give me a match and I'll see if there's any gas in the tank."

—Anonymous

Chapter 10
Getting the Words Right

. . . .

. . . .

*I*t's been said there are over ten thousand useless words in the English language, but a great many of them come in handy for writing computer manuals and political speeches. Some of them may come in handy for *your* presentations. It all depends on what you want to accomplish. Whatever your goal, there's no getting around the fact that words are the basic building blocks. If you want to give a successful presentation, you have to get the words right.

Tone and Style

A politician gave a speech denouncing the welfare nature of big government. His booming voice thundered across the room, "From federal payments for prenatal care to Social Security death benefits, the government is taking care of people from womb to tomb." The rhyming words of "womb" and "tomb" gave the line a nice ring and always got applause. But the politician got bored with the line, so he introduced a new version during a luncheon speech to a women's political club. Instead of "womb to tomb," he said he was sick of the government taking care of people from "sperm to worm." The audience silence was deafening.

What can we learn from this? Three things: Don't talk about sperm to a women's political club. Don't talk about worms while people are eating. And don't forget that tone and style are important — they have a major effect on how your ideas are received.

Word choice

Several years ago, I attended a seminar held by Ronald Carpenter, a professor in the English Department at the University of Florida at Gainesville. One of his major themes was that word choice is critical in the communication of ideas. To make the point, he posed a question. If a monument were built for John F. Kennedy, what Kennedy quote would be engraved on the monument? The seminar participants answered instantly and unanimously: "Ask not what your country can do for you, ask what you can do for your country."

That line was delivered by President Kennedy during his Inaugural Address on January 20th, 1961. It's a powerful arrangement of words that is universally associated with Kennedy.

Carpenter believes that the choice of words and their order has made that line immortal. His proof? He contrasted the famous quote with a line delivered by Kennedy several months earlier. During a campaign appearance on September 6th, 1960, Kennedy had said, "The New Frontier is not what I promise I am going to do for you, the New Frontier is what I am going to ask you to do for your country."

Huh? Come again. That's a clunker if there ever was one. Would that line appear on a Kennedy monument? Not a chance. In fact, it would never appear on any monument unless it was a monument to awkward phrasing. But substantively, this long forgotten line says *exactly the same thing* as the famous line. Word choice and arrangement made the critical difference. (Need another example? Imagine the "Gettysburg Address" beginning with the words "Eighty-seven years ago. . . .")

Use power words

Management communication counselor Jim Lukaszewski also places a heavy emphasis on the power of words. As principal of The Lukaszewski Group, he performs corporate troubleshooting for large companies throughout the United States. Much of his advice to executives involves how they can use language more effectively.

He divides words into three categories: blah words, color words, and power words. *Blah words* are just what you'd expect — blah. They're colorless filler that take up space without getting notice. *Color words* exist at the other end of the spectrum. They're colorful, but they generate an emotional reaction. "Color words can get you in trouble," Jim explains. "Every person in the audience interprets them differently, and they often overshadow anything else you say in a talk."

That's why Jim recommends using *power words* such as "interesting," "unusual," "decisive," "hot," "exciting," "new," "critical," "urgent," "compelling."

Power words grab attention without really saying anything. Jim's proof? "If I say 'This is an urgent matter' or 'This is really important,' I've said nothing to you, but I've got your attention," he observes. "That's what power words do. They grab attention without giving away what you want to talk about." Want to maintain an audience's attention throughout your presentation? Feed them a steady diet of power words.

How to use jargon

Real mode device drivers are fine, as long as you hook them up to a hybrid 16/32 bit OS, and retain control of the configuration of the SNMP agent and log-on domains.

Yeah, right. The traditional thinking on jargon in presentations can be summed up in two words — avoid it. Jargon is often incomprehensible. It's supposed to create a barrier with your audience.

Here's the uncommon knowledge — It can also create a bond. In order to explain why, I need to introduce an academic concept: the inclusionary and exclusionary functions of language. It sounds complicated but it's not. It simply means that one of the ways that groups of people define themselves is through the use of language. It's like knowing a secret password. If you speak the language, you're in (or *included*). If you don't speak the language, you're out (or *excluded*). Jargon is the language that's unique to each group.

Jargon is so widespread because every group creates its own jargon as a way of defining its membership. Each trade and profession has its own jargon. Many companies have their own jargon. Clubs and associations have their own jargon. Even individual families have their own jargon.

So what does this mean for presentations? Plenty. Are you an outsider in relation to the group you're addressing? You can create rapport with the audience by using some of its jargon in your talk. It is relatively easy to do, and it demonstrates that you made an effort to learn about the audience. It also suggests that you understand something about the audience. Talking to surgeons? Find out what a "lap chole" is and refer to it in your presentation. Talking to real estate agents? Find out what "FSBO" means and drop it into your talk.

What if you want to introduce jargon from *your* trade or profession that the audience will *not* know? Many speakers get themselves into trouble when they use their own jargon, and that's why the common knowledge says to avoid jargon. You really shouldn't have a problem with using your own jargon as long as you explain your jargon before you use it. Educate your audience. Tell them what it means. That's the secret. It's also the part that most speakers forget, which is why jargon has such a bad name.

How to Create Catch Phrases

The catch phrase provides a tried and true method for drawing attention to a key point and helping audiences remember it. Want some examples? Turn on your radio or television set. The advertisements are full of them. "When it absolutely, positively has to be there overnight." "Don't leave home without it." "Takes a licking and keeps on ticking." These phrases "catch" in your memory, and that's what they're designed to do. Every time you think about one of them, you automatically think about a product and its key sales point. Constant repetition of the phrase by advertisers augments this effect.

The catch phrase technique isn't limited to advertising. Anyone can use it in any type of presentation. Howard Nations, one of the country's leading trial lawyers, advises attorneys to create catch phrases that will stick in a juror's mind. And, of course, the most famous catch phrase from recent legal history comes from the O.J. Simpson trial: "If it doesn't fit, you must acquit."

Business leaders are also fond of this technique. In a speech about the future of telecommunications, William Esrey, Chairman of United Telecom/U.S. Sprint, coined a phrase to describe the marriage of the telephone and the computer. He called it "infonics." After defining his catch phrase, he repeated it more than 20 times throughout the rest of his speech.

You can apply this technique to emphasize points in your presentation too. Just pick an important point, build a catch phrase around it, and repeat it endlessly.

The Fog Factor and Other Measures of Clarity

In a speech about communication, Carl Wayne Hensley, Professor of Speech Communication at Bethel College, gives a great example of the need for clarity. He talks about a fellow named James Minor who taught writing classes to government bureaucrats. On the first day of class, Minor would read the following statement:

> We respectfully petition, request, and entreat that due and adequate provision be made, this day and date hereunder subscribed, for the satisfying of these petitioners' nutritional requirements and for the organizing of such methods of allocation and distribution as may be deemed necessary and proper to assure the reception by and for said petitioners of such quantities of cereal products as shall, in the judgment of the aforementioned petitioners, constitute a sufficient supply thereof.

That, said Minor, is how his students would have written, "Give us this day our daily bread."

It's not just bureaucrats who obfuscate and coat their communications with fog. Communication coach Alan Weiner offers this workplace example: A speaker says, "I'm here to suggest some modifications be implemented to achieve the goals of our strategic plan." Instead, the speaker could say, "We need a change. I'm going to talk to you about how to make that change that we talked about in our planning meeting." "There are so few people speaking plain English at work," Alan observes, "that any one who does will seem like a genius."

Want an easy test to help you blow away the fog? James Harris, General Manager of the Integrated Storage Products Division at Sony Electronics, suggests giving your presentation to a seventh grader. "If a seventh grader can understand it, then you're safe," he says. Why? "Your message competes for audience attention with a lot of distractions — noise, daydreaming, hunger, tiredness," he explains. "If you keep things on a seventh-grade level, there's a chance that your message will get through. The audience can't read your speech. It can't go back to something it didn't understand. It only gets to hear your message once as you say it."

Classic Rhetorical Tricks

There was some good news and some bad news if you had a dispute in ancient Greece. The good news: there were no lawyers. The bad news: you had to argue your own case. That's why the ancient Greeks developed all sorts of rhetorical devices to improve their presentations. They wanted to win.

This section presents a few of the classic devices. And don't worry, they still work today. (Your lawyer probably uses them.)

Hyperbole

Hyperbole is a fancy word for exaggeration. People use hyperbole instinctively in everyday conversation: "I was waiting a year for you to get off the phone." It's a wonderful device for emphasizing a point in a presentation. Here's an example from a speech that San Francisco comedy coach John Cantu gives about his roots in comedy:

> One of the first clubs I performed at was a small, dark place. It was so dark I could barely see the three people in the room — the two in the front row listening to me and the guy in the back row developing film.

Allusion

An allusion is a reference to a person, object, or event from the Bible, mythology, or literature. Here's an example from a speech about balancing work and family given by John Adams, Chairman and CEO of the Texas Commerce Bank.

> Opponents of work and family programs say that employers should not involve themselves more deeply in workers' lives, that to do so opens a Pandora's box of raised expectations, employer liability, invasion of privacy, and even accusations of unfairness in providing work-family programs

Alliteration

Alliteration refers to a phrase in which the words begin with the same sound. The classic example is former Vice President Spiro Agnew's description of the media as "nattering nabobs of negativism."

You can also use alliteration to make the title of your presentation more memorable. When I was in high school, an English teacher talked about a paper written by one of her college classmates. It was titled "Freshman Father of Four." She said that the alliteration had made the title stick in her mind for years. I can vouch for that because it's now stuck in my mind too — ever since high school. (By the way Mrs. Lifshey, if you're out there, everyone loved your class. Teachers need to hear that once in awhile.)

Metaphor

A metaphor is a short, implied comparison that transfers the properties of one item to another. A classic example comes from Martin Luther King's "I Have a Dream" speech:

> . . . the manacles of segregation and the chain of discrimination.

The metaphor can add a poetic quality to your presentation while still allowing you to make a point. Here's an example from a speech about our rapidly changing world given by Max Kampelman, Attorney, formerly in charge of U.S.-U.S.S.R. Arms Control Negotiation:

> Moreover, as we look ahead, we must agree that we have only the minutest glimpse of what our universe really is. Our science is indeed a drop, our ignorance a sea.

Not every metaphor has to be a poetic gem. A garden-variety metaphor can do a good, solid job of conveying your point as long as it creates a strong image. The following is an example from a speech about energy policy given by L.G. Rawls, Chairman of Exxon Corporation:

> Federal responsibility for energy rests in the hands of 51 committees and subcommittees of Congress, six Cabinet secretaries, three offices of the President, and four independent agencies. With so many cooks working on so many different recipes, it's not surprising that we face a smorgasbord of ill-conceived and inconsistent policies.

Simile

A simile is *like* a metaphor except it's a directly stated comparison of one thing to another. (It usually uses the words "like" or "as" to make the comparison.)

Here's an example from a speech about consumer protection given by Arthur Levitt, Chairman, United States Securities and Exchange Commission:

> A massive influx of inexperienced investors, and a real potential for conflicts of interest — it's like dry underbrush and a match. As SEC Chairman, I've seen too many people's life savings go up in smoke.

Here's another simile from a speech about the future of telecommunications given by William Esrey, Chairman of United Telecom/US Sprint:

> The flow of information has since swelled far over the traditional banks, flooding the social landscape such that today, countries . . . companies . . . even individuals . . . are like islands in a sea of information.

(Want a great source of similes? Find a copy of *The Book of Similes* by Robert Baldwin and Ruth Paris. It was published in 1982 by Routledge & Kegan Paul.)

Rhetorical question

A rhetorical question refers to a question that the speaker asks for effect. The audience isn't expected to answer. Rhetorical questions are designed to focus attention on the subject of the question. They are often used as introductions, conclusions, or transitions.

Mixed-up metaphors

Metaphors provide a colorful way of injecting some zest into a presentation — sometimes too colorful. Inspired by the passion of the moment, speakers may stumble when reaching for that perfect image to galvanize their audience. Instead of finding one metaphor, they grab two off their mental shelf and combine them. That's what's known as a mixed metaphor. Here are some examples of what can happen when words collide.

> We've got to seize the bull by the tail and look him in the eyes.

> From now on I'm watching everything you do with a finetooth comb.

That's the way the cookie bounces.

That's like the pot calling the kettle's bluff.

We'll burn that bridge when we come to it.

It'll be a dark day when you see a light at the end of the tunnel.

The big cheese smells a rat.

Don't put all the egg on your face in one basket.

He'd be spinning in his grave if he could see you now.

Don't cry over spilling the beans.

Here's an example from a speech by Benjamin H. Alexander, President of Drew-Dawn Enterprises, Inc.:

> Are we free when we can not leave our homes at night without fear of being assaulted, beaten, or robbed? Are we free when, as the richest nation in the world, we permit poverty, beggars, and homeless people everywhere amongst us?

> Are we brave or courageous when we are afraid to bring back the "Whipping Post" for hoodlums — one of whom, three months ago, in Washington, D.C., casually walked to a swimming pool crowded with youngsters; and for no reason began to shoot at children?

The rule of three

The rule of three refers to the technique of grouping together three words, phrases, or sentences. For some reason, a grouping of three items makes a powerful impression on the human mind. (Don't ask me why. It just does.)

Some of the most famous passages from the world's greatest oratory have used this technique.

- ✔ "I came. I saw. I conquered." (Julius Caesar)
- ✔ ". . . government of the people, by the people, for the people. . . ." (Abraham Lincoln)

Business speakers frequently use this technique. Here's an interesting example from a speech about the civil justice system given by Stephen Middlebrook, Sr. VP and Executive Counsel at Aetna Life & Casualty:

> Voltaire once said of the Holy Roman Empire that it was neither holy, nor roman, nor an empire. The same might also be said of the civil justice system in the United States: that it is neither civil, nor just, nor a system.

Here's another example from Dr. Robert McAfee's inaugural address as President of the American Medical Association:

> Since 1990, we've said 1,000 times in 1,000 forums the message you can boil down to three words: voice, choice, and coverage. Physician voice, patient choice, universal coverage. This is your agenda. This is my agenda. This is what we all stand for, and we will not stand for anything less.

The beauty of the rule of three is that it can work its magic on any topic — no matter how commonplace or mundane. Just take a few minutes to think about your subject. You can always come up with three items to group together. Are you talking about a new accounting procedure that must be followed by all employees? It effects managers, hourly staff, and temps. Is your subject quality management? It starts with awareness, training, and commitment.

Repetition

Repetition refers to repeating a group of words in an identical rhythm. This device draws attention to the phrase and can even be used to pull a whole speech together. Martin Luther King's "I Have a Dream" speech is a classic example. Dr. King repeated the phrase "I have a dream" throughout the speech.

But repetition doesn't have to run throughout an entire talk. It can be used to dramatize one section, or even one sentence, of your presentation. Here's how James Paul, President and Chief Executive Officer of the Coastal Corporation, used the device in a speech about the oil and gas industry:

> It's a system with inferior public services; at the same time there are more government employees in the country than manufacturing.

It's a system with intrusive government meddling increasing by the hour into every phase of your business and your private life.

It's a system with entitlement programs gobbling up 49 percent of the national budget.

So repetition is a dramatic way to create a rhythm. It's a dramatic way to make a point. It's a dramatic way to show your style. It's a dramatic way to be dramatic.

Antithesis

Antithesis refers to putting two opposites near each other in a sentence. The classic example is the opening paragraph of *A Tale of Two Cities* by Charles Dickens.

> It was the best of times, it was the worst of times, it was the age of wisdom, it was the age of foolishness, it was the epoch of belief, it was the epoch of incredulity, it was the season of Light, it was the season of Darkness, it was the spring of hope, it was the winter of despair, we had everything before us, we had nothing before us, we were all going direct to Heaven, we were all going direct the other way. . . .

Gets your attention doesn't it?

There's just something about an antithesis that makes it stand out. John F. Kennedy used them all the time: "If a free society cannot help the men who are poor, it cannot save the few who are rich." They're catchy, and they make the speaker sound eloquent. Just listen to this:

> We find ourselves rich in goods, but ragged in spirit; reaching with magnificent precision for the moon, but falling into raucous discord on earth.

> We are caught in war, wanting peace. We're torn by division, wanting unity. We see around us empty lives, wanting fulfillment. We see tasks that need doing, waiting for hands to do them.

Sounds pretty good, right? Want to know who said it? President Richard M. Nixon. And that's my point — Nixon was known for many things, but inspirational public speaking wasn't one of them. Yet this passage from his inaugural address sounds terrific. Why? Antithesis. It can make *anyone* sound great. There's probably some jazzy psychological explanation about why this is so, but who cares? All you need to know is that it works.

Now here's some uncommon knowledge courtesy of Professor Ronald Carpenter: Antithesis is one of the easiest rhetorical devices to use in a presentation. When I attended his seminar, he even offered a step-by-step formula for writing one.

1. Pick two opposites. (Words, phrases or concepts.)

2. Write a sentence with one of the opposites in each half of the sentence.

3. Make it sound balanced. (Put an equal number of words in each half of the sentence. Locate the opposites in approximately identical positions in their halves of the sentence.)

4. The closer together the opposites are placed, the more dramatic the antithesis will sound.

5. An antithesis generally works better if it's short and simple rather than long and cluttered. (Edmund Gwynn's famous line is a good example: "Dying is easy, comedy is hard.")

6. The antithesis will be more effective if it ends on a positive note. (The classic example is John F. Kennedy's, "Ask not what your country can do for you, ask what you can do for your country." Let's reverse it. "Ask what you can do for your country, ask not what your country can do for you." It just doesn't have the same impact.)

You can use an antithesis in a garden-variety speech. If you're speaking about the need to increase membership in a club or association, you might say, "We must stop talking and start acting." If you're presenting the quarterly results of your business operations, you could say, "Our profits are down but our sales are up." If you're talking about the multimillion dollar inheritance you dribbled away, you might say, "Easy come, easy go."

Now you're ready for Professor Carpenter's advanced formula. First, there's the *double antithesis*. You put *two* opposites in each half of the sentence.

We're so good at making war and so bad at keeping peace.

In this sentence, "good" plays off of "bad" and "war" plays off of "peace." Does it get twice as much attention as a single antithesis? Maybe not. But it does get your attention.

And finally, there's the ABBA antithesis. (No, this has nothing to do with the Swedish musical group that was big in the seventies.) ABBA is a formula that Professor Carpenter uses to describe an antithesis where the opposite in each half of the sentence is *the word order itself.* He cites a classic example which comes from the oratory of John F. Kennedy.

Let us never negotiate out of fear, but let us never fear to negotiate.

A = negotiate. B = fear. The first half has these words aligned as "AB" ("negotiate" precedes "fear"). In the second half, they're aligned as "BA" ("fear" precedes "negotiate").

Here's another example, from a speech by David Boaz, Executive Vice President of the Cato Institute.

> I heard a talented educator say recently, "We don't need to get kids ready for school, we need to get schools ready for kids."

Painless Editing Techniques

W. Somerset Maugham once said, "There are three rules for writing a novel. Unfortunately no one knows what they are." Fortunately the rules for *editing* are better known. This section contains a few that apply to presentations.

Read it out loud

If you write for the ear, you need to hear what you're writing. There's only one way to do that. Read your speech out loud. How does it sound? Does it have a good rhythm? Can you communicate each idea without running out of breath? Have you cut out all the tongue-twisters? Have you eliminated phrases that appear harmless on paper but are embarrassing when spoken? (Here's a classic example: "One smart fellow, he felt smart. Two smart fellows, they both felt smart. Three smart fellows, they all felt smart." Say it aloud quickly a few times. You'll find out why it's cherished by little kids throughout the English-speaking world.)

John Cantu suggests that you use a tape recorder as an editing tool. Talk your speech into the recorder. When you play it back, you'll hear exactly how your speech sounds. Many of the spots that need editing will probably leap out at you.

Keep the language simple

Many speakers feel they have to throw in a lot of big words to show how smart they are. Wrong. Smart speakers do just the opposite. Abraham Lincoln is a good example. Smart guy, right? Well, check out his "Gettysburg Address." Most of the words aren't more than five letters long. Or how about Franklin D. Roosevelt? Legend has it that one of his speechwriters wrote, "We're endeavoring to create a more inclusive society." Roosevelt changed it to: "We're going to make a country in which no one is left out." Which one sounds smarter to you?

Avoid long sentences

Brevity is the soul of understanding. No, that's *not* a mistake. I know the expression is really "brevity is the soul of wit," but I want *you* to know that brevity also has a big impact on comprehension. The more words a sentence contains, the more difficult it is to understand. Look through your speech. If you find a lot of sentences with more than twenty words, your audience had better be Ph.Ds. If you're talking to anyone else, start rewriting (and shorten those sentences).

Use the active voice

The active voice makes your sentences more forceful and powerful. The passive voice makes them sound whimpy. But you be the judge. Here's an example of the passive voice: "There's a bonus given by the boss once a year." Here's the same idea rewritten in the active voice: "The boss gives a bonus once a year." The passive voice is like a weed that creeps into your writing. You must keep pruning it out.

Be specific

Writing instructors have an old saying that also applies to speeches — specific is terrific. It means that concrete words and examples are more effective than vague words and descriptions. Contrast "I went to the store" with "I went to Safeway." The word "Safeway" is more specific than "store." It creates a stronger image. Or let's say you're talking about an accident that occurred in a schoolyard. You could say, "A boy ran into the wall and got hurt." You could also say, "A boy ran into the wall and scraped his arm in three places. The school nurse had to apply gauze and bandages to stop the bleeding." Be specific.

Use exciting verbs

Verbs are where the action is. So make them exciting. Let them help create a picture for your listeners. Let's say you're telling some war story from work: "I asked Smith to give me the file." Asked? Why not begged, pleaded, or implored? A good thesaurus can do wonders.

Get rid of clichés

"People are our most important resource." "We partner with our customers." "Synergy." "Re-engineering." "Excellence." "Strategic." Enough already. Give everyone a break. Instead of parroting the latest corporate clichés, come up with something fresh. It's not that difficult. Just take a few moments to think about what you're really saying.

Vary the pace

If all your sentences are the same length, your audience will fall asleep. So vary the pace. Use short sentences and long sentences. Throw in a rhetorical question. Don't let the rhythm become monotonous.

Avoid foreign words and phrases

So you were a French major in college. Good for you. But if you want to speak French, go to France. (Or to paraphrase a quote attributed to Dan Quayle — if you want to speak Latin, go to Latin America.) Here's the point: Dropping a bunch of foreign phrases into your talk doesn't impress anybody but yourself. It just makes you appear pompous. (Besides, English was good enough for Shakespeare.)

Be careful with abbreviations

There's nothing wrong with using a few abbreviations — if your audience knows them. CIA. FBI. IRS. No problem. But when you get into esoteric abbreviations (economic, scientific, governmental), make sure that everyone knows what the abbreviations mean. Don't load too many of them into one speech or you'll sound like you're reading from alphabet soup.

Put it aside and come back to it

The most effective technique for editing a presentation is also the simplest — put it aside and come back to it later. It's amazing how a short time away from a presentation will change your perspective. Both problem spots and solutions become obvious when you look at your presentation with "fresh eyes." Is this just common sense? Absolutely. Do most people do it? No. Why? Because they wait till the last minute to prepare their talk. So there's no time left to put it aside. Do yourself a favor. Build time into your schedule to put it aside and come back to it. That's one of the smartest decisions you can make regarding your presentation.

Chapter 11

Visual Aids: The Eye Contact That Really Counts

● ●

In This Chapter

▶ Deciding when to use visual aids

▶ Designing visuals aids for maximum impact

▶ Preparing slides and overheads

▶ Finding a useful prop

▶ Working with a flipchart

▶ Integrating audio and video into your presentation

● ●

*E*veryone's heard the old saying, "One picture is worth a thousand words." If that's true, then the average 20-minute talk can be reduced to two slides or overheads. We can spend 40 seconds looking at them and go home. But it doesn't quite work that way, does it? Here's why. One picture isn't always worth a thousand words. It's only worth a thousand words under certain circumstances. This chapter explores the nature of those circumstances. When do visual aids help? When do they hurt? What can they really do for you? (Get the picture?)

The Pros and Cons of Using Visual Aids

The term *visual aids* encompasses a wide range of items. The more common ones include slides, overheads, charts, videos, flipcharts, and props. Many props have come to be almost required at the modern day business presentation. (When's the last time you attended a training session that didn't include a flipchart? Or a sales presentation, strategic briefing, or financial talk that didn't include slides or overheads?)

But here's some uncommon knowledge from executive speechwriter John Austin. Visual aids don't automatically improve a presentation. "Many of us have endured sessions where someone has written an endless number of points on slides or overheads and then read them to the audience," he says. "It's really very tiresome." In fact, visual aids are essential only when you're discussing highly complex material that wouldn't otherwise be clear to the audience. "Presentations about DNA testing probably require a visual," says John. "But most topics can be handled successfully without one." (In fact, the highest paid speakers on the lecture circuit, the ones who fetch between $20,000 and $50,000 per speech, rarely use visual aids.)

So the key question becomes does a particular visual aid improve your particular presentation? What follows are some pros and cons you'll want to consider.

The cons

"There are two things you need to remember about visual aids," says Allatia Harris, Dean of the Communications Division at Mountain View Community College. "Number one, they should be visible. Number two, they should aid."

Allatia's point is well taken. It reflects the two biggest mistakes speakers make with visual aids. They use aids that are so small and poorly done that no one can see them, and they allow visual aids to take over their presentation, instead of just supporting it. This second mistake has become a growing trend.

Allatia traces the growth of this problem to the increased popularity of computer-generated slide shows. "People get carried away with all the slick slides and overheads they can get a computer to spit out," she observes. And that's the ironic part. Computer-generated slides and overheads are definitely visual. It's just not clear that they aid.

Here are a few other pitfalls associated with visual aids:

Distracted Audience. Even if the visual aids don't overwhelm your presentation, they can still distract the audience from your message — particularly if the visual aid is inappropriate or poorly executed.

Talking to them. Many speakers fall into the trap of talking to their visual aids instead of talking to their audience. Even if your back is your best side, the audience still wants some eye contact.

Equipment worries. Using visual aids means worrying about equipment. Will the slide or overhead projector be available as promised? Will it operate properly? Will the layout of the room accommodate slides and overheads? Even simple visual aids like flipcharts can provoke equipment anxiety. (Will the marker dry out?) All of these extra pressures serve only as distractions from your main task — giving a great presentation.

The pros

Visual aids can gain attention, help your audience remember key points, and help it better understand the flow of your talk. (You figured there must be some reason they're so popular, right?) They can also save a lot of time when it comes to descriptions. (In one of my talks, I discuss the layout of an intersection near my home — where the stop signs are located, where traffic bars might be painted, and so on. Showing an overhead with a picture of the intersection saves a lot of time.)

Some subjects of discussion really do require a visual. For example, I have a slide of a funny brochure sent out by a real estate broker. You have to *see* it to understand why it's funny. Are you talking about damage from a hurricane, earthquake, or other disaster? A slide of a single dramatic photograph will be far more powerful than almost anything you can say. Are you doing a "This Is Your Life" type presentation as a surprise birthday tribute to your boss? Everyone in the department will want to see a slide of that baby photo you got from the boss's mom. The list goes on.

Two other benefits of visual aids are less well known. First, they can replace speaker notes. If your visual aids cover all the points of your presentation, they can function as an outline. Can't remember what you were going to say? Just talk from the visuals. (That's why I like to use them.) Second and more important, visual aids help ensure that the entire audience receives your message in a uniform way. For example, say you talk about an accident that totaled an automobile. People in the audience will have their own picture of that in their heads. If you show a photo of the wreck, then everyone will see it the same way — your way.

Charts and Graphs

Charts and graphs are commonly used to depict numerical data. They're also useful for expressing such non-numerical relationships as organizational structure, procedures, and lines of authority. Although they appear most often on slides and overheads, they've become increasingly popular in hard copy versions that can be placed on an easel.

Common types of charts and graphs

Here are some of the most common types of charts and graphs and how you might want to use them:

> ✔ **Line graphs:** These are good for showing changes over a period of time. Any kind of trend data works well — stock market prices, voting patterns, productivity gains. That sort of thing.

- **Bar graphs:** These are handy for comparing all kinds of data — sales of widgets versus gadgets, defect totals under various quality management programs, drug reactions in infants versus adults.

- **Pie charts:** These are good for showing percentages in relation to each other. (The western region generated 80 percent of the revenue; the east 10 percent; the south 7 percent; and the north 3 percent.)

- **Organizational charts:** Who reports to whom? What's the exact relationship between the telecommunications department and the information services department? Is the European operation an independent unit or part of the main corporation? These types of questions can be answered with organizational charts.

- **Flow charts:** These are good for depicting any series of steps — company procedures, how a bill becomes a law, where a 911 call gets routed.

- **Tables of numerical data:** This is your basic spreadsheet layout. It's a boring format, but sometimes the numbers are so dramatic that the format doesn't matter. ("As you can see from the numbers in column three, half of you will be laid off next week.")

Tips and tricks

The following are a few pointers to keep in mind when you use a chart or graph:

- **Limit the data.** The more items included on a chart or graph, the more difficult it becomes to understand. If you have a lot of items that must be represented, rethink the graph. Maybe you can split the data into several graphs.

- **Size pie slices accurately.** The audience gets confused when you show a pie chart with a slice labeled "10 percent" that looks like a quarter of the pie. If you use a pie chart, make sure the slices of the pie correspond to the real numbers. (Unless you're speaking at a multilevel marketing recruitment meeting.)

- **Make absolutely sure the numbers are correct.** Check the numbers. Recheck them. And check them again. It's a credibility issue. If one number is incorrect, it can undermine your entire presentation.

- **Avoid three-dimensional bars.** Don't make bar charts with three-dimensional bars. "They're not precise," explains Marcia Lemmons, a marketing director at Andersen Consulting. "No one can tell exactly where they end. So you don't know what numbers they're supposed to represent."

- **Jazz them up.** Use graphics to add some pizzazz to your graphs and charts. Are you showing the price trends for the wholesale price of rubber chickens? Put images of rubber chickens on the graph, as illustrated in Figure 11-1.

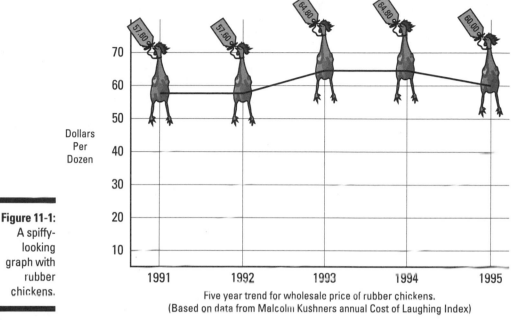

Figure 11-1:
A spiffy-
looking
graph with
rubber
chickens.

Dollars
Per
Dozen

Five year trend for wholesale price of rubber chickens.
(Based on data from Malcolm Kushners annual Cost of Laughing Index)

A coverup that's *not* a crime

The court was in Dallas. The case involved an employee suing a large company for wrongful termination. The jury included Allatia Harris. The defendant company's attorneys produced a chart with a timeline of everything that allegedly happened.

"The chart was a great visual," recalls Allatia. "It was very impressive." But in cross examination, the plaintiff's attorney pointed out that the timeline on the chart was inaccurate. It didn't represent the facts of the testimony, and the defendant company conceded that point. Unfortunately, the chart wasn't taken down. It remained in full view of the jury throughout the rest of the trial.

"When we deliberated in the jury room, I kept saying that the timeline on the chart wasn't factual," recalls Allatia. "That we had to base our decision on the testimony. And even though the other jurors knew that, it didn't matter. Those visuals were implanted in their brains and you couldn't undo it." So the plaintiff got shafted because of the chart. The plaintiff's attorney should have had the chart covered up as soon as the defendant conceded its inaccuracy.

Here's the lesson. If you're in a speaking situation where other speakers have preceded you, make sure their flipcharts and other visuals are out of view before you begin. Even if those visuals don't directly attack your message (like the chart in the courtroom), they'll still distract your audience. (You don't want them reading the previous speaker's flipcharts. You want them listening to you.)

Slides and Overheads

Slides and overheads have emerged from a checkered past to become the two most popular visual aids of our time. It wasn't that long ago that the bulk of these aids were associated with boring college lectures and recaps of family vacations. Their amateurish content was only exceeded by their amateurish quality. The high-powered slide or overhead presentation with snappy graphics was limited to top level executives and their ilk. No one else could justify the expense. That all changed with the desktop publishing revolution. Computers made slick quality slides and overheads available to everyone. You can't attend a business presentation without tripping over the slides and overheads. (Measured at a per person rate of growth, the U.S. may soon have more slides and overheads than lawyers.)

Slides

Well-designed slides can highlight your key points, add variety to your talk, and capture audience attention. But slides also have two big disadvantages. Projecting them requires you to darken at least part of the room. (That invites the audience to snooze.) And their order is inflexible once you place them in a carousel. (So you can't rearrange them as you're speaking.)

Another disadvantage, which can be easily avoided, is the tendency some speakers have to run through slides too rapidly. "If you're flipping slides every two seconds, that's too fast," says Steve Fraticelli, a professional designer based in Cupertino, California. "You've got to leave them up long enough to register with the human eye." His rule of thumb: allow at least 20 seconds for your audience to view and digest each slide. Steve also notes that people often rush through their slides because they have too many of them. "Speakers who have a lot of slides will zip through them to make sure they get to show them all," Steve explains. "But if you're doing a 20-minute talk, perhaps having 150 slides is a bit much." Point taken.

Overheads

When I have a choice between slides and overheads, I choose overheads every time. You can project them without turning down the room lights. (So the audience isn't invited to snooze.) You can write notes to yourself on the cardboard frames around the transparencies. And most important, you can reorder them as you speak. (You're not locked into the inflexible sequence of the slide carousel.)

I also like overheads because they're easier to create than slides. They don't need to be sent out to a photo lab for development. You can make them yourself with a copy machine.

Copy machines make great design tools. You can cut pictures, charts, and graphs out of a magazine or newspaper, then resize them on a copier. Paste them in place on a piece of paper. Add some text. And then copy it onto an overhead transparency. (But remember, you must get any necessary permission. Otherwise, it's called copyright infringement.) Want it in color? Use a color copier. Or apply colored markers directly to the transparency.

Here's the bad news. There's one very major disadvantage to overheads. They don't work well for a large audience because everyone won't be able to see them clearly.

Dos and don'ts for preparing slides and overheads

Are you making your own slides or overheads? Here are a few dos and don'ts to keep in mind:

Do leave enough time

People frequently forget to leave enough time to both design *and produce* their slides or overheads. "Don't forget about the production time," warns Steve Fraticelli. "If you wait until the last minute, you'll spend a lot of extra money on rush charges, and you won't have any time to make changes if you don't like what's been produced." So build some extra time into the schedule. You'll usually end up needing it.

Do check for spelling errors

There's nothing more embarrassing than a typo projected onto a large screen. So make absolutely sure that you've eliminated all spelling errors from your slides and overheads. If you made them on a computer, run them through a spell checker. And no matter how many times *you* proof them, have someone else take a look at them.

Don't overemphasize your logo

If you're going to use a logo on every slide, make it small. "It shouldn't be screaming at everyone," says Rachael Brune of Canyon Design in Palo Alto, California. "Otherwise that's all they'll notice slide after slide." A logo should simply be a little element that says this is a presentation from your company or organization.

Don't use all upper- or lowercase text

A mixture of upper and lower case text is easier to read. All upper case may be OK for headings or subheadings, but don't use it for the body of the text.

Do use relevant graphics

Graphics are good, but only if they support a point. "You need a reason for using them other than they're pretty," says Steve Fraticelli. "Too many people throw graphics onto a text slide just to fill space. The image draws your eye to it. But if it doesn't relate to the bullet points, then it doesn't make any sense." Want some examples? "I've seen text slides that had silhouettes of people or stick figures in the corner," Steve recalls. "But those graphics didn't really say anything. They were just distracting."

Do number your slides and overheads

Have you ever dropped a large stack of slides or overheads that weren't numbered? I rest my case.

Do be consistent

Visually, it's very important to be consistent. It shows organization. Or as Steve Fraticelli puts it, "If your visuals are kind of scattered, you come off as scattered." What does being consistent mean? Don't mix and match slides or overheads from different presentations if they have different design styles. "You're showing one type of template and then all of a sudden there's a different kind," says Steve. "It's jarring and distracting." If you use color overheads, don't suddenly throw in a black and white one. If you're preparing a slide show of photos, take Marcia Lemmons's advice and make sure they're all shot the same way (horizontally or vertically).

Do take advantage of templates

Many software programs for creating slides and overheads include predesigned templates. You just choose a style, and the program cranks out all your slides in that design. "Take advantage of the templates if you're a beginner," says Steve Fraticelli. "They'll help you achieve consistency." (But use your judgment, warns Rachael Brune. "Most of the templates are pretty good," she says. "But some use colors that make you want to gag.")

Don't use too much text

"Speakers tend to think everything they say has to be on a slide or overhead," says Steve Fraticelli. "But if it's too text-intensive, people won't read it — no matter how nice it looks. It's just too overwhelming. You don't want to ask your audience to read a novel on the screen."

So what should you do? "Let the slides or overheads reflect the basic outline," he advises. "Just put down the key things and then fill in the blanks as you speak." Marcia Lemmons calls this the 4 x 4 rule. Don't put more than four lines on a slide or four words in a line. Other authorities place the numbers as 6 x 6. It's not set in cement. The point is don't cram too much information onto one slide or overhead.

Do keep the text style simple

Many speakers feel compelled to "pretty up" their visuals with fancy text. Don't fall prey to this temptation; it makes your slides and overheads difficult to read. "I'd rather look at a simple blocky type than something artsy like old English lettering," says Steve Fraticelli. And here's another reason to keep it simple. "An artsy text style that works on a white background might be unreadable on a colored background," says Steve. "Then your points don't come across."

Don't mix a lot of fonts

"Try not to use more than two fonts," says Steve. "It just clutters things up too much." His major exception: slides that display a company logo, product name, or similar item that's identified by a specific font. Those items don't count toward your limit of two fonts.

Don't emphasize everything

Have you ever seen college students who use a yellow highlighter to mark up 95 percent of every page in a textbook? What are they trying to emphasize — the stuff that's not yellowed in? If you want to visually direct attention to certain points, go ahead. But don't dilute your message by emphasizing everything.

Do look at the big picture

Philosophers often claim that the whole is greater than the sum of its parts. With slide and overhead shows, the whole can be *worse* than the sum of its parts. "You can have slides that look good individually," explains Steve Fraticelli. "But when you click through them, they don't work well together. They make your eyes bounce all over the place." How can you prevent this problem? Many software programs have a slide show feature that will run your slides on the computer screen. If you have one of these programs, use it. If not, make hard copies of your slides or overheads and flip through them to simulate the presentation.

Do use builds

A *build* is a series of slides or overheads in which each successive slide contains the bullet points from the preceding slides plus a new bullet point. Builds have become a standard part of business presentations. They provide a good way to emphasize key points. (The down side is that you'll need more slides. For example, say you want to make six points. You can put all six points on one slide. Or you can do them as a build, which means using six slides.)

Before you go berserk with builds, here's a warning from Rachael Brune: Don't overdo them or put them into your talk just for the sake of having them. "Builds should be used only to emphasize important points," she says. "Otherwise, it's just a waste of slides and audience attention." She also says the points on the build should relate to each other. It shouldn't just be a list of things. "If it's the four components of your business, that makes sense," she explains. "But if it's just four points that happen to follow each other, then don't do a build."

Don't use too many colors

The rule of thumb is a maximum of four colors per visual — one color for the background, one color for headlines, one color for body copy, and perhaps a color for emphasis. (Graphs and complex images are exceptions to this rule. You may need more colors to make a pie chart or line graph understandable.) "Use a dark color for the background — maybe blue or purple — with yellow headlines and white body copy," recommends Rachael Brune. "And you might use red bullets for emphasis, but don't get insane."

Don't expect your slide and overhead colors to look like they do on your computer screen

Here's some very important uncommon knowledge if you design your slides and overheads on a computer: The colors you see on your computer monitor are not going to be the exact colors that appear on your overhead or 35mm slide. (The printout from your color printer will be yet another set of colors.) "It's something people don't think about," explains Rachael Brune. "You really need to run a few samples to see how they'll actually look. Then if the colors make you sick, you can change them." Overheads present the biggest problem. "There's usually a big difference between the way colors appear on an actual overhead versus the way they look on a computer screen," she warns. Slides present less of a variation, but they won't be a perfect match either.

Do rehearse

Practice using your slides and overheads until you're thoroughly familiar with their content and you feel comfortable using them. The slide show feature on Persuasion and other software programs makes a great rehearsal tool.

Do talk about what's on the slide or overhead

Talk about the slide or overhead that's on the screen. If you don't, the audience will get confused. They'll be looking at one thing, and you'll be talking about something else. Sound farfetched? It happens all the time. The speaker moves on to the next point without changing the overhead. Or the speaker doesn't stick to the script and goes off on a tangent. Either way, the audience ends up looking at a visual that's irrelevant to what the speaker is saying.

Fortunately, there's an easy solution to this problem. Turn off the overhead projector while you're talking about material that isn't on the overheads. What if you're using slides? No problem. Just insert blank slides in the carousel for the times you'll talk about material that isn't on a slide. (The blank slides will block the light of the slide projector so that it will appear as though the projector has been turned off.)

Computer software that helps

Can't design your way out of a paper bag? Don't worry. If you have access to a computer, you can find lots of software that can turn you into a fairly decent graphic artist.

Word processors. Most of the leading word processors such as WordPerfect and Microsoft Word include rudimentary desktop publishing features. You can create attractive overheads with the fonts and clip art available with the programs.

Presentation programs. These software products are designed specifically for creating slides and overheads. The leaders in this category are Persuasion, PowerPoint, and Harvard Graphics.

Desktop publishing programs. You're supposed to use these programs for brochures and newsletters, but they also work well for slides and overheads. The two big guns are PageMaker and QuarkXPress. But I use Microsoft Publisher. It works fine for me.

Drawing programs. The biggest name in this category is CorelDRAW!, but if you use a PC with Windows, then you already have a drawing program — Paintbrush. (I know this will ruin my macho image, but I've even designed overheads with KidPix. I used them in a seminar for lawyers.)

Working with designers and production people

If you don't want to create the slides and overheads yourself, you'll have to work with a designer. After the designer designs the slides or overheads, you'll have to have them physically produced by other people. (Usually in a photo lab or service bureau.) As in any creative collaboration, opinions can differ, miscommunications can occur, and tempers can flare. But professional designer Steve Fraticelli believes much of that tension is easily avoidable. Here are some of his tips for working efficiently and effectively with designers and production people:

Let the designer design

Many people have a tendency to micromanage the work of their designers. This behavior drives designers nuts and prevents them from giving you the full benefit of their creativity. "If you hire experts to work on your visuals, let them be the experts," says Steve. "They make their living at providing the service you hired them to do. They really do know what works, so trust them."

Give the designer your bullet points

The best input you can give to a designer is an outline of your bullet points — the text that you want on the slides or overheads. The designer can then make suggestions. ("Let's split these seven bullets into two slides rather than one.") "What we don't want is the detailed outline of your entire speech," says Steve. "It's not our job to figure out what the bullet points should be. The speaker has to make that decision. After the speaker decides on the bullet points, the designer arranges them so they look good on the visuals."

Be decisive

Have you ever worked for people who keep changing their minds about what they want? It's frustrating, right? Even though you're getting paid for your time, you still get angry after awhile. Well, join the designers' club. Designers may be the victims of indecisiveness more than any other occupation. "Designers aren't in a position to make the judgement calls on a presentation," explains Steve. "Only the presenter can do that. So we hate it when a presenter is indecisive. We know that revisions are part of the process. That's fine. But patience does wear out." The more decisive a presenter can be, the less frustrating the production will become.

Let the designer know what's coming

Want to have a good working relationship with designers? Let them know what's coming ahead of time. "Charts and graphs tend to be last-minute items," says Steve. "At least if we know what's coming, we can plan for it." Designers are only human. Want them to work all night tonight to finish the last minute slides for your presentation tomorrow? They'll be a lot more receptive if you tell them a day or two in advance than if you tell them at 4:00 p.m. today.

Don't forget about imaging time

No matter how fast you think you can force a designer to design, there's a physical limit to how fast the visuals can be produced. It's called *imaging time*. Forgetting about it is a common mistake. "Let's say you're doing 35mm slides from computer files," explains Steve. "Depending how big the file is, one slide can take 10 or 15 minutes just to image on the camera. Just a plain text file image takes 3 to 4 minutes. So multiply that by 30 slides." Even if your slides are being done in rush mode, there's still a minimum amount of time it takes to produce them. (You can also save yourself some money if you plan ahead. Standard production of slides or overheads is 48 hours. If you want them in 24 hours, you'll pay a rush charge.)

Neat ideas for slides and overheads

Tired of slide after slide of boring bullet points? Here are a few less conventional approaches you may want to try:

Cartoons

The common knowledge is that a funny cartoon that makes a point is usually a big hit with an audience. Well, the common knowledge is right for a change. (It can't be wrong every time.) So why don't more speakers use cartoons? Laziness. Lack of imagination. Stick figure phobia. Who knows? The point is that it's worth taking the time to find some cartoons to work into your presentation.

Here's a word of caution. Many speakers who use cartoons do so illegally. They reproduce cartoons found in books, newspapers, and magazines without permission of the copyright holder. One way around the problem comes from Marcia Lemmons of Andersen Consulting. "We subscribe to a cartoon service that allows us to reproduce the cartoons," she says. Another way is to create your own cartoons. Can't draw? No problem. You can compose a cartoon scene with computer clip art. Then add a caption and you're in business.

Headlines of the future

Are you giving a talk that will present your audience with a goal, mission, or vision? Write it as if it were a front-page headline on your favorite newspaper or magazine, and then make a slide or overhead that shows it that way.

Suppose that the goal is to diversify your company. You want to expand from manufacturing medical equipment in Hoboken to operating hospitals, running ambulance services, and distributing drugs around the world. A headline might say "Thousands Cheer as Health Giant XYZ Corporation Opens a Third Office in China." You can make it look like it's on the cover of *Time* Magazine.

"It's a way of summarizing your vision," explains Marcia Lemmons. "I've seen it used both as an opener to set the theme of a presentation and as a closer to help the audience remember the main message." Wouldn't it be simpler to just make the goal a bullet point instead of a headline? Something like "Goal — open three offices in China." Yes, but the headline has more impact. "It helps people project into the future," says Marcia. "Seeing the goal as a headline makes it seem real, more attainable." And it's a heck of a lot more interesting to look at than another bullet point.

Rearranged images

Have you ever gotten your photo taken while sticking your face through a giant cardboard scene? You know, the kind of thing you find at amusement parks. You end up with a photo that looks like you're some celebrity or historic figure. Or you're riding a surfboard or doing some other activity. Well, you can use this technique to liven up your slides and overheads. Just cut out the head from a photo of your organization's leader (or whomever) and attach it to a different body. (Yes, it sounds corny, but people love this stuff.)

Brains: a case study

There was some good news and some bad news for Neil Baron when he was Digital Equipment Corporation's manager of semiconductor CIM marketing. The good news: Baron had been selected as kickoff speaker for one of Digital's most important customer events for semiconductor manufacturers. The bad news: Pressure! Now he had to set the tone for the entire conference while explaining Digital's position to an audience of senior level Fab (fabrication) and MIS managers.

"One of the major goals of the conference was to create interest in our consulting services," Neil explains. "Specifically, we wanted conference attendees to invite us to make sales presentations to the top executives of their companies."

His work was cut out for him. He had to hit home on a number of issues while giving his audience a reason to sit through the day-and-a-half long conference. "I had a 'strategic directions' speech that I had given many times," he recalls. "But I wanted to add something humorous to make it more interesting and memorable." He didn't want to present bullet point after bullet point — better known as "dry tech." "People burn out looking at slides of endless bullet points," he explains.

So what did he do? He called me (smart man that he is). I told him to make slides depicting audience members' brains. "I took that idea and adapted it to the conference," Neil recalls. "I ended up creating slides contrasting the brains of a Fab manager and an MIS manager. (See Figures 11-2 and 11-3.) It was a great way to highlight the key issues without resorting to a bunch of boring bullet points."

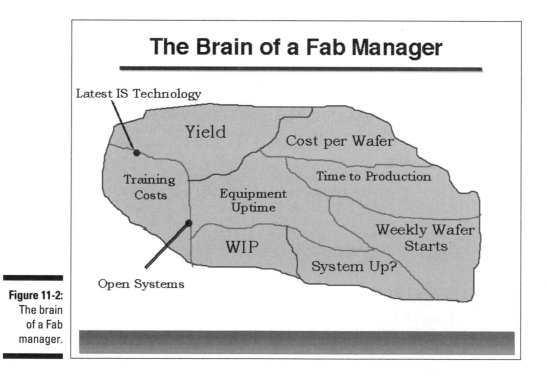

Figure 11-2:
The brain of a Fab manager.

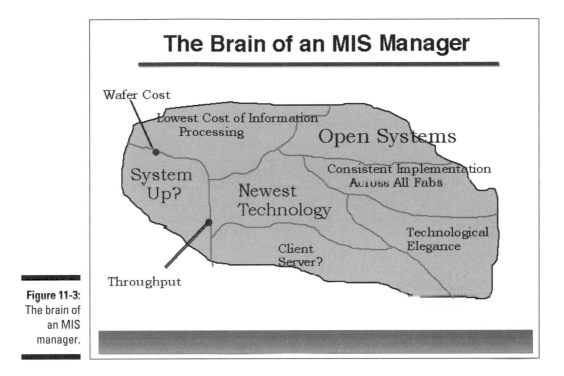

Figure 11-3:
The brain of
an MIS
manager.

And it worked. "People looked at those slides and really identified with the issues," he says. "After the presentation, everyone kept talking about the brains. I was repeatedly complimented on my effective use of humor." It didn't hurt that he also made a self-effacing reference to marketing. After showing the Fab manager brain and the MIS manager brain, he said, "I'd love to show you a marketing manager's brain, but frankly, I couldn't find one." Conference attendees "thought that was just the greatest," Neil recalls.

Every feedback form rated the presentation "very good" or "excellent." Most important, the presentation accomplished its primary sales goal. "As soon as I finished speaking, I immediately received about a dozen invitations to give the speech again at customer sites for CEOs and top-level management," he notes. "I was even asked to speak in France."

Epilogue: When Neil gave the presentation in France, he added a slide of a U.S. politician's brain (see Figure 11-4). The French loved it.

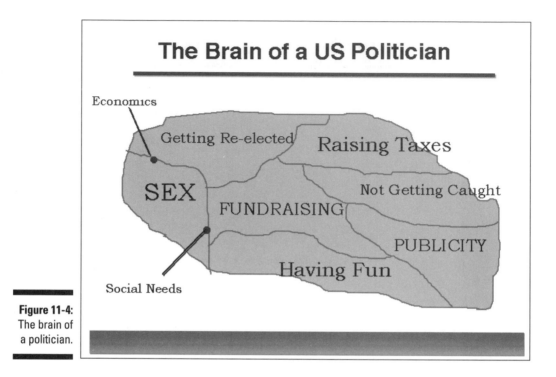

Figure 11-4:
The brain of
a politician.

How to work with an overhead projector

Have you ever watched a speaker fumble around with an overhead projector? It's not a pretty sight. Just when it's time for the first overhead, the speaker realizes that the projector isn't plugged in, or that it's out of focus, or that a bulb is burned out. (And my personal favorite: the speaker can't figure out where the on/off switch is located.)

Slick, well-designed overheads don't do much good if you don't know how to display them properly. What follows are a few suggestions to ensure that your overhead delivery is as slick as your overhead content.

The basics

These rules will save you a lot of potential hassle. They'll also make the "overhead viewing experience" more enjoyable for your audience.

- **Use a projector with two bulbs.** You can instantly click the spare one into place if the first one burns out. (So make sure that both bulbs work before you begin.)
- **Bring an extension cord and an adapter.** You can't fit a square peg in a round hole and you can't fit a three-pronged plug into a two-pronged outlet — especially if the projector cord is ten feet long and the outlet is 12 feet away.

✔ **Avoid projector glare.** Put masking tape along the edges of the projector so that light doesn't glare out around the edges of your overheads. When there's no transparency on the projector, turn it off. Don't just leave the light glaring on the screen.

✔ **Use fewer overheads by showing only parts of them.** The buzzword in training circles is "gradual revelation." You gradually reveal what's on the overhead. For example, I often talk about five types of humor anyone can use. I used to list them on five overheads — one per humor type. Now they're all on one overhead. When I put the overhead on the projector, I cover it with a piece of paper. Then as I talk about each type of humor, I slide the paper down to reveal the relevant section of the overhead. Why bother? The fewer overheads you need to make and handle, the fewer problems you'll have.

Where to stand

According to Alan Weiner, it makes a difference where you stand when you use an overhead projector. "Our research says you have to be standing next to the screen, not the machine," he says. "If the audience members look up at the screen and you're not standing by it, they have to split their attention between you and the screen." And you don't want that. "The theory comes straight out of advertising," notes Alan. "A driver going past a billboard is supposed to see the product and the celebrity in one glance. He shouldn't have to split his attention between the two." (For all you perceptual psychology buffs out there, it has to do with the theory of contiguity and splitting attention between figure and ground.)

Talking to the visuals

The common knowledge is that you shouldn't talk to the visuals. It puts your back facing the audience, breaks off eye contact and all that good stuff, and makes it difficult for the audience to hear you if you don't have a microphone. You know what? I don't think it's the big deal that everyone makes out of it. No, you shouldn't make a habit of talking to the visuals.

But here's the uncommon knowledge — it works great for emphasis. People will instinctively look at whatever you're looking at. When I want to direct their attention to something important on the screen, I twist my body to the side and talk to the visual. Guess what? They all look at it.

Use two overhead projectors

Here's a great idea from management communication expert Jim Lukaszewski: Use two overhead projectors at the same time. Just put one on each side of the room. "I use one for serious stuff and the other for funny stuff," he explains. (Of course, he breaks that routine every so often to keep the audience on its toes.) He also finds that two projectors help the audience take notes. "I cover a lot of material," he says. "With two projectors, I can keep up an overhead of important points for a long time. A lot longer than if I was using only one projector."

Two projectors also allow him to design overheads using very large type. "If I have a list of seven items, I can put 1–3 on the lefthand overhead and 4–7 on the righthand overhead," he explains. "It makes it very easy for the audience to see."

Flipcharts

A flipchart is a very large pad of paper that sits on an easel. It's become ubiquitous at business meetings — and for good reason. The flipchart is a very versatile visual aid. You can write on it as you speak or have pages prepared in advance. It's easy to use. You don't have to find any on/off switches, electrical outlets, or replacements for burned out lightbulbs. It always operates properly (unless your magic marker goes dry) and is easy to transport. Plus it's very inexpensive.

That's the good news. The bad news is that flipcharts aren't really effective for audiences larger than 50 people. The people seated toward the back won't be able to see what's on the chart. And there's worse news. Many speakers misuse flipcharts so badly that people in the front row can't decipher what the chart is supposed to say.

Common mistakes

Here's a checklist of common flipchart mistakes. Make sure you avoid them.

- **Too many words.** I've seen flipcharts covered with writing from top to bottom. It looks like a cave wall crammed with hieroglyphics, and it's about as easy to read. So do your audience a favor. Leave some white space.

- **Don't write all over the entire sheet.** Restrict yourself to the top two-thirds.

- **Tiny writing.** Maybe some people in your audience can read the bottom line of an eye chart. But it's not your job to test them. Make your letters large enough so that they can be read easily from the back of the room. And leave a couple of inches between lines.

- **Skinny writing.** Even when the letters are large, they can be difficult to see if they're really skinny. So don't make letters that look like stick figures. Make them thick enough so that they can be read easily from the back of the room.

- **Colors that are difficult to see.** There must be something about flipcharts that bring out the artist in speakers. Control the urge. Don't use a magenta marker to write notes on the flipchart. Yellow, pink, and orange are also bad. In fact, if you want to make sure that your audience can see what you're writing, stick with black or blue. Those two colors can always be seen from the back of the room.

✔ **Too many colors.** A rainbow is nice to look at in the sky, but not on a flipchart. You can use a few different colors to highlight various points and add emphasis. But if you use too many colors, they lose their impact and become distracting. (Especially when the colors start vibrating in the audience's eyes. That's a clue that your color scheme is a tad busy.)

Tips and tricks

Want to turn your flipchart into a powerful presentation tool? Here are a few tips and tricks that separate the masters from the disasters:

Use flipcharts with paper divided into small squares. Each page should look like a piece of graph paper. Here's the advantage: you can use the boxes as a guide when you write. That way you know your writing will be large enough to see. The boxes can also help you keep your writing evenly spaced.

Correct mistakes with white out. Have you ever spent a lot of time preparing a very detailed page in your flipchart presentation only to make a minor mistake when you were just about done? Don't pull out your hair and *don't* throw away the page. Put some white out over the mistake just like you would on a sheet of typing paper. Then make your correction. No one in the audience will be able to see it. (Unless you're speaking to Superman.)

Write secret notes on the flipchart pages. Worried that you'll forget to discuss important points? Use your flipchart pages as cheatsheets. Lightly pencil in a few key words or phrases on the appropriate page. No one in the audience will be able to see them. This technique can also improve the text and drawings that you do want the audience to view. Do you need to write or draw something as you speak? Draw it lightly in pencil beforehand. When you come to that point in your talk, you can just trace over it with a marker. (It will look a lot better than if you start it from scratch while you're speaking.)

Draw pictures from coloring books. Drawing simple pictures can add a lot of interest to your flipcharts. Can't draw? Here's some uncommon knowledge from Steve Fraticelli: Children's coloring books provide a great source of simple line drawings that are easy to copy. "Find characters you like and change them around to suit your purpose," he advises.

Use human figures. Are you drawing pictures on your flipcharts? Use human figures whenever possible. People respond to humans. (We're a narcissistic species.)

Leave two blank sheets between each sheet you use. If you prepare your flipchart in advance, don't use each page. Why? The paper is so thin that the audience can see through to the next sheet. And they can often see through that sheet also. So leave two blank sheets between each page that you use. Then you know you're safe.

Video (and Audio)

Video is a very powerful, yet overlooked, visual aid. Today's audiences are supposed to have a short attention span due to the influence of television. So why not capture what little attention they possess with the medium they love — video? This section also discusses how to use audio to break through the attention barrier. (While audio is not technically a visual aid, it can create pictures in your mind. Besides, this seemed like a good place to throw it in.)

Video

Video is so powerful that it should only be used in small doses. The danger is that it will take over your presentation. It will make the non-video portions (in other words — you talking) seem boring by comparison. That's exactly what you *don't* want.

Use videos in short bursts to emphasize key points and heighten audience interest. If you're speaking to a small group, just bring a VCR and TV monitor. You can work them like an overhead projector, turning them on and off when appropriate. If you're speaking to a large audience, you'll need to arrange for the videos to be projected onto a large screen. (That task usually requires some professional help.)

Testimonials

"Want to convince people about something you believe in?" asks Joe DiNucci. "Then have someone else tell it to them." Joe's absolutely right. No matter what you're selling — yourself, your ideas, or your products — it's hard to top the persuasive power of third-party credibility. What's this got to do with video? I'm glad you asked.

Suppose that I'm going to give you a sales presentation. It's much more persuasive for you to hear about the greatness of my products from some of my customers than from me. Unfortunately, they usually have better things to do and don't generally accompany me on my sales calls. (It's hard to believe but true.) That's where video comes in. I can videotape a customer singing my praises and show it to you. "I can talk all day," says Joe DiNucci. "And I can't have the impact of a 30-second video testimonial from a customer."

Here are a few tips from Joe for putting together video testimonials:

Get the right testimony. "Think about the people who can best corroborate your points," says Joe. "What will it take to get them on the record?"

It's OK to do it yourself. You don't have to hire an expensive camera crew and create a broadcast quality tape. "You can film it yourself with a shaky hand-held home camcorder," says Joe. "What counts is content." (In fact, the shaky home video look may actually increase the video's credibility.)

Boil it down. If you film long interviews, pick out the best stuff and turn it into a short video clip. (Between 15 and 60 seconds is a good length — just like a TV ad.)

Make a composite video. Did you get 30 seconds from an academic, 30 seconds from a customer, and 30 seconds from an analyst? Put them all on one tape. It's much easier to handle that way. (There's less chance of losing one, forgetting one, or cueing up the wrong one.) Make sure you know the order that the clips appear on your tape. Write a cue sheet so that you know exactly when to turn the VCR on and off during your presentation.

Other video ideas

When commercial television first took root in the 1940s, one Hollywood executive reportedly said that video wouldn't last more than six months — people would get tired of staring at a box. (His prediction displayed the usual amount of imagination associated with Hollywood executives.) He didn't realize that video would evolve into a wide variety of imaginative forms — all of which were designed to capture audience attention. Unless you're a Hollywood executive (or otherwise imagination-impaired), you should be able to work video into your presentation in lots of clever ways.

Television commercials. I saw someone give a speech about creativity. The speaker talked about different types of creativity and various techniques for being creative, and he illustrated the techniques with TV commercials. (I assume he obtained permission to show them.) The audience loved watching the commercials. (They were very funny.) The commercials did a good job of bringing home the points about creativity. The speaker appropriately spaced the commercials throughout his presentation. The speaker would talk awhile, show a commercial, talk some more, and show another commercial. The commercials helped maintain audience interest and energy till the end of the talk. Given the range of subject matter covered in TV commercials, you can probably find one or two (hundred) that can illustrate some points in your next presentation.

Filmed vignettes. A speaker made a presentation about crosscultural communication. He emphasized how Americans could avoid gaffes when doing business with people from other countries. He covered the usual stuff — differences in directness between Americans and Japanese, differences in time concept between Americans and Mexicans, differences in significance of male hand-holding between Americans and Arabs. Nothing new there. But he made it more interesting by introducing each segment with a short video. Actors portraying businesspeople from America and another country would act out a brief scene of a business meeting. The actor portraying the American would make every gaffe possible. (The audience responded with laughter to each gaffe. So the videos were entertaining, as well as educational.)

After each video, the speaker asked the audience to identify the gaffes, and then he'd elaborate on their causes. The videos kept the audience members engaged throughout the entire presentation and helped them understand the speaker's points. Do you have a presentation that lends itself to videotaping a few vignettes? Yes, you'll need to allocate some time and budget some money for it. But it's something to think about — especially if it's a presentation that you'll repeat frequently.

Person-on-the-street interviews. I've seen these used for comic relief in various types of presentations. You ask a four-year-old what he or she thinks the CEO of your company does all day and videotape the answer. Or you ask people at a trade show unrelated to your industry (gourmet coffees) what they think of your latest product (a hydraulic pump). Or you ask people in your organization to sing happy birthday to someone. You get the idea.

Audio

Music and sound effects can greatly enhance your presentation no matter what you're discussing. They can energize your audience, set a mood, and emphasize a point. Here are a few ideas to consider:

Set the mood with music

Audience members are walking into the room where they'll hear you give a speech. You have a choice. You can arrange for them to hear the "Theme From Rocky" as they enter. Or they can hear nothing. Do you think it makes any difference? You bet it does. If you play the "Theme From Rocky," they'll get pumped up and energized. And that's probably the way you want them. (No? Then play something else. Want them in a contemplative mood? Try some new age, cosmic music. Want them inflamed with patriotism? Play a Sousa march.) The point is that music can provide a wonderful warm-up act. Take advantage of it.

Add a beat to slide shows

People love to look at themselves. That's why multi-day meetings often conclude with slide shows of photos taken earlier in the meeting. (The meeting participants see themselves arriving, attending sessions, partying, and so on.) These slide shows are inevitably accompanied by loud music with a heavy bass beat. (Disco music is popular.) Why? It generates energy and enthusiasm. It makes the slide show come alive. (The slides will seem to synchronize with the beat of the music.) You can adapt this technique to your own presentations. Are you giving a talk about the completion of some project? (Completion of a new building, graduation from a school or program, release of a new product. Whatever.) Do you have photos documenting the project's progress? Put together a short slide show and add some music. It's simple to do and very effective.

Fill time when people are thinking or writing

Do you have a spot in your presentation when everything comes to a halt? Maybe you ask the audience members to do some exercise in which they have to think about something. Or maybe you've asked them to take a few minutes to write something. In any event, you stop talking and silence fills the room. It can become oppressive after awhile, and it definitely lowers the energy level. Want a simple solution? Play some music during this interlude. (Whatever you feel is appropriate.) It will help maintain a minimal energy level. It will also be appreciated by audience members who finish early. They'll have something to listen to while the slowpokes finish.

Props

Throughout much of the 1950s, Senator Joe McCarthy gave stinging speeches from the Senate floor denouncing alleged communists in the U.S. government. He always claimed to have a list of these offenders. His claim was always bolstered by the sheet of paper he would wave in the air while making his accusations. It was a dramatic flourish that added authenticity to his claims. It wasn't until after his downfall that the sheet of paper was revealed to be blank.

Joe McCarthy has long since become a discredited figure in American history. But there's one thing you have to say for him: he knew how to use a prop. He also illustrated some uncommon knowledge about props — they don't have to be very elaborate.

Simple props for fancy effects

When people think about props, they frequently conjure up images of large, complex pieces of equipment. (Like the giant glass tank of water with a series of pulleys and chains used by Houdini-type escape artists.) But almost any simple household item can become a riveting object of attention if you use a little imagination.

Newspapers

Here's some uncommon knowledge from Marcia Lemmons of Anderson Consulting: One of the most effective props you can use for any presentation is a current copy of a daily newspaper. "One of our business development directors begins every meeting by holding up *USA Today* and reading from it," says Marcia. "He always finds something that he can tie into his talk." What's the advantage? "It makes everything that he's going to talk about seem fresh," she explains. "Holding up a newspaper makes his message seem timely and important."

Hats

Want to instantly transform your public image? Put on a hat. And if you really want to make an impression, put on several in rapid succession. That's how Marcia gained attention when she taught a seminar about how to land a job in marketing. "I'd open with a quick overview of the traits that employers were looking for," she recalls. "And I'd put on a hat to illustrate each trait." A baseball cap showed you need to be a team player. A propeller hat showed flexibility. ("It goes where the wind blows," she explains.) A dunce hat showed a willingness to ask questions no matter how stupid. And a two visor hat (a baseball cap with a visor in front and back) showed the ability to move in two different directions at once. "I spent about a minute wearing each hat and talking about what it represented," she says. "People always commented on it afterwards. They said it helped them remember the skills they needed."

Gag items

Gag items can make good props — if they're used appropriately. Marcia recalls a meeting in which a new director was introduced to his group for the first time. "We presented him with gifts that we thought would be useful for his new job," she explains. These included a construction hard hat, a whip, a whistle, and a vest emblazoned with a firing range target.

Magic tricks

Magic tricks make great props for presentations especially when you tie them to a point. But aren't magic tricks difficult to learn and perform? Don't worry. Just read Chapter 25. It discusses simple magic tricks that anyone can perform in a presentation.

Dos and Don'ts

No matter what types of props you decide to use, a few general rules will apply. Here are some dos and don'ts:

Don't milk it

A major mistake in using a prop is using it too long during your presentation. "Most props have a joke or point attached to them that the audience can get in under a minute," says computer executive Joe DiNucci. "But because the speaker goes to the trouble of preparing the prop and schlepping it to the presentation, there's a tendency to keep it center stage too long." It's like when a baseball player tries to stretch a triple into a home run and gets tagged out at homeplate. So don't belabor your props. A triple is a lot better than an out.

Don't force it

If your prop doesn't operate correctly, don't force it — especially if it could be hazardous. "I had a student who gave a demonstration of a Vegematic or some slicing and dicing gizzmo," recalls Allatia Harris. "And something didn't work, but he forced the blade in anyway. He sliced a big chunk out of his finger. And it's very distracting to the audience when you're bleeding all over the place."

Do use them yourself if you want others to use them

When it comes to props, there's a thin line between what's hokey and what works — particularly if you want your audience to use them. If you give out hats or masks or clown noses, don't expect anyone to put them on unless you're willing to do so yourself. "We had a meeting celebrating a 60 percent sales improvement," recalls Marcia Lemmons. "So we put sunglasses on each chair and played the song 'The Future's So Bright I Gotta Wear Shades.' As people arrived, we asked them to put on the sunglasses." And they did. Why? Marcia and her boss (who was running the meeting) were wearing giant wraparound sunglasses. "Leadership style makes a big difference," notes Marcia. "The presenter has to lead the way."

Don't gag on the gifts

My customer was the chairman of a Silicon Valley company. The chairman wanted to present gag gifts as awards to executives during a speech at an annual shareholder meeting. My assignment was to come up with ideas. I jokingly suggested that the VP of Sales, a notorious womanizer, be given an inflatable doll. The chairman thought this was great and couldn't be talked out of it. And I was told to purchase the thing.

It was late in the afternoon and the shareholder meeting was early the next morning. So I called around and found a store that had the item. The owner gave me directions and said the store closed at 5 o'clock. It was 4:30. I could just make it.

Unfortunately, I got caught in traffic. At five to five, I was still 15 minutes away. With the clock relentlessly ticking down, I pulled off the freeway to call the store. The owner said that he would wait for me. "Just come around the back and knock on the window," he instructed.

Twenty minutes later, after a lot of horn honking and lane changing, I finally arrived at the store. I ran around the back and knocked on the window. The owner let me in.

"I'm the one who called," I panted, short of breath from running. "I need the inflatable doll."

"No problem," he said. "You want the cheap one without any openings or the anatomically correct one?"

It took me a moment to recognize the implications of his question. "Wait a minute," I exploded, "you don't understand. This is for a corporate meeting!"

"Riiiiiiight," he said.

"Just give me the cheap one," I fumed.

"Are you sure?" he asked.

"Just give me the cheap one."

"You called twice. You wanted me to stay open late. You were panting when you came in here.

(continued)

(continued)

Are you sure you don't need an anatomically correct one?"

"It's for a corporate meeting," I screamed.

"Riiiiiiiight."

The next day, the chairman presented the inflatable doll to the VP of Sales during the annual shareholder meeting. This simultaneously augmented the chairman's reputation for showmanship and raised the bar for outrageousness in corporate events — no small accomplishment in Silicon Valley. What did the shareholders think? One venture capitalist speaking to an analyst in the back of the room summed it up: "As long as they keep making their numbers, we don't care what they do."

What can we learn from all this? Three lessons: There's safety in numbers. Two heads are better than one — unless they're inflatable. And . . . corporate politics makes strange bedfellows.

Chapter 12

Multimedia Presentations: From Voodoo to Can Do

. . . .

In This Chapter

▶ Why multimedia can make you a star

▶ Hardware and software that you'll need

▶ Where to find great graphics, audio, and video

▶ Designing an incredible presentation

▶ How to run a multimedia presentation

▶ Really simple stuff that will blow your audience away

. . . .

*U*nless you've been living under a rock for the past few years, you've probably heard the buzzword "multimedia." It's difficult to escape. It appears ubiquitously in ads, articles, editorials, lectures, conversations, explanations, and prognostications about the information revolution. (In fact, you've probably heard the word even if you have been under a rock.)

Multimedia refers to the combination of video, text, graphics, and sound. (These are the "multiple media.") If you're like me, you've got a vague idea of what it all means. You know that the latest and greatest software is all multimedia. (It has text, graphic, video, and audio components.) You may have seen people use computers to project text, graphics, and video clips, as well as to play audio clips for multimedia presentations at business conferences.

While still far from standard, multimedia presentations will grow in popularity over the next several years as people discover the capabilities of the new technology. That's why I've included this chapter. It's important for you to understand how multimedia can enhance your presentations and what options you have available. I'm *not* going to go into every last bit of technical minutia involving multimedia. (See *Multimedia and CD-ROMs For Dummies* for an extensive discussion of this topic.) My goal is to give you an overview. I want you to know what multimedia can do for you, the basic tools needed to make a multimedia presentation, and how to get started quickly and simply. (For simplicity's sake, I'm going to discuss these items solely in terms of PCs, but much of the discussion also applies to Macs.)

In order to accomplish my goal, I talked extensively with three multimedia gurus. Jackie Roach and David Schmidt work for Silicon Graphics — one of the pioneers in the development and use of multimedia. (It's the company that made the computers used to produce the special effects for the movie *Jurassic Park*.) N.R. Mitgang, one of the industry's most prominent consultants, started the electronic publishing division of a major New York publisher. These people know multimedia.

Why Bother with Multimedia

You're up at the podium. A laptop computer is sitting where your notes would normally be. Behind you and toward the middle of the stage, a large, white screen is set up. (It's the kind of screen you project slides onto.) You tap a few keys on the computer, and a slide listing ten of your major customers appears on the screen.

In the corner of the slide is your company logo. You tell the audience you'll be telling a few customer success stories, but first you want to tell them a little about your company.

Turning to the computer, you use a mouse to click on your company logo. A video pops up and fills the screen. The 15-second video is a welcome message from your company's CEO. It disappears when it's done. You then say you'll talk about one of your customers in the aerospace industry. You click on the name of the company, and a slide of an airplane fills the screen. You click on the wheel of the plane, and a diagram of the wheel pops up. You talk about how your company helped design the wheels of the plane.

You tap a key and return to the slide listing your ten major customers. You say that you'll talk about a customer in the food industry. An audience member shouts out, "How about talking about the apparel industry." You agree. Instead of clicking on the name of your food customer, you click on the name of your apparel customer. A giant logo of your apparel customer appears. You click on the logo, and a video of the apparel company's CEO pops up. The CEO talks about what a great job your company did for him.

Flexibility

Flexibility is the biggest advantage of a multimedia presentation. You don't have to stick to a limited set of materials that must be displayed in a pre-arranged order. (To use a bit of technical jargon, it's *non-linear*.) If someone asks about your new product as you're speaking about your old product, no problem. You can click on the screen and have a slide, video, or audio about your new product appear (as long as you've planned to have that link available on that particular screen). Or you never have to click on it and the audience will never know it was even available. As N.R. Mitgang explains, "There is an order to multimedia material, but you can fast forward through it to get what you want. Or you can change your mind and skip things you don't want to use. Or you can have things ready to use in case you need them. You can't do any of that with a traditional slide show."

Other advantages

Flexibility is only one of several advantages associated with multimedia. Here are a few others:

Customization. Multimedia presentations are easy to customize to a particular audience. Because you're not locked into a set order, you can pick and choose whatever is appropriate. So you can customize on the fly as you speak. (In contrast, a 35mm slide show forces you to go in sequential order.)

Speed. A multimedia presentation can be altered in the time it takes to scan in an image. You don't have to send slides out to be developed, and there's no rush charge. If you discover some late-breaking news that affects your presentation, you can just digitize it in.

Credibility. Multimedia presentations can deliver instant third-party credibility. You can spend all day telling your audience how great you are, but a 30-second video clip of someone else singing your praises is a lot more convincing.

Translation. In today's global economy, more and more business is being conducted on a worldwide basis. That means presentations must often be given in more than one language. Multimedia simplifies this process immensely. "We did a sales presentation to a company in Florida that also had offices in Austria," recalls David Schmidt. "The company had a transcript made of the audio portion of the presentation, translated it, and spoke it back into the computer in German. Then the company shipped the presentation to Europe to play in its Austrian office."

Non-artists can do it. "You don't need any great artistic ability to put together a good multimedia presentation," asserts Jackie Roach. "Most people instinctively know how the screens should look. It comes from years of experience watching TV."

Disadvantages

There's one major disadvantage to multimedia, and it's a really big one. It can lull you into a false sense of security. You may develop a tendency to let the technology take over your presentation. So here's a warning: *Don't use multimedia as a crutch.* If the computer fails, *you* still have to give the talk. Having all the cool effects doesn't excuse you from being prepared.

Hardware

Putting together and running a multimedia presentation requires a lot of equipment, so I asked N.R. Mitgang to guide me through all the hoopla and hype.

Computer stuff

The rule of thumb for computers is very simple — get the fastest one you can afford.

"That means you want a fast hard drive and a fast processor," explains Mitgang. "It's the combination of those speeds that determines how fast the screens will pop up in your presentation."

Here's his minimum recommendations for computer configuration to create a multimedia presentation:

- **Memory:** at least 8 to 16 megabytes
- **Processor:** Pentium (at least 120 megahertz)
- **Hard drive speed:** in the 9 millisecond range (as opposed to 20 millisecond)
- **Hard drive size:** 1.2 gigabytes (or as much as you can afford to purchase beyond this minimum)

You'll also need a few other things:

- **Video display card.** Get as much memory on it as possible. Two megabytes is better than one megabyte.
- **Video capture card.** This card allows you to record and digitize video from sources such as TVs, VCRs, and camcorders. You want any card that will work with Microsoft Video One compression. (This card covers you for AVI video files — the current standard for computerized video — but Mitgang says these standards may soon change. New standards such as MPEG are coming soon.)
- **Sound card.** The sound card adds an audio dimension to your computer. It allows your computer to play sounds, and it also provides an audio input-output jack so that you can record sounds directly in digital form onto your hard drive. Look for cards that are Soundblaster and Soundblaster-Pro compatible.
- **CD-ROM drive.** Make sure it has Kodak CD capability. (A CD-ROM drive isn't absolutely necessary, but it's strongly recommended.)

Input devices: sound and image

Input devices allow you to get sound and images into your computer in a digitized format — everything from music and video images to photographs and business cards. Whatever you want to get in, there's a way to do it. Here are some of the more popular methods:

Service bureau

One of the simplest ways to get slides and photographs into digital form is to send them to a service bureau. Service bureaus usually charge less than $1 per picture. Bureaus use scanners to get each image into a form that will be recognized by your computer. Then they send you a disk or CD-ROM containing the computerized images. Which is better, the disk or CD-ROM? Here's a tip from N.R. Mitgang: Take the CD-ROM. "The images will have a higher resolution and a more professional level of quality," he explains.

Scanner

If you don't want to use a service bureau to digitize slides and photos, you can purchase your own scanner. The two major types are flatbed and slide scanners. The flatbed can be used to scan in photos and any other paper artwork — images from magagzines, brochures, business cards, and so on. The slide scanner can only scan in 35mm slides. (Some scanners can do both.)

VCR or TV

Do you have a video tape with a clip that you'd like to include in your multimedia presentation? (Home movies of your company's CEO as a baby are always a big hit.) Just plug your VCR into your computer. (You can find the inexpensive cables that you need for this operation at any Radio Shack.) Your cable from the "video out" jack on the VCR goes to the "video in" jack on the video capture card in your computer. (A *card* is a board that's installed inside your computer.) The same process works for capturing video from a TV.

Camcorder

You can also plug a camcorder directly into your computer and record video directly in digitized form. Once again, the cables go from the "video out" jack on the camcorder to the "video in" jack on the video capture card. (Here's the good news — the cables are often included free of charge when you purchase the camcorder.)

Audio cassette player, CD player, stereo or radio

The cabling deal also works with audio devices. Whether it's an audio cassette player, CD player, stereo, or radio, the process is identical. You run a cable from the "headphone out" jack directly to the "audio in" jack on your computer's sound card. (You can also do this with a TV or VCR if you only want to capture a soundtrack.)

Microphone

You can also plug a microphone directly into the input jack on the back of your computer's audio card. Then you can record interviews directly in digitized form.

Projection devices: sound and image

You also need hardware that projects the sounds and images of your multimedia presentation. The sound part is easy. If the room where you will speak has a sound system, you can just plug your computer into that system. If the room doesn't contain a sound system, you'll have to bring your own speakers.

For image projection, you need an overhead projector and an LCD projection panel. The LCD panel is placed on the overhead projector (in the spot normally occupied by a transparency) and connected to your computer. An LCD panel allows anything displayed on your computer screen to be projected through the overhead onto a large screen or wall.

Here's a tip from Marcia Lemmons, Marketing Communications Director for Government Industry at Andersen Consulting. If you run your presentation from one of the newer notebook computers, you need a special adapter to make it work with most LCD panels. What if you forget to bring the adapter? Save the presentation to a floppy disk and run it off an older PC (assuming one is available).

Here's a tip from N.R. Mitgang: "Always bring extra cables and extension cords," he says, "because the one you'll need is the one they won't have."

Software

With so much hardware involved, did you think you'd get away without software? The basic requirements are Windows and Video for Windows. Beyond that, you need software to develop the individual pieces of your presentation and authoring software to put it all together.

Creating and editing images, sounds, and text

Your first task is to construct the various images, video clips, audio clips, and slides that will make up your presentation.

Graphics

You have a lot of choices when it comes to software for creating images. These range from simple graphics tools such as Paintbrush (which comes with every copy of Windows) to high powered packages such as CorelDRAW! and Micrografx. Two of the more popular programs for image creation are

Persuasion and PowerPoint. Both of these offer lots of help for the non-professional designer. Specifically, they provide templates that allow you to create slides that automatically conform to commonly accepted design standards. (In other words, your slides won't end up with words written in twelve different fonts and eight different colors.)

Audio and video

You also need special software for capturing and editing the audio and video clips that you want to use in your presentation. The good news is that you probably don't have to buy it. Almost any sound card or video capture card that you purchase comes with recording and editing software that covers your basic needs. But here's a tip from Mitgang: "If Adobe's Premier isn't bundled with your video capture card, buy it," he says. "That's the best software for editing video clips."

Text

Most word processing packages are capable of tagging your word processing files for multimedia access. Your multimedia authoring tool will determine how this should be accomplished.

Authoring systems

Once you've assembled the various pieces of your multimedia presentation, you need a method of putting them all together and controlling them. That's the function of software known as an *authoring system*. An authoring system allows you to *author* your multimedia presentation. It's easy to understand if you compare it with a slide carousel.

"If you put 36 slides into the carousel of a slide projector, you wouldn't put the 14th slide in first and then jump around," explains N.R. Mitgang. "You'd put them in the order that you want to present them. The same principles of organization apply to multimedia. But instead of just slides, you've also got video and audio. The authoring system puts those items into the order you designate for the easiest access. It also gives you the switch to say start playing this one or stop playing that one." In simple terms, it allows you to choreograph all the other programs into a coherent presentation.

What authoring system should you use? One of the most popular systems now on the market is Macromind Director. Other good ones include HyperWriter, Icon Author, and Toolbook.

Content

The good news about multimedia presentations is that you *can* use text, graphics, video, and audio. The bad news is that you have to come up with all those materials, and the really bad news is that you need the rights to use that stuff.

There's a widespread misconception that you can use anything you want in a multimedia presentation. People use VCRs to capture video clips of news items, sports events, and scenes from their favorite movies. They record audio clips of songs from their favorite CDs or cassettes. Or they record music from the radio. They digitize photos and images found in books and magazines. Technically those activities are known as copyright infringement — a federal offense punishable by fines and imprisonment. Consider yourself warned.

So where can you get the materials you need for a multimedia presentation? Remember these two magic words — *public domain.* (But public domain is a tricky issue — even for lawyers. So make sure your public domain materials really are in the public domain.) When an item is in the public domain, anyone is allowed to use it. No permission is required. Here are a few other ideas:

Videos

Get a camcorder and shoot some video yourself. Then there's no permission problem. Or purchase video that's been legally cleared for your use. (It's sold with the understanding that you can use it any way you wish. It's the video equivalent of *clip art* — books of images that are sold with the understanding that you can use them however you wish.)

And here's some uncommon knowledge from David Schmidt. Corporations are a great source of video. "Large companies have all kinds of promotional videos lying around in their storerooms," says David. "They're usually delighted to let you use these videos."

Audios

At Silicon Graphics, most of the audios used in multimedia presentations are testimonials from customers. "If we can't record them in person, we record them right off a speaker phone," says David Schmidt. "And of course, we get their permission." You can do the same thing. What about music and sound effects? No problem. Plenty of collections of music and sound effects automatically grant you the right to use them. (These collections are essentially audio clip art.) Many of them can be found in your local library.

Slides and photographs

Once again, you can purchase photos that have been cleared for your use or you can get a camera and take your own pictures. If you shoot them yourself, here's some uncommon knowledge from N.R. Mitgang: Get the pictures developed as slides rather than photographs.

"Slides provide high quality in a small space," explains Mitgang. "The image is sharper. The color is richer and denser, and the size of the computer file after it's digitized is a lot smaller." In contrast, an 8 × 10 glossy created from a 35mm negative is big and blah. "It will look grainy because it had to be projected into a larger size," says Mitgang. "And if you want it digitized at a very high quality level, the size of the computer file can become gigantic."

Other graphic images

Any image that you can get permission to use can be scanned into your computer. Many companies have brochures that they will allow you to use, and you can always go to the nearest art supply store and buy some clip art. Want to save some time and skip the scanner? Go to a software store and buy clip art on a disk or CD-ROM. (A typical example is Corel Gallery, one of the best selling CD-ROMs for the past several years. It contains 10,000 clip art images — everything from a map of the world to a caricature of Sigmund Freud. You can find many other products like it on the market.)

The World Wide Web

The World Wide Web is an excellent source for any type of material you might use in a multimedia presentation. It's loaded with text, photographs, and video and audio files — all of which you can download to your own computer. Jackie Roach finds it a big time-saver. "I was looking for a picture of a tiger," she recalls. "I didn't feel like going to the library, finding a picture of a tiger, and scanning it into my computer." So she surfed around the Web and found a feline page. "It had a picture of a tiger, which I downloaded and imported into my presentation," she says. (But remember, be careful about the rights. The Web is notorious for flagrant violations of copyright law. Just because you can download something from the Web doesn't automatically mean you have the right to use it.)

How to Design a Multimedia Presentation

Many people make one giant, very common mistake when they put together a multimedia presentation — they emphasize the multimedia and forget about the presentation. Avoiding this mistake will vastly increase your likelihood of success. Making this mistake will almost guarantee failure.

"Just because it's multimedia doesn't excuse you from the fact that it's a presentation," explains David Schmidt. "You still need an outline; a beginning, middle, and end; a structure; and a flow." Or as N.R. Mitgang puts it, "You can't get away from doing your homework."

Don't think you can get out of it by hiring a multimedia designer to do the work for you. "You still need to write, design, and understand the project yourself," warns Mitgang. "Designers will only give you back what you've asked for. They may make a few suggestions, but you're responsible for the final product."

So how do you start? Just like a regular presentation — figure out what you want to say and develop a well-organized outline. Then create a storyboard based on the outline. The storyboard should show each computer screen in your presentation. Write out exactly what you want to include on each screen. (The first screen may, for example, show your company logo and have a video welcome message from your CEO embedded in it. The second screen may list your leading customers. Each customer name will be linked to another screen devoted to that customer.) You need to decide what types of effects — audio, video, graphics — will best support each point that you're trying to make.

Always view your presentation from the perspective of an audience member. What will the audience members think of the information? What will they think of you? Are all the multimedia effects entertaining or annoying?

General design tips

Some of the rules in this section apply to any type of presentation. Some of them are unique to multimedia, but all of them apply to making your multimedia presentation a success.

Don't get carried away. There's a great temptation to use all kinds of video and audio effects simply because you can. Resist it. Look at each effect and decide if it enhances your message. If it's a distraction, get rid of it.

Keep it simple. That applies to both form and content. Don't clutter the screens with too much information. Let the screens breathe.

Make sure you can backtrack in your presentation. "Someone in the audience will always ask you to go back one screen," warns Mitgang. "So you've got to remember to build that capability into your presentation. It's very simple to do with the authoring system. But if you forget to do it, you'll blow your talk."

Keep your information organized. "Put all the clips used in the presentation into a single directory instead of keeping them in 40 million subdirectories," Mitgang advises. "Then if you have to reconstruct it or transfer it to another computer, it's not a large pain."

Video tips

Here are a few tips that apply specifically to using video clips in a multimedia presentation:

Don't use too many video clips. The audience will get bored with them. "They're cool at first," says Jackie Roach. "But it's better if you use them sporadically throughout your presentation. You want them to remain surprising and entertaining."

Don't use video clips longer than 30 seconds. Most of them should be shorter. (Think about television ads — many of them are only 15 seconds.) You may make an exception for the beginning and ending of the presentation. "A video clip at the beginning can be longer if you use it as a lead in," explains David. "Maybe you have your corporate logo spinning around and music playing for 60 to 90 seconds. It signals the audience that it's time to sit down because the presentation is about to begin." (For a very large audience — several hundred or a thousand — you may want the opening video clip to play for two or three minutes. Larger crowds need more time to get seated.)

Capture images from videos. Why bother making a slide or photograph from one of the frames of the videotape? It can create a neat special effect. "We'll use an image from a video — someone's face for example — as a slide in the presentation," David Schmidt explains. "Then we'll launch that video from right on top of the image. So it seems like the picture of the face suddenly springs to life." It also helps you remember where the video clip is embedded and when you're supposed to play it. And most important, if the video clip fails to play, the audience can still see the picture of the person who was on the clip.

Use the video without its soundtrack. If you like the images on a video clip, but not the sounds — edit out the sounds. "You can play the video without sound while the speaker talks about it," says David Schmidt. "Or you can add a different soundtrack — music or narration. It just depends what point you're trying to make."

Watch television news. N.R. Mitgang believes this a great education in how to use video clips. "Watch how they superimpose an audio clip over a visual image," he says. "And how they fade from one video image to another. It's a free graduate school in multimedia design."

Audio tips

Here are some tips for using audio clips:

Launch audio clips off a key word or phrase. "We like to use audio clips to emphasize points made by the presenter," says Jackie Roach. "So we'll launch an audio clip when the presenter says a key word or phrase. For example, let's say the presenter has just said that we make the best computers in the world. If we have a picture of a customer on the screen, we'll launch an audio clip of that customer talking about our products." The television news also provides a good example. A newscaster may be talking about a diasaster that occurred in the southwestern United States. In the background, a map of the U.S. with a photo of a reporter who is located at the disaster site appears. The newscaster says, "And here's the latest report from the scene of the disaster. You're listening to the voice of Mr. Intrepid." Then they launch an audio clip. You hear the reporter, but all you see is his photo on the map.

Use sound effects. Small touches can have a large effect in the quality of your presentation. One of the slides from a Silicon Graphics sales presentation depicts a game-show style question and answer board. Whenever the presenter says, "The answer is,"a "bing" sound gives the proceedings an authentic TV feel. "It's just a little detail," says David Schmidt. "But our audiences love it."

Edit out the ums and ahs. Want to make the people you interview sound better? Edit out the "ums," "ahs," and other awkward noises that they made when pausing between thoughts. Should you edit more than that? Is it OK to rearrange the words that they said? "It's an ethical issue," says David Schmidt. "We always show the final audio or video clip to the people interviewed. Then they can see exactly how we've edited it. That covers all the bases."

Running a Multimedia Presentation

Your multimedia presentation has been created. You like it. You're ready to deliver it. Your next decision is who will operate the computer. You can do it yourself or have someone else run it for you. If you run your own presentation, you need to know what you're doing. So here are a few dos and don'ts:

Do rehearse a lot. Run through your entire presentation several times.

Don't acknowledge any problems if possible. If something goes wrong, act like that's what was supposed to happen. (Unless the problem is extremely obvious.) If the entire system crashes, turn it off and just talk.

Do make sure you know where every link is located. You'll look disorganized and silly if you say "and now a word from our CEO" and then can't remember where the video is embedded. (You frantically click all over your computer screen and nothing appears. Or worse, you inadvertently click on a *different* video. So instead of a message from your CEO, up pops a clip of a baby crying.)

Want to minimize these problems? Here's a tip from Jackie Roach: Embed the video clips in logical locations that will jog your memory. "If you have a video clip of the CEO, have it pop up when you click on the CEO's name," she says. "Do you have an audio clip of your company's mission statement? Embed it in your company logo. If you take some time to think through the placement of the links on your screen, you'll save yourself a lot of potential embarrassment."

Do consider using a wireless mouse. A wireless mouse allows you to point and click at your computer screen from a distance. It frees you from having to stand right behind the podium to operate the computer.

Content is gold

Multimedia developers have a saying, "Content is gold." That's because it's often expensive to acquire rights for the content — audio, video and textual information — used in multimedia programs. But computer guru N.R. Mitgang defines the expression differently. He says content becomes gold when it's put in a multimedia computer format to make the information more useful. And the people who really know how to make content golden aren't doing it yet.

"Most people doing multimedia programs today are experts in electronic publishing," he explains. "They're not experts in the content that goes into their programs." For example, a multimedia program about American history is developed by a computer guru, not a historian. "The developer might work with a historian," acknowledges Mitgang, "but if historians could fully understand what the computer could do, the content could be accessed better." Why? "People who are experts in their fields, who have studied their subjects for forty years, are sitting on incredible amounts of high quality information," says Mitgang.

Here's the good news. More and more experts are learning how to put information into an electronic format. In fact, by the time you read this, Mitgang will have lectured historians on this subject at the American Historical Society's annual convention. He'll have given a demonstration of *Well...There You Go Again!: The Humor That Shaped America, Volume One* — a CD-ROM

that's the first multimedia product devoted solely to Ronald Reagan. (With over eight hours of audio and 30 minutes of video, you can see and hear nearly every quip, joke, and anecdote told by President Reagan during his first administration.) "The Reagan CD-ROM will give the historians a good idea about how historical information can come alive on a computer," Mitgang explains.

Now here's the obvious question. Mitgang is a computer guru, not a historian. So wouldn't the content of his Reagan humor CD-ROM have been better if it had been developed by an expert? The answer is yes. And it was developed by an expert — me. I'm an expert on humor and I'm the codeveloper of *Well...There You Go Again!*.

I won't go on and on about why this is a great CD-ROM. Let me just say that it's now on display at the Ronald Reagan Presidential Library. (In addition to the jokes, it contains the full text of fifty major Reagan speeches, 200 photographs, as well as biographical materials. It's a must have for any Reagan fan. Call 800-278-3245 for information. There's even an offer at the back of this book.)

"In the next few years, as more experts get involved, multimedia programs will achieve the full potential of their content," says Mitgang. That's why he believes that content may be gold today, but it will be platinum tomorrow.

Don't turn all the lights off. The area around the screen where the images will be projected must be dark. But you may be able to achieve enough darkness without turning off all the lights in the room. Test your options. See if you can leave the lights on in the back half of the room and still display your presentation effectively. You want to avoid having the audience sit in a completely darkened room if possible. (Because even a slick multimedia presentation won't automatically overcome a basic human instinct — the urge to sleep when it's dark.)

Do use a laser pointer. A laser pointer is like a tiny flashlight that emits a thin, red beam of light. It displays a bright, red dot on the surface of any object at which it's pointed. Marcia Lemmons of Andersen Consulting finds them useful for pointing out things during multimedia presentations. "It's dark up front where you're projecting the images," she explains. "And the speaker needs to stay by the podium to work the computer. So a regular pointer isn't very effective. A laser pointer solves those problems."

Cool Simple Stuff to Do

Want to get started fast? This section covers some things that are very easy to do. And they'll knock the socks off your audience (assuming that your audience wears socks).

A video or audio clip on command

Anyone who has never seen a multimedia presentation before will be amazed if you simply click on an audio or video that you've embedded under a word or image. Yes, that's as basic as it gets, but it's exciting when you see it for the first time. (Think of the first time you ever saw a hologram or an IMAX movie. It was a big deal.)

A testimonial from someone in your audience

Videotape or audiotape people from the organization that you'll be addressing. Then include the clip in your presentation. Nothing is more impressive to a group than suddenly seeing one of their own members pop up on the screen and talk about how great you are. Your credibility will rocket off the top of the chart.

A clip or image of something that just happened

One of the big advantages of multimedia is how rapidly you can change your presentation. Take advantage of this feature. It's easy to do.

"One time we videotaped someone making a major announcement in the morning at a trade show," recalls David Schmidt. "Nothing fancy. Just using a hand-held camcorder. Anyway, we edited it into the presentation that one of our vice presidents gave in the afternoon. The impact was incredible. Instead of saying, 'Remember that guy who announced all that stuff this morning,' the vice president said, 'Remember when that guy made an announcement this morning? Here's what he said.' Then he clicked on the video clip and *showed* the guy making the announcement. The audience was dazzled."

You can do the same thing. If you're speaking at some event, get there early, record people on audio or video, and work them into your presentation. Even a simple photograph can be impressive. Suppose that you will talk at a local service club function. Get there a few hours early and take a photo of one of the leading members showing off his new hat. Get it developed at some one-hour photo place, and scan it into your computer. When you give the presentation, up comes a picture of Joe Blow in his new hat. Obviously it was taken only hours ago. The audience will be amazed.

So here's the rule of thumb, courtesy of Jackie Roach: the more current, the better. "A clip that's a few hours old is more impressive than a clip that's a few days old," she observes. "And if you can get one that's a few minutes old — you'll blow them away."

A customized effect

The speed with which you can change a multimedia presentation creates one of its other big advantages — it's easy to customize. Put in as many images and audio and video files related to the audience as you can. Are you talking to car dealers? Scan in some pictures of cars.

Here's a great tip from Jackie Roach: Business cards are a great source of customization. "Get a business card from someone in the company that you'll be addressing and scan in his company's logo," she advises. "Then you can make it appear in the corner of every screen with your own logo. Customize as much as possible."

Multimedia is still in its infancy — that's why it's a great time to take advantage of it. When radio was first invented, people were excited to hear voices coming out of a box. No one cared what they said. The same was true for early television. Not any more. Today's radio and TV audiences are far more discerning. (That's why so many shows go off the air so quickly.)

Multimedia is now at the stage where radio and TV were when they were first invented. People are excited just to experience a multimedia presentation. That will change over the next several years as audiences come to expect more sophisticated content. But for now, you can do almost anything and look good. So what are you waiting for?

Chapter 13
Practice Makes Perfect

* *

* *

A tourist stops a police officer on the street in New York City. The tourist asks, "How do you get to Carnegie Hall?" The officer says, "Practice. Practice. Practice."

That joke is older than the leftovers wrapped in a little ball of tinfoil on the bottom shelf of my refrigerator and so is the advice it contains. But you know what? Its message is true. There are no magic shortcuts. If you want to give a successful presentation, you've got to practice. The real issue is *practice what*?

Memory, Script, or Notes

It was Sunday afternoon, and the new minister was talking to the local judge. The new minister asked, "What did you think of my first sermon?" The judge said, "Well, there were only three things wrong with it. First, you read it. Second, you didn't read it well. And third, it wasn't worth reading anyway." (Hey judge, don't candy-coat it. Tell us what you *really* think.)

The judge may need a course in diplomacy, but he does raise an important issue — should you deliver your presentation from a script, from notes, or from memory? The judge's comments reflect the traditional thinking. Reading a speech word for word is considered an option to avoid at all costs. The case against reading a prepared text can be summarized as follows: maintaining eye contact with the audience is difficult; you don't "connect" with the audience; and the speech sounds stilted (it *sounds* like you're reading it).

Memorizing a speech word for word receives similar criticisms. Even though you can establish eye contact with the audience, you still don't really connect. You're still "reading" the talk, but now the script is in your head. In contrast, becoming thoroughly familiar with your talk (memorizing it in general, but not word for word) receives high praise. An audience is always impressed by someone who gives a polished presentation without using notes. The reason for the audience's favorable attitude is that the audience recognizes memorization's most significant drawback — *you can forget what you were going to say*. Making a presentation without a script or notes is like walking the high wire without a net. The audience will applaud generously if you can do this trick (but many people can't do it).

And that leaves notes. Using notes is the overwhelmingly preferred method of delivering a presentation. You have something to refresh your memory, but you don't get tied into a word-for-word reading that creates a barrier between you and your audience. (At least that's the theory.) Of course, the results all depend on how you structure your notes and how detailed you make them — two major areas of dispute.

In this section, you can examine all of these methods, look at their pros and cons, and decide which techniques may work best for you.

Memorizing

It's been said that an elephant never forgets. Of course, an elephant doesn't have much to remember. That's not the case if you're making a major presentation. Here are some factors to consider in deciding whether to go the memorization route:

The entire presentation

Memorizing an entire presentation word for word isn't an option for most people. The process is extremely time-consuming. Unless you have a photographic memory, memorizing an entire presentation is not worth the effort. And unless you're a professional actor, a memorized presentation usually comes across as stiff and stilted. You don't connect with the audience. So leave this choice to the professionals.

The introduction and conclusion

An exception to the general rule against memorizing involves the introduction and conclusion. Many speakers commit these two sections of the presentation to memory — especially the introduction. Why? Because the beginning and ending are the most important parts of your talk. They're the two times when you have the most impact on your audience. They're also the most likely spots for you to get nervous and forget exactly what you were going to say.

Even more important, the introduction sets the whole tone for your presentation. Memorizing the introduction allows you to look at the audience and begin with a commanding presence. If you get off to a strong start, the audience will forgive a lot of transgressions. If you flub the opening, you may never get the audience back. Even if you're using notes or a script, memorizing the first few lines of the introduction pays off.

The key jokes and anecdotes

Are you using jokes or funny anecdotes? This type of material depends on exact wording, so memorize it word for word. The only thing worse than saying a joke or funny story incorrectly is reading it.

The main points

Memorizing the basic points of your talk also makes sense. This technique frees you to look up from your notes and talk directly to the audience. Actor and comedian Chuck McCann suggests breaking your speech into basic subparts and memorizing their order. "You don't memorize each paragraph," he explains. "You memorize each idea and the flow. That way you always know where you are in the presentation without looking at your notes."

Use it or lose it

If you do intend to memorize a large amount of material, then you need to keep your memory in shape. Keeping your memory in shape is like going to the gym every day. You have to exercise. Professional actors routinely confront this problem because of their unique work schedules. "I might do voice-overs for a month where I can just read from a script," says Chuck McCann. "Then suddenly I'll get an on-camera TV show. They'll hand me a 72-page script to memorize. If you're not used to memorizing, it's a shock. And if you haven't kept in practice, you get rusty." Chuck keeps his memory in shape by memorizing famous speeches, but you can memorize whatever you want — as long as you keep memorizing something. As Chuck explains, "If you don't use it, you lose it."

Working from a script

Although the gurus are unanimous in advising against speaking from a script, sometimes doing so is unavoidable. Are you speaking at a trade show or convention where the text of your speech is released in advance? Are you giving Congressional testimony? Are you holding a press conference? These types of situations require a script.

Such situations may not come up very often, but you need to be prepared for them if they do.

Preparing a script for reading

Here are a few dos and don'ts:

Do use stiff paper. You don't want the pages to rip and wrinkle when you touch them. To eliminate this problem, use 60-pound paper. (Sixty-pound paper is *not* as heavy as it sounds. You can run this weight of paper through a laser printer or copy machine without any trouble.)

Do use a large font size that's easy to read from a distance. If you've got access to a computer, you've got many choices. Whatever you pick, write the words in upper *and* lower case. The words are easier to read that way. Make the font large enough so that you can read the words while the script is on the podium and your head is raised. (It's bad enough that you're reading this script. Don't compound the problem by keeping your nose stuck in the script.) If you're limited to a typewriter, use the largest typeface available and make the words all uppercase.

Do use a great deal of white space in the page layout. Double space sentences and triple space paragraphs to make them easy to read. Leave wide margins at the top and sides of the page so that you have room to write notes. Leave the bottom quarter of the page blank. These steps help ensure that you don't drop your head too much while reading. (The audience wants to see your face, not the top of your head.)

Don't split a thought at the end of a line or page. Are you using a statistic? Are you using a hyphenated word or phrase? Are you using someone's name? Keep each of these items on a single line. If you split them between lines, you increase the chance of saying them incorrectly. Similarly, end each page with a complete sentence. If part of a sentence carries over to the next page, you have to pause as you turn the page. Such pauses sound awkward — as if you forgot what you were talking about in the middle of your thought.

Do use only one side of the paper. There's one exception. If you can fit your entire presentation on a single piece of paper by using both sides of the sheet, then do it.

Do highlight the script to aid your delivery. Write tough-to-pronounce words out phonetically. Put in marks where you want to pause for emphasis. Mark in any other special instructions or reminders. (I mark in the points where I'm going to show a slide.)

Don't highlight the script too much. If you mark the script up too much, you'll get confused. The marks will lose their meaning through overuse, and they won't stand out. (Highlighting too much is typical of college students who use yellow markers to highlight almost every sentence in a textbook. What's the important stuff? Anything that *isn't* yellowed in?) Which reminds me, if you're color coding your script, don't use more than a couple of colors. You don't want your script to be somewhere over the rainbow (unless you're Dorothy giving a speech in Oz).

And here's some uncommon knowledge. If you use only one color to highlight your script, try pink rather than yellow. Why? Pink is much easier on your eyes because it doesn't glare as much as yellow. (I made the switch years ago. Pink is definitely better.)

Do number each page. The top-right corner is a popular location. (When I ghostwrite speeches, I often put the number in the top center of the page. But hey, I'm just being wild and crazy when I do that.)

Don't staple the pages together. Doing so makes the pages difficult to separate while you're reading. You don't want to have to fold each page back. You want to slide the top one off the pile to reveal the next one. (Also, if you're a klutz and cut yourself on the staple, you may bleed all over the script.)

Do bring a spare copy. You're using a script because you haven't memorized the speech. If something happens to your only copy — it gets lost, it gets stolen, someone mistakes it for a napkin — you're in trouble. So you know what? Bring two extra copies.

Tips for reading a scripted speech

The trick to reading a scripted speech is to seem as though you're *not* reading it. That means making eye contact. The more you can free your eyes from the page and look at the audience, the better. (Of course, that's a great deal easier said than done.)

Start by becoming so familiar with your script that you don't have to look at every word you say. This familiarity allows you to deliver the talk in a more conversational style. Yes, you're still reading the script, but not as much. And make sure that you practice reading the script aloud. (Contrast the way you sound reading a script aloud for the first time with the way you sound reading it aloud for the third or fourth time. You sound smoother. You are more familiar with the words. You can concentrate a little more on the audience. That's the difference I'm talking about.)

Keep the sentences in the script as short as possible and look up at the audience at the end of each one. "The shorter the sentences, the more you end up looking at the audience," explains communication coach Alan Weiner. He recommends looking up at the audience as you say the last three or four words of a sentence and then holding your gaze for a second. "The worst thing you can do is look down for the next line just a little too soon," he cautions. "That trivializes the sentence that you've just said."

Why? Because looking is a form of nonverbal communication. Looking *up* at the end of a thought and holding your gaze suggests that the thought is important. Looking *down* suggests just the opposite.

One more item, though obvious, needs to be mentioned. If you're reading from a script, make sure that you have a podium or a lectern. These aids raise the script closer to your eyes. If the script is simply placed on a table, you have to bend over to read the script or pick it up. Neither choice is desirable. Both draw attention to the script when you're trying to make your presentation seem as if you're not reading one. (Finding yourself without a lectern isn't uncommon. If this situation happens to you, improvise. You may be amazed at what you can turn into a lectern. I've used everything from cardboard boxes to small trash cans. Fortunately, good advance planning usually eliminates this problem. See Chapter 14 for more information about adapting to different settings and equipment.)

Notes

Winston Churchill was once asked why he had notes during a speech but seldom looked at them. He said, "I carry fire insurance, but I don't expect my house to burn down." Churchill's reply illustrates the main advantage of using notes — they're an insurance policy against the fickleness of memory. If your mind goes blank, you've got your notes.

Another big advantage is flexibility. When you're not locked into a word-for-word script (either read or memorized), you can adapt quickly to audience reaction. You can add. You can cut. You can connect. Notes also allow you to maintain eye contact with the audience and speak in a conversational style while providing a basic structure for your message. In other words, notes strike a nice balance between memorizing a speech and reading it from a script.

When notes are properly executed, they provide an outline of your talk. Notes remind you of the points that you want to make and the order in which you want to make them. Notes don't spell out the points word for word — they just cue you to talk about those points. That's why you can "connect" with the audience: you're *talking* to them rather than *reciting* to them. What about items such as quotes and statistics that must be worded in a precise way? No problem. Write such items out word for word in your notes. Nothing is wrong with reading them to the audience.

What's the best form for notes?

You can prepare presentation notes in many different ways. No one right way or wrong way to prepare such notes exists. Whatever works best for you is the best solution. Here are some common methods that you may want to consider:

Roman-numeral outlines. Notes are very easy to prepare if you use a traditional, Roman-numeral outline to develop your talk. Just take that outline and use it as your notes. Even if you develop your speech by other methods, you can still take the finished talk and reduce it to a Roman-numeral outline. This type of outline ensures that your notes will always tell you where you are and what you're supposed to talk about. The downside is that such an outline can have a very cluttered appearance, making the outline more difficult to understand at a glance.

Key words. Some speakers just write a series of key words as their notes. In theory, this technique allows these speakers to glance quickly at their notes and see what they're supposed to be saying, so it minimizes the time that they spend looking away from the audience. But as Chuck Reid has observed, "In theory, there's no difference between theory and practice. In practice, there is." In the case of key words, the theory can be derailed by faulty memory. If you forget what ideas the key words represent, you're in trouble. So in practice, you may end up staring at your notes praying that you'll remember what the key words mean.

Key sentences. Some speakers write out key sentences. This practice overcomes the problem of forgetting what a key word represents, but it encourages the speaker to read from the notes like a script, which is its main disadvantage. The whole reason you want to use notes is so you *don't* disconnect from the audience by reading. Another disadvantage of key sentences is that they make the notes more cluttered and difficult to view quickly, so they cut down on eye contact with the audience.

All of the above. You can mix and match the various methods. That's what I do. I begin with a Roman-numeral outline as the skeleton of my notes. Then I insert key words and key sentences where I want them. I also write out jokes almost word for word — especially the punch lines. (Yes, I memorize the jokes, but I like to know that they're available if my memory fails. I won't reduce a joke to key words until I know it cold.) Experiment. Try various ways of making notes to find a method that works for you.

Paper vs. cards

Should you put your notes on sheets of paper or index cards? Many speakers favor index cards. Index cards don't make crinkly noises into the microphone or blow off the podium. And if you're nervous, index cards don't highlight the fact that your hands are shaking. Sheets of paper have all of these drawbacks. On the other hand, you can put many more notes on a sheet of paper than on an index card, so you don't need as many sheets of paper as you need index cards.

Which of the two should you choose? Whatever makes you feel comfortable. I use sheets of paper in a ring binder. It makes me feel professorial and gets me in the mood to lecture. But it does tie my notes to the podium. Index cards are much more transportable; you can keep them in your pocket (a tough trick with a ring binder).

Putting your notes on cards

Index cards are probably the most popular format for notes. Index cards are easy to handle, they're easy to carry in your pocket, and (if organized properly) they make it easy for you to restructure a speech in a hurry. (You just shuffle the deck.) The following are some dos and don'ts for putting your notes on cards:

Do pick a card size and orientation that you like. Should the index cards be 3×5 inches, 5×7 inches, or 5×8 inches? Should you use them vertically or horizontally? The gurus disagree, and I don't think that the direction in which you use index cards is a big deal. Do whatever you like. Just make sure that the cards are white and unlined so that they're easy to read.

Do use one side of the card. The exception is if you can fit all your notes for an entire presentation on both sides of a single card.

Do number each card. If you drop them, at least you'll be able to put them back in order.

Do code your cards for cutting. Mark your cards so that you can easily shorten your presentation as you deliver it. (Running low on time is quite common. The audience may react longer and more often than you had anticipated. You may decide to emphasize certain points more than you had planned. Or your allotted time may be reduced before you even begin speaking.) You can mark certain cards or sections of cards as nonessential. For example, anything written in dark blue is important, but anything written in light blue can be cut.

Don't go berserk with highlighting. If you use a color system to highlight your notes, don't go wild. If you use too many colors, you may forget what they mean.

Do lay out each card for easy reading. Leave lots of white space and make sure that your writing is large enough to read under actual speech conditions. That means that your cards should be readable if you have too little light (a common problem) or too much light (for example, if a spotlight is on you or you're speaking outside on a sunny day). And make sure that you can read the card at the distance that you'll hold it when you actually give your presentation.

Don't overload the cards. Some speakers put only one idea per card. (Of course, if you have an information-packed presentation, you may get a hernia carrying your cards.) That's a bit extreme. I say use your judgment. If you have a long quote that you'll say word for word, that alone may take up a single card. If you have three points that you can write in a few key words, that can go on a single card. If in doubt, err on the side of more cards with less information on each one.

Don't use abbreviations that you may forget. In the desire to reduce the number of cards, getting carried away devising key words and abbreviations is easy. Don't take chances. Use abbreviations with which you're familiar. Use a key phrase rather than a key word if you think that you may forget what the word represents.

Tips for reading from notes

Don't pretend that you have no notes. You don't want to draw undue attention to your notes, but acting as if you don't have any notes is silly. Yes, audiences are impressed by speakers who can deliver a great speech without notes, but audiences know that most people can't do that. (Most people can give a really *bad* speech without notes.) So the notes provide a certain level of reassurance. They show the audience that at least you've prepared.

Do begin without looking at your notes. It gets you off to a much stronger start. You look at the audience and take command.

Do be familiar with your notes. The first time you speak from your notes shouldn't be when you make your presentation. Your unfamiliarity with the notes will show. Rehearse with your notes so that you don't have to read them intently.

Don't keep your nose in your notes. If you're just going to read your notes, you may as well have a script.

Do read quotes and statistics. The audience will appreciate your effort to get this type of material exactly right. Reading also makes the quote or statistic more credible because the audience knows that you're not relying on the vagaries of memory.

And here's some uncommon knowledge. If the audience sees you read a quote from your notes, it justifies why you have the notes. (You don't need your notes for your outline. You just need them to get the quote correct.)

Don't play with your notes. Playing with your notes just tells the audience that you're nervous or neurotic, and it increases the chances that you may drop them (the notes, not the audience).

Do remove each note card from the pack after you use it. Many people who use note cards hold them in a pack and move the top card to the bottom as they finish with it. Here's a great suggestion from San Francisco comedy coach John Cantu: As you finish with each card, remove it from the pack. Put it in your pocket or anywhere else. Then if you drop the cards, your problem isn't as big. For example, if you were speaking from a pack of twenty cards and dropped them halfway through your talk, you'd only have to pick up and reorder ten cards rather than twenty.

Using overheads or slides as notes

Are you giving a presentation using slides or overheads? The material they contain may be all the notes you need. As the bullet points guide your audience through your talk, they can guide you as well.

Joe DiNucci, Vice President, Manufacturing Industries at Silicon Graphics, proved this point to a speaker by taking the text of his speech away. "The CEO of one of our customers was scheduled to speak in my marketing road show," Joe recalls. "In our first rehearsal, he had a prepared speech. It was terrible because he read it." During the second rehearsal, Joe grabbed the CEO's script as he went to the podium. Then Joe told him to look at the points on his slides and talk about them. "Once he stopped insisting he couldn't do it and started to talk, he gave an instantly better speech," says Joe.

But don't let the tail wag the dog. Slides and overheads shouldn't be designed for the purpose of replacing your notes. Their purpose is to visually support your message. (See Chapter 11.) And even when they also function perfectly as notes, you should still bring along a real set of notes. Why? Two reasons. First, you need a real set of notes as a backup in case the audiovisual equipment fails. (The only thing that sounds lamer than "the dog ate my notes" is "the slide projector ate my notes.") Second, you need the notes for material that must be worded in a very exact way such as jokes, quotes, and statistics. This material doesn't usually appear, word for word, on your slides or overheads.

Rehearsal Tips from the Pros

A man who studied opera for many years was finally invited to sing at the La Scala opera house in Milan — the pinnacle of the opera world. In his debut, he sang the beautiful aria "Vesti la Giubba" from the opera *Pagliacci*. When he finished, the applause was so thunderous that he had to do an encore. And then another. And then six more. Finally, he motioned for quiet. He said, "I've now sung 'Vesti la Giubba' nine times. My voice is gone. I can't sing it again." And a voice from the balcony said, "You'll sing it till you get it right!"

There's no doubt that, whether singing an aria or delivering a speech, repetition is the key to success in mastering any skill. But how much is too much? And what's the best way to go about rehearsing? Rehearsal is probably the most neglected area of speech-making. People run out of time. They think that rehearsing is unnecessary. They ignore it, and they pay the consequences.

How much should you rehearse?

This question evokes a split opinion from the gurus. Some authorities say that you can rehearse too much; others say that you can't rehearse enough. The divide centers around the issues of spontaneity and memorization.

Those authorities who say that you can over-practice recommend rehearsing a maximum of six times. They claim that any additional rehearsals cause the talk to become memorized. This over-rehearsal results in a decrease of spontaneity, and the talk sounds stilted.

Tell it 27 times to 27 different people

Allatia Harris, Dean of the Communication Division at Mountain View College, subscribes to the theory that you can't rehearse too much. She says that every time you practice a presentation, you become more familiar with it and you improve it. This lesson was brought home to her very dramatically after a hitchhiker fired a gun at one of her colleagues.

"It was a Thursday afternoon when the incident occurred," she recalls. "By the time he got to school to teach his Thursday night class, he had already told the police, his wife, and his kids. Then he told his class and a couple of other instructors. I didn't see him till Friday morning — that's when he told me. As we walked down the hall, he told a few other professors. Then we went to a class that we were team teaching. He told the class. After the class, he told someone else."

"At that point he'd told the story about eleven times," she notes. "I heard him tell it five times. Each time he told it, he paid attention to his listener's response. And each time the story got a little bit smoother. He was subconsciously editing the story every time he told it. Parts of the story stayed the same as he learned what listeners liked. Parts of the story changed as he learned what they didn't understand. By the end of the day, he had that story down — the timing and everything. He knew what worked and what would get his desired response."

The you-can't-rehearse-enough people disagree. They recommend rehearsing until you have your presentation down pat. They say that the spontaneity issue is a fallacy. "Yes, if you rehearse less, you may be more spontaneous," notes communications expert Jim Lukaszweski. "That's the problem! You may be remembered for your spontaneity, *not* what you said." (That's Jim's polite way of saying that you may be remembered for screwing up your talk because you didn't rehearse enough.) And there's no guarantee that you'll be spontaneous even if you don't rehearse. "It depends on how spontaneous you are to begin with," explains actor and comedian Chuck McCann. "If you're a dull person, there's no spontaneity to lose. It's like a match without a head."

Both of them also observe that the more you practice something, the better you get at it. "The thing that makes any professional good — athlete, speaker, anyone — is the willingness to do things again and again until you get it up to a professional level," says Jim. "And the secret of rehearsal is each time you say your presentation, you improve it. You find what works and doesn't work and you fix it." I agree.

Should you record yourself rehearsing?

Many professional speech coaches make a big deal out of recording their students rehearsing presentations. Do you need to record yourself practicing? Here are some thoughts on the subject:

Videotaping

If you have the time and equipment, videotape yourself. Reviewing the results can be a real eye-opener if you've never seen yourself on video before. But don't sweat the small stuff. If your hair is out of place or your clothes look wrinkled, those problems are easy to remedy. Concentrate on your message and delivery. Ask yourself the following:

- ✔ Am I speaking too slow or too fast?
- ✔ Am I speaking loud enough?
- ✔ Do I have any annoying nonverbal habits (hair pulling, coin jingling, and the like)?
- ✔ Do parts need to be rewritten to sound more conversational?
- ✔ Do I look animated and enthusiastic about my message?

Here's some uncommon knowledge from Allatia Harris, Dean of the Communications Division at Mountain View College. She recommends *not* videotaping yourself if you don't have much time until your presentation. "Some people get very depressed the first time they see themselves on videotape," she explains. "They need enough time to adjust and rebuild their confidence before they stand in front of an audience." Her recommendation: videotape yourself, but not at the last minute.

Audiotaping

If you don't videotape yourself, you should at least rehearse with a tape recorder. As with videotaping, you want to time your presentation, find out what words and phrases need to be changed, and check the rate, volume, and emphasis of your voice.

How should you rehearse?

Want to use your rehearsal time to maximum advantage? Here are some ideas for practicing your presentation profitably:

Rehearse out loud

The only way that you can tell how your presentation will sound is to listen to it. *That means that you have to say it out loud.* Listening to the voice in your head doesn't count — that's not the voice that your audience will hear. As management communications advisor Jim Lukaszweski points out, most of us have two voices — an outer voice and an inner voice. Our outer voice is the one that other people can hear. Our inner voice is the one in our head that coaches us.

"When you rehearse with your inner voice, it never makes a mistake, never mispronounces a word, always gets the stories and punch lines right, and it remembers everything," he explains. "The problem is you give your speech with your outer voice. So sitting down and reading intensely isn't a rehearsal — it doesn't help you. You've got to rehearse out loud."

Get an audience

Phase one: When you first begin developing your presentation, you can use yourself as an audience. As you create different parts of the talk, say them aloud. You may be able to detect problems and make changes. But this technique only goes so far. At some point you need an audience other than yourself.

Phase two: Practice *parts* of your presentation on a friend. Your goal is to polish each part — story, example, argument — into its best form. As you practice saying the words to a friend, you can get a sense of what works and what doesn't, and your friend can point out anything that's unclear. You can also become thoroughly familiar with each part.

Do this process over the telephone. Then your friend won't be distracted by your gestures and body language. In this phase, you want the focus to be totally on your words and voice.

Phase three: Talk through your entire presentation to a friend or colleague — three or four times. (Your audience doesn't have to be the same person each time. Audience duty does get old fast.) This process is still informal. You're just trying to familiarize yourself with the talk and work the bugs out.

Phase four: This phase is the dress rehearsal. Gather a small group of friends and do the presentation as if you're doing the real thing.

Simulate real conditions

The more closely you can simulate actual speaking conditions in your rehearsals, the better prepared you can be for the actual event. Use the actual notes that you'll use when you speak. Use the actual clothes that you'll wear. (At least wear them in your dress rehearsal. That's why dress rehearsals are called dress rehearsals.) Will you be using a handheld microphone for your talk? Most people don't have a sound system at home for rehearsal purposes. Don't worry. Here's a tip from comedy coach John Cantu: When you practice at home, use a hairbrush to simulate the microphone. The average hairbrush is about the same length as the average handheld mike.

Find someone to give you feedback

Writer Franklin P. Jones once said, "Honest criticism is hard to take, particularly from a relative, a friend, an acquaintance, or a stranger." He had a point. But if you really want to improve your presentation, you need some objective feedback. (Watching a videotape of yourself doesn't count.) You need someone who can give you honest feedback *and whose opinion you respect.*

How do you find such a person? John Cantu suggests listening to the feedback that your colleagues and acquaintances give to *other* people. Does a certain colleague or acquaintance see things from your perspective? Do you agree with that person's feedback? Do you agree with the advice that he or she gives? If the answers are affirmative, ask that person to listen to you rehearse your talk — and give you advice.

Don't use a mirror

One of the clichés of speech rehearsal is that you should practice in front of a mirror. This is another area where the experts disagree. The pro-mirror people say that practicing in front of a mirror helps you monitor your body language. The anti-mirror people say that practicing in front of a mirror is a distraction — you concentrate so much on your body language that you pay too little attention to what you're actually saying. Or as Chuck McCann observes, "Some people *shouldn't* see what they look like!"

I side with the anti-mirror people. Using a mirror is very unnatural. How many people look at themselves while they're talking? (Other than the evil queen from *Snow White*, I can't think of any, and she was really talking to the mirror.)

Time it

Time your talk. Do it while you're rehearsing in front of an audience. (Audience reactions can affect the length of your talk.) Everyone knows that you should time your entire presentation. Timing your presentation is the only way to determine whether your talk will fit its assigned time slot.

You should also time each major component of your talk — key examples, anecdotes, arguments. Then if you need to make cuts during your presentation, you can factor the length of various segments into your decision.

Part III
Delivering Your Presentation

The 5th Wave   By Rich Tennant

In this part . . .

1 t's show time. In this part, you'll learn how to deliver a presentation that wows an audience. That means managing stage fright, setting up the room to your advantage, and handling any audience no matter how tough or wacky. You'll also discover how to convey messages using your voice and body, how to handle a microphone, how to deal with a podium, and how to produce commanding eye contact. These chapters also cover impromptu speaking, serving on a panel, and introducing other presenters.

Chapter 14

Getting the Room Right

● ●

In This Chapter

▶ Arranging the room to your benefit

▶ Anticipating equipment problems

▶ Eliminating distractions

▶ Four reasons to arrive early

▶ Taking control of the set-up

● ●

*Y*ou prepare a fantastic presentation. You rehearse. You rehearse some more. You run it by your colleagues. Everyone says it's pure genius. Can't miss. You're going to be great. The big day arrives and you're psyched. You take your incredibly cool slides and go to the site of your soon-to-be-widely-acclaimed performance. You enter the room and you wish you were dead. The ceiling is too low for the screen you need for your slides. There's no slide projector anyway. And a tap dance festival is being held in the courtyard adjacent to your room.

Never take the room for granted. It can make or break your presentation. The world's most informative and entertaining talk can become torture in a bad room. If it's hot and stuffy, people go to sleep. If the sound system squeals with ear-splitting feedback, they get a headache. It doesn't matter what you say if everyone just wants to get out of there.

Always check the room before you speak. Several days ahead of time is preferable. If you can't do it in person, send someone you trust — a lot. At a minimum, pump your contact — the person who arranged for you to speak — for information and details. You want to know everything there is to know about the room. It will affect how you plan your presentation. And on the day of your talk, get to the room at least one hour before you're scheduled to begin. That leaves enough time to correct any mistakes and still get mentally prepared.

Seating Arrangements

One of the most important aspects of the room where you speak is the seating arrangement. It affects your entire relationship with the audience. Done correctly, they will sing your praises. Done incorrectly, they'll tell you to . . . sit on it.

The basics

When it comes to seating, three basic considerations apply to any type of presentation in any type of setting. First and most important, can everyone see you? Second, is the seating comfortable — both physically and psychologically? Third, is the arrangement of chairs suited to the size of the room, the size of the audience, and the purpose of your presentation?

In considering these factors, start with the room. Will you be in a banquet room? A conference room? A large meeting room? An auditorium? The room establishes the parameters for seating. Next, will the audience be seated at tables? If so, will they be round tables or rectangular tables? Once you have this information, you can arrange the seating pieces like a jigsaw puzzle until you get the picture you want.

Within the boundaries established by the room and furniture, you can arrange seating based on the size of the room and your purpose. Chairs arranged in a semi-circle provide a more informal atmosphere. This arrangement puts you directly in front of each audience member. It also allows all the audience members to see each other. If the audience is more than 30 people, the group is probably too large for a single semi-circle. In that case, you can stagger a second row of chairs behind the first row. Now you have a double semi-circle where the second row looks between the shoulders of the people in the first row. For large groups, or a more formal atmosphere, classroom style seating in rows is recommended.

If you're speaking at a breakfast, lunch, or dinner meeting, the audience will probably be seated at round tables, which means that half of them will have their backs to you when you begin to speak. Factor this in when you begin your presentation. Leave time for them to turn their seats around to face you, or solve the problem through seating. If the tables seat eight, then place only four chairs and four settings at each table — facing your podium. Alright, maybe you don't have that much control over the seating, but it doesn't hurt to ask.

The psychology of seating

Why should you care how the seats are arranged? Because there's a whole psychology to seating, and it can have a tremendous effect on how your audience perceives your presentation. (Maybe that's why psychiatrists make patients lie down on a couch.)

Think of the optical illusions you've seen in a college psychology class or in kindergarten. The teacher shows a small white square and a big white square, each containing a black dot. The dot looks bigger in the small square and smaller in the big square. But, surprise, the dots are really the same size. How you perceive the dots is affected by the space around them.

The same psychological principles apply to seating. We perceive audience size *not* by the actual number of people in the audience but by the number of empty chairs.

If there are 25 people in a room with 50 chairs, both you and your audience will perceive a small crowd. In contrast, if you set out 15 chairs and add 10 more as people arrive, everyone perceives a bigger turnout.

Why does this matter? Because the first situation — 25 people in a room of 50 chairs — is a horrible setting for making a presentation. Everyone wonders why more people didn't show up. Your audience thinks that maybe they made a mistake in coming — which is a major strike against you before you even begin to speak. Even worse, you have to deal with the "energy" problem. When people are scattered throughout a room, you won't receive as strong a response as when they're seated together. You will feel much less energy coming from the audience. Twenty five people sitting together and laughing sound a lot louder than 25 people scattered through the room.

The rule of thumb is the more densely packed the audience (in terms of seating, not intelligence), the better. When the audience is seated together, it makes them feel more like a group. It also makes it easier for you to maintain eye contact with them. Most important, it maximizes the energy of their response, and that energy is vital to your success.

How to get the seating the way you want it

Here's the secret to getting the audience placed to your liking: arrange the seating *before* they arrive. (Alright, so it's not such a big secret, but it's amazing how many people ignore this simple truth.) Once the audience shows up, it's too late to mess with the seats. That's just human nature. People hate being told to move after they've plopped their fannies into the chairs. It's like there's some mysterious bonding between the butt and the bench.

If you've ever been at a presentation where the crowd was smaller than expected, you know what I mean. Everyone is sitting toward the back of the room. The speaker is up on the stage gazing out over row after row of empty chairs. It's like the tide is out, and the speaker is waiting for a wave to send the audience crashing back to the front of the room. Of course, no wave is coming. So the speaker utters those dreaded words, "C'mon, there's lots of room up front. Why doesn't everyone move up? C'mon now, don't be shy." Lame. Lame. Lame. The speaker sounds lame — weak and begging. Even worse, no one moves. Would you?

How can you avoid the empty seat syndrome if the audience is smaller than anticipated? There are several ways to handle this problem. One technique that most people never consider is to monitor attendance. Call your contact a day or two before your presentation and find out how many people have registered, responded, or otherwise indicated that they'll show up. If the number is a lot smaller than you expected, get busy. Ask your contact about moving your presentation to a smaller room. Or seat people at rows of tables instead of just rows of chairs. Or set the room up banquet style with people seated at circular tables — even if no food is being served. The point is that you have lots of ways to arrange the seating to your advantage — if you know the size of the group in advance.

The first line of defense for a small crowd is to remove chairs. That lowers the odds of having empty seats. One friend of mine removes chairs even if he expects a large crowd. He likes to create excitement and energy by opening up chairs as people arrive. If he's expecting 100 people, he sets out 50 chairs. When the 51st person arrives, he makes a big deal out of opening up more chairs. It lends an air of importance to the event, the atmosphere of a sellout crowd.

What if you have no way of knowing the audience size in advance? Or you have to speak in a large auditorium no matter how few people show up? Don't worry. Here's what to do. Let's say the room is set for 100 people — ten rows of chairs with ten chairs to a row. Put masking tape along the edge of the chairs on both aisles — from the back row to the second row, leaving only the front row open. After people fill up the front row, pull the tape off the second row. You get the idea. This technique allows you to fill the rows from front to back.

The tape has tremendous psychological power. People won't break it. Early arrivals who don't want to sit in the front row may congregate outside the room or take a walk and come back later. But they won't break the tape to sit where they really want to — in the back. (For added insurance, use yellow tape that says "Crime Scene — Do Not Cross.")

An additional benefit of the tape technique involves late comers — those annoying audience members who can't show up on time. By placing the empty seats in the back, the tape technique gives latecomers a place to sit down without distracting you and the rest of the audience. They don't have to make the long trek to the front of the room — stepping on toes, banging into things, excusing themselves — while you're telling your best story.

What happens if the unthinkable occurs? Someone goofs up. You're facing a bunch of empty rows and everyone is sitting in the back. Don't panic, and don't ask the audience to move up! (They won't.) *Instead, you can move down.* Again, it doesn't take a rocket scientist to figure this out, but I can't tell you how many times I've seen speakers who won't make this adjustment. You can't just give your speech like there are 100 people filling the room if there are only 20 people in the two back rows. Adjust. Be flexible. Get off the stage and onto the floor level. Pick up your podium and move it with you. Clear away a few chairs so you can get even closer to your audience. If they're in the last two rows, go back there and stand right in front of them. And then give your speech.

The most important thing to remember is that seating arrangements aren't set in cement, and neither are the seats. Don't be afraid to move things around. Ask your contact for help.

Equipment Considerations: Testing, One, Two, Four

The communications revolution has taken us a long way from our cave-dwelling ancestors who, when giving a speech, would merely stand erect (a big deal at the time) and emit some Tarzan-like howls. Today, you need lots of equipment: microphones, slide projectors, sound systems, podiums. And you've got to be sure the equipment works. Murphy said everything that can go wrong will go wrong. Lincoln said you can't fool all of the people all of the time. Kushner says all the equipment that can go wrong will go wrong if it's set up by a fool.

One speech coming right up — hold the anchovies

Anyone who has ever made more than a handful of presentations has a "worst room" story. One of my favorites comes from San Francisco comedy coach John Cantu. He arranged for one of his clients to give a humorous talk at a college — specifically, in the pizza restaurant of the student union. Unfortunately, no one had thought to provide a separate sound system for the presenter. The college officials covered their mistake by patching the speaker's microphone into the room's regular sound system, which was used to announce diner's orders, and they didn't tell the speaker.

A crowd of students gathered as the time for the talk arrived. The speaker was introduced, took the mike and began. "I'm happy to be here tonight, in a college so well known for its. . . ." "TWO EXTRA LARGE VEGETARIANS," blared from the sound system, drowning out the speaker. And so it went for the rest of the performance. "The thing about students and sex is that everyone assumes that's all you think about. But we know that you spend a lot of time thinking about social issues, politics, and. . . ." "ALL MEAT COMBOS." "No matter how you slice it, you come up with. . . ." "ONE SLICE EXTRA GARLIC." "Thank you very much, you've been a great. . . ." "PEPPERONI."

The prime rule

Call me an ex-New Yorker. Call me paranoid. (But I repeat myself.) The prime rule when it comes to equipment of any sort is *trust no one but yourself*. You want a slide projector. You want a microphone. Then *you* take responsibility. Otherwise, you better be prepared to pass your slides around the audience as you yell your speech at them.

I've learned the hard way — through years of broken promises and broken equipment — don't trust anyone. The first corollary is this: always be prepared to do your presentation without equipment. And the second corollary: the person who screwed up your equipment request will not consider it a major problem.

Here's a great example: I gave a presentation to a group of lawyers who were holding a meeting in a restaurant in a small, remote town. If they didn't bring an overhead projector to the meeting, there was no way to get one from anywhere else in time, and my presentation was built around overheads. So in the weeks before the meeting, I told my contact about two million times that I absolutely had to have an overhead projector. He said, "No problem. I think I can borrow one from the courthouse." Naturally, when I showed up there was no overhead projector. Instead there was an *opaque* projector — a museum relic that only projects shadows of solid objects like rocks. (I wanted to put this guy's head on it.) My contact's response: "Well, everybody wants to hear what you have to say. You can just do your speech without overheads. It's OK." Yeah right, it's OK. The fact that the entire presentation was built around overheads was no big deal.

What can we learn from my experience? First, always be prepared to do your presentation without equipment. Second, never trust anyone else — especially when they say, "I think I can borrow...." Third, never trust a lawyer, period.

Six things you must always check

Everyone knows that you need to check all the equipment in advance and make sure everything is operating properly. So here's some uncommon knowledge: Make sure that *you* know how to operate the equipment; otherwise, you're begging for major embarrassment. There's nothing worse than having a technician approve a slide projector or microphone fit for use and later realize that you don't know how to turn them on. Believe me, I've done it. You lose a lot of credibility.

Here are six things you should always check before you begin your presentation:

Sound system

Is there a sound system and does it work? Make sure the volume is adjusted so that you can be heard by everyone in the room. *Test the microphone in the location where you'll actually use it.* I learned this lesson the hard way. Just before a speech to a group of Defense Department managers, I tested the microphone while standing in the front of the room. It worked fine. But I didn't go up behind the podium where I'd actually be speaking. Big mistake. When I started my speech, the microphone erupted in screeching feedback. Great way to begin, right? Turns out the culprit was a metal sprinkler nozzle in the ceiling over the podium.

Make sure that you know how to work the microphone. Do you know how to turn it on and off? If there's a microphone stand, do you know how to adjust it? Different microphones pick up and broadcast your voice in different ways. Play with the microphone until you get a good idea of its range.

Podium

Is there a podium or lectern? And is it the right size? The *right size* is whatever suits your purposes. Do you want the audience to see you? Then make sure you're taller than the podium or that there's a box you can stand on behind it. Are you afraid the audience will throw things? Get a podium that's high and wide. In either case, make sure that the podium has a light that's in good working order — especially if you're going to darken the room for slides. You'll never get the audience to see the light if the podium leaves your notes in the dark.

Audiovisual equipment

You can't check slide or overhead projectors too many times. After you get your slides or overheads focused, walk around the room while one is projecting on the screen. Can it be seen from everywhere in the room? Overhead projectors often block the view of people seated in line with them. If that's the case, try to project your overhead higher up the screen — closer to the ceiling. And definitely use a screen. It will show your slides or overheads much better than a wall. Many slide and overhead projectors come equipped with a spare bulb. Make sure you know where it is.

Lighting

Test the "house lights" to see if they work and how the light fills the room. Find out if you can adjust their level of brightness. If they're adjustable, take advantage of this feature — especially if you're using slides.

The common knowledge is that slides require you to turn the lights off.

Here's the uncommon knowledge: If your slides are easy to see, you can show them with the lights turned down but *not* off. A small amount of light makes a tremendous difference in your interaction with the audience. They can't go to sleep under the cover of darkness.

Human equipment

If people are operating equipment for you, make sure that they know what they're doing. You don't need an Einstein to work a slide projector, but it does require a minimal level of competence. Also, make sure that you know who to contact for help with minor and major catastrophes — a lightbulb burns out, a microphone breaks, or your podium is destroyed by a UFO.

Electricity

Where are the electrical outlets in the room? Are there enough of them for your equipment? Are they two-prong or three-prong? Do yourself a favor. Always bring an adapter and an extension cord. You'll be glad you did.

How to Eliminate Distractions

If a tree falls in the forest and nobody hears your speech because they're watching the tree, did your speech occur? I'm no philosopher, but I say, "Darn right it did." You put a lot of work into that speech. You wrote it. You went to the forest. You delivered it. But nobody paid attention because they were distracted by the tree. The speech occurred whether the audience heard it or not. What *didn't* occur was your recognition of the need to anticipate and eliminate distractions.

A room with a view

If you're speaking at a restaurant or hotel or office building, chances are there's a nice view out the window of the meeting room. That's bad news because you want audience attention focused on you, not the view. What can you do? First, try to speak in a room that has no windows. If that's not possible, make sure that the windows are covered with drapes or curtains. What if they have no curtains? Improvise. I've seen speakers hang tablecloths over the windows — anything to eliminate the competition of the view.

If you're forbidden from covering the windows, then you must bear the consequences. And they're not pleasant. The worst audience reaction I ever got was during a speech I gave on a boat traveling around the nighttime harbor in Long Beach, California — home of the Queen Mary. Every time the boat passed the brightly lit Queen Mary, every head in the audience jerked around to look out the window. But the biggest jerk was me for agreeing to speak in such a distracting setting.

The view from the audience

If you want to know what your speech will seem like to your audience, you need to view things from their perspective — literally. Go sit in a few different sections of the audience. The front. The back. The sides. How does it look? Is anything blocking your view? If you're using slides or overheads, can they be seen from every angle? Low hanging chandeliers often cut off the top part of these projections for people sitting in the back.

Ask someone to stand up front and play the role of speaker. That way you can spot any weird distractions. A friend of mine once gave a speech on a stage that had been decorated with large, fancy potted plants. Unfortunately, one of them was positioned directly behind him. It wasn't until he was done that someone mentioned that it looked like he had a tree growing out of his head. Hey, it's a jungle out there — but that kind of jungle you don't need.

Look carefully at the background. Is there a black curtain on stage behind you? Then don't wear dark clothes because you'll blend in with the curtain. Are there stained glass windows behind you? Then don't wear stained clothes. (Just kidding.) The point is to discover potential distractions and neutralize them. The best way to do it? If at all possible, go watch someone else give a speech in the room you'll be using. Sit in a back corner. Then you'll know exactly how the audience perceives things.

The view from the podium

It's not just the audience that gets distracted during a speech. So can you. That's why you need to get up on the stage, or wherever you'll be speaking, and look around the room. Is there anything that will bother you? Now is the time to take care of it. Is there a mirror on the back wall reflecting light in your face? Is there a neon sculpture? Is the old Elvis staring at you from a crushed velvet painting? Get rid of it.

Noise

One of the worst distractions for any speaker is noise. It provides direct competition with your message. It obliterates what you're saying. Even if you're revealing how to make a million dollars, cure cancer, or stop Sylvester Stallone from filming another comedy, you won't get attention if no one can hear you. Your mission is to discover and control all noise sources — both inside and outside the room.

The only good way to control noise from outside the room is to get a sound-proof room. No, you don't have to give your speech in some vault beneath the Pentagon. But you should inquire about the thickness of the room walls. If someone in an adjacent meeting room sneezes, is your audience going to say "Gesundheit?"

I once gave a continuing education seminar on the very sensitive subject of racial and sexual harassment. The seminar was held in your basic downtown-hotel meeting room. Naturally, I was trying to establish a mood commensurate with the subject matter — serious and no-nonsense. Unfortunately, the room next door contained a motivational meeting for some multilevel marketing scam. And these people were loud. They must have been applauding anything and everything. Every few seconds, their room would erupt in a thundering ovation that instantly passed through my room like a shock wave. There I was, asking rhetorical questions to set the tone for my lecture: "How many of you feel that it's appropriate to stare at an attractive coworker?" The response: a wild burst of applause from the next room.

What if the room isn't soundproof? Sometimes it doesn't matter. Here's the trick: Find out what events will occur in the rooms surrounding your room at the time you'll be speaking. If nothing else is going on, you're OK. If the Marching Band Society will be having its monthly meeting, a red flag should go up. Get another room if possible.

A more common problem for speakers is noise from within the room. Again, the physical construction of the room is a factor. Bare walls, floors, and ceilings create echoes and poor acoustics. Carpets, wallpaper, drapes, curtains, and other sound absorbers go a long way in solving this problem.

If you're speaking at a grazing function — a breakfast, lunch, or dinner — don't start your presentation until the waiters have cleared the tables. The clatter of dishes is an intolerable distraction. Unfortunately, due to "time problems," your contact may insist that you begin speaking before the meal is concluded. Here's what to do. Suggest that the waiters serve desert and disappear. They can clear the desert plates *after* you're finished speaking. You start talking as soon as the waiters leave the room. The noise of people eating desert while you're speaking is a drag, but it's a lot better than trying to speak with waiters running around the room.

Doors are another important consideration for eliminating room noise. How many doors does the room have and where are they? Try to avoid having doors located behind you. You don't need the audience watching people going in and out of the room as you're speaking. And people *will* go in and out: latecomers, early leavers, bathroom visitors, telephone junkies. There's lots of potential traffic. That's why your ideal room has the doors in the back and you in the front. If there are doors behind you, find out if they can be locked. This request may be refused because of fire hazard rules, but it doesn't hurt to ask. It also doesn't hurt to have your contact place someone at each door to ensure that people enter and exit quietly.

One other source of room noise is music. Many restaurants and hotel banquet rooms use background music to create an ambiance for diners. (If you call violin renditions of "The Girl from Ipanema" ambiance.) This is deadly for you as a speaker. You want the music turned off as soon as you hear it. Don't believe facility managers who say, "Oh, don't worry. We'll turn it off when everyone is done eating, just before you start to speak." Uh-huh. How many times have I heard that one? Also, make sure that when they turn off the music, they don't shut off the whole sound system; otherwise, your microphone will be useless.

The Stuff Everyone Forgets

They say an elephant never forgets. Unfortunately people do. Of course, people give better presentations than elephants. But if you crossed an elephant with a person, there are certain things it would always remember about public speaking. Communication is like a circus — the audience wants to be entertained. Always start in the center ring, and never let a clown interfere with your message.

Getting there

Do you know exactly where you're giving your presentation, how to get there, and how long it takes to get there? Well, find out. It's amazing how little consideration people give to these basic concerns. You knock yourself out preparing a killer talk, and then you blow it by going to the wrong ballroom. It's not enough to know the hotel. You need to know the *exact* location. Why? Because by the time you get to the correct room, you're frazzled and possibly even late. The time you were going to spend getting used to the room and psyching yourself up is gone forever.

Related concerns are traffic and parking. Don't plan your timetable on some general notion of how long it takes to get to the meeting site. Plan specifically for the time you'll be traveling. Maybe it generally takes 30 minutes to get there. If you have to travel during rush hour, it's going to take longer. Plan for it.

Then there's the whole parking thing. Is it my imagination or is it taking longer and longer to find a place to park? (Except for certain parts of California where people are, like, into creating their own space.) You need to know in advance where to park. Hey, you're the speaker. Tell them to give you a special parking spot at the meeting site. You deserve it.

Four reasons to arrive early

Everyone knows you should arrive early so that you can rearrange the room if necessary. Here are four more reasons to get there early:

- ✔ Just looking at the room, seeing how it's laid out and where you'll be standing can help put you at ease. It removes the fear of the unknown. And the less fear you have, the better.

- ✔ You can stand at the podium and visualize success. The more realistic the setting, the more effective the visualization. And you can't get more realistic than standing where you'll actually be speaking.

- ✔ You can sit in the audience and discover last-minute distractions that must be corrected.

- ✔ You can meet and speak with members of your audience. Introduce yourself to them. Make a connection. When you start speaking, they will feel like they already know you — and vice versa. You may also pick up some information that you can work into your talk.

Temperature and ventilation

Mark Twain once said that everybody talks about the weather but nobody does anything about it. When it comes to the "weather" in your meeting room, nobody even talks about it, but maybe *you* should do something about it. The "weather" — temperature and ventilation — can have a greater effect on your audience than anything you say. Ever had to sit through a speech in a hot, stuffy room? Or a chilly room? It ain't fun. And it's certainly not conducive to listening to the speaker. If the room is hot and stuffy, get a maintenance person to turn up the air conditioning. If it's too cold, turn up the heat. Don't make the audience wait for your hot air.

You have more control than you think

Most speakers feel they have no control over the room. That's why room set up is one of the most overlooked parts of the public speaking process. Don't fall into this trap. Any influence that you can exert over the room will work to your benefit. And you *can* exert influence — even at the last minute.

Remember, the opposite of setup is upset. The more you control the former, the less you'll become the latter.

Chapter 15

Communicating with Confidence: How to Scare Away Stage Fright

*S*tage fright. The words themselves make me nervous. Maybe that's why social scientists have abandoned the term. First they changed it to "communication anxiety." Now they talk about "communication apprehension." (If you've ever heard a social scientist speak at an academic conference, you know why these people are apprehensive.) But whatever you want to call it, the symptoms are universally recognized. Your heart pounds. Your hands shake. Your forehead sweats. Your mouth goes dry. Your stomach feels like a blender on high speed. And that's just when you get asked to speak. It really gets bad when you absolutely dread the idea of getting up in front of people to speak.

Well, congratulations. You're in the majority. According to a frequently cited survey, most people consider public speaking more frightening than death. (How would they feel delivering a eulogy?) If misery loves company, you've got plenty of it. Celebrities alleged to suffer from this affliction include Abraham Lincoln, Mark Twain, Carol Burnett, Johnny Carson, Erma Bombeck, and Laurence Olivier. In fact, anyone who does *not* get at least a little nervous before a presentation is probably a few French fries short of a Happy Meal.

Stage fright is like an incurable disease. You have to accept that you will always have it. You have to learn to control it and use it to your advantage.

What is Stage Fright?

The term stage fright actually covers a wide range of reactions. It can run the gamut from a slight unease before speaking to a paralyzing fear of standing in front of an audience. Perhaps the most common description is feeling like you have butterflies in your stomach. (Many gurus say, "Don't get rid of the butterflies — make them fly in formation." That's a catchy line, but do you really want a bunch of butterflies flying in formation in your stomach?) The most useful way to understand stage fright is to think of it in terms of stress.

Much of today's knowledge of stress originated with Dr. Hans Selye. He defined stress as "the non-specific response of the body to any demand made upon it." (I have no idea what that means either.) So I asked prominent psychiatrist and stress management expert Dr. Steven Resnick to explain it in English.

"There are three key points," explains Dr. Resnick. "First, stress is your body's response to something *you* perceive as stressful. It's totally subjective. Second, what you perceive as stressful can be good or bad. Winning a million dollars can be just as stressful as losing a million dollars. Third, you'll get the same type of stress response — muscle tension, mental preoccupation, general body stimulation — no matter what's causing your stress."

So what's this got to do with stage fright? Plenty. "When you encounter a stressful situation, your body goes into a stress reaction," explains Dr. Resnick. "Your adrenaline starts flowing. You sweat. Your blood pressure and heart rate increase. Your muscles get tense." Sounds like the symptoms of stage fright to me, and it should. Giving a speech is a stressful situation for most people.

A Little Nervousness Is Good

Do you feel a little nervous before you speak? Don't worry. It's a normal human response. We're programmed that way, and it can actually benefit your presentation. You can use the nervous energy to give a more animated and enthusiastic performance. A little nervousness can give you an edge because it can help you focus on your talk.

Why does this occur? It's the tension of wanting to do a good job. You know you'll be speaking and people will be observing you. So you get a little adrenaline pumping. It's a perfectly natural reaction, and it's nothing to worry about.

Too much nervousness is another story. If you're so paralyzed with fear that you can't speak, then you've got a problem. That's *not* just normal tension.

What You're Nervous About

A woman entered a room at a posh hotel and saw a man pacing back and forth as he talked to himself. She said, "What are you doing here?" He said, "I'm the keynote speaker at a banquet, and I'm on in ten minutes." She said, "Do you always get so nervous?" He said, "I'm not nervous. What makes you say that?" She said, "You're pacing. You're talking to yourself, and in you're in the Women's Room."

Fortunately, most speakers don't get *that* nervous. But almost everyone who makes a presentation finds something to be nervous about. The first step to reducing stage fright is identifying and understanding your anxieties.

Common fears

Stage fright fantasies commonly fall into two categories: how badly you'll perform and how horribly the audience will react. You'll freeze up. You'll goof up. You'll throw up. The members of the audience will fall asleep. They'll walk out. They'll laugh (when they're not supposed to). Or maybe they'll even throw things — like rotten fruit.

Most of these fears bear little relationship to reality. The odds of the feared events occurring are very low. Let me put it this way: I've seen lots of presentations, and I have yet to see an audience throw fruit at a speaker. (Though I've seen a few speakers who deserved it.) In fact, I can't recall ever seeing an audience walk out or a speaker throw up. That's the good news.

The bad news is that there are some other common fears that are quite realistic. On the performance side, you may fear that you won't meet expectations — yours and the audience's. On the reaction side, you may fear the audience will lower its opinion of you, that your reputation will suffer. These fears are especially justified if your presentation will be evaluated in some way. For example, you'd have to be dead to avoid feeling some anxiety if you're speaking at a major business conference in front of your peers and boss.

You should remember that these fears are common. Just because they plague you doesn't mean you won't make an incredible presentation.

Analyzing your fears

Your anxiety level can be affected by a wide variety of factors. These can include the size of the audience, the length of your presentation, how well you know the audience, your experience as a speaker, how well you know your subject matter, and the importance of the occasion.

Specifically identifying your fears is the first step toward controlling them. Are you nervous about content? Are you nervous about standing in front of an audience? Are you nervous about not being prepared? Once you've analyzed what makes you nervous, you can do something about it. Remember, the first line of defense toward stopping the stress reaction is eliminating the stressor. If lack of preparation is stressing you out, maybe you can get more time. If the size of the audience makes you nervous, maybe you can limit its size.

Even if you can't completely eliminate the stressor, you might be able to make it less stressful. For stage fright situations, Dr. Resnick suggests bringing a familiar object with you during your presentation. "It's an adult version of a security blanket," he explains. "Having something familiar in a stressful environment is comforting and makes the environment a little less stressful. You can bring anything. Many speakers bring a favorite glass."

Nervous about being nervous

When Franklin Delano Roosevelt said, "We have nothing to fear but fear itself," he was talking about the depression. But because fear feeds on itself, he might have been talking about stage fright. Loyd Auerbach, a corporate trainer with Lexis/Nexis, has seen this phenomenon with many people he trains. He says most of them are more nervous about becoming nervous during their presentations than they are about not knowing their material. It becomes an endless loop. The worry about worrying causes more worrying. It all goes back to how you perceive the situation.

Loyd suggests two steps for recovery. (Hey, at least it's not a 12-step program.) The first step sounds easy — recognize what's going on, that you're worrying about worrying. It's harder than it sounds. Remember the old saying that it wasn't a fish who discovered water? If you're swimming in an ocean of worry, it's difficult to recognize your situation. Step two is to recognize that you should be more concerned with "knowing your stuff." As Loyd puts it, "The more you know, the more you're in charge, and the more comfortable you'll be."

The Self-Image Fulfilling Prophesy: Mental Readiness

Teacher to pupil: "Think positive." Pupil to teacher: "I am. I'm positive I'm going to fail." It's an old joke but it highlights an important point — stress is a mental phenomenon. However, if stress can be caused mentally, it can be cured mentally. It's all in the way you look at things.

Tea for two

Normally, I wouldn't drink much of anything before I speak, but this was a special case: I was scheduled to give a one hour seminar at the Ohio State Bar Association, and my voice was rapidly losing a battle with laryngitis. So I drank cup after cup of tea for about 30 minutes prior to my start time.

I downed the last cup and headed for the seminar room. Precision timing was the key. I wanted to get there right before I was on. That way the effect of the tea wouldn't wear off and maybe my voice would hold out. (Yeah, I know. You're always supposed to get to the room early to check things out. But this was a special case.)

I arrived, sat down in the front row, and waited to be introduced. The program chair walked to the podium, made some announcements and introduced the speaker — it wasn't me. Turns out I was to do the second hour of a two-hour program. No one had ever told me. Ordinarily, it wouldn't have mattered, but I'd been drinking a lot of tea.

You don't have to be a plumber to figure out what happened. I sat in the front row squirming through the first speaker's talk. (As much as I wanted to go to the bathroom, I felt it would be impolite to leave — especially because I was sitting in the front row.) Then it was my turn. My voice was hoarse but it held out. And finally the ordeal was over.

Afterwards, I asked people in the audience if they had noticed my voice problem. No one had, but they said it was the most animated body language they'd ever seen.

What can you learn from all this? First, audiences really don't notice the things speakers worry about. Second, you really can survive giving a speech even under the most trying circumstances. And third, you can lead the hoarse to water, but you shouldn't if he's not speaking first.

Four things you must realize about your audience

Stage fright is a very egocentric affliction. *I'm* scared. *I'm* nervous. *I'm* going to pass out. Me. Me. Me. It's easy to lose sight of your audience's interests, but the audience has as much at stake as you. In fact, your audience may be more scared than you. It may suffer from *seat fright* — the fear of wasting time listening to a bad speech. Here are four things you need to know about your audience:

The audience wants you to succeed

By showing up, members of your audience give you a tremendous vote of confidence. They don't want to spend their precious time to come and hear you fail. They want your presentation to be a success. Their success is linked to yours. When your presentation is terrific, people in the audience feel brilliant for attending.

You have knowledge the audience wants

There's a reason why you were asked to speak; it's probably because you have information desired by the audience. You're the expert. You're the person in the know. You have the data that they clamor for. Even on the rare occasion that the audience knows more than you about your topic, you can still provide new information. Only *you* can provide your own unique insights. No one else knows *your* view and interpretation of the material. View your role as that of an information provider. It's like I tell my five-year-old son — you have to share. Think of yourself as sharing valuable knowledge and ideas with your audience.

The audience doesn't know you're afraid

Social science research shows that the speaker and the audience have very different perceptions about stage fright. Often, an audience won't even detect anxiety in a speaker who claims to be extremely nervous. It's like the acne lotion commercial you see on TV. A teenager gets a pimple on his nose. He imagines the pimple is as big as a watermelon and that people are staring at it wherever he goes. Of course, no one even notices it. Stage fright works the same way. It's a mental pimple that seems a lot worse to you than to your audience.

The audience can be treated like an individual

Dr. Alan Weiner says his clients tell him all the time that "they love to answer questions, but they hate to give speeches." As president of Communication Development Associates, Alan gets paid a lot to advise these people. (And his clients include senior executives of Fortune 500 companies.) Here's some of his advice free of charge: View your presentation as the answer to an *implied* question. In other words, what question does your speech answer? Just make believe someone in your audience asked you that question and then give the speech as if you're answering that person's question. Instead of "making a speech," you're just "answering a question." Presentations are far less frightening when thought of this way.

How the pros visualize success

The next time you're on an airplane, pick up the in-flight magazine and flip through it. You'll find a lot of advertisements for products that tell you how to harness the power of visualization: special videos to play before you go to sleep, special books to read as you go to sleep, special audio cassettes to play after you're asleep. (These ads will probably put you to sleep.) All of these products make the same claim — they'll help you become more successful by visualizing success.

Do you really need all this stuff? Nope. Use your head. (That's where the visualization is supposed to take place anyway.) The concept of visualization is simple and straightforward. You just imagine yourself performing a task successfully. A number of athletes use this training technique. They imagine themselves hitting home runs, scoring touchdowns, or signing autographs for $100 apiece. They imagine these activities in vivid detail and try to remember past successes and build them into the image.

Apply visualization techniques to *your* presentation. Imagine yourself giving your talk. You're smooth, very smooth. Your voice fills the room with wisdom. People in the audience hang on your every word. (If they lean any further forward, they'll fall out of their chairs.) They take notes and want to remember every single thing you say. They interrupt their notetaking only to engage in lengthy rounds of applause. Your gestures and body language are flawless, and you work the people in the crowd into a frenzy. You build to a big finish and leave them with a conclusion they'll never forget. They give you a standing ovation and rush the stage to carry you out on their shoulders. (You get the idea.)

Your most important audience: talking to yourself

Your audience only has to hear you once. You have to hear yourself all the time, so the messages you send yourself are very important. I'm talking about your *internal dialogue* — the things you say to yourself in your head. When you repeat them over and over, you start to believe them. So you've got to be careful what you say. If you keep telling yourself that you'll flub your talk at a critical moment, you probably will.

(In a way, talking to yourself is the flip side of visualizing success — not talking yourself into failure. But it's more than that. Successful visualization techniques apply to a specific task — like making a presentation. Your internal dialogue has a much broader focus. It applies to *everything* you do.)

Avoid "awful-izing" and "absolute-izing"

Psychiatrist Steven Resnick says the two most common factors that turn self-talk negative are the tendency to "awful-ize" or "absolute-ize" our beliefs. What does that mean? "If you think how awful it would be to make a mistake while you're giving a speech, then you are awful-izing," he explains. "Or if you think that it's absolutely necessary for you to get a standing ovation, then you are absolute-izing." This type of irrational thinking leads to negative self messages. "You'll tell yourself that you can't do it," says Dr. Resnick. "So instead of boosting your self-confidence, you criticize yourself in advance for not achieving an irrational goal. And that helps ensure that you *won't* give a good performance."

Positive self-talk

So how can you keep the self-chatter positive? Here are a few techniques from Dr. Resnick:

Dispute irrational thoughts

Let's say you have the irrational thought "If I stand in front of an audience, I'll forget everything I know about the topic." A disputing thought could be "I'll have no reason to remember all that stuff if I *don't* tell it to an audience."

Use personal affirmations

"I'm the greatest speaker in the world." "My subject is fascinating and the audience will love it." "I'm an expert." If you're an optimist, you say these types of things to yourself naturally. If you're a pessimist, start forcing yourself to say them because they really do help. Yes, they're corny, but they build confidence. The more you talk yourself into believing them, the less stress you'll encounter with your presentation.

Imagine the worst case scenario

Face your fear directly. Think about the worst possible thing that could happen and realize that it's not that awful. If you make a mistake while you're speaking, you can correct it and continue. If the audience doesn't give you a standing ovation, it might still applaud. Even if the speech is a total disaster, it's not the end of the world. No one will shoot you. And besides, you'll get a great personal anecdote about "bombing" to use the next time you speak.

Transforming Terror to Terrific: Physical Symptoms

A man went to the doctor for a physical. He said, "I look in the mirror and I'm a mess. My jowls are sagging. I have blotches all over my face. My hair is falling out. What is it?" The doctor said, "I don't know, but your eyesight is perfect."

Unfortunately, a lot of other people have perfect eyesight too — especially when it involves examining your physical symptoms of stage fright. But here's the good news: It's not that hard to eliminate or disguise the sweating and shaking.

Stress-busting exercises

You understand mentally that stress is all in your head — that if you don't view a speech as stressful, it won't be. But darn it, you just can't seem to accept this belief emotionally. You've tried all the mental tricks — thinking positive, visualizing success, focusing away from yourself — and they haven't worked. Your heart is still pounding. You're still sweating profusely, and you still feel nauseous. Now what can you do?

Don't sweat it (so to speak). Even though stress is technically all in your head, its effects can be quite physical. So if you can't treat your mental state, treat your physical symptoms. Here are some recommendations from prominent stress expert Dr. Steven Resnick:

Breathing

Take a deep breath. Hold it. Hold it. Now let it out slowly. Good. Do it again. Breath deeply and slowly. Keep it up. Don't you feel better already? Dr. Resnick says breathing exercises are one of the world's oldest techniques for relieving stress. "We release carbon dioxide every time we exhale," he explains. "That decreases the acidity of our blood." It also increases the oxygen in your brain. (And gives a whole new meaning to the term "airhead.")

Stretching

Stretching is a great way to relieve muscle tension quickly, and it doesn't take long to do. Stretching for time periods as short as ten or fifteen seconds can be beneficial. Now you can't just do yoga in the middle of a banquet when you're the after-dinner speaker, but you can excuse yourself and do a few quick stretches in the restroom just before you speak. Here are a few exercises to get you down the home stretch:

- ✔ **Head rolls.** Slowly turn your head from side to side. That's the warm-up. Now move your head clockwise in a circle (look up, right, down and left). Do this three times then reverse it. You should feel the tension flowing out of your neck.

- ✔ **Arm lifts.** Stretch your right arm up into the air as far as it will go. Hold it a few seconds. Bring it back to your side. Now stretch your left arm up as far as it will go. Keep repeating the process. In high school, your gym teacher made you do this exercise as a form of torture. Now you're going to do it for relief. It helps stretch out your back.

- ✔ **Jaw breakers.** Open your mouth as wide as possible (as if you're going to scream).Then close your mouth. Keep opening and closing your mouth. This exercise helps relieve tension in the jaw. You can also use your fingers to massage the muscle that joins the jaw and the rest of the head.

Self-massage

Can't afford a masseuse? Don't worry. You can handle the job for yourself. Start with your arms at your sides. Then place the fingers of your right hand at the base of the left side of your neck. (Get the tips of your fingers on that area where the neck ends and the shoulder begins.) Now place the fingers of your left hand on that spot by the right side of your neck. (Your arms should be crossed at the wrists in front of your chest.) The fingers of both hands should now be over the muscles between your neck and shoulder — two of the tensest areas known to stage fright victims. Start squeezing yourself. Move your fingers around to cover the entire neck and shoulder areas.

Moving around

Some speakers like to take a quick walk or jog in place to get rid of nervous energy. Are there stairs in the building where you'll speak? A few trips up and down some flights of stairs may be helpful, but don't overdo it. You don't want to be sweaty and tired by the time you go on.

Progressive muscle relaxation

This exercise trains you to recognize when you're muscles become tense and helps you get rid of the tension. Start by tensing and untensing your forehead. Notice the difference between the tension and letting it go. Now tense your jaw and release the tension. Then repeat this process as you work your way down through your body — neck, shoulders, stomach, legs. Tighten and relax. Then just relax.

The real secret: don't look nervous

The common knowledge is that a little nervousness is good and a lot of nervousness is bad. So you're supposed to control your nervousness, keep it at an acceptable level. You do that by following all the standard techniques described in this chapter.

Here's the uncommon knowledge: It doesn't really matter how nervous you are — as *long as you appear calm.* As Dr. Alan Weiner puts it, "You have to look like you're under control, not be under control. As long as the audience thinks you're confident — that's what counts." Here are Alan's tips and tricks for disguising some of the common signs of stage fright:

✔ **Fidgeting.** Fidgeting is an announcement that you're anxious. Touching your face with your index finger or rubbing it under your nose or scratching above your lip are all signs of nervousness. The solution: keep your hands in front of you in the "steeple position." (See Chapter 16). If you're using a lectern place your hands on it as if you're playing the piano.

✔ **Pacing.** Pacing is another tip-off of anxiety. The solution: Move closer to the audience and then stop for a moment. Then move somewhere else and stop.

✔ **Drinking water.** Drinking a lot of water is a sign of a dry mouth that indicates nervousness. The solution: Don't keep a pitcher of water available. Place a small amount of water in a glass and ration yourself.

✔ **Sweating.** It's how you handle the sweating that counts. If you take a handkerchief, open it up and swipe at the sweat — you look like a nervous wreck. The solution: Never open the handkerchief. Keep it folded in a square. *Dab* at the sweat and then replace the handkerchief in your pocket.

✔ **Hands shaking.** If your hands are shaking like a leaf, that's a pretty good indication of stage fright. The solution: Use cards rather than sheets of paper for your notes. (Paper, which is larger and lighter weight than cards, highlights your shakiness.) Also, don't hold props or other items that emphasize that your hands are shaking.

Seven Tricks to Prevent and Handle Stage Fright

Are you worried about getting stage fright? Don't be. Just keep the next several tricks in mind and you'll be ready for anything. (Unless you get so nervous that you forget the tricks.)

Write out your intro and conclusion

The student was six feet two inches tall. He was standing in front of the class preparing to start his speech. You could tell he was nervous by the way he gripped the podium — the color had drained from his hands. He started to speak. He got out a few words, and then he fainted. As he fell to the ground, the podium went down with him. He never let go.

The student was in a class taught by speech expert Allatia Harris. She says it's a perfect example of why she advises speakers to write out the introductions to their presentations. "Nervousness is most intense just before you start talking," she says. "You see all those people looking at you and words start coming out of your mouth, but your mouth's not connected to your brain. You may not even be aware of what you're saying." That's why you have to give special attention to the introduction. You need to have it down cold so you don't fall down cold.

Similar preparation should be given to the conclusion — the second most anxiety-producing part of a presentation. (See Chapters 8 and 9.)

Anticipate problems and have solutions ready

Anticipate any problem that can arise and have a plan ready to deal with it. For example, whenever you stumble over a tongue-twisting name or phrase, you can have an all-purpose recovery line ready. "Let me try that again — in English."

What if you forget what point you were going to cover next? You can buy time by asking the audience a survey question that requires a show of hands. Or you can review what you've already covered. Or you can skip ahead to a different point. (I've done this lots of times. I'll talk about the six rules of using humor effectively, and after rule three, I'll go blank; I can't remember rule four for the life of me. So rule five becomes rule four, and rule six becomes rule five. By that time, I've usually remembered rule four, which then becomes rule six. No one except me knows the difference.)

Being prepared to handle the things that can go wrong will reduce a lot of anxiety, and it doesn't require an elaborate plan. You just need to know what you will do if disaster strikes. Be like the fellow who attended a seminar on computer data storage. The instructor asked how many people had a disaster recovery plan. One man raised his hand and said, "I've got a plan and it's just one page." The instructor said, "In just one page you can cover what you'd do if your computer center was flooded or hit by a tornado or sabotaged or disabled by an earthquake or a fire?" The man said, "Yes, it's very simple. It's a two-step plan. First, I maintain a copy of my résumé up to date at all times. Second, I always store a back-up copy off-site."

Get there early

Fear of the unknown probably produces more anxiety than any other cause. Until you get to the site where you'll speak, you face a lot of unknowns. Is the room set up correctly? Did they remember to give you an overhead projector? Is an audience actually going to show up? Plenty of little questions can add up to big sources of stress if you don't have answers for them.

You can get the answers simply by going to the room, so do it early. The earlier you arrive, the more time you have to correct any mistakes (see Chapter 14), and the more time you have to calm down. You also get a chance to meet members of the audience who arrive early, which can reduce stress by making the audience more familiar to you.

On a personal level, I can tell you that I'm always nervous until I get to the room and see the audience. Once I see the audience, I always feel a lot better. (I can see that everyone in the audience checked their guns at the door.)

Divide and conquer

Many speakers who suffer from stage fright claim it's a large audience that triggers their fear. A few people, no problem. A big group, forget it. Here's what to do: Look at one face in the audience at a time — especially faces that appear interested in what you're saying. Keep coming back to them. (No, normally you shouldn't stare at only a few people. That's a basic rule of eye contact as discussed in Chapter 16, but stage fright creates an exception. If the only way you can prevent yourself from passing out is to look at only a few people, then do it.)

Move

Find ways to channel your nervous energy constructively into your performance. Move around when you talk (but don't pace). Make dramatic gestures that support your message. Think of ways to keep moving that don't detract from your presentation.

Don't apologize for nervousness

Many speakers feel compelled to apologize for being nervous. Don't apologize for making a mistake, flub, or goof-up. Just let it go. You don't want to draw additional attention to your nervousness. As speech expert Allatia Harris says, "Never apologize to the audience unless you've injured someone."

Watch what you eat

It's been said that you are what you eat. Maybe and maybe not. But here's some food for thought — what you eat before you speak *will* affect your anxiety level. That's why you want to avoid drinking coffee, tea, and other caffeinated beverages before you go on. You'll be jittery enough without the added stimulation they supply. You also probably want to avoid carbonated beverages unless you're planning to speak about burping.

What about dairy products? Many people believe you shouldn't consume dairy products before a speech. They're supposed to generate mucus that causes speakers to keep clearing their throats.

Here's some uncommon knowledge: Dr. Christine Griger says that unless you're personally allergic to dairy products, the mucus-causing properties of dairy products are a myth. So if drinking milk before a talk makes you feel better — go right ahead.

Two Popular Cures That Don't Work

Throughout history, human maladies have inspired remedies that claimed fantastic curative powers but actually proved worthless. Snake oil for the common cold. Blood-sucking leaches for fevers. Ear plugs for political speeches. Here are two such "cures" for stage fright:

Imagine the audience naked

An alleged cure for stage fright that's probably as old as human speech itself is to imagine your audience naked. (I can just see this advice being dispensed by one caveman to another. Caveman #1: "Don't be nervous; just imagine that the audience is naked." Caveman #2: "But they are naked.")

As speech expert Allatia Harris observes, this "cure" doesn't work for a couple of reasons. "First, there are some folks in the audience I wouldn't want to see naked — especially if I'm trying *not* to be frightened. Second, there might be a few I'd *really* like to see naked." Either way, the effect isn't calming.

Booze and pills

Another folk remedy often suggested for stage fright is to have a drink or take a tranquilizer. This is supposed to help you calm down. Here's the problem: The desired effects normally wear off just before you get in front of an audience — especially if you consume the drink or pill 30 to 60 minutes before you're scheduled to speak. Then the fear returns with a vengeance, and it makes the speaking experience much worse instead of better. In addition, you won't be at your best because you'll still be a bit groggy.

Parting Thoughts

In ancient Rome, the Coliseum was full as a Christian was thrown to a lion. The crowd cheered as the lion ran up to the Christian, bent over him, and prepared to eat him. Just when the end seemed imminent, the Christian whispered something and the lion bolted away in fear. The Emperor, clearly impressed, asked the Christian how he performed this miracle. The Christian said, "It was easy. I told the lion that after dinner, he'd be expected to say a few words."

Yes, making a presentation can be scary. But don't let that deter you. Unlike the lion, you can learn to handle your fear. And there's definitely no reason to lose your dinner over it.

Chapter 16

How to Stand Up and Stand Out

In This Chapter

▶ Understanding nonverbal communication

▶ Harnessing the power of body language

▶ Establishing commanding eye contact

▶ Physical positioning and movement

▶ Dressing for impact

▶ Working from a podium

▶ Handling a microphone

▶ Using your voice strategically

*A*n old philosopher once said that public speakers should speak up so they can be heard, stand up so they can be seen, and shut up so they can be enjoyed. That advice may be harsh, but it does highlight a very important aspect of public speaking: Much of your presentation's impact comes from how you look and sound.

The Role of Nonverbal Communication

Nonverbal communication is said to account for as much as 93 percent of a speaker's message. The numbers usually cited are 38 percent for vocal qualities and 55 percent for facial expressions, gestures, and movements. Only 7 percent of the message is attributed to the words that are actually spoken. Professional presenters and communication coaches have seized upon these findings to proclaim that your body language is far more important than the words you actually say. (If this is true, you have to wonder why these people spend so much time training their students how to write a speech.)

Here's the uncommon knowledge. Nonverbal communication is very important — but its importance is overrated. (I've never heard anyone quote a gesture.) *You can give a successful presentation without having perfect gestures, eye contact, and body language.* The secret lies in matching your message to audience needs.

Let's say you're a Nobel Prize-winning cancer researcher speaking to a group of cancer patients. You tell them that you've just discovered the cure for cancer and that you will present it to them. You know what? Those cancer patients don't care if you gesture or make eye contact. They don't care if you mumble. They don't care if you face the wall and spit wooden nickels. Just tell them the cure.

And you don't have to be a Nobel Prize winner to take this approach. You just need credibility with your audience. Here's a great example: When I taught freshman speech at USC, my students had to give an informative speech. Their average age was eighteen, and the drinking age in California was twenty-one. Most of them talked about the usual boring stuff: how to bake a cake or how to change a flat tire. When the class wise-guy took his turn, he said, "Today I will teach you how to fake an ID." Before he uttered another word, every student in the class opened a notebook and prepared to write. And they took notes throughout his entire presentation. He could have looked at the floor and whispered. No one would have cared. His audience wanted to know how to fake an ID. And they knew, by his reputation, that he knew how to do it.

Now don't get me wrong. I'm not saying that nonverbal communication isn't very important. It is. I'm just saying that you don't have to be discouraged if you don't have the moves and delivery of an Academy Award winner. You can still make a successful presentation if you match your topic to audience needs and you have a lot of credibility.

The impact on credibility

The reason I acknowledge the importance of nonverbal communication is its effect on your credibility. Try a little experiment. Tell someone to meet you for lunch while shaking your head "no." Your verbal and nonverbal messages conflict. Which will your listener believe? Let's put it this way: I don't think you'll be having a companion for lunch today. When verbal and nonverbal messages conflict, we believe the nonverbal.

Why do nonverbal cues affect credibility? Because a common mistake speakers make is presenting nonverbal messages that undermine the believability of what they're actually saying. A classic example occurred during a presidential campaign debate between George Bush and Bill Clinton. Although George Bush spoke about how important certain issues were for the American people, he kept looking at his watch. He gave the impression that he was bored and couldn't wait for the debate to end. Many observers felt that this action undermined his credibility. He sure didn't *look* like he thought the issues were very important.

You can talk the talk. But you also have to walk the walk. Your gestures, body language, and facial expressions must support what you're saying. Otherwise, you lose credibility.

Command performance vs. commanding performance

Now I've said that nonverbal communication is overrated in importance. But it's still very important, especially if you can't make an exact match between your topic and the needs of your audience, or if you don't have a lot of credibility. Then your delivery becomes critical. It can make the difference between your audience dreaming about what you say or falling asleep as you say it.

If a picture is worth a thousand words, then your body language must be worth a billion. The cliché is "You are your most important visual." It's a cliché but it's true. The way you carry yourself and project your message will have a big effect on how that message is received. Have you ever listened to a speaker talk about a topic that held no interest for you? If the speaker droned from a script and never looked at the audience, made a gesture, or changed position, you probably dreaded the experience — if you stayed awake. If the speaker was dynamic — moved around, made dramatic gestures, engaged the eyes of the audience — you may have enjoyed the speech despite your lack of interest in the topic.

When you have to give a talk that you don't want to give, that's a command performance. When you give it and get the audience to pay attention, that's a commanding performance. The difference between the two comes down to one word — enthusiasm. If you're enthusiastic, your audience will be too. It's contagious. And it's communicated nonverbally.

Body Language

Body language refers to the messages you send through facial expression, posture, and gesture. You don't need a Berlitz course to learn this language. You already use it every day, and most of the meanings are obvious. A smile indicates happiness. A frown means disapproval. Leaning forward means active engagement in the discussion.

What's not as obvious is how *you* employ body language. It's amazing what watching a videotape of yourself will reveal. That's the quickest way to improve your body language — because the camera doesn't lie. It will show you movements and gestures that you may not be aware you were making. Ask someone to videotape you giving a presentation. Then watch the video with the sound off. Common sense will tell you most of what you need to correct. Other things to keep in mind are facial expressions, posture, and gestures.

Facial expressions

If the eyes are the windows to the soul, then the face is the front of the house. Its appearance says a lot. And how you make it appear says a lot about your message.

The single most important facial expression is the smile. Simply smiling at an audience can create instant rapport. Unfortunately, many speakers — particularly business speakers — feel they must wear their "game face" at all times. They're *serious* businesspeople. They have facts and figures. They have bottom-line responsibilities. If they smiled, they might seem . . . human.

That's not to say you should smile all the time. There's no need to be an advertisement for your dentist. In fact, inappropriate smiling can undermine your entire message. The classic example is former President Jimmy Carter. He used to punctuate his sentences with smiles. Every time he finished a sentence, he'd beam a big warm smile at the audience. While the smiles revealed his warm, compassionate nature, they were often disconcerting. He'd be talking about nuclear war and the need for disarmament and the threat of global annihilation. And he'd smile after each sentence. What was wrong with *that* picture?

Use your face to accentuate key points. Act out what you're saying. Are you incredulous about a statistic you've just cited? Raise your eyebrows in disbelief. Are you briefing the audience on a strategy that you disagree with? Frown. Are you telling a group of kindergarten students that they will be getting more homework in first grade? Stick your tongue out at them. (Just kidding.)

Posture

Your mother was right. You should always stand up straight — especially when you're making a presentation. Sloppy posture invites negative judgments from the audience.

Is the speaker lazy? Sick? Tired? Contrast those reactions with the expressions associated with good posture. The speaker is upright, a straight arrow, a straight shooter, a standup person. Every presentation involves a lot of posturing. Make yours the anatomical kind.

Posture dos and don'ts

Don't lean on the podium. Once in a while for effect is OK. But planting yourself on the podium makes you look weak.

Don't stand with your hands on your hips. You'll come across as a bossy gym teacher. Besides, it makes you look like you're leading a game of Simon Says.

Don't sway back and forth. Unless you're talking about how to use a metronome or the finer points of sea sickness, no one wants to watch you sway back and forth. It's very distracting.

Don't stand with your arms folded across your chest. You'll look like a goon from a gangster movie. What are you going to do? Beat up the audience?

Don't stand with your arms behind your back. It's a tad limiting on your ability to gesture. And if you clasp your hands together, it makes you look like you've been handcuffed and arrested.

Do stand up straight with your feet slightly apart and your arms ready to gesture. This is the basic, preferred posture for any presentation.

Don't stand in the fig leaf position. That's when a speaker holds both hands together over his or her crotch — like the fig leaves that Adam and Eve wore. It's fine if you're posing for a Renaissance style painting of blushing modesty. It looks really stupid in any other circumstance. It's like you've just discovered your nakedness (or lack of anything intelligent to say) and you want to hide it from your audience.

Do lean slightly toward the audience. Leaning forward shows that you're actively engaged with them. Leaning back signals retreat.

Don't bury your hands in your pockets. People will wonder what they're doing down there. It's OK to put one hand in your pocket from time to time. But don't park it there.

Gestures

A cynic once suggested that speakers who don't know what to do with their hands should try clamping them over their mouths. That suggestion, though mean-spirited, does highlight a common problem for presenters — what to do with your hands. There's no getting around the fact that you have to do *something* with them. And your choice will have important consequences for your presentation.

Gesture dos and don'ts

Using gestures properly in a presentation means breaking one of your mother's basic rules: you *don't* want to keep your hands to yourself. You want to share them with your audience. How do you do that? Just follow these simple guidelines and you'll do fine:

Don't memorize gestures

Think about the gestures you'll use. Think about where they might fit into your presentation. But don't plan them out in specific detail. And don't memorize them. Allatia Harris, Dean of Communication at Mountain View College, observes that you can always tell which speakers went to gesture school — because they look ridiculous. "Their gestures trail two seconds behind their words," she says. "You can see them fishing around in their brains to remember they were supposed to make a gesture. It's like they're dubbing their own speech." And it just looks dumb.

Do create opportunities to use gestures

If you're worried that gestures won't occur to you naturally, then stack the deck in your favor. Include a few items in your talk that beg for gestures. Talk about alternative courses of action — "on the one hand . . . and on the other hand." Talk about how large or small something is. Talk about how many points you'll make and hold up your fingers. (This technique works best if the number is ten or less.)

Do vary your gestures

If you make the same gestures over and over, you start to look like a robot. And the predictability lowers audience attention levels. Don't let your gestures fall into a pattern. Keep the audience guessing. It will keep them watching.

Do put your hands in the steeple position

Your hands really will take care of themselves as you speak. But if you insist on guidance, here's what to do — put your hands in the steeple position. Just put them together in front of you as if you're applauding. That's the steeple position. Now you don't keep them like that. It's just a rest stop. As you talk, your hands will naturally split apart from the steeple. Sometimes they split widely. Sometimes they split narrowly. That's why Alan Weiner, President of Communication Development Associates, calls the steeple the secret to good gesturing. It places your hands in a position where they'll move without your thinking about them.

Do make your gestures fit the space

A common mistake speakers make is transferring gestures used in small, intimate settings to large, formal settings. For example, people at a cocktail party gesture by moving their arms from the elbow to the end of the hand. "That's fine for a small audience," notes comedy coach John Cantu. "But those gestures will seem very limited and closed when performed in front of a large group of people."

If you're speaking to a large audience in a large space, you must adjust your gestures. You must open them up and make them larger. Are you going to emphasize a point? Move your arms from the *shoulders* to the ends of your hands instead of from the elbows.

Do make bold gestures

Your gestures should communicate confidence and authority. Tentative, half-hearted attempts at gesturing make you look weak and indecisive. Get your hands up. (No, I'm not about to rob you.) You'll look more assured if your hands are higher than your elbows. Be bold. Don't use a finger if a fist is more dramatic. Watch the Sunday morning evangelists on television. They know how to gesture with authority.

Don't let your gestures turn you into any of these types of speakers:

- ✔ **The banker:** These speakers keep rattling coins in their pockets. They sound like a change machine. It's very distracting.

- ✔ **The optician:** These speakers constantly adjust their glasses. They're on. They're off. They're slipping down their noses. Do everyone a favor and get some contact lenses.

- ✔ **The tailor:** These speakers fiddle with their clothing. The tie is a big object of affection for male speakers in this category. They twist it. And pinch it. And rub it. No one listens to the talk. We're all waiting to see if the speaker will choke himself.

- ✔ **The jeweler:** These speakers fiddle with their jewelry. Necklaces are a big attraction for female speakers in this category. And you'll find ring twisters from both sexes.

- ✔ **The lonely lover:** These speakers hug themselves. It looks really weird. They stand up in front of the audience and hug themselves while they speak. They lose a lot of credibility.

- ✔ **The beggar:** These speakers clasp their hands together and thrust them toward the audience as if they're begging for something. They probably are — a miracle.

- ✔ **The hygenicist:** These speakers keep rubbing their hands together like they're washing them. It looks weird for a few reasons. There's no soap. No water. No sink. And a bunch of people called an audience are watching.

- ✔ **The toy maker:** These speakers love to play with their little toys — pens, markers, pointers — whatever happens to be around. They turn them in their hands. They squeeze them. And they distract the audience.

- ✔ **The bug collector:** These speakers keep pulling at the hair on the back of their necks or their heads. Yes, the audience knows it's just a nervous habit, but they still wonder when was the last time you washed your hair.

Eye Contact

There's a point in many old tearjerker romantic movies where the heroine tells the hero (or vice versa) that she doesn't love him anymore. (Usually the villain has forced this situation upon them.) The violins come up strongly on the soundtrack. The camera pans in for a close-up. Shock and disbelief register across the hero's face. And inevitably he utters this immortal line: "Look me in the eye and say that." In other words, it's not true until she says it while making eye contact.

What is it about eye contact that so affects our perception of human veracity? Think about it. We've got lots of expressions linking eye contact to believability. "The eyes are the window to the soul." "The heart's letters are read in the eyes." "The ear is less trustworthy than the eye." "The eyes have it." (Just kidding about that last one.) Put simply, eye contact is a major factor in credibility. It's often more persuasive to look people straight in the eye and lie than to tell the truth and gaze elsewhere. Poor eye contact lowers your credibility.

Eye contact also serves other important functions. It officially initiates communication. You can talk to people, but it doesn't really count until eye contact is established. Don't believe me? Try getting a cranky waiter's attention in a busy restaurant. You can yell "Waiter!" all night. It doesn't count. The waiter can act like he didn't hear you. Communication doesn't officially begin until you "catch his eye." In a presentation situation, that means maintaining eye contact with your entire audience. You want all of them to know you're talking to them.

And eye contact is a two-way street. The eye contact that your audience provides is crucial feedback about your presentation. Do their eyes show boredom, enthusiasm, interest, anger? Are their eyes focused on you? Are their eyes open or closed? You need to know this stuff in order to make adjustments as you go along.

Eye contact dos and don'ts

"If looks could kill." We've all been glad they can't when we've been on the receiving end, but when you make a presentation, looks *can* kill. Depending on what you do or don't look at, looks can kill your entire presentation. Here are a few rules to prevent you from committing a capital offense:

Don't look out the window

If you look out the window, so will your audience. This is also true for looking at the ceiling, the walls, or the floor. The audience plays follow the leader, and you're the leader. Look at them so they'll look at you.

Don't look at one spot

Make sure that you establish eye contact with all parts of your audience. Cover the entire room. Too many speakers face straight ahead and never look toward the sides. No, you don't want your head to look like a machine gun pivoting back and forth as it sprays eye contact at the crowd. But you do want to keep your gaze rotating from one part of the audience to another.

Do look at individuals

As you gaze around the room, make eye contact with as many individuals as possible. A common myth is to pick out a friendly face and look at it. That gets weird fast. This poor person wonders why you're staring at him or her, and so does the rest of the audience. Look at a variety of individuals. Remember, you want to be a search light, not a laser beam.

Don't forget to look at the back rows

If you look only at people seated toward the front, you risk losing a major portion of your audience because everyone in the back feels left out. Besides, as Loyd Auerbach explains, you get more bang for your eye contact buck by looking at people in the back. "When you talk to a large group and catch someone's eye in the distance, the five people seated around that person also think you're looking at them," he says. "If you look at someone in the front, no one else thinks you're looking their way."

Don't let notes ruin your eye contact

Some speakers get so hung up looking at their notes that they don't look at their audience. Big mistake. The notes aren't going to applaud when you're done. And neither will the audience if you haven't looked at them. What can you do? First, make sure your notes are easy to read — large print, legible, only a few key words per card. Second, watch how your favorite TV news anchors read from their notes. They look down. They read the notes. They look up. They look into the camera. They tell you one thought. Then they repeat the process. Head up. Head down. Head up. Head down. (Just don't do it too fast or you'll look like one of those little statues you see in car rear windows.)

Don't look over the heads of the audience

A big myth that originated in a lot of grade school public speaking classes is it's OK to gaze over the heads of your audience. Nervous about looking them in the eye? Just look over their heads. They won't know the difference. Wrong. People can tell if you're speaking to the clock on the wall behind them. And the smaller the audience, the more obvious this technique becomes.

So what should you do if you're too nervous to look in their eyes? Look at the tips of their noses. Loyd Auerbach, corporate trainer and magician, swears it works. "They can't tell you're not looking them in the eye," he says, "especially if you're on a stage." So next time you want to go nose-to-nose with an audience with whom you can't see eye-to-eye, go eye-to-nose with them. (Sorry, I couldn't resist.)

Image: Dress to Impress

As the saying goes, clothes make the man (or woman). The question is what do they make you? The answer: credible — if you dress appropriately.

A single article of clothing can change your entire image and have a large effect on how an audience receives your message. When Dan Rather first became anchor of the CBS Evening News, his ratings weren't as high as desired. He was perceived as too stiff, especially when compared with his predecessor, the legendary Walter Cronkite. The problem was partially solved when Rather began wearing a sweater under his jacket. It softened his image and improved his ratings.

People make all kinds of judgments based on clothes. It's human nature. Many studies of retail outlets have shown that well-dressed customers receive better service than poorly-dressed customers. And it's common sense. If you saw someone walking into your store in checked pants, a striped jacket, white socks and black shoes, you'd make some assumptions, too. (And they wouldn't be very positive.)

The point is that your attire is part of your message. It should augment what you say, not detract from it.

Image dos and don'ts

Do dress conservatively. You want your audience to focus on you — not on what you're wearing.

Don't have pencils, pens, and markers peeking out of your shirt or jacket pockets. It makes you look like a nerd.

Don't wear distracting jewelry. Distraction is defined as when your jewelry is louder than you are (both to the eye and ear).

Do shine your shoes. The audience will look at them — especially if you're on a stage.

Do wear comfortable clothes. That doesn't mean old clothes or informal clothes. It means that maybe the time to break in that new pair of shoes isn't the day you're giving your speech.

Don't take a purse to the podium. It's a distraction. Ask a trusted member of the audience to guard it.

Don't keep bulky stuff in your pockets. Remember Mae West's famous line, "Is that a pistol in your pocket or are you just happy to see me?" You don't want the audience mentally asking that question. (This applies to both men and women. You don't want the audience wondering what's in your pockets; you want them wondering what you're going to say next.)

What about informal meetings?

Let's say you're speaking at an event where the audience will be dressed casually — golf clothes, shorts, and T-shirts, maybe even bathing suits. Is it OK for you to dress casually? Great minds diverge, but if it's a business event, I say "No." Wear business clothes. I always do — even if the meeting planner says it's not necessary. Even if the whole audience is wearing beach attire. (Beach attire isn't that unusual. Many companies hold sales or management retreats at oceanfront hotels where meetings are followed by recreation.)

Here's why you ought to wear business clothes: The audience will take your message more seriously if you wear business clothes. And speakers who dress casually may fall into the trap of speaking too casually. Besides, I don't look that great in a bathing suit.

The exception is when you're also a member of the audience you'll be addressing. Let's say a group of managers is dressed in golf clothes because golf is scheduled right after the meeting. You're one of the managers in the meeting, so you'll be playing golf just like everyone else, and you're scheduled to make a presentation during the meeting. In that situation, you probably want to be wearing golf clothes. *Not* wearing them would seem odd and detract from your talk.

Whatever the situation, the criterion is always identical. What attire will most enhance your message? That's what you should wear.

Physical Positioning and Movement

Where do you stand? The question usually refers to a speaker's position on an issue. I'm posing it in reference to your position on stage. Where do you stand? How do you get there? And how do you move from there? The answers to all of these question will have important consequences for your presentation.

Entrances and Exits

"Time for my close-up, Mr. DeMille." Those immortal words belong to the character of Norma Desmond in the film *Sunset Boulevard.* Desmond, an elderly, washed-up silent film star, lives in a fantasy world in which she's the toast of

Hollywood. She becomes involved with a younger man and kills him. In the final scene, police gather at the foot of a long staircase inside her decaying mansion. Desmond appears at the top of the stairs, sweeps halfway down, and utters her immortal line. She then slowly descends the remaining stairs and is swept off by the police. Desmond understands the importance of an entrance and an exit. She performs both simultaneously and makes them among the most famous in movie history.

Getting on with class

The beginning of a presentation is its most critical part. Everyone knows that. But when does it begin? This is a question of great philosophical dispute. Does it begin when you start speaking? When you walk to the podium? When you enter the room?

Great minds disagree, but I say play it safe. I say your presentation starts when you leave your home.

My position can be explained by a classic episode of *The Honeymooners*. Bus driver Ralph Kramden is scheduled to receive a safe driving award. En route to the award ceremony, he gets into a fender bender. Kramden and the driver of the other vehicle have a huge argument about who's at fault. When Kramden arrives at the ceremony, the VIP presenting the award turns out to be the driver of the other vehicle.

Once you leave your home, you never know when a member of your audience may see you. And if you're observed engaging in some dubious activity, your image may suffer. Remember what it was like in first grade when you saw your teacher in the supermarket for the first time? Wow. You mean she has to shop for food just like an ordinary mortal? It totally destroyed the teacher's all-powerful image. When you ascend the stage to speak, you want to project an aura of confidence and command.

You want to be all-powerful. You don't want any audience members to recall that an hour ago they saw you picking your teeth in the parking lot.

At a minimum, consider yourself "on" when you arrive at the site of your presentation. Be dressed and ready to go. A common mistake is to arrive in grungy clothes (guys) or without makeup (women). Yes, you may be able to dress at the site — in a bathroom or wherever. But someone will see you arrive and it will ruin your image. (Gee, how come this high-powered guy in the three-piece gray flannel suit who's analyzing economic trends was wearing tie-dyed jeans when he arrived?)

Get to the room early and make sure that the podium, microphone, and any audiovisual equipment are arranged properly. Pay particular attention to microphone cords and power cords. You don't want to open your talk by tripping and falling. If you're speaking on a stage, check where the stairs are located. Plan your route to the podium.

While you're waiting to speak, listen attentively to any speakers preceding you. When you're introduced, rise confidently and walk assuredly to the podium. Shaking hands with the person who introduced you is optional. (Unless the person extends his or her hand!)

When you arrive at the podium, place your notes where you want them. Open them. Look out at the audience. Pause. Then give one heck of a speech.

Getting off in style

Saying the last words of your presentation is only the beginning of the end. You still have a lot to do. And that doesn't mean hurriedly gathering up your notes and getting the heck out of there. First and foremost, you must bask in the thundering ovation that your audience will no doubt deliver. (If for some unfathomable reason they're not immediately forthcoming with applause, then you can give them a hint. At least that's what I do. On the rare occasions when a deafening roar of approval doesn't greet my closing, I make a short bowing motion. They usually get the message.)

After you've accepted your ovation (and answered any questions), you must disconnect yourself from the microphone (if you were using a lavaliere or wireless). Many speakers forget this step, and it can be quite embarrassing. Even if you don't wear the mike into the bathroom, everyone still hears you breathing. You lose credibility.

Once the microphone is detached, gather your speaking materials and depart from the podium in a confident manner. Stride purposefully back to your seat. Smile and acknowledge audience kudos along the way. If there's to be another speaker, become a model audience member. Wait expectantly for the speaker with your full attention directed at the podium.

Act this way even if you've just given the world's worst speech. It's amazing how people will give you the reaction you ask for. If *you* act like the presentation was a success (even if it wasn't), there's a better than average chance that the audience will play along. It makes *everybody* feel better.

One last reminder: you're never really finished until you've left the site of your speech, you no longer have contact with any audience members (like in a hotel bar after your talk), and you're home in bed.

Moving around

American wit Franklin P. Jones once observed, "Veteran speakers usually gesture vigorously and walk around. A moving target is harder to hit." Maybe so. But a moving speaker has a better chance of *being* a hit. Movement helps maintain audience attention. Of course, speakers who move endlessly and erratically will distract from their message. Here's how you can have all the right moves:

Do use up and down movements. Find a reason to bend over close to the floor or reach up into the air. Watch the televangelists on Sunday morning. They kneel down. They point up. This kind of movement makes you look more interesting to the audience.

Do move purposefully. Make every movement count. Whether you're gesturing, changing position, or walking from one location to another, the movement must support your message. Pacing is an example of *non*-purposeful movement that should be avoided.

Don't move in a regular pattern. A major value of movement is that it helps maintain audience attention. But moving in a regular pattern has an opposite effect. The predictability of any regular pattern lulls the audience into a semi-hypnotic state (that's also known as sleep). You want to keep moving. Just make sure no one else knows where you're going.

Do be aware of audience depth perception. Here's some uncommon knowledge. If you're speaking from a stage in a large room, moving left or right will have much more impact than moving forward or back. (It has to do with depth perception. Don't ask me to explain it.) This is important to remember because it goes against instinct. You'd assume that moving toward or away from the audience would have the bigger effect. It doesn't. A step forward or back doesn't have half the impact of a step left or right. Keep that in mind when you want to emphasize a point.

Don't make nervous movements. Speakers who constantly pull at their hair, shift from foot to foot, play with their notes, scratch themselves, and adjust their clothes are very distracting. So don't do any of that stuff. Don't be a perpetual motion machine. You'll end up looking very nervous or like you have to go the bathroom. Either way, the audience won't focus on what you're saying.

Basics of stage positioning

Assume the position. (No, don't put your hands behind your head and lay face down on the ground. You're not under arrest.) I'm talking about the power position if you're speaking from a stage. What's the power position? Divide the stage into a nine square grid: back left, back center, back right, left center, center center, right center, right front, center front, left front. The power position is center front.

But don't just stand there. Move into different squares as you speak. If you want a mechanical formula, find cues in your talk that suggest moves. "I was in a cattle store looking at bulls. And over on the right I saw (move to a square on the right) a beautiful set of china teacups. I took one to the proprietor (move into another square) and I said, 'Is this the famous china in a bull shop?'" (Now you better move to a rear square because with puns like that, the audience may start throwing things.)

This process of moving from square to square is called making an active stage picture. It ensures that you don't just stand in one place, and it makes you more interesting for the audience to watch. Just remember to return frequently to the power square.

Working from a podium

The common wisdom on podiums is that they act as a barrier between the speaker and the audience. The speaker is "hiding" behind the podium. So many public speaking teachers, communication coaches, and other professional presenter types give this advice: don't use one. And if you do use a podium, get out from behind it as often as possible.

The big deal that's made out of the podium being a barrier is a lot of baloney. My advice: if you want to use a podium, go right ahead.

Here are two reasons why, and the first is common sense:

- ✔ If you're comfortable behind a podium and nervous in front of it, then stay behind it. You'll give a better presentation. There's no point getting out from behind the podium to "eliminate a barrier with your audience" if doing so creates a bigger barrier — stage fright. (It's interesting how the same people who say the podium is a barrier also say that most people fear public speaking more than death. Don't they realize that speaking without a podium is even scarier? The lack of internal logic never ceases to amaze me.)

- ✔ The "barrier" argument is a myth. Alan Weiner, President of Communication Development Associates, says that a speaker's first connection with an audience is facial expression and eye contact. "I've seen studies," he says, "where the speaker's facial expressions and eye contact were so good that two weeks later the audience didn't remember whether a podium had been used." What about the argument that stepping away from the podium every so often gets attention because it eliminates the barrier? Alan's response: "It doesn't get attention because they can now see your whole body. It gets attention because it's a change. You've been standing behind the podium for awhile. Suddenly you're not. Any change gets attention."

Here's one more thing to think about: When the President of the United States gives a speech, he always uses a podium. John F. Kennedy and Ronald Reagan gave pretty good speeches — some of the best in this century. If a podium was good enough for them, I wouldn't worry about using one if it makes you feel comfortable.

Podium dos and don'ts

Do use the podium as a strategic tool. The podium doesn't just have to be a place where you dump your notes and make your speech. It can play a much more active role in your presentation. Timing is a perfect example. Comedian George Burns uses a cigar as a timing device. He puffs when he needs a pause for effect. Jim Lukaszewski uses a podium. "If I walk into the audience and make a point I want them to think about, they can't unless I stop talking," he says. So what does he do? He makes his point, turns his back to the audience, walks back to the podium. The time it takes him to move around allows the audience to think about the point he made. Jim plans these moments in advance just like George Burns plans when he'll puff his cigar. You can too.

Don't press or grip the podium. It's OK to use a podium — but not as a crutch. When I taught speech at USC, I had a student who wanted to do a reverse bench press with the podium. His hands were placed palms down on the podium, and he looked like he was trying to push it through the floor. He did this through his entire speech. It was a tad distracting.

The other common mistake is gripping the podium for dear life — like you'll float away if you let go. Again, it's disconcerting for the audience because it's an obvious indication of stage fright. So instead of concentrating on what the speaker is saying, the audience is mentally placing bets on when he or she will pass out.

Do look at your notes while you're moving behind the podium. Want to disguise your reliance on notes? Look at your notes whenever you move. When you make a gesture, shift position, turn your head, take a quick peek at your notes. The audience will focus on your movement rather than your reading.

Do use a podium to "hide" when appropriate. Even if you don't like to stay behind a podium, there may be times when you want to draw audience attention to something other than yourself. Are you using slides, overheads, or a volunteer from the audience? Standing behind a podium makes perfect sense for these situations, especially if the podium is placed off to the side.

How to Handle a Microphone

Tap. Tap. Tap. "Can you hear me? Is the mike workingggggggg?" Buzzz. Screeeeech. If I had a nickel for every time I've witnessed this scene, I could . . . well, I could buy a new microphone. There's no problem that makes a speaker look more like an amateur than inability to handle a mike, and there's no problem that's easier to correct. You just have to . . . buzzzzzzz. Screeeeeeech.

Should you use a mike?

The simple answer to the question of should you use a mike is "Yes." Unfortunately, an epidemic of mike-shunning has spread across the land. "No thanks, Mr. Meeting Organizer. I have a great voice. I don't need a microphone." Famous last words — at least the last ones that anyone hears. Why would anyone speaking to more than a handful of people ever refuse a microphone? Perhaps it's a backlash to technology. Perhaps it's some macho thing. Perhaps it's just a sincere desire to eliminate potential equipment hassles. Whatever the reason, it's a big mistake.

First, you lose the ability to augment your message with the subtle nuances of your voice. There isn't anything subtle about screaming your speech so that everyone can hear it. Second, you strain your vocal chords needlessly. And third, well, I'll let veteran speaker Jim Lukaszewski give the third reason: "It's the height of arrogance," he explains. "You immediately cut off audience members over fifty years old — a growing segment of the audience. Their hearing is less acute than younger audience members."

So don't reject the microphone. Embrace it. Move it close to your lips and talk to it softly. You'll sound like you're having an intimate conversation with the audience.

The microphone is your friend. Use it to your advantage.

Types of mikes

Microphone selection is important for much more than sound quality. The type of microphone you use can dictate many other aspects of your presentation. For example, a wireless mike lets you walk into the crowd. A mike with a cord puts you at the end of a leash. And a mike built into the podium means you can't move at all. This can be a problem if you're flipping your own overheads and the projector is located ten feet away. Here's a rundown of the mikes you're likely to encounter:

Built-in podium mike

Many podiums come with a built-in mike. This kind of mike has a major disadvantage, as it limits your movements severely. You can't walk around. You can't even come out from behind the podium. You're stuck there. When Loyd Auerbach gets into this situation, he lets the audience know: "I'd love to move around here, folks, but carrying this podium just isn't going to make it for me." The line gets a laugh and absolves Loyd of potential criticism for not walking around. Another problem with built-in podium mikes is that you're limited by their physical dimensions. If you're tall and the mike is short, you have to bend down to speak into it. Kind of a dumb-looking way to give a speech, but what's your choice? The choice, as always, is advance planning. Tell the meeting organizers you want a detachable mike. Even if the podium has a built-in mike, they can still get you another one. I do this all the time. I speak from a podium with a built-in, but I use a lavaliere or wireless mike. (One thing to remember if you do this: turn off the built-in podium mike. Otherwise, you may get ear-splitting feedback when you get near it with the mike you are using.)

Hand-held mike

A hand-held mike lets you move around. Many speakers like this mike because it gives them a place to put one of their hands. But that cuts both ways. It means you can't gesture with both hands while you're speaking. (Otherwise the audience can't hear you because the mike is away from your mouth.) You also have to contend with a cord, which limits how far you can move and requires you to avoid tripping over it. But what bugs me the most about hand-held mikes is that you always have to be aware of how far you're holding the mike from your mouth. If you hold it a fraction of an inch out of range, the mike won't pick up anything you say. It's like not having a mike at all. I'd rather not have to think about this problem while I'm speaking. There are enough other things to think about.

Lavaliere mike

The lavaliere mike (also called a lapel mike) clips onto your shirt, blouse, jacket, or tie. Sometimes it's also worn necklace style. The mike is attached to a loop of string which is placed over your head. The mike then rests on your chest like a pendant. In either case, a cord runs from the mike back to a power source. The cord is the only disadvantage of the lavaliere mike. It acts like a leash, letting you move only as far as its length. And you have to avoid tripping over it. I've seen speakers who move back and forth as they speak get their legs completely tangled in lavaliere mike cords. Then they have to disentangle themselves while still speaking and hope no one notices. (All right, I admit it — I've done this more than once.) The big advantages of the lavaliere mike are that you can gesture with both hands, you don't have to worry about where it is in relation to your mouth after its initial positioning, and you *can* walk around — even if it's a limited distance.

Wireless mike

The wireless mike is like a lavaliere mike but without the cord. The mike clips onto your shirt, blouse, jacket, or tie. A thin wire runs from the mike to a small box (like a beeper) that clips onto your belt or pocket. The wireless is always my first choice. There's no cord to trip over or limit your movements. Both your hands are free to gesture. And you don't have to worry about whether the mike is close enough to your mouth (assuming you've clipped it on properly). If anyone ever tries to talk you out of using a wireless mike, be suspicious. They often cost more to rent and the person running the meeting may just be trying to save money. That shouldn't be your problem.

Tricks and Tips

John Cantu is a San Francisco comedy coach with more than twenty years of professional experience. He has worked with everyone from nationally known business speakers and entertainers to aspiring lecturers and presenters of every type. Here are some of his tricks and tips for using a microphone:

How to check the mike

Familiarize yourself with the sound system well in advance of your presentation. Learn how the mike turns on and off and how far you can hold it from your mouth and still be heard. When you test a mike to see if it's live, don't bark, "Is this thing on?" (Unless you want to be heard by everyone within a ten mile radius.) Instead, just tap the head of the mike. If it's on, you'll hear a metallic "thunk, thunk."

How to take control of the mike

The speaker, who is six feet tall, is introduced and walks on stage. The mike is only adjusted to a height of five feet, eight inches. What happens next is critical. The speaker should adjust the mike up to the proper height. But what often happens is the speaker will bend over to speak into the mike — and stay that way for the entire presentation. "It sends a message of weakness," notes John Cantu. "You must control the mike, not be controlled by it." (Plus you end up with a terrible neckache the next day.)

If the mike goes dead

You can usually tell when the mike goes dead. If this happens when you're speaking, *drop the mike*. It looks really dumb to speak into a dead mike. You might tell the audience you're sorry the sound went out. (Or you might have some funny lines ready for this situation. See Chapter 22.) Then, if you have the lungs for it, continue your talk without the mike. Assume that someone will take care of getting the sound system corrected. How do you know if the sound comes back on? Tap the head of the mike about once a minute. When you hear a metallic "thunk, thunk," it's live again. So bring the mike back to your mouth and talk into it.

How loud to speak if you have no mike

If the mike goes dead and you continue without one, you must speak loud enough to be heard by the entire audience. But how loud do you need to be? Sometimes it's difficult to judge. Here's what to do: Look out at the last row and speak as if you were having a conversation with someone in that row. Use whatever volume you would use if you were both separated by the length of the room. Even if it seems too loud to you, it will sound natural to the audience. If you speak to the last row, everyone else can also hear.

How to hold the mike in relation to your face

If you stick the microphone right in front of your face, it creates a barrier with the audience. Remember that you're trying to have a conversation with them. As John Cantu points out, "Most people who have a conversation with you don't do it with a metal object stuck to their face." His solution: Hold the microphone about a half inch below your chin. "It will essentially disappear," he says.

How to gesture while holding a mike

If you're using a hand-held mike, gesturing can be a problem. Don't worry. You've got two choices for handling the situation. You can limit your gestures to one arm and hand while you speak. (The other hand holds the mike to your mouth). Or you can gesture with both arms and hands — *if you stop talking while you're gesturing*. If you don't stop talking, no one will hear you because the mike will be away from your mouth (in one of your gesturing hands). This is a very common mistake. You'll hear the speaker's voice fading in and out as his gestures move the mike closer or farther from his mouth. Just remember: one hand, keep talking; two hands, stop talking. Either choice is acceptable as long as you do it correctly.

Paralanguage: What Your Voice Says about You

In the mid-1970s, I moved from New York to Los Angeles to teach freshman speech at the University of Southern California. I was quite a role model for my students. "Tawk like dis or ya flunk." (Fortunately, it didn't matter. I had the football team as students — they couldn't talk anyway.) But my accent was an endless source of amusement to my colleagues. Luckily a grad student from Dallas showed up. Once they heard her, my accent was quickly forgotten.

A popular radio commercial says that people judge you by the words you use. Well, they also judge by how you use them. Do you say the words loudly? Rapidly? Monotonously? Do you have an accent? Do you mispronounce them? All of these factors — *how* you say things, *not what* you say — are known as *paralanguage*.

I didn't know it was on

The invention of the modern sound system was a great advance in the history of public speaking. People giving presentations didn't have to worry whether their voice could cover an entire room. The microphone eliminated the problem. But there was a down side. You had to be constantly aware whether the mike was on or off. And it was easy to forget when it was on. Three famous examples illustrate the danger of not knowing that the mike was on.

✓ Uncle Don was an entertainer who had one of the most successful radio programs for children in the 1930s and 1940s. His career took an abrupt downward spiral after one of his popular broadcasts. Unaware that the mike was still on, Uncle Don was allegedly heard by a nationwide audience as he spoke to a colleague in his studio. He said, "I guess that'll hold the little bastards for another night."

✓ Former President Ronald Reagan, often called the Great Communicator, should have known better. He was preparing for his weekly, presidential radio broadcast when he picked up a microphone to do a voice level check. Unfortunately, he didn't say, "Testing, one, two, three." Instead, he said, "My fellow Americans, I am pleased to tell you today I've signed legislation that will outlaw Russia forever. We begin bombing in five minutes." You guessed it. The mike was live and the remark went out on the airwaves. The Russians didn't find it amusing.

✓ Senator Bob Kerry of Nebraska was running for President in 1991. During a campaign appearance in New Hampshire, he told an off-color joke involving lesbians to another candidate. The joke was told in a private conversation. Unfortunately, Senator Kerry was unaware of the C-Span microphone nearby. It accidentally picked up the conversation. Although the tape was never broadcast, the incident and the joke were reported widely in the press — much to the embarrassment of the Kerry campaign.

So be advised. Don't say anything confidential or controversial near a microphone. Don't tell offensive jokes. And never call children little . . . well, you know.

Tricks and tips

My friend Loyd Auerbach is a corporate trainer for Lexis/Nexis as well as a professional magician. So he makes a lot of presentations. Here are some of his tricks and tips for using your voice:

Warm up your voice

You're about to speak. You're opening line is a gem. People will be quoting it for years. You're introduced. You get to the podium. You open your mouth to deliver your bon mots and . . . your voice cracks. So much for the brilliant opening. That's why you need to warm up your voice. Go into the bathroom before you speak and do some vocal exercises. Hum. Talk to yourself. Get your voice going. (But make sure that no one is in there with you. You *don't* want anyone in the audience to remember you as the person talking to himself in the bathroom.)

Don't mumble

You know that it's not polite to speak with your mouth full. Well, it's also not polite to sound like you're speaking with your mouth full — especially if you have an audience. It's hard enough for one person to understand another even when they each know exactly what was said. Don't make it even more difficult. Pronounce your words clearly.

Don't say ah or um — OK?

Get rid of filler sounds and phrases. They take up space for no reason, sound dumb, and distract the audience from your message. Banish these words and phrases from your vocal vocabulary: like, you know, um, okay, ugh, ah, actually, interestingly enough.

Don't be monotonous

It's common knowledge that a monotonous voice is boring. Here's the uncommon knowledge: monotony refers to more than just tone of voice. Yes, a monotonous voice may be the result of speaking in one tone. But it may also result from speaking at one rate of speed, in one volume, or in one pitch. If you're monotonous in any of those ways, you have a problem. If you're monotonous in all of those ways, the audience will fall asleep. The cure is vocal variety.

Use your voice for emphasis

You can completely alter the meaning of a sentence simply by changing the words you emphasize. Say the following line aloud and emphasize the word in italics. "Are you talking to *me*?" "Are *you* talking to me?" "Are you *talking* to me?" All right, enough with the Robert DeNiro impressions. You get the idea. Use vocal emphasis to reinforce the meanings you wish to communicate.

Slow down for flubs

No this isn't a road sign from Burma Shave. It refers to flubs you make when you speak. No one is perfect. Everyone makes mistakes. (You can quote me on that. It's a real insight, right?) Inevitably, you will mispronounce a word or stumble through a tongue-twisting phrase. The natural instinct is to speed up when you make a mistake. Don't. It highlights your error and increases your chances for making additional errors. Just slow down.

Don't discount volume

Volume is a powerful tool that's easy to manipulate. It may be tough to change your pitch or tone, but anyone can talk louder or softer. And it can have an amazing effect on an audience.

Let's clear up a big myth. Many speakers think you should never speak softly. Wrong. Speaking softly can be incredibly effective. I've seen speakers whisper and draw in an entire audience. People lean forward in their seats. How can they hear? As the current White House staff might say, "It's the microphone, stupid!" If you're speaking into a microphone, it doesn't matter if you speak softly. That's the whole point of using the microphone — it allows you to speak in a full range of volumes.

Speaking at a high volume can also be used dramatically. There's a point in one of my presentations where I talk about a man who's engaged in a full-scale domestic squabble (furniture being thrown around and stuff like that). A police officer rings his doorbell, and he yells, "Who is it?" When I tell this story, I calmly and quietly describe the police officer ringing the doorbell. Then I scream, "Who is it?" into the microphone. The audience is always stunned. It gets their attention. (And no, I don't blow out their eardrums.)

Any time you shift your volume, people will pay attention. It's an easy way to vary your speech pattern. So use it.

Don't be afraid to pause

A common mistake of inexperienced (and nervous) speakers is to speak without pausing. They just rush though their presentations, one thought merging into another. The audience *listens* to a lot of words but doesn't *hear* a thing. They become clogged with information.

The pause is a vital part of the communication process. "It leaves time for the meaning of what's been said to sink in," explains speech guru Jim Lukaszewski. "And it clears the way for the importance of what comes next." He also notes that pausing before a change of subject, major point, or interesting fact creates an impression of confidence. It also highlights the point. Loyd Auerbach believes a pause should always precede an important point. In fact, he suggests actively looking for opportunities to build pauses into your presentation.

So don't be afraid to pause. And don't forget: Your audience is like a bunch of McDonald's customers — they deserve a break today.

Vary your repetitions

An old adage on the lecture circuit says if you want people to really get a point, then you need to repeat it — but in a different way. You're supposed to repeat the point using different words.

Here's the uncommon knowledge courtesy of Loyd Auerbach: Use different vocal characteristics as well. Repeat the point using a different volume, rate, or tone. "It gives your words another path into the listener's brain," Loyd explains.

Listen to William Shatner

You can learn a lot about speaking patterns by observing professional performers. How do your favorite actors and actresses use their voices? What do they do vocally that affects their message?

Loyd Auerbach believes every speaker should observe William Shatner, best known as the actor who played Captain Kirk in *Star Trek*. Comedians have long poked fun at Shatner's delivery — especially his use of pauses and phrasing. He'll start . . . a sentence with a pause right near the beginning and thennn do a long discussionnnn where he slowssss downnnnn and stretechesssss out every wordddddd and then suddenly he'll speak really fast. "He's a clinic in how to use vocal variety to gain and hold attention," says Loyd. "Every time he pauses or shifts his speed or changes his volume, it's an unexpected stimulus that arouses audience attention. These are all tools that keep people listening."

Chapter 17

How to Handle an Audience (Without Leaving Fingerprints)

● ●

In This Chapter

▶ How to "read" an audience's reaction

▶ The most common types of tough audiences

▶ Dealing with hecklers and other pains in the neck

▶ What to do when you're losing the audience

▶ Surefire audience involvement techniques

● ●

*Y*ou can have the world's greatest presentation, but that may not mean very much if you have the world's worst audience. An audience is like a thorny, long-stemmed rose. Handled properly, it's a thing of beauty that can blossom as you speak. Handled improperly, it will prick you severely.

How to "Read" an Audience's Reaction

Many professional speakers claim they can "read" an audience like a book. I've always wondered what that means. They read a little of the audience at bedtime, drift off to sleep, and read some more the next day? They mark up the audience with a yellow highlighter? They put a bookmark down the audience's throat? In any event, it makes a lot more sense to read an audience like an audience — a group of people who have to listen to your presentation. What follows are a few ways to gauge their reactions.

Energy level

One of the easiest ways to read an audience is by observing its energy level. Are people talking and laughing as they wait for the event to begin? That's a high-energy audience, and that's what you hope for. It'll be much more receptive to your presentation. A high-energy audience is basically yours to lose. If you have a high-energy audience, you don't have to be high-energy yourself. (Although it doesn't hurt.)

Here's a tip from San Francisco comedy coach John Cantu: A high-energy audience will laugh and applaud longer than a low-energy audience. Therefore, you need to allow extra time for laughter and applause when you calculate how much you can say in the time you've been allotted. (See his formula in Chapter 6.)

A low-energy audience is just the opposite. No one's talking, and the mood is kind of blah. (This mood often correlates to specific times of the day and week. For example, Monday night audiences are typically low energy.) This audience will be tough. You have to be high energy. You have to ignite the audience.

Body language

The nonverbal behavior of your audience can tell you an enormous amount about the effectiveness of your presentation. Are people nodding at what you say? Are they looking up at you? Are they leaning forward? Are they smiling? Or are they squirming in their seats, nudging each other, looking at their watches, and staring out the windows? (You don't need a Ph.D. to interpret these signals.)

Don't judge the entire audience by the reactions of a single person. This tip sounds obvious, but speakers do it all the time. There'll be one sourpuss who won't crack a smile. You'll become obsessed with this person and make all of your speaking decisions based on the sourpuss' reaction. That's usually a mistake. Because nothing you do will work with the sourpuss, you'll get nervous, feel you're bombing, and screw up. If you look at the other 99 percent of the audience, you see that it is enjoying your talk — at least until you screw it up by focusing on the sourpuss.

Questions

If you don't know if people in an audience agree with you, disagree with you, or even understand what you're saying, ask them. That's the direct method of reading audience reaction. ("How many of you are familiar with the large oil spill that I was just talking about?" "How many of you disagree with what I just said?" "How many of you have never heard any of these arguments before?")

Giving Permission

Most people are cautious in an unfamiliar situation. If they're interacting with a stranger, they assume a conservative demeanor. They don't let their guard down and kick back until they're sure that it's a safe behavior. Audiences react in much the same way. If Bob Hope steps up to a podium, the audience knows it's OK to laugh. If someone the audience doesn't know steps up to the podium, people in the audience don't know how they're expected to behave. You have to tell them.

Management communication counselor Jim Lukaszewski calls this process giving permission. "Most of us are strangers in front of crowds," he explains. "So you have to give the audience permission to enjoy your speech." Jim likens this process to having a continuing side conversation with the audience. "I give them substantive information in my speeches," he explains. "But I also keep giving them permission to react in various ways."

What kind of permissions must audiences receive? It all depends on what you want to accomplish and how you want them to react. Here are three of the more important permissions you can bestow on your listeners:

Permission to laugh

Do you want to use humor successfully in your talk? Then one of the most important permissions you can give your audience is permission to laugh. Joe DiNucci, Vice President of Manufacturing Industries at Silicon Graphics, is famous for his humor-filled talks to customers and employees. He starts by telling them it's OK to enjoy themselves. He'll say something like, "I intend to communicate and inform and enlighten and bring insight, but it is an explicit goal that you be entertained. So loosen up your tie. Loosen up your mind. Turn off the immune system that rejects anything that's amusing. I promise you there's a lot of meat in this material, but we also put some fun in with it too."

Permission to learn

Jim Lukaszewski likes to give his audiences permission to learn. He'll say, "I believe this is a really important speech. I'm going to be talking about three sensitive, important topics. I'll go into more detail later. But I think when you leave here today, the things you'll really remember about this talk are these key areas. . . ." By telling the audience what's important, Jim gives the audience insight into his interpretation of his own talk. "I've given them permission to enter my psychological being," he explains. "Now they can actively follow the outline with me — not just react to it as I dump it out there."

Permission to write

Now here's some uncommon knowledge from Jim — one of the most important permissions that you can give your audience is the permission to take notes. He'll start by saying something like, "My speech is packed with information you'll want to remember. That's why there are pencils and paper at your seats. And if you don't have some, please make friends immediately with someone who does because you'll need them."

This permission flies in the face of the traditional wisdom that considers writing to be a distraction. "A lot of trainers believe you can't have people writing and paying attention to you at the same time," says Jim. "That's dumb. What is greater than having hundreds of people writing things down as you speak?" How does he make sure they won't miss anything? "I shut up and let them write," he explains. "And guess what — if I stop talking, they start writing."

How to Handle a Tough Audience

The audience was so tough, when they gave the speaker a standing ovation they were standing on his chest. When the speaker began to talk, the audience took their seats — and everything else that wasn't nailed down. When the speaker asked, "Am I on target?" the audience said, "Bullseye!" and took aim.

Not every audience you ever address will be an absolute delight. When you face a tough crowd you have some choices. You can figure out the problem and handle it, or you can wait for a standing ovation — on your chest.

The most common types of tough audiences

Easy audiences are all alike; but every tough audience is tough in its own way. (My apologies to Leo Tolstoy.) Here are some of the varieties you may encounter:

Offbeat audience

An offbeat audience responds in ways that you don't anticipate. They laugh or applaud when you don't expect it, and they're silent when you expect applause.

That's why they're tough. They throw off your entire rhythm. There's nothing you can do besides go with the flow. Just don't cue the audience members that you find their responses unusual. Pause for their applause when you get it and keep speaking when you don't.

Captive audience

The captive audience is tough because it's not there by choice. Attendance at your presentation has been forced upon these people for one reason or another, and they resent it. So they're in a foul mood before you ever begin. It's not your fault. It has nothing to do with you, but you'll have to bear the brunt of their anger. What can you do? Acknowledge the situation up front and appeal to their sense of fairness. Tell them what benefits they can expect to receive if they simply take the chips off their shoulders and give you a fair chance.

More educated or experienced than you audience

A classic joke from the lecture circuit tells of the last living survivor of the Johnstown flood who finally came to the end of his days. Saint Peter greeted him at the Pearly Gates and said some old timers would like to gather and hear the latest word from earth. Did he have anything interesting to talk about? The new arrival said he'd been a major attraction on the lecture circuit on earth with his tales about the Johnstown flood. So Saint Peter brought him in, introduced him, and said he had something very interesting to say. And then just as Saint Peter turned to leave, he whispered in the fellow's ear, "That man second from the left in the front row — his name is Noah."

What can you do when your audience knows more about your subject than you do? You can reframe your entire presentation as a review of the basics. As an alternative, you may decide to make the talk intensely personal. The presentation becomes a description of *your* feelings, ideas, and reactions regarding the subject matter. Or you can elevate the discussion to a higher, "big picture" level. (I'm not here to talk about floods today. Obviously Mr. Noah knows a lot more about them than I do. My comments today will examine the basic relationship between man and nature and how mankind responds to adverse circumstances. Into each life a little rain must fall. . . .)

Hostile to your position audience

You're speaking pro or con about a controversial issue — gun control, abortion, Burt Reynolds' hairpiece, whatever. Your audience holds an opinion that's the opposite of yours. So you know it'll be hostile to what you have to say. This will be a tough crowd.

The best approach is to try to disarm the audience members immediately. Begin by acknowledging that you have a difference of opinion. (And don't apologize for your opinion; you're entitled to it.) Then appeal to the traditional values of fairness, free speech, and dialogue. Let them know that they'll have a chance to air their views after you're finished speaking. ("We are going to disagree on some fundamental issues. But that's why I'm here today — to have a dialogue about the effects of the hole in the ozone layer. If we all believed the same thing, we couldn't have much of a dialogue. And we will have one because after I'm done speaking, anyone who wishes to express an opinion will have an opportunity to do so. I only ask that you give me a fair chance to make my case without interrupting me. You don't need to let me know how much you disagree with me. I already know.")

Didn't come to see you audience

The keynote speaker may be the latest business babble guru who has written a best-selling book on leadership, the latest politician with his own personality cult, or the latest celebrity in the limelight. That's who the audience has come to see. Unfortunately, the audience has to sit through a few other speakers before it gets to hear the guru. Even more unfortunate, *you* are one of the speakers that must precede the guru.

These audiences are tough because they want you to be finished before you've even started. You can't do very much about it, but you may find some relief by referring to the guru in your remarks as often as possible. That may be the only thing you can say to get a positive response from the audience. (I'm honored to be here today, speaking in the same program as Mr. Guru. In fact, many of my ideas have been influenced directly by Mr. Guru's work. How many of you would agree with me that Mr. Guru's book *Babble Your Way to Leadership* is the most important business book of the century? Later on today, you'll hear Mr. Guru speak about leadership. But right now I'd like to discuss a few concepts that will give you a deeper insight into Mr. Guru's ideas.) Is this pandering to the audience? You bet it is. Do you have any other choice? Yes. You can give your presentation as planned to the accompaniment of audience hoots and jeers. ("Hey, shut up and sit down." "Get off the stage." "We want the Guru.") It's up to you.

The current event distracted audience

You're speaking to a group of fund raisers about new techniques to increase donations, and you're an expert on the topic. It's a perfect match between speaker, topic, and audience. Your audience members should pay undivided attention and take notes, but they aren't. They seem distracted; they're definitely not listening. What's the problem? Two hours before you started speaking, the space shuttle Challenger exploded, or the Oklahoma City Federal Building was bombed, or the President was shot. Some major event has usurped the consciousness of the audience, and everything else — especially your speech — seems unimportant by comparison.

The distracting event need not be national in scope. It may be very local. In fact, it may be specific to your audience. (You're scheduled to give a brown bag lunch presentation about investment opportunities to a group of employees from Thud-Tech, Inc. That morning, Thud-Tech's CEO projects a record quarterly loss and indicates that massive layoffs will be forthcoming. Thud-Tech employees will *not* be focusing on your talk.)

What if you're scheduled to speak on the day that a distracting event has occurred? Try to get your speech canceled or changed to another time. If neither is possible, be prepared to talk about the distracting event because that may be the only subject that will interest your audience.

Mirror image audience

You're the only male at a female event or vice versa. You're the only Black at a Caucasian event or vice versa. You're the only Jew at a Christian event or vice versa.

You get the idea. You're the mirror image of your audience. Audience members will be tough if they assume that you can't possibly understand their point of view. After all, you're different from them.

Start by breaking the tension. Acknowledge your difference. If appropriate, poke fun at it. Then establish your common ground. You are speaking to this audience for a reason. Members of the audience can receive some benefit from listening to you. Let them know what it is — fast.

Angry at previous speaker audience

The speaker before you has really riled up the audience members. In fact, they're mad as hell. Maybe the speaker was controversial. Maybe he was insulting. Maybe she was offensive. Whatever the case, the audience is in a vile mood, and they want to take it out on you. The most important thing you can do in this situation is *be aware of it*. You need to know that the audience is angry at the prior speaker, not you.

Failure to recognize this situation can jeopardize your entire presentation. You'll assume that *you* are the problem and adjust your performance accordingly. That won't work because you're *not* the problem. It's imperative to learn what any previous speakers said to your audience. Attend their presentations if possible. If not, find out what happened. Then, if there's been a problem, you can address it immediately in the opening of your talk.

I found myself in this situation several years ago when I gave a talk to a group of law firm administrators. The speaker before me was scheduled to talk about financial planning. It had been promoted as a nuts-and-bolts session, and the administrators had anticipated receiving a lot of useful information. Unfortunately, it turned out to be a two-hour sales pitch to hire the speaker as a personal financial planner. (I caught the last half hour, and it was like the Twilight Zone. It felt like being trapped inside an infomercial.) Well, to say that the audience was a tad upset would be putting it mildly. Especially at the end, when the speaker passed out contracts and tried to sign up new clients on the spot.

The audience still had a foul taste in its mouth when I approached the podium to talk about humor. The antagonism in the room was palpable. Having been burned once, the audience radiated distrust. If looks could kill, I would have been dead — many times over. Fortunately, I had seen part of the previous speaker's presentation and knew what had happened. My opening line became, "I'd like to sell you some personal financial planning." The audience laughed. I followed up with some comments showing my empathy for what they'd gone through. And I assured the audience that the only thing I had to sell was "the idea that humor is a powerful communication tool." Then I spent an hour giving the audience nuts-and-bolts information on how to use humor in a business context.

Already heard it audience

The speakers before you have made acceptable presentations. They've left the audience in decent shape for your talk. The audience isn't angry or upset about anything. But that can change rapidly if you get up and repeat what the previous speakers have already said.

Why would anyone do that? It happens all the time, and there are two major causes. Either you're unaware of what the previous speakers said. Or despite the fact that you know they've already said what you planned to say, you plow ahead with your prepared remarks anyway. Audiences absolutely hate this. (That's why so many people try to avoid all-day business conferences. When the fifth speaker in a row gets up and talks about the importance of synergy, commitment to change, and the globalization of business, you just want to puke.)

If you find yourself in this situation, don't just do your presentation as if the audience members haven't already heard the same thing. You'll lose them instantly. You have to adapt. At a minimum, you have to acknowledge that you'll be saying things that they've already heard. A much more effective strategy is to abandon your prepared remarks entirely. Just wing it. Think of a different angle and speak about it on an impromptu basis. Comment on what the previous speakers have already said. Or solicit participation from the audience.

Computer guru N. R. Mitgang found himself facing this situation when he was a speaker at the PC Expo — one of the largest technical conferences in New York. He was supposed to speak about the pros and cons of commercial publishers producing CD-ROMs in-house versus out-of-house. He was scheduled to be the first of three speakers. Unfortunately, he was provided with a computer that malfunctioned. By the time he repaired it, the other two speakers had made their presentations — and covered everything Mitgang had planned to say. So he opened by telling the audience that everything he'd planned to say had already been said, and given that fact, he would tell them "what the industry is really all about." He then told a series of war stories from his work publishing CD-ROMs. It was the highlight of the session.

Sick audience

The sick audience is literally ill. Numerous members of this audience cough and sneeze loudly throughout your presentation. It's quite a distraction, but there's not much you can do about it. You can try using humor to deal with the situation. ("Please hold your applause and coughing till the end.") If that doesn't work, you're out of luck. (Anyway, that's what you get for volunteering to speak at a meeting of AA — Allergics Anonymous.)

Hecklers and other pains in the neck

The traditional notion of a heckler is someone who interrupts a speaker by shouting out hostile remarks or questions. (Of course, that definition could also apply to the White House press corps.) I'm going to define heckling a little more broadly. My definition of heckling is anything someone does to purposely distract you or the audience from your talk. Here are some of the hecklers you may encounter:

The non-heckler

I want to start with some uncommon knowledge from San Francisco comedy coach John Cantu. *The most common distractions caused by audience members may seem like heckling, but they're not.* "Speakers have a tendency to think that anyone who is talking or not paying attention is purposely trying to be a distraction," he explains. "I've seen speakers get very insulted. Then it turns out that the person talking was asking someone how to get to the bathroom. Or someone had to leave the room to call a baby-sitter." Perhaps the most unusual example is one that occurred at one of John's lectures. "One of my students had a heart attack," he recalls. "When he closed his eyes, he wasn't heckling me." So take a tip from John. Don't assume you're being heckled. Your audience is innocent until proven otherwise.

The dweeb

The dweeb is someone who unintentionally engages in distracting behavior. Suppose you ask a rhetorical question. The dweeb will shout out an answer. Technically, it's not heckling because dweebs aren't purposely trying to disrupt the proceedings. They just don't know any better.

The one-upper

The one-upper is a heckler who wants attention. If you ask the audience for questions, the one-upper will jump in with some sarcastic comment or tough question designed to embarrass you. It's not that the one-upper dislikes you personally or even disagrees with your positions. You're just a prop for the one-upper to manipulate in an unending quest for attention.

The under-the-influence heckler

If you speak at enough dinner meetings, you'll eventually run into an under-the-influence heckler. These people have had a few too many, and they exhibit the typical effects of alcohol (or drugs) — they get very angry, sad, or happy. Whichever mood it is, they display it to an exaggerated degree. They shout or cry or laugh in a way that completely disrupts your presentation.

The attack dog

The attack dog is the traditional heckler. This person doesn't like you or your opinions and is determined to stop you from speaking. He or she will try to shout you down, insult you, and do whatever it takes to cause a commotion. These people want to fight — with *you*.

Dealing with hecklers

Although many speakers fantasize and worry about facing hecklers, the situation isn't really that common. If you're not speaking about a controversial issue, the problem usually won't arise. But if you ever do find yourself confronting hecklers, here are a few dos and don'ts for handling them:

Don't get angry. Hecklers want control. If you get angry, you give them exactly what they want — a negative reaction (and confirmation that you've lost control). So stay calm at all times. If nothing else, it will drive the heckler nuts.

Do identify the type of heckler. Why are you being heckled? Is the heckler drunk? Is she opposed to you or your views? Does he simply want attention? You need to know why the heckling started so you can determine how you'll end it.

Do be empathic. Sometimes you can defuse hecklers just by acknowledging their point of view. Let them know that you understand their position, even though you don't agree with it.

Do suggest that the heckler speak with you after your presentation. Here's how Jeff Raleigh does it: "Listen my friend, this is my speech. If you want to argue with me afterwards, you're more than welcome. I'll be glad to talk to you later, but right now, you're insulting the rest of the audience."

Don't argue. It just gives legitimacy to the heckler and makes you look bad. And that's exactly what the heckler wants you to do.

Do look for help. You shouldn't have to deal with audience members who are out of control. Seek help from the person running the meeting or the person who invited you to speak. You can also appeal to the audience members for assistance. (Let them tell the heckler to shut up.)

Heckling the hecklers

The greatest nightmare for many speakers is the prospect of being interrupted by a heckler. But here's what's overlooked — being heckled provides a great opportunity for the speaker to respond with wit and acumen. In fact, a good retort is usually remembered long after the actual presentation is forgotten. What follows are some examples.

Al Smith was a popular governor of New York and a presidential candidate. During a campaign speech, he was interrupted by a heckler who yelled, "Tell 'em what's on your mind, Al. It shouldn't take long." Smith didn't miss a beat. He replied, "I'll tell 'em what's on both of our minds. It won't take any longer."

William Gladstone and Benjamin Disraeli were archrivals in the British Parliament. During one of their many debates, Gladstone yelled at Disraeli, "You, sir, will die either on the gallows or of some loathsome disease." Disraeli responded, "That, sir, depends upon whether I embrace your principles or your mistress."

President William Howard Taft received the ultimate heckle during a campaign appearance. Someone threw a cabbage at him. Taft evaded the projectile and said, ""One of my opponents has apparently lost his head."

Nancy Astor, the first woman to sit in the British House of Commons, was an outspoken proponent of women's rights. During one of her speeches on the subject, a heckler interrupted with comments about Lady Astor's numerous bracelets and necklace. The heckler said, "You have enough brass on you, Lady Astor, to make a kettle." Astor's reply was quick and devastating: "And you have enough water in your head to fill it."

During a campaign speech, Al Smith was repeatedly interrupted by a heckler who shouted, "Liar!" After ignoring the heckler proved fruitless, Smith replied, "If the gentleman would be so kind as to give us his name as well as his calling, we should be happy to hear from him."

Don't feel obligated to continue. If the heckler won't stop and no one will help you, then end your presentation. Tell the audience that you can't proceed due to the disruption. Then exit gracefully.

Dealing with other distractions

Hecklers will probably remain a rare occurrence at your presentations; other distractions will be far more common. If you're speaking at a lunch or dinner, a waiter will inevitably drop some dishes during your talk. If there are children present, a baby will cry. The audience member with the loudest ringing cellular phone will receive a call while you're speaking. The list goes on.

When these types of distractions occur, an audience will often react with laughter. If that happens, you have to laugh right along with the audience. Once again it's a control issue. You have to show the audience that you're handling the problem and that you remain in control. (It's analogous to skidding while driving a car. If you steer into the skid, you regain control.) If you get upset about the distraction, the audience will become uncomfortable, and you'll lose momentum.

Anticipate things that can go wrong and have some quips ready to deal with them. For example, assume the room lights go out because of a power failure. You might say, "Now I'm really going to have to shed some light on the subject." (No it's not hilarious, but it doesn't have to be. It communicates that you're not upset and that you're still in control.)

How to Handle a Non-Responsive Audience

There are subtle clues that tell you when you're not clicking with an audience. (People don't nod in agreement, but they do nod out.) If you want to save your presentation, then you have to take charge. It's like working in an emergency room. You need to figure out what's wrong with the patients, but first you have to revive them — before its too late. So let's look at some resuscitation techniques for non-responsive audiences.

What to do if you're losing them

An audience first-aid kit includes a variety of devices for reviving interest in your talk. Like the contents of a real first-aid kit, these devices range in strength from band aids to adrenaline shots. You have to know how to use the appropriate device for the audience in front of you. I find it convenient to diagnose a dying audience by sorting it into one of three categories.

Level one: you've still got their attention, but they look bored or puzzled

The audience is still watching you speak, but you can sense that you're not connecting. They're fidgeting. They're not responding. What can you do? You must break out of the pattern you're in. Talk directly to the audience like it's a real conversation. Ask them if they understand what you're talking about. Ask if they'd like you to give another example. Or tell them that what you're about to say is very important. Emphasize a key benefit that really puts them in the picture. ("Now I'd like to tell you the only guaranteed way to prevent yourself from being laid off in the next two years.")

Or you can say something that you feel is guaranteed to get applause. (The energy of their hands clapping will help prevent the onset of lethargy.) What if you're waiting for applause and you don't get it? Say something like, "Oh, I guess you didn't think that was as important as I did." If they laugh, you've connected with them. If they don't, you're not any worse off.

John Cantu says that if you want to maximize your chances of getting applause, you should ask the audience some questions and tell them to respond with applause instead of a show of hands. ("How many of you can't wait until my speech is finished?" Thundering ovation.)

Level two: their attention is waning

The audience is starting to drift off. People are staring at the ceiling, out the windows, and at their watches. The only thing they're not looking at is you. One of the simplest things you can do to revive this audience is also one of the most effective — just ask them to stand up. Say something like, "You've been sitting down for awhile now. And I think we could all use a short stretch. Everyone stand up. . . . OK, sit back down. Feel better?" It's amazing how this can transform the energy level in the room. (That's why they have a seventh inning stretch at baseball games.) But let me add a word of caution. The effect is temporary. When the audience members retake their seats they will pay attention for a minute or two. That's your opening. It's your chance to get your talk back on track with some exiting, dynamic stuff. If you don't, you'll lose the audience again.

Level three: code blue, they're about to become comatose

The audience is falling asleep or in a trance-like state or just plain dazed. You don't have time to ask them to stand up or applaud. You need to do something immediately that will jar it out of its stupor. It must be loud or dramatic or both. Here are a few things to consider:

- Pound your fist on the podium
- Beat your chest like a gorilla
- Move the mike toward a sound-system speaker to cause loud feedback
- Wave a $20 bill in the air and then rip it up
- Throw your notes on the floor
- Light the podium on fire

Any of these should wake up the audience. But here's the trick. You need to tie these actions into your speech so that they make a point. Otherwise, it looks like you were just trying to wake up the audience members. (You can't admit that your goal was to wake them up. They would resent that. It has to appear that you were just giving your talk and part of it happened to revive them.)

For example, you pound your fist on the podium. (Do it near the mike so it really makes a loud noise.) Then you tie it into whatever you're talking about. "That's the sound of people beating their head against a wall because they're frustrated with government regulations." "That's the sound of your heart beating when you go on a job interview." "That's the sound your car makes after you try to save $150 by going to the lowball mechanic." "That's the sound of Tonya Harding having a reunion with Nancy Kerrigan."

Get a volunteer from the audience

One of the best ways to coax a response out of an audience is to put people in the audience into your act. It's an ego thing. They identify with the audience member who stands before them. Suddenly your presentation becomes a lot more personal. (There but for the grace of God, and someone dumb enough to volunteer, could have been me.)

In my presentations on humor in business, I often ask a volunteer to share a personal anecdote with the audience. This is usually a highlight of the day. The volunteer always receives a high level of attention and a great response. Why? The audience considers the volunteer one of their own. The trick is getting someone to volunteer.

I use what's known as the "beg and sweat" method. I announce that I need a volunteer. Immediately, every person in the audience simulates a state of non-existence. Breaths are held, eye contact is avoided, and bodies become perfectly still. (It's an automatic response learned in high school. You did it in the class where you never wanted to get called on.) That's when I start to beg and sweat. "C'mon. Someone volunteer. Here's a chance to shine in front of your peers. What an opportunity. Somebody help me out. Please." Then I start to sweat — profusely. After I'm about to drown in my own perspiration, someone will volunteer simply to put me out of my misery. (All right, it's not the classiest way to get a volunteer, but it works.)

Meeting members of your audience before you speak will help you get a volunteer. Whenever I've had to beg and sweat for a long time, the person who volunteered has always been someone I'd spoken with earlier. Why does this happen? Your guess is as good as mine. Maybe some kind of bonding takes place. The person now feels like we're friends and feels obligated to help out. Who knows? I can only tell you that it happens consistently.

If you don't want to beg and sweat, try getting the audience to pick a volunteer for you. Ask who would be good for whatever you want the volunteer to do. Sometimes you can identify a volunteer just by watching the audience's body language. When you say you need a volunteer, see if everyone instinctively turns to look at someone. If they do, there's a good chance that person is the workplace equivalent of the class clown. Focus your efforts on that person. He or she will probably volunteer if you ask nicely. (If not, you can always beg and sweat.)

Surefire Audience Involvement Techniques

An old Chinese proverb says, "I hear and I forget, I see and I remember, I do and I understand." The point is that your presentation will be more successful if you get your audience members involved. They'll learn more and remember more—two of your major objectives.

Social scientists explain this phenomenon as the difference between active and passive learning. Their studies show that people engaged in active forms of learning retain a lot more information. (A 3M brochure says people retain 10 percent of what they read, 20 percent of what they hear, 30 percent of what they see, 50 percent of what they see and hear, and 90 percent of what they see, hear, and do.) It's common sense. Think about the most exciting learning experience you've ever had. You were probably *doing* something. As Alan Weiner puts it, "You can sit and read about what it takes to run a marathon. But until you do it, you don't really understand it."

Psychological involvement

Now here's some uncommon knowledge. Involving an audience isn't limited to having it do physical activities. You can also do things to get an audience psychologically involved.

San Francisco comedy coach John Cantu suggests involving your audience by activating their emotional connections. "There are certain things that mean a lot to people — their high school, their first car, their first date," he says. "Find a way to bring those things into your talk." It can be as simple as telling the audience to think about the first person they ever dated. "Anyone who hears you will automatically start thinking about this person," John explains. "They'll become very involved in your talk."

There's just one catch — you have to justify why you asked the audience to think about the emotional subject. "It must relate to your talk and make a point," says John. Fortunately, that's easy to do. Just find something in your talk that evokes similar emotions and link it to what you've asked the audience to think about. ("Think about your first date. Remember how you felt excited, scared and happy, all at the same time? That's how I felt when I went to the bank to apply for a loan to start my company. . . .")

Use all the senses

John Cantu also recommends involving your audience members by engaging all of their sense memories. He deliberately describes events by using all the senses. ("Do you remember being in high school? Everybody's walking down the hall. Everyone's talking around you. The place smells like a public restroom.") "You don't want to overload it," he cautions. "But it does help keep the audience involved."

Ice breakers and other gimmicks

Many speakers rely on audience participation exercises and other gimmicks to keep their audiences engaged. Why bother? "Once you get audience members to speak, they become much more receptive to you," says Loyd Auerbach. That's why many of these gimmicks are called ice breakers. They warm up the audience. Here are a few that you may want to try:

The table card

Are you speaking at a breakfast, lunch, or dinner? Then your audience will be sitting around tables, talking and eating before you begin. Here's what to do. Put a card on each table or at each place setting. The card should contain something that will provoke a discussion about your topic — a quote, a question, a prediction, whatever. Your audience will get involved in your presentation before you even begin to speak.

The greeting

Ask the people in your audience to turn to the person next to them and say hello or shake hands. Is this corny? Absolutely. Does it work? Most of the time. It depends a lot on the type of audience and event. If you have a bunch of yuppie types who think they're too sophisticated for this kind of ice breaker, make a slight adjustment. Instead of asking them to shake hands with their neighbors, ask them to exchange business cards. They'll think you're a genius.

The game

Ask the audience to play some type of game. (The game usually involves interacting with other members of the audience. "Everyone put your finger on the nose of the person on your left.") Again, this is very corny. But it usually works. (Yes, there's usually one member of the audience who says, "Touch my nose and I'll break your finger.")

The magic trick

Loyd Auerbach, a corporate trainer for Lexis/Nexis, often opens his training presentations with magic tricks. They inevitably receive applause. He then says, "I'm doing this magic so I can get applause now because you may not applaud at the end of the speech." The line gets a laugh and puts the audience in a positive mood. (See Chapter 25 for a discussion of simple magic tricks that you can perform in your next presentation.)

The question

One of the simplest ways to involve people in an audience is to ask for a show of hands in response to a non-threatening question. Just the physical act of raising their hands can boost their energy level and receptivity. (It may be the most exercise they've had all day — especially if you're the last in a series of speakers.)

What should you ask? Many presenters like to ask questions that will give them a better handle on the audience. How many of you are here from out of town? How many of you work in high tech? (How many of you wish the speaker would stop asking dumb questions?) As trite as this "survey" technique may seem, it works. Believe me, I know. I've used it for years. I always start by asking my audiences a series of questions regarding their beliefs about humor. Do they have a sense of humor? Do they believe humor can be useful in a business context? Can they tell jokes? That sort of thing. It gets the audience thinking about my topic and anticipating my talk.

But here's an important reminder from Allatia Harris, Dean of the Communication Division at Mountain View Community College. *After people in an audience respond to your questions, you have to acknowledge their response.* "Some speakers ask questions, don't pay attention to the answers, and just plow ahead with their next scripted comment," she explains. "That's a big turn-off. It makes the audience feel like they're just props in your slick presentation."

The group order

Comedy coach John Cantu believes the key to successful audience participation exercises is getting everyone involved. "People are more likely to do something if everybody is doing it," he explains. "Tell *everybody* to put their hand in the air."

Management communication counselor Jim Lukaszewski agrees. "Audiences will do anything that you ask them to do if it's moral and legal, the instructions are simple, and they won't be embarrassed." He cites a speech he gave to an audience of 750 people. "I wanted to demonstrate that audiences will respond to a speaker's directions," he recalls. So he asked them to stand up. And they stood up. He asked them to take one step to the left, turn and face the row behind them. They did. Then he said, "Now there's a gentleman entering the room who is late for my speech, would you mind waving to that gentleman." And they all did. Then he told them to sit down. And they did. "You can move an audience with your words in lots of different ways," Jim observes.

The experiment

Here's a Loyd Auerbach original that he's graciously allowed me to share with you:

Tell the audience that you would like their assistance in an experiment in mind control. (Or call it whatever you'd like.) Then say: "Everybody stand up. Now that you're all standing up, here's what I'd like you to do. Take your right arm. Bend it at the elbow, and let your palm face your left side with your thumb straight up toward the ceiling. Take your left arm. Bend it at the elbow so your palm faces right with thumb up. So now your hands are facing palm to palm. They're a little spread apart, and your thumbs are pointing up to the ceiling. Look at the ceiling. Look back to your thumbs. Look at both of your palms. Now very quickly strike your palms against each other. Keep striking them against each other . . . . Thank you very much ladies and gentlemen. I just wanted to make sure I got a standing ovation before you heard the rest of my speech."

This gimmick is especially useful because it will fit anywhere in a presentation. You can use it as an opening. ("I'd like to start with a little audience participation. I'm going to get you all moving and get your energy flowing. So follow my instructions because you'll feel a lot better for it. I know I will.") You can use it anytime during your presentation — especially if you start to lose the audience. ("Let's take a little break for a minute. Everyone stand up," and so on.) Or you can use it as a close. Just change the last line. ("I just wanted to make sure I got a standing ovation.")

The invitation

You've given your presentation. You've asked for questions. No one responds. Here's some uncommon knowledge from Loyd Auerbach — expand your invitation. Don't just ask for questions. Invite questions *and comments*. "Your speech may have been so great that no one has any questions," explains Loyd. That's why he always says something like, "I'll be happy to take questions now. And if anyone has an experience that's related to the subject matter that you would like me to comment on, please speak up. Because I'm sure other people here would like to hear about it." The invitation for comments often sparks a discussion.

Handling an audience is like handling a porcupine — you've got to do both with great care. But neither is really as frightening as it may first appear. After all, underneath that prickly exterior, both audience members and porcupines are soft and cuddly creatures. Keep them involved and deal with them fairly, and they won't "stick it" to you.

Chapter 18

You Want to Know What? How to Handle Questions

A professor traveled from university to university speaking about quantum physics. One day his chauffeur said, "Professor, I've heard your lecture so many times I could give it myself." The professor said, "Fine. Give it tonight." When they got to the university, the chauffeur was introduced as the professor. The chauffeur delivered the lecture, and nobody knew the difference. Afterwards, someone in the audience asked a long question about Boolean algebra and quantum mechanics. The chauffeur didn't miss a beat. He said, "I can't believe you asked that question. It's so simple I'm going to let my chauffeur answer it."

Unfortunately, most people don't have a chauffeur who can answer tough questions. So you have to drive yourself through the maze known as the question-and-answer period. Many speakers let their guard down during this period. It's a big mistake. Even if you've given a great presentation, a poor performance during the Q&A can totally change the audience's perceptions of you and your topic. That's the bad news. The good news is if you're presentation was mediocre, a strong performance during the Q&A can leave the audience with a very positive impression.

The Basics

Want to give a sparkling performance during a question and answer session? You can stack the odds in your favor by following a few basic rules.

Anticipate questions

As any high school student can tell you, the secret to giving brilliant answers is knowing the questions in advance. In some circles, this is called clairvoyance. (In high school, it's called cheating.) In my system, it's called anticipation. You anticipate the questions that you'll be asked.

How do you anticipate questions? Just use your common sense. Think about your presentation and your audience. Then generate a list of every possible question that they might ask. Don't pull any punches. Think of the toughest questions that might come up. Then ask your friends and colleagues to think of the toughest questions they can devise.

After you've compiled a comprehensive list of questions, prepare an answer for each one. Then practice till you've got them down cold.

Answer questions at the end

It's generally better to take questions *after* you've made your presentation than while you're giving it. If you take questions during your presentation, it distracts both you and the audience, it makes your presentation harder to follow, and it ruins your rhythm. (It's always a thrill when someone asks a question just as you're building to the climax of your most dramatic story.) Tell the audience in the beginning that you will take questions at the end.

Don't let a few people dominate

Every so often, you'll get an audience from which one or two people will ask questions — endlessly. The moment you've finished answering their first question, they're asking another. What's their story anyway? Are they really that interested in your topic? Or do they just like to hear themselves talk? Whatever their motivation, it's not your job to play twenty questions with them. You want to have a conversation with the *entire* audience, not just one or two members of it.

Don't let a couple of people ask all the questions (unless they're the only ones with questions). Why? It frustrates everyone else who wants to ask you something. Their hands are raised. They're waiting their turn, but it never comes. Eventually they just give up. One big mouth with endless questions is getting all your attention.

You want to take questions from as many different audience members as time permits. And be fair. Don't favor one section of the room over another. Try to call on people in the order they raised their hands. (Yes, it's tough to do it, but try anyway.) Don't give in to bullies who won't wait their turn and shout out questions. It's the oral equivalent of cutting ahead in line, and it's definitely not fair to the people who have been patiently waiting for you to call on them.

Establish the ground rules early. When you open the session up for questions tell the audience that everyone will initially be limited to a single question. Then if time permits, you'll take a second round of questions.

Don't let the questioner give a speech

You've just asked for questions. Despite the fact that you're standing at a podium and you've just made a lengthy presentation, someone in the audience will want to give a speech. There's one in every crowd.

These people just don't get it. Are they naive? Out of touch? Or just raging egomaniacs? (I think it's usually an ego problem.) No one came to hear them give a speech. No one wants to hear them give a speech. And it's your job to make sure they don't.

You're the speaker. You've opened up the session for questions — not speeches. When one of these people starts giving a speech, you must cut it off. How do you do it? Watch CNN star Larry King. Callers to his show are supposed to ask questions to his guests. If a caller launches into a speech, King immediately says, "Will you state your question, please." Want to be more diplomatic? Say "Do you have a question?" If you want to be very diplomatic, you can gently interrupt the person and suggest a question: "So what you're really asking is. . . ." (If the reply is, "No, that's not what I'm asking," then immediately say, "Will you state your question, please.")

Listen to the question

A young psychiatrist and an old psychiatrist had offices in the same building. Every morning, they'd meet in the elevator, both looking fresh and dapper. But by day's end, the young man looked exhausted while the old man still looked fresh and dapper. Finally, the young psychiatrist said to the old one, "I don't understand how you look so fresh all the time. How do you put up with listening to those patients all day?" The old man shrugged his shoulders and said, "So who listens?"

If you want to be successful in a question and answer period, then you need to be like the *young* psychiatrist — you've got to listen. I mean *really* listen. Yes, it will be exhausting, and you may not look fresh and dapper, but your answers will be infinitely better if you really listen to every question.

By really listening, I mean going below the surface of the words used by the questioner. Read between the lines. Watch the body language. Listen to the tone of voice. What is the questioner really asking? That's the question that you want to identify and answer.

Repeat the question

One of the biggest mistakes speakers make is *not* repeating the question. And it's an enormous mistake. There's nothing more frustrating than giving a brilliant answer to a question that wasn't asked.

There are three major reasons why you should *always* repeat the question.

- ✔ You make sure that everyone in the audience heard the question.
- ✔ You make sure that *you* heard the question correctly.
- ✔ You buy yourself some time to think about your answer. (If you want even more time, rephrase the question slightly and say, "Is that the essence of what you're asking?")

Don't guess

If you don't know the answer to a question, never guess. *Never.* It's a one-way ticket to zero credibility. Once in awhile you may get lucky, beat the odds and bluff the audience. But most of the time, someone will call your bluff. Then you have a big problem. First, you'll be exposed as not knowing the answer you claim to know. More important, the audience will wonder if you bluffed about anything else. And they will project their doubts backward to encompass your entire presentation.

If you don't know, admit it. Then take one, some, or all of the following actions:

- ✔ Ask if anyone in the audience can answer the question.
- ✔ Suggest a resource where the questioner can find the answer.
- ✔ Offer to learn the answer yourself and get it to the questioner.

Remember, nobody knows everything (except my grandmother).

End the Q&A strongly

The Q&A session is your last chance to influence audience opinion — of your topic, your ideas, and you. So you want a strong ending. That's why there are two things you shouldn't do. Don't wait for audience questions to peter out and say, "Well, I guess that's it." You'll look weak and not in control. And don't say, "We only have time for one more question." It may be a question you can't answer or handle well. Again, it will make you look weak.

How do you achieve a forceful finish? Simple. After you've answered a reasonable number of questions, start looking for an opportunity to end the session. Wait till you get a question that you answer brilliantly. Then announce that time has run out. Of course, you'll be happy to stick around and speak with anyone who still has a question.

What if you don't get any questions that you can answer brilliantly? Don't worry. Just make the last question one that you ask yourself. "Thank you. We've run out of time. Well, actually you're probably still wondering about [fill in your question]." Then give your brilliant answer. It works every time.

One more word (actually four more words) about ending the Q&A session: end it on time. Some audience members come solely for your presentation. They don't care about the Q&A. (Or they don't care about the questions being asked.) They just want to leave, but they're too polite to go before it's all over. So stick to the schedule. You can make yourself available afterwards for anyone who wants to keep the discussion going.

Coming Up with a Perfect Answer Every Time

It's been said that experts are people who know all the right answers — if they're asked the right questions. Unfortunately, your audience may not always ask the right questions. This section presents some ways to make sure your answers will be expert no matter what you're asked.

How to treat the questioner

Questioners may be rude, obnoxious, opinionated, egomaniacal, inane, obtuse, antagonistic, befuddled, illiterate, or incomprehensible. You still have to treat them nicely. Why? Because they're members of the audience, and the audience identifies with them — at least initially. Here are some suggestions for dealing with someone who asks you a question:

Don't make the questioner feel embarrassed or stupid. Remember your grade school teacher saying there's no such thing as a dumb question? She was wrong. There are plenty of dumb questions, and speakers get asked them all the time. But you don't want to be the one to point them out. No matter how idiotic the query, treat the questioner with dignity. If you go into a scathing riff about the stupidity of the question, you'll make yourself look bad, generate sympathy for the questioner, and discourage anyone else from asking a question.

Do assist a nervous questioner. Some audience members who ask questions may suffer from stage fright. These people want to ask their question so much that they try to ignore their pounding hearts, sweaty palms, and stomach cramps. As they ask their questions, they try to forget that all eyes in the room are on them, but it's often difficult to ignore this situation. So it's not unusual for anxious audience members to have trouble getting out their questions. They'll stammer and stutter, they'll lose their train of thought, and they'll make the rest of the audience extremely uncomfortable. So help these people out. Finish asking their questions for them if you can. Otherwise, offer some gentle encouragement. By breaking in and speaking yourself, you give nervous questioners time to collect themselves. They'll be grateful. And so will everyone else.

Do recognize the questioner by name. If you know the name of the person asking the question, use it. This has a powerful effect on the audience. It makes you seem much more knowledgeable and in control. And the people whose names you say love the recognition.

Don't send the questioner a negative non-verbal message. It can take a lot of guts to rise out of the anonymity of the audience to ask a question, so don't discourage questioners by looking bored or condescending while they're speaking. Even if you think the question is imbecilic, look fascinated. Shower each questioner with attention. Give full eye contact. Lean forward. Show that there's nothing more important to you than listening to the question. There's nothing more insulting or dispiriting than a speaker who looks around the audience for the next question while the current question is being asked. And it's not only the questioner who gets offended. The whole audience picks up on it.

Do compliment the questioner if appropriate. If the question is particularly interesting or intelligent, it's OK to say so. But be specific and say why. Some communication gurus advise never to say, "Good question" because it implies that the other questions weren't. If you're worried about this, then say, "That's an especially interesting question because. . . ." This statement implies that the other questions were interesting — a compliment. It also eliminates all the value judgments attached to the word "good."

Don't attack the questioner. No matter how offensive the question or questioner, stay calm and in control. Use diplomacy and finesse to dispose of such annoyances. If the questioner is a major jerk, the audience will recognize it. Don't become a jerk yourself by getting defensive. The questioner wants to provoke you. Don't take the bait.

How to design your answer

You never know exactly how to answer until you receive the question, but that's not really helpful if you're trying to prepare in advance. Here are some general guidelines — dos and don'ts — to help you formulate your answers:

Don't assume you know the question. Unless the questioners are rambling or they need help, let them finish asking their questions. Too many speakers jump in before the question is fully stated. They *think* they know what the question will be, and they start giving an answer. They look very foolish when the questioner interrupts saying, "That's not what I was asking."

Do keep it brief. Your answer should be a simple, succinct response to the question asked. Too many speakers use their answer as an excuse to give a second speech. Give everyone a break. If the audience wanted an encore, they would have asked for one. And remember, many members of the audience may not even be interested in the question you're answering. They're waiting to hear the next question — or ask one.

Don't let the questioner define your position. An alarm should go off when you hear a questioner say something like "Well, based on your presentation, it's obvious that you think. . . ." Typically, what the questioner says that you think *isn't* what you think at all. Don't let anyone put words in your mouth. If this occurs, address the problem immediately — as soon as the questioner finishes asking the question. Point out the misconception contained in the question. Then firmly state your actual position.

Do refer back to your presentation. Tieing your answers back to your presentation reinforces the points you made earlier. It also makes you seem omniscient. (You somehow foresaw these questions and planted the seeds of their answers in your presentation.)

Don't get locked into the questioner's facts or premises. If the questioner makes assumptions with which you disagree, politely say so. If you dispute the questioner's statistics, say so. Don't build a nice answer on a faulty question. Start by dismantling the question.

Do define the terms under discussion. Let's say someone asks if you think the middle class deserves a tax cut. You say "yes." The questioner immediately disagrees by arguing that it's unfair to give a tax break to the middle class. After a ten-minute debate, everyone realizes that there's no real disagreement. You don't think any family making more than $100,000 deserves a tax break, and neither does the questioner, but you define such families as "rich." The questioner defines them as "middle class." Make sure that everyone is on the same wavelength. Define the terms up front.

Don't make promises you won't keep. Don't say that anyone can call you at your office to ask questions if you know you won't take their calls. Don't say you'll find out the answer to a question if you know you won't. Don't offer to send information to someone if you know you'll never get around to it.

Do refer to your experience. It's not bragging to refer to your personal and professional experience in your answer. That experience is one of the reasons you've been invited to speak. It's part of what makes you an expert. The audience *wants* to hear about your experience.

Don't evade questions by acting like you're answering them. You're not obligated to answer every question. (You're *really not* under interrogation although it may sometimes seem that way.) But if you evade questions, you lose credibility. It looks like you're ducking the issues. If you don't want to answer a question, say so firmly and politely. State the reasons why and move on to the next question.

Don't depend on being asked a particular question. It might not get asked. And definitely don't leave important points out of your presentation because you want to save them for the Q&A session. You may never get a chance to raise them.

How to deliver your answer

Don't assume a new persona. Many speakers undergo a transformation at the conclusion of their presentation. I call it the Cinderella effect. The speaker's brilliant, thoughtful, formal persona of the presentation is stripped away to reveal someone who is relieved to be done. It's like the clock struck twelve and the spell wore off. What happened to that confident expert who just delivered the presentation? All that's left is a glass slipper which the speaker is rapidly putting in his or her mouth. The moral of this story is stay in character. If you assume a new persona during the Q&A, you lose credibility. Which is the real you? Are you a chameleon? Was the confidence you showed during your presentation fake?

Don't limit eye contact to the questioner. Start off by looking at the questioner, but as you give your answer, direct your eye contact to the entire audience. That's who you're speaking to — not just the questioner.

Don't be smug. It doesn't win any accolades from the audience, and it just creates a barrier. It can also backfire in a big way: the audience will start rooting for you to screw up. The first time you fumble an answer — even if it's just misstating an insignificant detail — smugness will come back to haunt you.

Do be appropriate. Match your demeanor to the substance of the question and your answer. If someone is confused, be understanding. If someone is blatantly offensive, be forceful and disapproving (without counter-attacking). If someone is seeking information, be professorial. Never lose control of yourself. Never be discourteous.

Six Great Question Handling Techniques

How do you become an expert in deftly fielding questions? Practice. Practice. Practice. Practice what? The following six basic techniques (most of which were provided by my old friend Dr. Barbara Howard, a Denver-based corporate facilitator).

Reverse the question

Someone in your audience may ask you a question for the express purpose of putting you on the spot. No sweat. Just reverse it. For example, the questioner makes a big show of appearing bored and asks, "What time are we going to take a break?" Don't get defensive. Just respond, "What time would you like to take a break?" It's mental judo. You use the weight of the questioner's own question against him.

Redirect the question

Someone asks a question. You don't have the vaguest idea how to answer it. What can you do? Get the audience involved. Redirect the question to the entire group. "That's an interesting question. Does anyone have any thoughts on the subject?" Or, "Does anyone have any experience with that situation?"

"When I speak, I never set myself up as the only expert on the subject," explains Barbara Howard. "So in the Q&A period, answers can come from anywhere. If I can't respond, I facilitate people's questions being answered by someone else." The audience is a tremendous resource — a veritable repository of knowledge and information. Take advantage of it.

Rephrase the question

"Last week's indictment of your chief lobbyist for bribing a Senator has finally revealed how your parasitic company got federal approval for a drug that's already killed 200 people. Will you now issue a recall to remove it from the market?" Hmmmmm. Are you really supposed to repeat this question for the audience? I don't think so. In fact, you never want to repeat a question that presents a problem — doing so is embarrassing, difficult, hard to follow, whatever. Here's the solution: Don't repeat the question word for word. Rephrase it to your advantage. "The question is about how we will convert our concern for public safety into action. Here are the steps we are taking to protect the public. . . ."

Keep in mind that a question can be a problem just because it's worded in an obtuse manner. "In your opinion, will the actions of the Federal Reserve Board to control inflation through monetary policy, combined with global financial trends — particularly the devaluation of the Mexican peso — result in economic forces that validate or prove wrong the Wall Street bulls in the short term?" Huh? Rephrase the question so that the audience can understand it (assuming *you* can understand it). "The question is whether the stock market will go up or down in the next few months."

Expose a hidden agenda

Sometimes a question contains a hidden (or not so hidden) agenda. It may be a loaded question. It may be some other type of trick question. It may be a question containing an accusation. ("How could anyone in good conscience possibly suggest cutting funds for the nursing department?") No matter the method, the question has a "hook" in it. The questioner wants to provoke a certain answer so that he or she can argue with it. The question is just a setup for a fight.

Don't fall for this trap. Instead of launching into an answer, acknowledge your suspicions. Here's how Barbara Howard does it: "I'll just say, 'Wow, that one feels like it's got a hook in it. Tell me, what's your stake in this question? What's of interest to you in it?'" This forces questioners to put their agenda on the table. Then you can deal with it in a straightforward manner.

Other responses that work well for this type of question include

> "Do you have some thoughts on that?"

> "It sounds like you're expecting me to give you a certain answer. What is it you're trying to get me to say?

The point is to politely expose the hidden agenda and get the questioner to speak about it first.

Put the question in context

"Isn't it true that you were in Mr. Smith's bedroom the night he was found stabbed to death in his bed?" This is known as a loaded question. It's framed in a way that makes the audience jump to very specific conclusions that make you look bad. Your response has to broaden their frame of reference. You have to provide the missing information that "unloads" the question. "Well, yes, as a police photographer, I did take pictures of the crime scene a few hours after Mr. Smith died. That's why I was in his bedroom the night he was stabbed to death." The meaning of any words or behaviors can be distorted if they're taken out of context. It's up to you to give a context to any question that needs one.

Build a bridge

Let's watch a politician evade a question. "Senator Blowhard, are you going to vote against a tax increase?" "Well sir, you want to know if I'm going to vote against a tax increase. What you're really asking is how can we get more money into the pockets of more Americans? Let me tell you about my twelve-step plan for reviving the economy. . . ."

The senator has built a bridge. He's constructed a phrase that allows him to move from a question he wants to ignore to a topic he wants to address. In this case, the bridge is, "What you're really asking is. . . ." There are lots of bridges of this sort:

> "It makes much more sense to talk about . . ."

> "The real issue is . . ."

> "The essential question is . . ."

> "What you should be asking is . . ."

> "If you look at the big picture, your question becomes . . ."

A word of caution about using a bridge: Use it to move a short distance away from a question you dislike, rather than to evade it completely. You lose credibility when you evade a question. (Politicians don't care because they have none to lose.) You have to give the appearance of at least attempting to answer.

Common Types of Questions

Certain types of questions are designed to put you at a disadvantage. What follows are some you must be ready to identify and handle.

The yes or no question

"Is your company going to form an alliance with the Okkie Corporation, yes or no?" Don't get trapped by this type of question. Unless you're under oath on a witness stand, you're not required to provide a yes or no answer. If the question requires a more complex answer, don't hesitate to say what needs to be said. "The formation of an alliance between our company and Okkie depends on a number of factors. . . ." Does this kind of response evade the question? Not really. It evades *the form of the question* that the questioner is trying to force on you, but your answer does address the question.

The forced choice question

This is a close relative of the yes or no question. Here, the questioner wants to force you to choose between two alternatives, and like the yes or no question, you're not obligated to do so. Sometimes both alternatives offered are bad. ("Does your plan omit security guards because they're too expensive or because you forgot to include them?" "Neither. I didn't include them because they're not needed.") Sometimes you just don't want to choose between the alternatives. ("What is the main focus of your growth strategy — developing new products or cutting costs?" "Actually, we intend to do both of those and more. We will also be acquiring new products, expanding our sales force. . . .")

The classic response to a forced choice question is contained in an old joke. A senator is asked, "Are you for the war or against the war?" He replies, "Some of my friends are for it and some of my friends are against it. I stand with my friends." (Of course, this response evades the question, but it was a senator answering.)

The hypothetical question

What if . . . the product doesn't sell up to your expectations? . . . the board turns down your proposal? . . . pigs could fly? Don't get sucked into the morass of hypothetical questions. You've got enough "real" things to worry about. Just say something like, "I don't anticipate that happening, so we'll cross that bridge if we come to it."

The top question

"What are the top five challenges facing your industry?" "Which will be the best ten fields for finding a job ten years from now?" "What are the three most useful features of your software?" Your answer will be "wrong" no matter what choices you make because someone will argue about your selections. Here's an easy fix for this problem: Anytime you get this type of question, purge the number from your answer. "Well, we can debate all day about what the top five challenges are, but I can tell you that some of the major challenges facing the industry are. . . ."

The false assumption question

The classic example is "Have you stopped beating your wife yet?" The question assumes that you've been beating your wife. (And you may not even be married.) False assumptions can also include incorrect facts and statistics, as well as incorrect conclusions that the questioner has drawn from your talk. The solution: point out the false assumption and correct it immediately.

The implied question

"The time frame you outlined for the product release just doesn't seem like it will work." This is a comment, not a question, but that's OK. Many Q&A sessions begin with a request for questions *or comments*. In some cases — like this one — the comment will imply a question. It's your job to flush it out. "It sounds like you really want to know how we'll get the product fully tested in only two months. Here's our plan. . . ."

The multipart question

"Could you tell me if we'll be receiving raises this year, and if not, why not, and if so, how big will they be?" Whoa. Slow down there, pardner. That's what's known as a multipart question. When you get one like this, divide it up and answer one part at a time.

Nine Special Situations and How to Respond

Handling questions from the audience is a very delicate situation. You often need to take a firm hand, but you don't want to alienate your listeners. Here are some ways to handle common "problem" situations:

A questioner interrupts you

Don't interrupt the interrupter. Stop talking and let this boor finish what he or she is saying. Then say something like, "Please wait until I've finished." Then complete your answer. If the person interrupts again, repeat the process. Don't get into a fight. If the interrupter continues, other members of the audience will eventually intercede on your behalf. (If they don't, then they don't deserve to hear your pearls of wisdom.)

Someone asks about something you covered in your presentation

Don't say, "I already covered that in my presentation." Perhaps you did, but maybe you didn't cover it clearly. If the person asking the question missed the answer in your speech, then others might have missed it too. And if it was important enough to include in your initial presentation, then you can spend time going over it again. So answer the question. Try explaining it a different way this time.

Someone asks a question that was already asked

If your answer will take more than ten seconds, politely refuse to answer. Say something like, "We've already addressed that question." This situation is completely different than getting a question about something covered in your presentation. Here, the audience member simply hasn't been paying attention. If you answer the question, then you're being rude to the rest of the audience. You're wasting their time. Want to be nice? Offer to talk with the questioner individually after the Q&A session is concluded.

Someone asks a completely irrelevant question

You can point out that it's not germane to the discussion and go on to the next questioner. You can give the questioner a chance to ask a relevant question, or you can use the question as a springboard to raise a topic you want to discuss.

Someone asks a completely disorganized question

You've got a couple of choices. You can ask the person to restate the question (not a good idea because you'll probably get a question more disorganized than the first attempt). You can respond to part of the question (a part that you liked), or you can offer to talk with the person individually after the Q&A session is concluded.

Someone asks a question to promote him or herself

"I have a question about your point about marketing trends. Having held positions with leading market research companies for the past 20 years — I'm now Vice President of Polling and Surveys at the Blab Brothers Consulting Group — I've found that trends can be difficult to quantify. In fact, that was the exact problem I ran into in a survey I did for a Fortune 500 company. This was a multimillion dollar project — which is small for our firm, but we did it anyway as a favor to the CEO. And we conducted the survey over a period of two years. So by the time you spot the trend, it may already be out of date. How do you factor that into your marketing equation?"

This stuffed shirt probably doesn't care what you answer. I'm sure he thinks he knows the answer anyway. He's only asking the question so that he can pump himself up in front of *your* audience. Here's what to do. Answer the question as succinctly as possible. Then call on the next questioner quickly, before this whale ego has a chance to spout off again.

Someone asks a rathole question

"Why did you change the bitmap for the icons on your menu screen for the financial applications in Release 3.1?" Watch out! This is a rathole question. It's of interest to only one person in the audience — the questioner. It's a painful distraction for everyone else. That's why it's called a rathole question. Any time and effort you put into answering it goes down a rathole.

"I've seen speakers bore an audience to tears because they spend ten minutes discussing some arcane point related to only one person," says Neil Baron, a Sybase marketing manager. His solution: After the question is asked, answer it briefly. Then ask for a show of hands to learn if anyone else is interested in the topic. If there's significant audience interest, continue your answer. If not, offer to resume the discussion after the Q&A session has concluded.

Someone asks multiple questions

You have a few options for handling this situation. You can tell the questioner that you'll only answer one of the questions due to time constraints and fairness to other audience members. (Offer to answer the other questions later after everyone else has had a turn to ask one.) You can answer all of the questions in the order asked, or you can answer all of them in an order you choose. (Exercise these last two options when you feel that answering the questions is to your advantage.)

Someone asks a long, rambling question

If you see where the question is going, gently interrupt (citing time considerations) and pose the question concisely in your own words. Confirm that you've understood what the questioner wants to know. Then answer it. If you don't see where it's going, use the Larry King technique. Say "Can you state your question, please?"

Handling Hostile Questions

One of the great fears facing many speakers is the prospect of dealing with hostile questions. Stop worrying. There are tried and true techniques for handling this problem. In fact, a little advance planning can significantly reduce your chance of receiving these pesky questions.

Identifying hostile questions

Don't put a chip on your shoulder and assume that anyone who disagrees with you is hostile. Even people who disagree can have a legitimate question. They don't necessarily want to argue with you. They may just want information.

Also, don't assume that someone who asks pointed questions disagrees with you. The exact opposite may be true. This happens at the U.S. Supreme Court all the time. A justice who agrees with a certain position will ask the lawyer representing that position an incredibly tough question. Why? The justice hopes that a good answer will help persuade the other justices to agree with the position too. This process can occur in your audience. Someone who agrees with you may ask a tough question, hoping your answer will persuade others in the audience. So some of your toughest questions can come from your biggest allies. Don't assume they're hostile.

If someone asks you a trick question — that's hostile. "Have you stopped beating your wife yet?" "Do you think you'll get 10 years or 20 years for income tax evasion?" "Isn't this an amazing achievement — for a woman?" It's safe to assume these questioners are out to get you.

Heading them off at the pass

The simplest way to handle hostile questions is to not get any. Unfortunately, I can't guarantee that you won't, but here are some techniques for minimizing the number you do receive:

The inoculation. Can you anticipate specific hostile questions that you'll receive? Then raise them and answer them during your presentation. By beating your antagonists to the punch, you leave them with nothing to ask you.

The admission. Admit at the outset of the Q&A session that you're not the world authority on everything. Set audience expectations properly regarding the extent and areas of your expertise. Tell the audience what you don't know. This technique will help defuse potential hostility and disappointment resulting from your inability to answer specific questions.

The revelation. At the outset of the Q&A session, announce that the people who ask questions must begin by identifying themselves. They must reveal their name, organization, and anything else you want to require. Having to reveal this information is a major barrier to hostile questioners. They don't like losing the cloak of audience anonymity. It's much easier to act like a jerk, be hostile, and get confrontational with the speaker if no one knows who you are.

Dealing with hostile questions

Receiving a hostile question is like being tossed a bomb. You need to know how to defuse it before it blows up in your face.

Empathize with the questioner. Start by recognizing that the questioner is upset and emphasize that you *understand* his or her point of view even if you don't agree with it. Make sure you communicate that you bear no personal animosity toward the questioner. Your disagreement is solely about the issue in question. "I can see that you feel strongly about this issue, and I understand where you're coming from. Let me give you a few more facts that may affect your opinion. . . ."

Establish common ground. Find an area where you and the questioner can agree and build your answer from there. "Then we agree that the budget will have to be limited to 75 percent of what we spent last year. We just differ on how to allocate the money. . . ." If you're really stuck for finding common ground, here's the all-purpose (albeit somewhat lame) response that works for any hostile question: "Well, at least we agree that this is a controversial issue. . . ."

Put the question in neutral. If you get a question loaded with emotionally charged words or phrases, rephrase the question in neutral terms. (See the "Rephrase the question" section earlier in this chapter.)

Be very specific. Talk about specific facts and figures. Be concrete. The more you get into theory, speculation, and opinion, the more opportunity you provide for disagreement. You want to limit the opportunities for arguments.

Ask why they're asking. What if you're on the receiving end of a loaded question or any other blatantly hostile query? Don't even bother giving an answer. Just say, "Why did you ask that?" This can go a long way to defusing the situation. The questioner, often embarrassed that you've spotted the trap, may withdraw or modify the question. (See "Expose a hidden agenda" earlier in this chapter.)

Elude the jerks. Don't allow continued follow-up questions from people who just want to interrogate you in a hostile manner. (Unless they've got a badge.) There's no reason for it. You should be giving everyone in the audience a chance to ask questions. And if you're going to let one person dominate (which you shouldn't), why on earth would you give this opportunity to a hostile questioner? If you want to go one-on-one with someone, do it one-on-one — after the Q&A session is concluded.

How to Get Your Audience to Ask Questions

You've given a brilliant presentation. The audience is applauding so hard that their hands may fall off. You love it. (And you deserve it.) As the thunderous ovation subsides, you pick up the microphone and ask, "Are there any questions?" There's no response. Nothing. No one raises a hand. No one shouts out a query. There's just dead silence. Uh-oh. You've gone from toast of the town to burnt toast in less than five seconds.

There's one item that every question and answer session requires — questions. It really shouldn't be your fault if there aren't any, but it's a psychological thing. If you make a big deal of asking for questions and no one responds, it seems like you've somehow failed. Here are a few ways to eliminate this problem:

Plant a question

Arrange in advance for someone in the audience to ask you a question. (Just make sure it's someone you can trust.) Or go all out. Plant several people throughout the audience. (For maximum impact, don't tell them about each other.)

Ask yourself a question

No one wants to break the ice? Break it yourself. "When I talk about this topic, the one thing everyone usually wants to know is. . . ."

Ask a question you were asked privately by an audience member

If you get to the site of your presentation well in advance of your talk (as you should), you may get to speak with members of your audience — the early arrivers. And you'll certainly touch base with the person responsible for your presentation. During these conversations, you will often receive questions about your topic. Just because they're asked before you speak doesn't mean they can't be used after. "When I arrived here today, I had an opportunity to meet some of you and chat a little bit. And someone asked me. . . ." (You can also make up questions and say someone asked them to you.)

Solicit written questions in advance

Want to guarantee that you get questions? Arrange for the audience to submit written questions before you start speaking. There are several benefits to this arrangement. Audience members who are uncomfortable asking a question in public have no problem submitting anonymous questions. Also, you get to pick the questions that you want to answer. And you can "submit" your own questions (and act like they came from the audience).

Ask the audience a question

Get the audience involved in the question process in a nonthreatening way. Ask a survey-type question that can be answered with a show of hands. Then use the response to generate a discussion. "Lets see by a show of hands. How many of you think that. . . ."

Refer jokingly to the dearth of questions

Not getting any questions? Use Barbara Howard's line. She says, "Well, I've either made this completely clear or it's so confusing that you don't know what you don't know." It usually gets someone to ask a question.

Offer to take questions privately

Sometimes a lack of questions stems from the nature of your topic. If you're dealing with a sensitive issue, don't expect people to discuss their questions and concerns in public. Barbara Howard's presentations to battered women are a good example. "I always offer to talk with people individually after the presentation," she says. "They're much more willing to ask questions privately." A good idea for *any* topic or audience.

Use your intuition

Shortly after abandoning my career as an attorney and becoming a humor consultant, I was scheduled to be interviewed on National Public Radio. Naturally, I was very excited. (Even my parents were impressed, and they weren't particularly thrilled with me at the time. Hey, I'd left a great job at an international corporate law firm to become a humor consultant — whatever that was. How would your parents feel?)

Unfortunately, my enthusiasm quickly evaporated once the interview began. The interviewer opened with a few innocuous questions. Where had I practiced law? How long had I practiced? Why did I become a humor consultant? But he asked these questions in a way that sounded both bored and superior, like he thought the whole interview was a stupid waste of his time. What a snob!

My suspicions were confirmed when he summoned his most sneering tone of voice and said, "This country has functioned perfectly well without a humor consultant for more than 200 years. Do you really think we need one now?"

Now the common wisdom would say that you shouldn't embarrass the person asking you the question. The audience doesn't like it, and it just makes you look bad. But my intuition told me that this case was an exception. This guy was already making me look bad, and the interview had only just begun. I really didn't want to find out where it would end if I kept following his path, so I decided to take a different tack.

"Well, quite frankly," I stated, "you may not realize that what I'm doing as a humor consultant has its roots in the origin of Western civilization. The sophists of ancient Greece were the first paid teachers. In that society, which originated democracy, there were no lawyers, and everyone pled their own cases. So the ability to give a persuasive speech was essential. That's why people paid the sophists to teach them to speak." From there, I traced the history of speech education through Socrates, Plato, and Aristotle to the Middle Ages and Renaissance (when rhetoric was considered one of the three pillars of learning) and through modern times. Finally, I explained how my work teaching businesspeople to use humor in presentations was a natural extension of the work begun by the sophists. In fact, as anyone could plainly see, I was the natural heir to the entire educational tradition of Western civilization.

Well, I don't know if the interviewer was embarrassed or not. But suddenly the whole tone of the interview changed. He started treating me with respect.

What can you learn from this? First, there are exceptions to every rule. Second, follow your intuition. Third, if you're going to answer questions on National Public Radio, be prepared to drop a few names — Socrates, Plato, and Aristotle.

Chapter 19

Panels and Other Special Situations

● ●

In This Chapter

▶ Unique challenges of panel presentations

▶ Maintaining control of your message

▶ Being a panelist with pizzazz

▶ Introducing other presenters

▶ Organizing an impromptu speech

▶ Thinking on your feet

● ●

Being on a Panel

Many people who don't enjoy making presentations say they would rather speak as part of a panel than as a sole presenter. (Misery loves company.) Panelists usually don't have to speak as long as a sole presenter, and they can pass tough audience questions to other panelists. That's the good news. The bad news is that the panel format has its own unique set of challenges. If you're ready for them, you'll shine. If you're not, you'll get shined.

The inevitable comparison

Compared with a sole presenter, panelists have much less control over their message and image. Why? The audience *compares* panelists to each other as they speak. So how a panelist is perceived depends on who else is on the panel, which means that your presentation — which might be considered good if the audience hears no one else — could come off poorly if you're on a panel with high-powered presenters. You need to be aware of the factors that affect the comparison and learn to control them. It's not that you want the other panelists to look bad (although that could be a goal); you want to make sure that *you* look good.

Who else is on the panel?

Finding out who else will be on your panel sounds pretty basic, and it is. But it's amazing how many people don't bother to do it. They're invited to be on a panel. They say "OK." And a few days, weeks, or months later (whenever the panel is held), they show up. They never ask for any details. It's essential to find out who else is on your panel. How can you influence the comparison if you don't know who you'll be compared to?

Find out everything you can about the other panelists: their names, their qualifications, their jobs, their knowledge of the topic, their reputation as speakers, and so on. And don't forget to ask about the moderator. Will there be one? If so, you want to know everything about this person, too.

Sometimes the entire panel hasn't been selected when you agree to serve on it. Maybe you're the first person invited. Fine. That's no excuse for not knowing who else is on the panel. Wait a few days, weeks, or months (whatever is appropriate) and call the organizer. Get an update. Ask who else is on the panel. (If you're still the only panelist, then expect to get a new title — keynote speaker.)

What are the rules?

Every panel operates within some set of rules. (All right, once in a while, there's a panel that doesn't, but it's not very pretty.) You need to know those rules. Will everyone on the panel make their remarks before the audience asks questions? Or will the audience ask questions after each panelist speaks? Are the panelists even expected to make remarks? How much time is allotted for the entire session? How much time will be given to each panelist? Will there be a moderator, or is it a free for all? What's the physical setup? Will each panelist have a microphone, or do they have to pass one around? Whether you want to follow the rules, bend the rules, or break the rules, you have to know the rules.

What is the speaking order?

The order in which panelists speak is a major factor in determining how you will be perceived. Here are some things to think about:

First speaker. The advantage of going first is that there's no one to compare you with — yet. So if you're on a panel with several strong speakers, going first makes a lot of sense. Another advantage is that the first speaker can set the tone for the entire panel. Go first, give a well-structured talk, and you set the standard. The audience now expects the other speakers to do at least as well as you did.

The disadvantage of going first is that you can't react to the other panelists. They haven't said anything yet.

Last speaker. The biggest advantage of going last is that you can comment on what all of the other panelists have said. This allows you to have the final word in defining the discussion. Going last is also the best position if you're not prepared. You can formulate your remarks while the earlier panelists are speaking, and you can just comment on what they said.

Middle speakers. The advantage of going in the middle is that you can comment on any panelists that spoke before you, and you can still shape the discussion of the panelists that go after you. The disadvantage is that you may get lost in the shuffle. A basic principle of psychology is that people most strongly remember things that come first or last. In a panel situation, that's the first speaker and the last speaker.

Other considerations

How big is the panel? What time of day will the session occur? The answers to these questions may affect your choice of when you want to speak (if you have a choice). A large panel with many speakers increases the chance that the audience will burn out by the time the last speaker gets a turn. Similarly, a panel held in the late afternoon means that the audience won't be focused on the last speaker (except for wondering when he or she will end so that everyone can go eat dinner). With an early morning panel, the audience may still be waking up while the first panelist is speaking.

Maintaining control of your message

Panel discussions create special obstacles to getting your message across the way you want. Many of these obstacles are beyond your control, so it's even more important than usual to identify your goals clearly and construct your message carefully. You want to maintain as much control as possible. Paying attention to the following factors will help you achieve that goal.

Why are you on the panel?

Why am I here? This question has haunted philosophers for centuries. Now *you* have to answer it. (Fortunately, you just need to figure out why you're on the panel — not why you exist.) Your answer to this question will shape your message strategy. Are you on the panel as a favor to the moderator? Are you there to showcase yourself and your ideas? Are you there to gain recognition for your company or organization? Who, if anyone, are you trying to impress? You need to know what you want to accomplish.

Preparing your message

Any presentation requires you to decide how you'll get the audience to remember your key messages. This goal is even more challenging in a panel presentation because there's a lot of "noise in the channel." The audience is bombarded by messages from your co-panelists. And the audience itself may offer statements or questions that provide further distraction from your key ideas. Your messages have a lot of competition, so you have to make them powerful, persuasive, and to the point.

Start by learning who is in the audience. What organizations do they represent? What are their jobs? What positions do they hold? You can involve them in your remarks by speaking directly to their interests. Then they don't have to wait for the Q&A period to get involved.

Anticipate where you'll be challenged on particular issues. You don't need co-panelists or audience members sinking your entire message by torpedoing you on one point — especially if you know it's coming. Defuse the issue by addressing it in your remarks before the Q&A period.

And listen to the other panelists. I mean really listen. Be prepared to refer back to specific things they've said. This tip is especially effective if you get their names right. ("As Heather and Amy said earlier. . . .")

Timing

Panelists get many opportunities to present information: when they make their remarks, answer questions from co-panelists, answer audience questions, and even when they tag statements onto the end of co-panelists' answers to audience questions. But not all opportunities to present information are created equal. Depending on what you want to say, certain times to say it are better than others.

If you have important information for the audience, don't convey it right away. Let them settle down first and get used to the panelists. And don't wait till the end. You may run out of time, or the audience may be distracted by their preparations to leave. Key information is best presented after the audience has heard you for a few minutes or a few times.

Another aspect of timing has to do with whom the audience credits with an idea. It's not always the panelist who said it first. More often, it's the panelist who talks about an idea second — who takes the idea and runs with it. This second panelist expands the idea, puts it into new words, and makes it his or her own. The audience never remembers that someone else mentioned the idea first. Keep this in mind when you toss your gems into the discussion. If it's a diamond in the rough, don't wait for a fellow panelist to polish it. They'll be polishing off your credit.

Timing also applies to how much you speak. If you speak every time a question or issue is raised, you'll seem pompous, and your answers will lose their impact. People will stop listening to you. But if you never speak up, you'll seem weak and irrelevant — if the audience even remembers you're there. So monitor yourself. Be aware of how much time you've spent speaking. Assert yourself but don't go wild.

Delivery

It's easy to forget about the audience if you get into a debate with another panelist. That's a mistake. The majority of your eye contact and "face time" should be with the audience. Focus on different sections of the room as you answer different questions. Make everyone feel like you're talking to them.

And don't become a victim of microphone placement. If there's only one mike for all the panelists, make sure that you have access to it. And please, don't lean forward to use it. Lift it up and bring it close to your mouth. Too many speakers seem like they're bowing at the altar of the microphone. It's not a deity. You should control it — not the other way around.

Interacting with other panelists

Your interaction with other panelists will have a major effect on how the audience perceives you. Everyone assumes that panelists will have disagreements. (Otherwise, the panel would be fairly boring.) It's *how* you disagree that's important. So here are two words of advice: be diplomatic.

If you want to point out an inaccuracy stated by another panelist, say something like, "I understand how Matt's experience could lead to his conclusion. However, I have found that. . . ." Don't say that Matt is an idiot. The audience will get the idea. They don't want to see you mud wrestling with the other panelists — especially if you threw the mud at them first.

Sony Electronics executive James Harris III often speaks on panels populated with his competitors. Naturally, each panelist wants to outdo the other, but James shuns the direct attack. "The key in those situations isn't to get me going against the other panelists," he explains. "It's to get the crowd going against them." He does this subtly and indirectly. By emphasizing strengths of Sony products and strategies, he highlights his competitors' weaknesses. He also moves the discussion in directions that encourage the audience to ask tough questions to the other panelists.

You should also know where to turn for help. Which panelists are your allies? Which of them will support your positions? Communications guru Barbara Howard calls this "knowing your second." In other words, who will "second" your motion. "If you're going to be the first person to take a certain position, you need to know who to turn to for confirmation," she explains. "And you've got to force them to provide it." She suggests two methods. Nonverbally, you can turn to your "second," establish eye contact, and put him or her on the spot to offer support. Verbally, you can do this by saying something like, "Matt, haven't you found what I've said to be true?" The main point is don't leave it up to chance. Don't just make your statement and hope someone will jump in to support it. Make them jump in.

Answering questions when you don't get any

Answering questions from the audience is prime time for a panelist. It's your chance to shine. But what if the other panelists get all the questions? What if none are directed to you? Don't worry. It just means that it's time to play tag. As other panelists finish their answers, you can tag on your own statement: "I'd like to add one thing to what Sam just said. . . ." Is it aggressive? Yes. But it's better than sitting around after the session is over wishing someone had asked you something. If you want to make an impression, you need to have your say.

Dealing with a moderator

There's some good news and bad news about panel moderators. The good news is that a good moderator can make the panel a pleasure. The bad news is that a lot of them are clueless. They see their function solely as introducing the panel members. When hassles occur — inappropriate questions from the audience, fist fights among the panelists — the moderator is nowhere to be found. And sometimes they even screw up the introductions.

Assume that moderators will be incompetent and celebrate if they're not. That means you must be prepared. Prepared to reintroduce yourself to the audience. Prepared to take charge if other panelists hog your time. Prepared to grab the microphone. And if you get a good moderator who runs a tight ship, be prepared to finish on time.

Have a secret weapon ready

Smart panelists carry a secret weapon in reserve — the *sound bite*. That's a short line or phrase designed to capture audience attention. It gets its name from the radio and television news business. A reporter will interview someone for an hour. That night on the news, you hear the person for 30 seconds. That's the sound bite.

Speech guru Jim Lukaszewski makes frequent panel presentations to audiences of information systems personnel. One of the sound bites he brings is that the average tenure of a chief information officer is eighteen months. He explains why it's a great sound bite: "It's catchy. I've seen it in the press, and people remember it because it hits close to home."

Sony Electronics executive James Harris III also has sound bites ready for panel presentations. If the discussion involves products and product futures, he'll mention the "field of dreams engineering vision — if we build it they will buy." Another line that stirs up the audience is "People win business, not products. Products enable you to get in the door." He also likes to toss in a tag line from a Pacific Bell ad: "You never get a second chance to make a first impression."

Introducing Other Presenters

Several years ago, I was an after-dinner speaker at a Digital Equipment Corporation sales meeting. Sales representatives had flown in from around the world on the day of the dinner. They were tired and jet-lagged, but they were required to attend the dinner. It was the first event in their multiday meeting.

The meeting organizer knew that the sales reps would be tired and factored that into his plans. He put together a tightly scheduled event. Dinner would be served from 7:00 to 8:00. I would speak from 8:00 to 9:00. Then everyone could hit the bar or go to sleep.

The organizer had selected me as the speaker because he wanted to set an upbeat tone for the meeting. My topic — using humor in sales presentations — would be both entertaining and useful. It would get the sales reps laughing *and* thinking. And it would get the meeting off to a good start.

Everything proceeded as planned. The dinner was served at 7:00. The plates were cleared by 8:00. And the person introducing me stepped up to the podium. He welcomed everyone to the meeting, made some remarks about the next day's schedule, and said that the evening's speaker would teach everyone how to use humor. I prepared to stand up and walk to the podium. But then he told a joke. It was long and irrelevant. The silence when he finished telling it was deafening.

I thought maybe he'd told a pointless joke on purpose to highlight my topic. He hadn't — because he told another one, and it was worse than the first. The audience was squirming. He'd now been introducing me for fifteen minutes and he still wasn't done. Next he launched into a long riff about why humor was important to him, to the company, and to the world. People in the audience looked at each other in disbelief. And they all started glaring at the meeting planner who looked like he wanted to disappear. A few more "jokes" followed. Finally, he actually introduced me. It was 8:37. The audience was bored and angry. So much for starting on an upbeat tone. (Fortunately, I got them recharged and laughing. But let me tell you, it was tough.)

When you introduce speakers, you need to say who they are and what they'll talk about. But you also need to do several other things. A good introduction should warm up the audience and get them excited about the speaker. It should set a positive tone for the event, and it shouldn't discourage the speaker from speaking. (Most speakers are nervous enough without the added pressure of a lousy introduction.)

If you're asked to introduce someone, take the time to do a good job with it. The better you make the speaker look, the better you make yourself look.

How to get the information you need

Information is the key to making an appropriate introduction. The introduction you do will only be as good as the information you get. And that can be a problem, especially if all you have to work with is a speaker's official company biography.

Just listen to John Austin, speechwriter extraordinaire: "Most official company bios are as interesting and clear as hieroglyphics. They just list dates and titles. They don't tell you anything about the person." How true. So what can you do about it? Plenty.

Start by finding out if there are any other written materials about the speaker. Was she profiled in a company or association newsletter? Was he written up in the local paper? Your goal is to get *too much* information. Then you can pick and choose the best stuff.

No written materials? Don't worry. That's only a starting point. Now it's interview time. Interview the speaker. Interview people who know the speaker. (Or interview people who used to know the speaker. One of the most interesting introductions I've ever heard included quotes from one of the speaker's old girlfriends.) Talk to the speaker's friends, relatives, and coworkers. Talk to the speaker's clients and customers. That's where you'll get good stories and quotes.

Checklist of speaker interview questions

Interviewing the person you'll introduce is one of the best ways to get the material you'll need. Here are a few questions to get your interview started:

Why are you making your presentation?

What do you want to accomplish with your presentation?

What is your expertise regarding the topic of your talk?

How did you get interested in your topic?

What are the two or three most important things for the audience to know about you? What are the two or three most important things for the audience to know about your presentation?

Whom should I contact to get some good stories about you?

Are there any interesting organizations that you belong to?

Do you have any hobbies?

Is there anything that you specifically want me to mention?

Is there anything that you specifically don't want mentioned?

Is there anything you thought I was going to ask or that I should have asked you?

Six ways to make them (and you) look good

The way that you introduce other speakers says as much about you as it does about them. The following are some tips to ensure that you both come out looking good.

Make it interesting

Anyone can get a speaker's résumé, stand at a podium, and read it. But it's boring, and it's a disservice to the speaker and your audience. It means that you didn't take the time to put together an introduction that will set a great tone and turn on the crowd.

Make the speaker real. Quote the speaker. Tell some anecdotes about the speaker. Let the audience see the speaker as a human being — not a résumé.

Now that doesn't mean you should ignore the speaker's accomplishments. Pick out a few of the major ones and show how they relate to the speaker's topic. The audience wants to know what the speaker will talk about and why he or she is qualified. So tell them.

Get the name right

There's nothing more embarrassing than mispronouncing the name of the person you're introducing. (Maybe there are a few more embarrassing things, but they're too gross to mention.) The point is you lose a lot of credibility if you get the name wrong. You look sloppy, silly, and unprepared.

How do you learn the proper pronunciation of a speaker's name? Ask the speaker. And if it's a real tongue twister, write it down phonetically. The other reason to ask speakers about their names is to find out what they like to be called. If you're introducing a former President of the United States named James Earl Carter, you'd want to know that he likes to be called Jimmy Carter. And if you introduce Dr. Samuel Bloom, find out if he prefers Sam or Samuel and if he wants his title used. (Surprisingly, some people with doctorates don't want to be called Dr.)

And while I'm on the subject of names, don't forget to verify the names and pronunciations of any geographic entities you'll mention. If you're going to say the speaker was born in the city of Sarajevo in Bosnia-Herzegovina and then moved to a town near China's border with Kazakhstan, you'd better know how to pronounce all that stuff.

Keep it brief

The introduction should be short and sweet. If you're introducing a head of state or similar dignitary, maybe you can go as long as three to four minutes. (And that's really pushing the limit.) For anyone else, one to two minutes is plenty.

Coordinate with the person you're introducing

Check your introduction with the person you're introducing. Make sure you've got all the information correct and find out if there's anything the speaker wants *omitted*.

You've done a lot of research and found out lots of things about the speaker, but the speaker may feel strongly that some of these things shouldn't be mentioned. Or the speaker may want to mention these things within his or her speech.

Most important, if speakers ask you to include certain information in their introduction and you don't, then let them know beforehand. Otherwise, you may destroy their presentation. They may plan their entire opening on the assumption that the audience will get a key fact from your introduction. This often occurs when speakers want to open with a self-effacing joke referring to something in their background. If the introducer didn't give the audience the background information, they can't "get" the joke.

Talk to the audience

The person doing the introduction gets to the podium, takes out some notes, and gives the introduction. But he looks only at the speaker he's introducing. It's a common mistake. Don't make it. When you introduce someone, look at the audience. The people you're introducing already know all about themselves. They don't need your eye contact. Why look at them, anyway? Do introducers want the speaker's approval? Do they want to make sure the speaker won't disappear?

And while you're talking to the audience, tell them to put their hands together for the person you're introducing. Do it at the end. Let them know when they're supposed to burst into a welcoming round of applause. Heck, you can lead the applause yourself. It can only make you look good.

Announce if there will be a question-and-answer period

The audience wants to know when they can ask questions. Will there be a Q&A session after the speaker's presentation? Or do audience members have to buttonhole the speaker on an individual basis? Either way, it's one less chore the speaker must deal with if you let the audience know when you introduce the speaker.

What not to do

Don't give the speaker's speech. You're supposed to announce what the speaker will talk about, but that's all. Don't go into minute detail about what the speaker will cover — or there'll be nothing left to cover.

Don't give your own speech. Again, you're just supposed to announce what the speaker will talk about. While your views on the subject may be fascinating, no one came to hear them. Holding a microphone is not a license to give a speech. Get on with the intro and get off.

Don't overpromise. You want to get the audience excited about the speaker and the topic — but not overexcited. Raising the audience's expectations too much makes things tougher for the speaker. If you say that the speaker is a brilliant orator who will make the audience laugh while tugging at their heartstrings and changing their lives, you're setting the speaker up for a fall. Give a good buildup but don't go crazy.

Don't gush. I don't know who gets more embarrassed by a gushing introduction — the person being introduced or the audience. Either way, the person doing the introduction looks ridiculous. Yes, you're supposed to praise the speaker, but don't go overboard. It's a common malady. That's why so many professional speakers have lines ready to deal with this situation. "After hearing that introduction, I'm not sure if I'm supposed to speak or be buried." "Thanks for that fantastic introduction. You read it just like my mother wrote it."

Don't highlight deficiencies. You want to put the audience in a receptive mood, so don't remind them about problems. "We're lucky our speaker agreed to come from out of town today even though the river is supposed to reach flood level in an hour." Thanks a lot. That really makes everyone want to hear the speech. You're supposed to put the audience on the edge of their seats — not on edge.

Don't wing it. You've done a lot of research. You have some great stories about the speaker. You've edited the speaker's list of achievements down to the ones relevant to the audience. Don't blow it now by winging it. Write out the introduction and stick to it.

Say a Few Words: Giving Impromptu Speeches

"Say a few words." This phrase can strike terror into the hearts of the bravest souls. But view it as an opportunity. Really. Everyone knows that you've had no time to prepare, so no one expects you to deliver a presentation on the level of Lincoln's "Gettysburg Address" or Martin Luther King's "I Have a Dream." You're held to a much lower standard. That's the opportunity. If you say anything remotely well-organized and intelligent, you'll be perceived as a genius.

Of course, there are a few tricks to help you succeed. The first is to realize that you're not likely to be asked to give an impromptu speech unless you know about the subject. So you really do have a good head start. The second is to be ready when you are asked. As comedy coach John Cantu has observed, "Ad-libs work best when they're written down."

ANECDOTE

Thou shalt not steal

Several years ago, I was asked to speak at a university's public affairs club. It was one of those deals where each week a local luminary is brought in to be an after-luncheon speaker. It was actually a fairly prestigious invitation. Previous speakers had included leading business and political figures.

Naturally, a big deal is made out of introducing the speaker, and I was no exception. The person who introduced me gave a very elaborate description of my topic and credentials. He said that I would talk about using humor in business. He said that I had a background in communications. He said that I was a lawyer. And he said that I had served as a humor consultant to numerous Fortune 500 corporations. It was a big build-up. It got the audience excited. It was a text-book perfect intro. Except for one thing — his last line.

He said, "As Malcolm likes to say, whether or not you think the world needs a humor consultant, he's sure you'll agree it can use one less attorney." The line got a big laugh (as it always does). Then he said, "Please welcome Malcolm Kushner."

Here's the problem: That line about one less attorney is my trademark. I always use it as my opening line. (That's how I know it always gets a big laugh.) The person introducing me *knew* that it was my opening line. He had heard me speak before. (In fact, that's why he had begged me to speak at this luncheon where he was introducing me.) So let's not mince words — he stole my line.

Why did he do it? Who knows. Fortunately, I'd designed my presentation so that my second line could serve as the opener. The audience was none the wiser. No one knew that I hadn't used my real opening line except me and my "pal" the introducer. (As you can tell, I still think highly of him to this day.)

So do the people you're introducing a big favor: don't steal their material. If you even think there's a possibility that you're infringing on their turf, check with them. They'll appreciate it.

Be Prepared

One of Winston Churchill's critics once said, "Winston has devoted the best years of his life to preparing his impromptu speeches." Intended as a cutting remark, it's actually a compliment. Because smart speakers are always prepared — to speak.

Yes, the whole idea of an impromptu talk is you don't know that you'll be asked to speak. But that doesn't mean you can't *anticipate* the possibility. Watch the Academy Awards some time. Only one person will win best actor, but five nominees have acceptance speeches sticking out of their pockets. Take a cue from the professionals: Be ready to speak.

How can you anticipate when you may be asked to vocally bestow your wisdom? Use your common sense. Are you going to an event honoring a friend, coworker, or relative? It's not a big stretch to assume you may be asked to make a toast or utter a few words of praise.

Are you going to a business meeting? What's on the agenda? It may suggest topics you'd better be prepared to discuss — even though you're *not* a scheduled speaker.

Agenda's have been known to change. Think about what issues might arise. Would you need to respond to any of them? By the way, who else will be at the meeting? Anyone who will try to embarrass you by catching you off guard? Assume the worst and be prepared to do your best.

How to buy time

There's an old saying that nothing makes time pass faster than vacations and short-term loans. Here's a third item for the list: being asked to give an impromptu speech. Because the time between when you're asked to "say a few words" and when you start talking can go by faster than a prayer at an atheists convention. Yet this time is crucial to the success of your impromptu remarks. It's when you will plan and organize your entire presentation.

Your goal is to lengthen this time period as much as possible. Do it any way you can. Here are a few ideas to get you started:

Pause thoughtfully

When someone asks you to say a few words, you're not required to immediately start talking. You can pause and think. This technique actually increases your credibility. The audience assumes that your words will now be carefully considered rather than the first thoughts that flew into your head. (Little do they know.) You can even use some showmanship. Tilt your head slightly to one side. Furrow your brow. Squint a bit. Let the audience know that they're in the presence of some incredibly powerful thinking.

Repeat the question

This technique is the traditional stalling device, but there's a good reason to do it aside from gaining more time. You always want to make sure that you understand what was asked. There's no point knocking yourself out to give a fabulous impromptu talk if it turns out to be on the wrong subject. (And you'll look fairly foolish.) Put the question in your own words. Then get confirmation that you've stated it correctly. (And run the clock as long as possible in the process.)

Be ready with an all-purpose quote

It doesn't hurt to memorize a few all-purpose quotes — lines that you can use to begin *any* impromptu presentation. Quoting someone makes you sound smart, and you get a little extra time to think about what you really want to say. Here are a few quotes to keep in reserve:

To paraphrase Richard Nixon, "Let's get one thing perfectly clear. In this case, I mean your question."

To paraphrase Robert Frost, "The brain is a wonderful organ; it starts working the moment you get up in the morning and doesn't stop until you get asked to make a speech."

As legendary baseball manager Casey Stengel once said, "If you don't know where you're going, you might end up somewhere else." So let me just make sure where I'm going so that we don't end up someplace else. Did you want me to speak about. . . .

Organizing your thoughts

Samuel Johnson once said that "when a man knows he is to be hanged in a fortnight, it concentrates his mind wonderfully." Well, when you know you have to give a speech in twenty seconds, you may feel like you're about to be hanged, and you definitely need to concentrate your mind.

Make a quick decision

Do you remember Aesop's fable of the fox and the cat? One day the fox and the cat are discussing how they avoid their common enemy — the hound. The fox brags that he has at least a hundred tricks for avoiding the hound. The cat says he has only one — jumping into a tree. Suddenly they hear the hound. The cat jumps into a tree. The fox stands around trying to decide which of his one hundred tricks to use. The fox gets eaten.

Here's the moral as applied to impromptu speaking: When a hound asks you to speak, decide quickly what direction you'll take and keep it simple — or bear the consequences.

The big myth with impromptu speaking is that your mind will go blank as soon as you're asked to speak. It's really just the opposite. Most people get an overwhelming number of ideas, and almost any of them will do the job. You need to pick one idea and stick with it. That's the secret. Commit to one main point — quickly.

Pick a pattern

Once you've selected your main point, you have to organize your presentation. What are your subpoints? How will you support them? Do you have examples or anecdotes? You need to pick a pattern of organization — something that will allow you to quickly sort out your information. The following are two popular approaches:

✓ **Organize around the conclusion.** Decide on a conclusion. Organize all your information so that it supports your conclusion. Then start speaking. Everything you say should be designed to move your message toward the conclusion you select.

✓ **Organize around a standard pattern.** Pick one of the standard presentation patterns — past, present, future; problem, solution; cause and effect — and quickly fit its structure to your message. Many speakers find the chronological pattern easiest to use.

Find an opening

There are many ways to begin an impromptu speech. But if the audience doesn't know that you're speaking impromptu, then there's only one way to begin — tell them. Make absolutely sure that they know. Otherwise, they'll apply a higher standard to your remarks. And when you're speaking off the cuff, you don't want to be judged as if you had months to prepare.

Usually the audience will realize that your presentation is impromptu. Then how do you begin?

✓ **Tie into previous speakers.** This is probably the easiest opening. You just react to what's already been said.

✓ **Be candid.** If you really don't know much about the subject, admit that you're not an expert. Then offer whatever information you can contribute to the discussion. If you're completely clueless, offer to gather information and provide it in the future.

✓ **Tell a personal anecdote.** Think of a war story that's relevant to the issue at hand and makes your point. "That reminds me of the time I worked at Company X. We faced a similar issue. . . ."

✓ **Switch the topic.** This method is popular with politicians. They're asked for their opinion on a tax increase. And they reply, "Taxes are one of the controversial areas of any system of government. When the ancient Greeks invented democracy, they had to find a way to pay for it. In those days, government was a deliberative force to carry out the will of the people. Today, government does many additional things. As your representative in Congress, I've been proud of the accomplishments our government has achieved, particularly here in our district. . . ." By the time Congressman Blab is finished, most of the audience won't remember that the question had nothing to do with the role of government in our lives.

✓ **Create a catchy analogy.** Pick anything — an object, a celebrity, something in the news — and attach it to an item related to the topic under discussion. Here's an example: You're asked to speak about quality management in your company. Pick an object. I'll pick "orange juice." Then you need an item related to quality management. There are lots of theories about quality, so I'll pick "theory" as the item. Now attach orange juice to theory and make up an analogy. "At my company we subscribe to the orange juice theory of quality management. You squeeze the best performance out of everyone and get rid of the pits." You don't like that one? Make up your own. The Madonna philosophy of quality management: Don't wait to correct problems later. It's better to reveal everything up front. The Jeopardy approach to quality management: We ask the questions *after* we have the answers. That's why we have such poor quality. You get the idea. The audience loves this kind of opening because they have no idea where you're going with it. It gets them curious. As long as you make the analogy relevant to the discussion, it will work.

One final word of advice on openings. There's one thing you should never do — apologize. What would you apologize for anyway? Not having a carefully polished talk ready? It's an impromptu speech! By definition, it's off the cuff.

Simplify your support

When you make your point, don't support it with endless details. Limit yourself to two or three key items of evidence. Make them as specific as possible and simplify them where appropriate. For example, if you can round off statistics without distorting them — do it.

Stop talking

Stop when you're finished. It sounds obvious — but most people don't. The most common mistake related to impromptu speaking is rambling. The way to avoid this problem is to know where you're going. Make sure that you think about a conclusion in the short time you have to organize your thoughts. Then stick to your plan. When you get to the conclusion — stop.

Part IV

Scoring Points with Humor

The 5th Wave   By Rich Tennant

"NOW THAT I'VE LIGHTENED UP THE ROOM,..."

In this part . . .

Laugh and the world laughs with you. It's absolutely true, and that's the point I try to get across in this part of the book. Anyone can learn to use humor effectively. You don't have to be "naturally funny" or know how to tell jokes. In these chapters, you'll discover how to transform your sense of humor into a powerful presentation asset. You'll also learn to use humor to gain attention, create rapport, make your message more memorable, and motivate an audience. And that's no joke.

Chapter 20
Making Your Point with Humor

● ●

In This Chapter

▶ Making humor work even if you're not "naturally funny"

▶ Gaining audience attention and creating rapport

▶ Avoiding offensive humor

● ●

*H*umor is a powerful communication tool. It can gain attention, create rapport, and make a presentation more memorable. It can also relieve tension, motivate an audience, and enhance your reputation if it's used appropriately. If it's not used appropriately, it can sink a presentation faster than a politician can make an excuse. In this chapter, you'll discover what humor can do for you as a speaker and how to avoid its major pitfalls.

The Common Fears

If humor can provide benefits like gaining attention and creating rapport, why don't more speakers attempt to harness its power. One word — fear. Professional speakers like to cite surveys showing that speaking in public is feared more than anything else, including death.

But let me suggest that there's another fear even greater than giving a speech — telling a speech with a joke in it. Why? Because if humor is used inappropriately, it can cause lots of serious problems. These include

✔ Losing credibility

✔ Being misinterpreted

✔ Increasing tension

✔ Offending audience members

✔ Distracting attention from key points

But the biggest fear of all is *bombing* — standing before a silent audience after a joke has flopped. Fortunately, you can read the rest of this chapter to find out how to avoid these problems.

Why You Don't Have to Be "Naturally Funny"

How many times have you heard someone say about humor, "Either you have it or you don't"? (If I had a million dollars for every time that I have heard it, I'd be a millionaire by now.) Here's some very uncommon knowledge: *Anyone can learn to use humor effectively.* You don't have to be naturally funny; you don't have to be a comedian; and you don't even have to know how to tell a joke. If you have a sense of humor, then you can apply it in a presentation.

Being funny versus communicating a sense of humor

You should learn to distinguish between being funny and communicating a sense of humor. Some people are born with a gift for being funny. They grow up to work in a circus, comedy club, or Congress. But all of us know people who have a good sense of humor yet can't tell a joke. They can't make you guffaw with laughter, but they can communicate a certain warmth and make you smile. That's the quality you want to get across during your presentation. You can learn to communicate your natural sense of humor without telling jokes. (See Chapter 21.)

Why bother? The benefits of humor

Lots of studies attest to the benefits of using humor in a presentation. Most important, audiences tend to like speakers who use humor. Audiences don't automatically accept these speakers' words as gospel, but they'll be more favorably disposed to receiving the speakers' messages.

Humor woven artfully into a talk can also draw attention to key points. Social science research has shown that information put into a humorous form such as a joke or anecdote is remembered a little longer than non-humorous material. (My ideal is always to build informational points right into a joke. Then if people remember the joke to tell their friends, they're automatically remembering my points.)

Getting serious about humor

Humor is no laughing matter — especially to researchers who study it. Why is humor funny? How does humor affect personality? What's the relationship between humor and hockey? These are just a few of the questions that an army of social scientists have investigated over the past several years. Want more information? Here are a few articles to get you started. (I'm waiting for the movie versions.)

"Effects of Dyadic Participation and Awareness of Being Monitored on Facial Action During Exposure to Humor," Alexander J. Dale, Mary A. Hudak and Paul Wasikowski, *Perceptual and Motor Skills* (December 1991), p. 984 (3 pages).

"Preliminary Validation of a Multidimensional Model of Wittiness," Alan Feingold and Ronald Mazzella, *Journal of Personality* (September 1993), p. 439 (18 pages).

"An Exploratory Factor Analysis of the Sense of Humour Personality Construct: A Pilot Project," David Korotkov, *Personality & Individual Differences* (1991 v.12 n. 5) pp. 395–397.

"Presentation of Humor and Facilitation of a Relaxation Response Among Internal and External Scorers on Rotter's Scale," Frank J. Prerost, *Psychological Reports* (June 1993), p. 1248 (3 pages).

"Organ Donation, Authoritarianism, and Perspective-Taking Humor," Herbert M. Lefcourt and Robert S. Shepherd, *Journal of Research in Personality* (March 1995), pp. 121–138.

"Anger, Aggression, and Humor in Newfoundland Floor Hockey: An Evolutionary Analysis," Craig T. Palmer, *Aggressive Behavior* (May–June 1993), p. 167 (7 pages).

The other big benefit of humor in a public speaking setting is its ability to reduce tension. An appropriate joke can be very effective at breaking the ice with an audience, and it can be even more effective as a response to a hostile question. Humor can help set a positive tone for a presentation. It can foster a lighter atmosphere that's more conducive to the exchange of ideas.

Avoiding the Biggest Mistake

Have you ever heard a speaker start a presentation with a joke that had nothing to do with anything? I'm talking about an absolutely pointless, no connection to anything, completely irrelevant joke. What was your reaction? If the joke was funny, maybe you laughed. But even if you did, the joke was still just a distraction because it didn't make any point. It just wasted your time.

And if you didn't laugh? Well, that's called *bombing*. Everyone knows the speaker was trying to be funny, but no one laughed. So the speaker was left facing that deafening silence emanating from the audience, and the audience began to feel uncomfortable because the speaker seemed uncomfortable. (Perhaps the audience noticed the torrents of perspiration pouring forth from the speaker's brow.) The speaker was trapped in that peculiar twilight zone known as bombing and had no way out.

If you use humor to make a point, then you won't bomb. Now let me be perfectly clear. I'm not saying that your audience will laugh at your joke. I *am* saying that you won't bomb. Here's why: When you tell a joke that makes a point, people recognize that fact. So even if they don't find the joke funny, they still realize that you're making a point. If they don't laugh, it doesn't matter. The joke still serves a purpose and moves the presentation forward. After the joke, you just go on to your next point. When you tell a pointless joke, people realize that too. If no one laughs, then the joke serves no purpose whatsoever, and you're stuck with no place to go.

You may also want to make a point with humor because doing so increases the chances that your audience will find your humor funny. Why? It's basic audience psychology. People are resistant if they think you're trying to make them laugh. Think of the last time you saw a comedian stride up to a microphone. Your first thought was probably, "You think you're funny — prove it!" That mindset is quite different when you know that the speaker is trying to make a point. You have much less resistance, and you're much more open to responding with laughter.

How to Make Humor Relevant

If you want to make humor relevant, you must tie it to a point in your presentation. You must do more than simply select jokes that reflect the topic of your talk. Just because you're talking about computers, doesn't make any computer joke automatically relevant. If you make the point that computers aren't infallible, a joke about computer error is relevant. A joke about computer costs is not. Here are some ideas for making your humor relevant.

The analogy method

An analogy allows you to compare two different objects and show how they're related. Establishing this relationship is at the heart of the creative process, and it's quite useful for ensuring that your humor is relevant. The trick is to analogize your humor to a point in your presentation.

To see the analogy method in action, read the following example from a speech made by Robert Clarke, former Comptroller of the Currency. Speaking to the National Council of Savings Institutions in 1990, he discussed how regulatory tools could be used to promote a sound banking system.

A friend of mine, an honors graduate of Texas Agricultural and Mechanical University, an "aggie," spent the first half of the 1980s lusting for a car phone. Finally, he convinced himself that it was a necessity, not a luxury, so he bought one. The day he bought it, he called me from his car to tell me the news. And I didn't hear from him again for about a month. Finally I saw him on the street and he seemed really down in the dumps. I asked him what was wrong and he said it was the car phone. "What do you mean?" I asked. "You wanted that phone more than anything you ever did." And he said: "Yeah, but it's wearing me down having to run to the garage every time it rings."

Regulations — like telephones — are instruments. They can be used effectively. They can be used adequately. Or they can be misused.

The story is effective because it illustrates a key point — that regulations are merely tools. You should notice two other things. First, this story would never be listed under "regulations" in any jokebook. The speaker used analogical thinking to relate the joke to his point about regulations. Second, the story could illustrate other ideas. It would be equally effective for making points about office automation, productivity, and training. In fact, the story can be used to illustrate any point to which you can analogize it. The process is limited only by your imagination.

How to find new uses for old jokes

Another way to make humor relevant is to switch old jokes. Just change them around to apply to points in your presentation. For example, here's an old one about Congress.

Believe it or not, they have a Dial-a-Joke service in Washington D.C. You call it up, and they give you the number of Congress.

If you have to give a consumer-tips talk about automobile repairs and not about Congress, no problem — just switch the joke.

Believe it or not, they have a Dial-a-Prayer service along Interstate 80. You call it up, and they give you the number of the local auto repair shop.

It's time we stopped acting on faith when it comes to auto repairs.

Any joke can be switched in numerous ways. Once again, your imagination is your only limit.

Avoiding Humor That Hurts

When you use humor appropriately, you create rapport with your audience. Many speakers achieve the exact opposite effect when they use humor. Why? They tell offensive jokes. Inappropriate humor can be very hurtful — and not just to audience members. It can hurt the speaker too. Offensive humor makes speakers look bad, lowers their credibility, and turns off the audience in a big way. Humor should be used to build bridges, not burn them. This section contains a few suggestions for making sure that *you* don't get burned.

The three most offensive categories of humor

Forget about political correctness. It's just common courtesy not to insult an audience by using offensive humor. But as with many things common — common sense, common decency, common touch — common courtesy is not so common. Want to make sure that you don't become an offender? Then you must avoid three major types of humor: ethnic, racist, and sexist humor; off-color humor; and sarcasm.

Ethnic, racist, and sexist humor

Jokes based upon an individual's gender, race, ethnicity, or sexual identity are taboo — plain and simple. It doesn't matter what the speaker thinks. ("Gee, I don't understand why those people are offended. It's just a joke.") All that counts is the opinion of the audience. Rest assured, some of them will be offended — and not just members of the group targeted by the joke. Many people find any ethnic, racist, or sexist humor offensive. And here's a tip to help you avoid being unintentionally offensive: AIDs jokes are as offensive as ethnic jokes.

What if you're a member of the group you're joking about? Is it OK to tell Irish jokes if you're Irish? The experts are split on this, but why take a chance? Someone will always find it offensive. Remember, you want to use humor to win friends, not create enemies.

Off-color humor

Have you ever heard a speaker use the phrase "mixed company"? (The speaker may say something like, "There's a great joke about this, but I can't tell it in mixed company.") I always get a kick out of that phrase. It's supposed to refer to an audience of males and females. Presumably if the company weren't "mixed" — if it were males only — the speaker could tell the joke because the joke is probably off-color and therefore assumed to be offensive to women but not men.

Plenty of men, as well as women, are offended by off-color jokes. (Would you tell one to your clergyman?) That's why my lexicon defines "mixed company" as a mix of people who possess good taste and people who don't. Because no audience will ever contain only people with good taste, you'll always be speaking in mixed company, so you'll always offend someone if you tell an off-color joke.

Sarcasm

The word *sarcasm* has its roots in ancient Greece and translated literally means "to tear flesh apart." Today, sarcasm leaves its wounds in the ego rather than the flesh, but that doesn't make it any less painful. (It may be even more painful.) Speakers who use a lot of sarcasm tend to be showoffs. They think sarcastic remarks reveal their great wit. Unfortunately, it reveals much more — a big ego coupled with an obnoxious personality.

While sarcasm can sometimes be used effectively to attack an enemy that's common to the speaker and audience, it still sends a red flag to audience members. They know that the sarcasm may be turned on them at any time — especially if they ask a tough question. People never feel quite at ease around a sarcastic speaker. While many speakers use humor to decrease tension, sarcasm has the opposite effect.

A simple test to determine offensiveness

In today's politically correct universe, many people honestly don't know what's offensive anymore. When I lecture about this topic, I hear their frustration. Someone will always say, "Then I just can't ever use humor again. It's not safe. I might offend someone." Well, I disagree. You don't have to go to such extremes. Just because food might spoil in your refrigerator doesn't mean you should never eat refrigerated food again. You use your common sense and test it. You smell the food. If it stinks, you throw it out. That's what you do with humor too. You test it. And if it stinks, then don't use it.

How do you know if it stinks? Here's a very simple test: Picture a front page headline in your hometown newspaper describing your use of the joke in a presentation. Would you be embarrassed? If the answer is "yes," then don't use the joke.

I have an ever-growing collection of articles involving people who should have applied this test. Perhaps the saddest is the one about the high school principal who made "amusing" references to San Francisco and Oakland during a local service club speech. Unfortunately, the amusing references were homophobic and racist. And that's exactly how they came across in the newspaper headlines the next day. The really sad part is that the principal was well regarded in the community. No one thinks he is, or ever was, racist or homophobic, but his insensitive remarks caused a wound in the community that will take a long time to heal. It could have easily been avoided if he had just pictured those headlines before he spoke.

And that brings me to the prime rule for evaluating potentially offensive humor: *When in doubt, leave it out.* It's that simple.

How to transform ethnic jokes into usable material

The common knowledge is that ethnic jokes should be avoided because they're offensive. That's absolutely true. But here's the uncommon knowledge: They're easy to switch into a non-offensive format.

The vast majority of ethnic jokes are based on the assumption that the group in question is dumb. So the jokes can work with *any* group. It doesn't have to be an ethnic group. Here are a few examples.

> Q: Why did 18 Competitor Company executives go to the movies?
>
> A: The sign said "17 and under not admitted."
>
> Q: How can you tell if a Competitor Company executive has been using the computer?
>
> A: There's white-out on the screen.
>
> Q: How can you tell if another Competitor Company executive has been using the computer?
>
> A: There's writing on the white-out.
>
> Q: Why did the Competitor Company executive stare at the frozen orange juice can for two hours?
>
> A: Because it said "concentrate."
>
> Q: What do you call an intelligent person at Competitor Company head-quarters?
>
> A: A visitor.

I first heard these jokes made about ethnic groups. In their original format, they were offensive and insulting. (And also the potential basis for lawsuits.) In their "switched" format, they poke fun at one of your company's competitors — an acceptable target.

Chapter 21

Simple Types of Humor Anyone Can Use

"**S**o these three guys walked into a bar and the bartender had a parrot on his shoulder. No wait, I mean one of the guys had a parrot on his shoulder. And the bartender wanted to know why the parrot was on his shoulder. And the guy said . . . no wait, I mean the parrot said . . . umm one second, it will come to me in a moment. Oh yeah, I forgot to say that the parrot was wearing a little hat and singing the national anthem."

Can't tell a joke? Don't worry. You have lots of other options for incorporating humor into your presentation.

How to Use Personal Anecdotes

A personal anecdote is a story based on a real experience — yours or someone else's. It's a story about something that happened with friends or relatives. It's a war story from work. It's an incident that occurred at school or home or anywhere. It's your life. These stories provide an absolute gold mine of humorous material for any presentation. And here's their best feature — *you can tell them*. You've already been telling them for years. So you don't have to worry about delivery.

Instead of telling these stories for no particular reason while conversing with friends or acquaintances, use them for a purpose: use them to make a point. (For a full discussion of the importance of tying humor to a point, see Chapter 20.) What follows is an example from a commencement address given by Alexander Sanders, Jr., Chief Judge of the South Carolina Court of Appeals. The judge's daughter Zoe was among the graduates.

I am reminded today of something that happened when Zoe was just a little girl. When she was three years old, I came home from work to find a crisis in my household. Zoe's pet turtle had died. And she was crying as if her heart would break. Her mother, having coped with the problems of the home all day, turned that one over to me to solve. At the time, I was practicing law and serving in the Legislature. Frankly, it was a problem a lawyer politician was not up to solving.

The mysteries of life and death are difficult, if not impossible for the mature mind to fathom. The task of explaining them to a three-year-old was completely beyond either my confidence or experience. But I tried. First, I made the obvious argument that we would get another turtle to replace the one that died. We would go down to the pet store and buy another one just like the one who was gone.

I got nowhere with that argument. Even at three years old, Zoe was smart enough to know that there is a certain nontransferability about living things. A turtle is not a toy. There's really no such thing as getting another one just like the one who died. Zoe's tears continued.

Finally, in desperation, I said, "I tell you what, we'll have a funeral for the turtle." Well, being only three years old, she didn't know what a funeral was. So I quickly proceeded to expand on my theme. You see, I was employing the typical lawyer's tactic of diversion. If you can't win on the issue at hand, take off on something completely beside the point.

"A funeral," I explained, "is a great festival in honor of the turtle." Well, being only three years old, she didn't know what a festival was either. So, I quickly proceeded to explain further. And, as I did so, I began to depart from the lawyer's tactic of diversion and engage in the politician's prerogative of outright lying. "Actually," I said, "a funeral is like a birthday party. We'll have ice cream and cake and lemonade and balloons, and all the children in the neighborhood will come over to our house to play. All because the turtle has died."

Success at last! Zoe's tears began to dry, and she quickly returned to her happy, smiling self again. Now, happy. Now, joyous. At the prospect of all that was going to happen. All because the turtle had died.

Then an utterly unforeseen thing happened. We looked down, and lo and behold, the turtle began to move. He was not dead after all. In a matter of seconds, he was crawling away as lively as ever. For once, a lawyer politician was struck dumb for words.

I just didn't know what to say. But, Zoe appraised the situation perfectly. And, although this happened more than twenty years ago, I remember what she said as though it was yesterday. With all the innocence of her tender years, she looked up at me and said, "Daddy," she said, "Daddy, let's kill it."

The judge used the story to make a point about the lengths to which parents will go to make their children happy. But it could also be used to make points about knowing your priorities, analyzing a situation for maximum advantage, and learning that appearances can be deceiving.

Why Personal Anecdotes Get Attention

Personal anecdotes are real. Audiences instinctively recognize this quality, and they literally hang on every word of these stories. Let's face it — most people enjoy gossip. That's why the *National Enquirer* and *People* magazine are so popular (not to mention TV talk shows that feature gender-bending guests who describe their most intimate experiences). Personal anecdotes are a form of gossip. They're *personal,* and they always get attention.

Personal anecdotes also receive attention because your audience can't hear them from anyone else. They're *your* personal anecdotes. You're the only one in the world who has them. Talk about positioning. The more personal anecdotes you use, the more you differentiate yourself from other presenters. In the jargon of modern business babble, that means they give you a "strategic competitive advantage."

That's why I strongly recommend that you mine yourself for these stories. They're pure gold. Did a relative walk out of a bathroom at a formal event trailing a roll of toilet paper? Did you think your car was stolen when it rolled down the street because you forgot to engage the parking brake? Did your kid ask why you always say your neighbor smells — while you were talking to the neighbor? People love this stuff. You have them in your head; now get them in your talk. (Need help jogging your memory? See the personal anecdote checklist in Chapter 8.)

Fifteen More Types of Non-Joke Humor

What if you don't have an endless supply of personal anecdotes? No problem. Most people don't. Fortunately there are lots of other simple types of non-joke humor that don't require any special comic delivery. Here are fifteen of them.

Analogies

An analogy is a comparison between two objects or concepts. A funny analogy makes the comparison in an entertaining way. And analogies don't require comic delivery because they are so short.

Full deckisms

Have you ever had to make a presentation arguing that someone's position or idea didn't make any sense? It was inane, idiotic, preposterous, unintelligible, ridiculous, and absurd. (Now don't candycoat it. Say what you really think.) The next time you need to make this point try using a "full deckism." Full deckisms are euphemisms for saying that people are stupid or illogical — that they're "not playing with a full deck." Here are a few to get you started:

✓ One Fruit Loop shy of a full bowl.

✓ A couplet short of a sonnet.

✓ Has it floored in neutral.

✓ Left the store without all of his groceries.

✓ Missing a few buttons on her remote control.

✓ Two socks short of a pair.

✓ A few clowns short of a circus.

✓ A few tiles missing from his space shuttle.

✓ Goalie for the dart team.

Here's an example from a speech about regulatory reform given by Eugene Ludwig, Comptroller of the Currency of the United States:

> Being a regulator these days is a lot like being the nearest fire hydrant to the dog pound. You know they'll have to turn to you in an emergency, but it's sure tough dealing with those daily indignities.

Here's another example from a speech about teaching virtue given by Todd Buchholz, Associate Director of the Economic Policy Council at The White House:

> Frankly, blaming Columbus, the Pilgrims, and George Washington for all the trouble that followed is like blaming Marco Polo because yuppie restaurants charge $20 for a bowl of pasta.

Now I admit that funny analogies are difficult to think up yourself, but you can use other people's analogies in your own speeches by switching some of the facts. The analogy about the regulator and the fire hydrant is a perfect example. It could apply to a secretary, a manager, or anyone who feels that his or her work is important but unrespected. So anytime you come across a funny analogy, write it down and file it away. You can never have too many at your fingertips.

Quotes

Funny quotes provide an easy way to get attention. Call it the cult of celebrity. Call it a fascination with the quoteworthy. Whatever you want to call it, the phenomenon remains the same — as soon as an audience hears a famous name, it perks up. If the famous name is followed by a really funny quote, then you've got them. (At least for a few seconds. But in today's computer age, that's a long time.)

A few amusing analogies

Need an amusing analogy for your next presentation? Here are a few you may be able to use. See if you can tie one into a point you'll be making.

> I feel like Elizabeth Taylor's seventh husband. I think I know what to do, but I don't know if I can make it interesting.

> Trying to analyze leadership is like studying the Abominable Snowman. You see footprints . . . but never the thing itself.

> It's like a Pia Zadora movie. Everybody's heard of it, but nobody's seen one.

> It's like the suicide bomber who did 35 missions. He was interested in his work, but he wasn't really involved.

Here's an example of a funny quote used by Richard Lidstad, Vice President of Human Resources for 3M, in a speech about success:

> Second, you need to know that I don't consider myself an intellectual. I don't know everything. That's not all bad, however, since President Dwight Eisenhower once said, "An intellectual is a man who takes more words than necessary to tell more than he knows."

And here's another example from a speech about medical progress by James Todd, Senior Deputy Executive Vice President of the American Medical Association:

> It is only natural to wonder when it happened, why the American conquest of progress went so far astray from our concepts of humanity and social responsibility.

> It makes me think of Samuel Butler, who said that, "all progress is based upon a universal innate desire on the part of every organism to live beyond its income."

Let's do one more. In this next example, Mark Schannon, Director of Public Relations at the Monsanto Company, uses a quote from a comedian to make a point in a speech about the ecology crisis:

> We have come a long way in twenty short years — our ability to continue to make progress will depend in large part on our willingness to acknowledge and address the complexity of the world around us.

> As Woody Allen once said, "More than at any time in history, mankind faces a crossroads. One path leads to despair and utter hopelessness, the other to total extinction. Let us pray we have the wisdom to choose correctly."

If you can't find a funny quote that fits your point, you can make one up. Why isn't this an ethical problem? Because if you do it correctly, it's *obvious* that you made up the quote. This advice comes courtesy of Loyd Auerbach, a corporate trainer and professional speaker. He cites the *Myth Adventures* series of humorous fantasy novels written by Robert Lynn Aspirin as an example. "Each chapter begins with a made-up quote from a real or fictional character," Loyd explains. "They're funny precisely because you know they're made up." Some of his favorites from the series include the following:

- "90 percent of all business transactions are selling yourself to the customer." (Xavier Hollander)
- "No venture succeeds without good planning." (Christopher Columbus)
- "The best laid plans often go afowl." (Wylie Coyote)

"I've used these quotes on slides and overheads in lots of presentations," Loyd says. "I throw them in where appropriate because people get a laugh out of them." But he adds a word of warning: You must make sure your audience can get the joke. "Most people are familiar with Wylie Coyote and Christopher Columbus," he observes. "Not everyone knows Xavier Hollander." (Ms. Hollander is better known as "The Happy Hooker.")

Fulfilling your quota of quotes

Want to display a touch of erudition in your next presentation? Quote a few quips from some modern day sages. Here are a few pearls of wisdom to get you started:

"If you can keep your head while all about you are losing theirs, it's just possible you haven't grasped the situation."

—Jean Kerr

"Anywhere is walking distance if you've got the time."

—Steven Wright

"Power corrupts. Absolute power is kind of neat."

—John Lehman

"Life is what happens when you are making other plans."

—John Lennon

"Football incorporates the two worst elements of American society: violence punctuated by committee meetings."

—George Will

"I think of my boss as a father figure. That really irritates her."

—Mary Jo Crowley

Cartoons

Even people who insist that they can't tell a joke will admit that they can describe a cartoon that appeared in a newspaper or magazine. I see people do this all the time. Someone joins a gathering of coworkers taking a coffee break. The conversation turns to some business topic, and the person describes a cartoon from *The Wall Street Journal* that relates to the discussion. The coworkers laugh, and the conversation continues. If you can do this (and I know you can), you can use cartoons to make points in a presentation.

One of my favorite cartoons is a picture of two shipwrecked survivors standing on a tiny island. One of the survivors is holding a bottle that floated onto the shore. He looks at the note that was in it and says to his companion, "It's from your alumni association." I can use this cartoon to make points about relentlessly pursuing an objective, finding what you're looking for, and how you can run but you can't hide.

You can even describe an entire comic strip in your presentation — if it makes a point. The next quote shows how Professor James V. Schall of Georgetown University's Department of Government used a *Peanuts* comic strip in a speech titled "On Wasting the Best Years of Our Lives: Christianity Is a Religion of Joy."

> Sally and Charlie Brown are seen standing by a telephone pole waiting for the school bus one morning. Charlie is gazing down the empty street while back of him we hear Sally exclaim, "Someday there's going to be a monument here, and you know what will be on it?" Charlie continues looking down the street in silence. Sally continues to explain. It will read. "This is where Sally Brown wasted the best years of her life waiting for the school bus. . . ." Finally, Charlie turns around to look at her with some considerable perplexity as she describes what she would proceed to do with the wasted time. She would have "slept another ten minutes."

> Clearly Sally did not think sleeping another ten minutes each school day morning constituted a waste of her time. The question of whether we are "wasting our time" by sleeping or waiting for school buses, however, is one of considerable interest if we think about the issue of human priorities.

Definitions

Funny definitions are extremely easy to use. Just pick a word or phrase from your presentation and define it in an amusing way. Here's an example from a speech to the Ag Bankers Association given by Dale Miller, President and CEO of the Sandoz Crop Protection Corporation:

> A cynic once defined a farm as an irregular patch of nettles bounded by short term notes.

Here's another example from a speech by Norman Augustine, President and CEO of Lockheed-Martin:

> I bring you greetings from my home town, "America's Most Confused City," Washington, D.C., which I have occasionally referred to as "a diamond-shaped city surrounded on all four sides by reality."

Want a formula for inserting funny definitions into your presentation? Try the old "dictionary bit." You pick out a word or phrase that you look up in the dictionary and then state the meaning. Here's an example from a speech about biotechnology given by Richard Mahoney, Chairman of the Monsanto Company:

> For those six weeks I spent splicing genes in the lab, the scientists presented me with a certificate, designating me an official "journeyman in gene splicing." I was quite pleased, until I looked up "journeyman" in the dictionary: "An experienced, reliable worker, especially as distinguished from one who is brilliant."

Where do you find funny definitions? Most "treasury of funny stuff for public speakers" type books contain them. Just look in your local library or bookstore. Trade journals and professional magazines are also good sources. These types of publications often have a humor page that will include amusing definitions related to their readers' occupations. And don't forget *The Wall Street Journal*. It's "Pepper . . . and Salt" feature, which appears in the bottom-left corner of the op-ed page, often includes a "daffynition."

Some of the best sources for funny definitions are little kids — anyone from preschool to the lower elementary grades. Just ask a young child to define a big word and see what happens; you might be able to use the result in a speech.

For example, Thais Billing has a two-year-old daughter who went shopping with her grandmother. When they returned home, Thais asked if grandma had bought anything. The two-year-old said, "No. It was too expensive." Thais thought that was a big word for a two-year-old. So she asked "What does expensive mean?" The two-year-old said, "It means you don't get one."

Thais is a manager for a high-tech company. The next time she gives a talk about why her department can't afford a certain budget item, she has a great definition to use.

Abbreviations and Acronyms

An abbreviation is formed by combining the first letters of a series of words. Two familiar (but boring) examples are IRS (Internal Revenue Service) and the accounting principle known as LIFO (Last In First Out). Funny abbreviations are much more entertaining.

You can make abbreviations funny in a variety of ways. The simplest way is to change the meaning of the underlying words. For example, PBS usually refers to Public Broadcasting System, but that's not how Daniel Brenner, Director of the Communications Law Program at the UCLA School of Law, used it in a speech about the information revolution:

> I've just come from a meeting of the Corporation for Public Broadcasting in Washington. Public broadcasting has its own problems. Most people think PBS stands for Plenty of British Shows.

Acronyms (abbreviations that form a word) can also be used in a humorous way. You can make up funny ones by abbreviating a funny phrase. Here's an example from a speech about corporate ethics given by William Dimma, Deputy Chairman of Royal Lepage Limited:

> Ten or fifteen years ago, corporate ethics was a MEGO topic . . . My Eyes Glaze Over . . . but not today and not likely ever again.

Another way to add humor is to redefine a negative word by making it an acronym for something positive. I recently heard an engineer use this technique after his department was referred to as a bunch of nerds. He said that NERDS stood for "Nouveau Engineering Research and Development Stars."

Computer viruses

During the past year or so, a list of funny computer viruses has been circulating by fax and e-mail through offices around the world. (The list is also on the Internet, so it's been everywhere.) Before I suggest how you can use these viruses for comic effect, let's look at some examples.

> AIRLINE VIRUS: You're in Dallas, but your data is in Singapore.

> GOVERNMENT ECONOMIST VIRUS: Nothing works, but all your diagnostic software says everything is fine.

> POLITICALLY CORRECT VIRUS: Never calls itself a "virus," but instead refers to itself as an "electronic microorganism."

OK, you get the idea. The "virus" combines traits of computer technology with traits of something else (airlines, government economists, political correctness, and so on) to produce a funny result. How can you use this device? Create your own "viruses" related to things or people who you'll talk about.

Has your company begun a new expense reporting procedure that everyone thinks is ridiculous? Talk about the (NAME OF EXPENSE REPORTING PROCE-DURE) VIRUS: It's probably harmless, but it makes a lot of people really mad just thinking about it. Is the chief executive of your competitor telling analysts that he'll blow your company out of the water? Talk about the (NAME OF COMPETITOR'S CEO) VIRUS: Sounds dangerous but doesn't do anything.

Lists

Anytime your presentation includes a list, you have an opportunity to include some humor by adding an incongruous item to the end of the list. Your audience won't expect the item, so it'll be surprised and amused.

Here's an example from a speech about the information revolution given by Daniel Brenner, Director of the Communications Law Program at the UCLA School of Law:

> It's a pleasure to be in Detroit. When I think of Detroit, I think of your city's great institutions: the Detroit Tigers, the Motown sound, Lee Iacocca's press agent, to name but a few.

Look for lists that occur naturally within your presentation — lists of budget items, product features, names of people, rhetorical questions. (Remember, a list must be at least two items long or it's not a list. The funny item that you add at the end can't be less than the third item, and it can always be a higher number — fourth, fifth, or hundredth item — as long as it's the last.)

Letters

The funny letter is a wonderful device to use in a presentation. It doesn't require comic delivery. It gives you a prop to hold. And you don't have to worry about forgetting what you'll say — you just read the letter.

Politicians have always had a special fondness for the funny letter. The following is an example from a speech given by President Ronald Reagan to a joint session of Congress. It was his first major address after being hit by an assassin's bullet. He used a letter from a child as a way of thanking the country for its support during his time of crisis:

> The society we heard from is made up of millions of compassionate Americans and their children, from college age to kindergarten. As a matter of fact, as evidence of that, I have a letter with me. The letter came from Peter Sweeney. He's in the second grade in the Riverside School in Rockville Centre, and he said, "I hope you get well quick or you might have to make a speech in your pajamas." He added a postscript. "P.S. If you have to make a speech in your pajamas, I warned you."

But you don't have to be a politician to use a funny letter effectively. Here's an example from a speech about wasteful federal spending given by the late J. Peter Grace when he was Chairman and Chief Executive Officer of W. R. Grace & Co.:

> This letter was sent to me by one of our supporters as a glaring example of waste, and it's addressed to the Secretary of Agriculture. It reads as follows:

"Dear Sir:

"My friend, Ed Peterson, over at Wells, Iowa, received a check for $1,000 from the government for not raising hogs. So I want to go into the 'not raising hogs' business next year. . . .

"As I see it, the hardest part of the program will be in keeping an accurate inventory of how many hogs I haven't raised.

"My friend, Peterson, is very joyful about the future of the business. He has been raising hogs for twenty years or so, and the best he ever made on them was $422 in 1968, until this year, when he got your check for $1,000 for not raising hogs.

"If I get $1,000 for not raising 50 hogs, will I get $2,000 for not raising 100 hogs? I plan to operate on a small scale at first, holding myself down to about 4,000 hogs not raised, which will mean about $80,000 the first year.

"Now another thing, these hogs I will not raise will not eat 100,000 bushels of corn. I understand that you also pay farmers for not raising corn or wheat. Will I qualify for payments for not raising wheat and corn not to feed the 4,000 hogs I am not going to raise?

"Also, I am considering the 'not milking cows' business, so please send me any information on that, too.

"In view of these circumstances, you understand that I will be totally unemployed and therefore plan to file for unemployment and food stamps.

"Be assured you will have my vote in the next election.

Patriotically yours,
/s/ John Partridge"

Now some of you may think this letter is apocryphal, and maybe it is, but it gives you a good idea of what we're looking for.

How do you obtain funny letters? Start with a trip to a library or bookstore and look in the humor section for books that collect amusing letters. (One of my favorites is *Dear Sir: Drop Dead!* It bills itself as "the first ever collection of hate mail." It's edited by Donald Carroll and published by Magnum Books.) Do an author search for the name Juliett Lowell. In the 1950s and '60s, she wrote a series of books collecting funny letters by various themes. (It was called the "Dear" series. Titles included *Dear Doctor, Dear Candidate, Dear Hollywood, Dear Justice, Dear Man of Affairs,* and so on.) Bill Adler is another name to find. His books included *Love Letters to the Beatles, Love Letters to the Mets, Letters From Camp, More Letters From Camp,* and *Kids Letters to President Kennedy.*

Some of the funniest letters can be found right in your own mailbox. I'm talking about the "personal" letters you get from politicians, actors, and other celebrities asking you to support their causes. Quoting excerpts from these letters can provide great comic effect in a presentation. (Here's a letter I received from the President of the United States. He says that a $5 donation from me is crucial to the preservation of the free world, and so on.)

Want to ensure a steady supply of funny material? Write ridiculous letters to prominent executives and politicians. The form letters that they'll send back will be highly entertaining — especially when worked into a talk. (Here's a letter I recently received from the chief executive officer of the Sudso Detergent Corporation thanking me for an idea I sent him. "Thanks for your suggestion that we make a product that turns all clothes black in the wash so that they won't show dirt. We have submitted your idea to our product review committee. They will study it carefully and give it thorough consideration. Your ideas are important to us.) If you want to see exactly what type of letters this process can produce, get a copy of the *Lazlo Letters* by Don Novello. Don Novello, posing as Lazlo Toth, sent absurd letters to some of the most prominent people in the world. The book is a collection of his letters and the responses they generated.

Observations

The funny observation is a wry look at our everyday fortunes and foibles. It's an amusing line that doesn't require comic delivery and can fit almost anywhere in a presentation.

Here's an example from a speech given by Walter Wriston, Former Chairman and CEO of City Corp and City Bank, N.A.:

> We live in a world of people who make projections about the future. Most of these futurists use straight-line projections of today's data to paint a picture of tomorrow. My favorite illustration of this is the recent statement that if George Steinbrenner continues to behave as he has in the past, 70 percent of the male population of New York will have managed the Yankees by the year 2020.

Here's another example from a speech given by Benjamin Alexander, President of Drew-Dawn Enterprises, Inc.:

> Let me reflect now on our city. Many times D.C. is in real trouble only because of its city council. If it had been around when the good Lord said let there be light, eternal darkness would have won by a vote of 6–5.

Parody news headlines

Creating parodies of newspaper and magazine headlines provides two opportunities to make points with humor. You can choose a headline topic related to your talk and poke fun at it. You can also choose the publications that you wish to satirize.

Here's an example from a speech given by William Schreyer, Chairman of the Board of Merrill Lynch & Company, Inc.:

I know you folks in Washington always keep up with the news, so I'm sure you saw some of the headlines the other day, just before the world came to an end.

The New York *Daily News* proclaimed: "God to World: Drop Dead!"

The New Yorker magazine used a very short, simple heading: "Good Riddance."

The Boston Globe said: "World Coming to an End — Harvard and MIT Economists Say 'We Told You So.'"

The Washington Post bantered: "World Will End Tomorrow — Senate Demands Special Prosecutor."

Those of you who know me know I'm not much of a pessimist. It's probably good I went into the securities business and not journalism. But one thing we do learn from reading the papers and watching TV every day is that this year, the conventional political wisdom has been turned upside down.

Don't limit yourself to newspapers and magazines — or even headlines. Anything with a distinctive style can be parodied for a presentation.

You can invent headlines in the style of your company's employee newsletter or your association's monthly bulletin. You can create parody movie reviews. (What would Siskel and Ebert say about your company's new product?) You can invent song titles that various pop stars would sing about your product or issue. The possibilities are endless.

Predictions

K. William Kapp once said, "Had there been a computer a hundred years ago, it would probably have predicted that by now there would be so many horse-drawn vehicles it would be impossible to clean up all the manure." If a computer had made that prediction, it wouldn't have done much worse than many of its human counterparts. Throughout history, leading authorities in every field of endeavor have felt compelled to make predictions that were dramatic, bold, and wrong. While these pronouncements haven't served as a useful guide to the future, they do provide great comic material for presentations. They're particularly good for illustrating points about making predictions, the future, expertise, analysis, and change.

The following is an example from a speech about competition and education given by Joseph Gorman, Chairman and CEO of TRW, Inc.:

Unfortunately, many of those charged with addressing these critical issues are all too reminiscent of past well-known nay-sayers. I offer a few illustrative quotes:

"Heavier than air flying machines are impossible" (Lord Kelvin, President, Royal Society, 1895).

"Everything that can be invented has been invented" (Charles Duell, Director of U.S. Patent Office, 1899).

"Sensible and responsible women do not want to vote" (Grover Cleveland, 1905).

"There is no likelihood man can ever tap the power of the atom" (Robert Millikan, Nobel Prize in Physics, 1923).

"Who the hell wants to hear actors talk?" (Harry M. Warner, Warner Brothers Pictures, 1927).

And those of you who are baseball fans will love this one: "Babe Ruth made a big mistake when he gave up pitching" (Tris Speaker, 1921).

Now plainly implicit in my talk is the notion of change — change of profound and revolutionary proportion.

(Want to see more inane predictions? The best source is *The Experts Speak: The Definitive Compendium of Authoritative Misinformation,* by Christopher Cerf and Benjamin Navasky, published by Pantheon.)

Signs

Have you ever seen a sign that made you laugh? They're all over the place these days. The "You Want It When?" sign posted in a secretary's cubicle. The "Mistakes Made While You Wait" sign hanging by a bank teller's window. The "Your Failure to Plan Does Not Constitute an Emergency on Our Part" sign taped to the wall of a printer's shop. All of these are potential material for a presentation. You just describe the sign and where you saw it. Then tie it to a point.

Here's an example from a speech about health data given by James O. Mason when he was Head of the U.S. Public Health Service:

> I was driving through a small town in Maryland the other day when I saw a sign on a home/office that said, "Veterinarian and Taxidermist." Underneath in very small letters it said, "Either way you get your pet back." I thought if we collected data and analyzed it that way, we all would be successful. Everyone would have the data they needed to get the decision or policy done in a way that they wanted it done.

And here's an example from a speech about image building given by David D'Alessandro, President of the Corporate Sector at John Hancock Financial Services:

> Executives often conclude:

> "The media's out to get us, so we're not saying anything."

That attitude reminds me of a sign I saw in the customer service department of a store recently. It read, "Answers $1, Answers Requiring Thought $2, Correct Answers $5, Dumb Looks Are Still Free." Too many otherwise bright executives are giving dumb looks these days.

Laws

We live in a world of laws — civil laws, criminal laws, scientific laws. But no matter where we live, all of us answer to a higher law — Murphy's. That's the famous law that anything that can go wrong will go wrong. This "mother of all laws" has spawned quite a brood. You can find entire books of Murphy-style laws, which is good because it means you can probably find a law that will fit your subject matter. Why bother? Because funny laws provide a simple way to add humor to a presentation.

Here's an example from Norman Augustine, President and CEO of Lockheed-Martin:

> I have recently branched out from the rather narrow confines of laws governing aerospace management to promulgating the more general laws of nature. My latest endeavor in this arena has been the law, derived from a considerable base of empirical evidence, that "Tornadoes are caused by trailer parks."

Where can you find funny laws? One of the best sources is *The Official Rules* by Paul Dickson, published by Dell Publishing. But don't rely solely on books. Make up your own laws specifically related to your topic and audience. (Like Kushner's Law of Advice: It is better to give than receive.)

Karnak

Johnny Carson, longtime host of *The Tonight Show*, used to do a comedy bit called Karnak the Magnificent. He would "telepathically sense" the answers to questions that were contained in a sealed envelope. After saying the answers aloud, he would open the envelope and read the questions. The results were always extremely funny.

This bit can be easily adapted to any presentation. The humor comes from the structure of the questions and answers — not from any special comic delivery. If the material is written correctly, you can read it deadpan and still get a laugh.

What follows is an excellent example from a speech by Peter Peterson, Chairman of the Blackstone Group. (It gets extra credit for being self-effacing.)

We have an annual Christmas party in which the young professionals can express their unbridled hostilities to the partners. They play a game called Karnak that you may remember from Johnny Carson, in which they give the answers and you have to guess the questions. The answers at last year's Christmas party, shortly after my book came out, were 100,000, 99,999, one, and zero. What were the questions? The questions were: "How many books did Peterson print?" "How many did he sign and give away?" "How many were bought and paid for by someone else?" And "How many were read?"

Lightbulb jokes

Lightbulb jokes refer to variations of the question, "How many whatevers (doctors, teachers, rabbits) does it take to change a lightbulb?" (All right, I said that I would provide only types of *non-joke* humor. So sue me. My lawyer will argue they're not really jokes; they're riddles.) I've included lightbulb jokes as a non-joke type of humor because they don't require any special comic delivery. They're also easy to fit into almost any presentation. If you can't find a lightbulb joke that applies to your topic, you can make one up. Just focus on the key traits of the person who will change the lightbulb and emphasize those traits in the answer. Here are two examples of this technique applied to MBAs and economists:

Q: How many Harvard MBAs does it take to change a light bulb?

A: Only one, if you hire me. I can actually change the light bulb by myself. As you can see from my resume, I've had extensive experience changing light bulbs in my previous positions. I've also been named to the Harvard Light Bulb list, and am presently a teaching assistant for Light Bulb Management 101. My only weakness is that I'm compulsive about changing light bulbs in my spare time.

Q: How many Chicago School economists does it take to change a light bulb?

A: None. If the light bulb needed changing, the market would have already done it.

So there you have it. There's help for the humor-impaired. If you can't tell a joke, you can still tell a personal anecdote, make an amusing observation, quote a funny line, or employ many other simple types of humor. Any of them can enhance your next presentation. After all, how many presenters does it take to tell a joke about changing a lightbulb? One — but it may take a while if the broken lightbulb is in the overhead projector.

Chapter 22

Building Yourself Up by Putting Yourself Down

*P*resident Ronald Reagan was fond of telling stories about his experiences as an actor, lecturer, and politician. Both his supporters and detractors were fond of hearing them. Why? Read the following example, and you will know why.

> While I was Governor of California, I was asked on several occasions to represent the United States in functions across the border in Mexico. And at one of these at which I spoke to a rather large audience, I made my speech, and then I sat down to rather unenthusiastic and scattered applause. And I was a little embarrassed. In fact, I was very self-conscious. I thought maybe I'd said something wrong. I was doubly embarrassed when the next speaker got up and, speaking in Spanish, which I didn't understand, he was getting enthusiastic applause almost every other line. Well, to hide my own embarrassment, I decided that I'd start clapping before anyone else, and I'd clap louder and longer than anyone else. And a few minutes of that, and our Ambassador leaned over to me and said, "I wouldn't do that if I were you. He's interpreting your speech."

Why did people like this story? For the same reason they liked most of Ronald Reagan's stories — he was willing to poke fun at himself.

The Power of Self-Effacing Humor

Many of the world's most highly acclaimed speakers have shared one trait in common — a good sense of humor and the ability to direct it at themselves.

Self-effacing humor lowers the barrier between speaker and audience. It helps create rapport. And most importantly, it tells the audience that the speaker has some perspective on life — always a plus. (It's the people who can't laugh at themselves that you have to worry about.)

In a world teeming with big egos, posturing, and pompousness, poking a little fun at yourself makes you stand out. It reflects confidence and security. Audiences love self-effacing humor. (They're usually astounded because it's such a rare occurrence. That's why it's so effective.) You just have to go about it in the right way.

How to Poke Fun at Yourself

Management communications consultant Jim Lukaszewski gives a lot of speeches. Like many speakers, he asks the person introducing him to read an introduction about how great he is. But unlike other speakers, Jim begins by poking fun at his credentials.

Here's what he says when he steps up to the podium: "Thanks for reading that material that I provided. But the fact of the matter is my mother still has no idea what I do." Then he shows an overhead transparency of a man standing next to a roadway with a sign that says, "Will consult for food." People laugh and settle back. What message have they received? They've learned that Jim is an expert in management communications (as described in the introduction), but that he's not a pompous, self-important, stuffed shirt (as reflected by his opening comments).

Now let me issue a word of caution. Don't go overboard with self-effacing humor. If you use it too often or make it too personal, you'll appear neurotic. Poking a little fun at yourself doesn't mean maligning or degrading yourself. I've seen seriously overweight speakers launch into ten minute routines that make fun of their rotund demeanor. Unless you are a comedian, you shouldn't bombard yourself with disparaging remarks. Rather than creating rapport, it creates embarrassment. No one wants to hear you barrage yourself with put-downs about your weight or other physical traits. Your quips should be designed to put people at ease, not to make them uncomfortable.

So what can you poke fun at? Here are a few ideas.

Your status as a speaker

The fact that you've been asked to speak gives you a certain inflated status. Many speakers take themselves down a peg by making fun of their role as presenters.

TIP

Poke fun at your mistakes

Have you ever made a mistake during a presentation? You know, you mispronounce a name, misstate a fact, trip over a microphone cord, or lose the audience with a complicated example. These common goofs provide a great opportunity to use self-effacing humor. Instead of standing there looking embarrassed, poke fun at your mistake. Here are two good lines to get you started:

"I feel like the javelin thrower who won the coin toss and elected to receive."

"I can explain your difficulty understanding my [last point, chart, plan, whatever]. Before I held my current position, I wrote instructions for putting together childrens' toys."

Here's an example from a speech given by Lee Hoskins, President of the Federal Reserve Bank of Cleveland:

> As a closing speaker at a multi-day session, I am always a little anxious about the attendance, especially in such a beautiful resort as the Greenbrier. So, I was relieved and, to be honest, feeling a little smug when I saw the size of today's turnout; that is, until I learned about the wonderful drawing for prizes and the condition that you must be present to win.

And here's one more from a speech about the lead business given by Jeffrey Zelms, President of the Doe Run Company. He was speaking to the Battery Council International (BCI) in San Francisco.

> Recently my wife and I ate at one of this city's fine Chinese restaurants. When it came time for the fortune cookies to be served, I opened my cookie, and the fortune read, "Closed mouths don't gather feet."

> I thought, that's surely a coincidence. It can't have anything to do with me addressing the BCI. So I opened a second cookie. This time the fortune read, "Your ideas appeal to a small, select group of confused people."

> While I was trying to figure the odds of two consecutive negative fortune cookie messages, my wife spoke up and asked, "What are you going to say at the BCI?"

> I told her, "I'm just going to tell them what's on my mind."

> "Good," she answered, "you have nothing to lose."

The length of your talk

The long-winded speaker is a stereotype long associated with public speaking. (If the first phrase learned by our cave-dwelling ancestors was "Say a few words," the second phrase was "Get to the point.") This fear of a lengthy talk has been passed down to modern day audiences, and it's always a fit subject for self-effacing humor. Here's an example from a commencement address given by Philip Burgess:

> When I asked President Horton what I should talk about today, he said, with tight lips and a fierce gaze, "Talk about 15 minutes."

> I am the last lecturer you will have to endure. I promise to be brief.

Here's another example from a commencement address given by Daniel Evans, a Public Leadership Fellow at the University of Washington and a former U.S. Senator from Washington:

> I've also struggled with my message for today. Should it be serious or funny? Challenging or comfortable? My wife said — compromise — "be mercifully short."

Your profession or occupation

If you occupy a position of high status by virtue of your job or profession, your audience may expect you to be pompous or arrogant. (Certain occupations generate this expectation due to commonly accepted stereotypes. Lawyers, surgeons, venture capitalists, and investment bankers come to mind immediately.) Poking fun at your big shot status is one way to shatter the stereotype and let the audience know that you're really an OK person.

The following is an example from a speech that Karl Otto Poehl, President of the Deutsche Bundesbank, delivered to the Economic Club of New York:

> Montesquieu, the eighteenth-century French writer and philosopher, said about economists and bankers: "For a country everything will be lost when the jobs of an economist and a banker become highly respected professions." I am not sure whether the Board of the Economic Club was aware of this judgment when they decided to invite John Reed and myself as guest speakers for tonight.

And here's an example from a speech by Joseph Gorman, Chairman and CEO of TRW, Inc.:

> At the same time, I'm not sure that you are doing me a favor to mention my background in law . . . which reminds me of a recent statement by the Dean of Harvard Law School, where he said that if we continue to grow lawyers at our current rate, by the year 2005, we'll have more lawyers than people.

Your public image

If you're strongly identified with a particular trait, especially a negative trait, make fun of it. Sometimes that's the best way to improve your image. A good example comes from Al Gore, Vice President of the United States. He has had a reputation for being stiff and wooden in his public appearances. He's turned that image to his advantage by poking fun at it. Here's an example from a speech he gave to the Television Academy at the University of California Los Angeles:

> It's great to be here at the Television Academy today. I feel I have a lot in common with those of you who are members of the Academy. I was on Letterman. I wrote my own lines.
>
> I'm still waiting for the residuals.
>
> At first, I thought this could lead to a whole new image. And maybe a new career. No more Leno jokes about being stiffer than the Secret Service. Maybe an opportunity to do other shows. I was elated when *Star Trek: The Next Generation* wanted me to do a guest shot — until I learned they wanted me to replace Lieutenant Commander Data.

Your less-than-lofty experiences

Have you ever had to change a diaper, unplug a toilet, or clean up after a puking pet? Any experience of this nature can become great material for self-effacing humor. It shows that you're not too high and mighty to perform a menial task — an endearing trait. The following is an example from a speech about saving the environment given by Fred Krupp, Executive Director, Environmental Defense Fund:

> Thank you for that kind introduction. I'm a little surprised that you left out my most important qualifying credential. I have three small sons — ages 7, 4, and 14 months. So I do know a great deal about cleaning up after environmental disasters.

Your memberships and associations

Have you made poor choices when it comes to associating yourself with various organizations? Are you a member of the wrong club? A fan of the wrong team? Acknowledge that fact and laugh at it. Here's an example from a speech given by Reed Hundt, Chairman of the Federal Communications Commission, to a group of radio broadcasters:

> I love radio. I grew up on AM, listening to the Washington Senators losing to everybody, the Washington Redskins losing to everybody, the Baltimore Bullets losing to everybody. So with all this experience in losing, I was well prepared to be a life-long Democrat.

Defusing controversy with self-directed humor

One of the most powerful aspects of self-directed humor is its ability to defuse controversial issues. A good example comes once again from Ronald Reagan. As the oldest president in the history of the United States, his age was an issue of concern to many people — particularly his detractors. While his opponents fanned the flames on this issue, Reagan used self-directed humor to extinguish the fire. In his numerous public appearances as president, he never missed an opportunity to poke fun at his advanced age. Here are a few representative examples:

> I want to begin by saying how grateful I am that you've asked me here to participate in the celebration of the 100th anniversary of the Knights of Columbus. Now, it isn't true that I was present at the first anniversary.

> Yes, we have a trade deficit, but this isn't entirely new. The United States had a merchandise trade deficit in almost all of the years between 1790 and 1875. I remember them well. Of course, I was only a boy at the time.

> There was a very prominent Democrat who reportedly told a large group, "Don't worry. I've seen Ronald Reagan, and he looks like a million." He was talking about my age.

Did the self-effacing lines work? In 1980, when Ronald Reagan ran for president, his age was a major issue in the campaign. In 1984, when he ran for re-election, age wasn't a factor — *even though he was four years older.* His "age lines" completely defused the issue.

Stockpile humorous acknowledgments

Are you the victim of a controversial issue? An issue that embarrasses or angers you when it's raised? Something that you get hounded about constantly? Well, follow the Reagan example. Be prepared to acknowledge the issue by poking fun at it and yourself.

Broadway star Tommy Tune (he's an actor, dancer, director, and producer) follows this advice. At six feet, six and a half inches, his height is a source of constant comment by reporters and other interviewers. Tune, knowing that the issue will come up, handles it with humor. When asked how tall he is (and he's asked a lot), he replies "I'm 5 feet, $18^1/_2$ inches."

President Bill Clinton also uses this device to address the issue of his long-winded speaking style. According to *The Wall Street Journal*, he began a speech to the Democratic National Committee by saying he was "supposed to talk about the future here today, but instead [he] decided to finish a speech" that he'd made at the Democratic convention in 1988.

Part V
The Part of Tens

In this part . . .

You've heard of the seven deadly sins? In the first chapter of this part, I cover the ten fatal flaws — surefire ways to screw up any presentation. But don't worry, I also help you avoid them. You'll also find a list of great stories, ideas, and concepts to use in a presentation; a list of web sites for locating good material; and a list that will help you to literally add magic to your presentations.

Chapter 23

The Ten Biggest Mistakes Presenters Make

● ●

In This Chapter

▶ Common mistakes that are easy to avoid

● ●

Starting with an inappropriate joke: Unless the humor is in good taste and makes a point, resist the urge to regale people with your wit.

Going too long: Don't exceed your allotted time. There are few transgressions that an audience is less willing to forgive.

Using poor visual aids: Don't clutter slides and overheads with too many words, and don't make the words too small to see. You're trying to deliver information, not administer a driver's license vision test. Use a few lines with a few words in a large font.

Not rehearsing with the visual aids: If you go to the trouble of making visual aids, take the time to make sure that you can display them properly.

Ignoring audience interests: If you want to guarantee that your speech is a flop, don't bother learning anything about your audience members. Just assume that they'll be absolutely fascinated by anything you might choose to discuss.

Faking it: If an audience member asks a question that you can't answer, admit it. You can ask if someone else in the audience knows the answer, or you can offer to find the answer and get back to the questioner.

Looking at notes instead of the audience: People want to see your face as you speak — especially your eyes. It's when eye contact is established that the audience feels engaged in an act of communication. So don't overdo the notes. Keep them brief and easy to read.

Trying to be something you're not: Making a presentation doesn't require using big words and a formal oratorical style. If that's how you normally talk, fine. If it's not, you'll sound phony, and no one will know what the heck you're talking about.

Not practicing out loud: The time to discover tongue twisters, stories that don't work, and sections that don't flow isn't when you're in front of an audience. Practice your presentation out loud.

Forgetting to check the room: A bad room can turn the best speech into a disaster. If you don't want that to happen to you, get to the room early and make sure that the arrangements meet your specifications.

Chapter 24

Ten Great Stories, Ideas, and Concepts to Use in Any Presentation

*P*eople who have to give presentations often ask me where they can find good material. Chapter 7 describes a variety of sources. If you're like me, you may be too lazy to explore those resources. So as a public service for the energy challenged, I've done the work for you. I've reviewed thousands of pages of speech transcripts in order to collect incisive and amusing observations and anecdotes. This chapter contains material that can brighten, lighten, and heighten your next presentation.

I selected these items based on a variety of criteria. First, they were relatively fresh. (By that I mean they haven't already been used by every speaker in the world. I admit that's a judgment call. But as a professional speaker I hear and read a lot of speeches. After awhile, it's easy to spot certain jokes, analogies, and quotes that get used over and over again.) Second, they can be easily adapted to make a wide variety of points. Third, they represent a variety of styles — humorous, inspirational, motivational, and so on. Fourth, and most important, I liked them. Simply put, I responded to them, so I thought you would find them useful.

The Lesson of the Bamboo Seed

The bamboo seed is a nut, enclosed by a very hard skin. You plant it the first year, and add fertilizer and water. Nothing happens. You water and fertilize it for the second year, the third year, and the fourth year, and nothing happens. But when the fifth year arrives, the bamboo grows 90 feet in six weeks.

So now we are watering and fertilizing, and so should you. When your business grows 90 feet in six weeks, and someone asks you how you did it in such a short time, you'll have the right answer.

This fascinating tidbit comes from a speech given by Susan Au Allen, President of the United States Pan Asian American Chamber of Commerce. She used it to encourage businesspeople to expand their trade in Asia. I think you'll find it useful, too, when you want to make points that frequently appear in a wide variety of presentations — hard work pays off, success doesn't come overnight, you've got to toil in the garden before you reap the fruit. Whether you're speaking to businesspeople, volunteers, or schoolchildren, you'll eventually want to make one of those points. You can now use the example of the bamboo seed to inspire and motivate your audience, instead of mouthing the usual clichés about hard work.

The King and his Advisor

There once lived a king, a very benevolent fellow, loved by his community. He ruled a little kingdom tucked away in a pleasant corner of one of those European regions that used to have little kingdoms tucked away in its corners.

One day an army came and overran the castle, making off with half the treasury. The king decided to tell the people he must increase taxes to make up for the loss. He called in one of the court wise men.

"How can I break the news without inciting a revolt?" he asked.

The wise man pondered — that's his job — and came up with a gentle way of explaining the theft as a tragedy for the entire kingdom, imploring the people for their support. It went over well.

Time passed, and once again the neighboring army raided the castle, this time carting away much of the food stored for the winter. Once again, the king called upon his wise man — by this time, he was known as the Director of Wisdom — and laid bare the facts.

"What can I tell my subjects this time?" the king asked. "They will lose confidence in me if I can't defend the kingdom's food and money."

Again, the wise man pondered. He advised the king to be frank about the loss, but to say only that it had gone to a neighboring kingdom that seemed to need it desperately. And the king told the people and asked them to work even harder on the year's harvest. And they did, and all was well.

By this time, the neighboring army was getting rather good at raids. Once again they struck, hauling away horses, hay, other foodstock, and most of the royal jewels. Once again, the king summoned his trusted advisor, the VP of Wisdom and Sagely Advice. This time, the king was despondent.

"They raid the treasury. They take our food. They steal our livestock," the king wailed. "And the queen's going to kill me about those jewels. You are my most trusted advisor. What shall I do?"

The wise man hesitated. "I think," he said, "I think the time has come for Your Highness to put the water back in the moat."

The moral of the story is simple: solve a basic problem, and you won't have as many public relations problems.

This story comes from a speech given by Harold Burson, Chairman of Burson-Marsteller. He used it to make a point about the changing role of public relations advisors. You're not talking about public relations? Don't worry. There are a lot of other morals that this story can have: Don't overlook the obvious. The best offense is a good defense. Think for yourself. You've got to fill the moat if you want to walk on water. It's time to sink or swim.

Asking Good Questions

All innovation starts with a question. Isidor Rabi said it was his mother who led him to science rather than other professions — though she never intended it. Instead of asking him after school what he had learned that day, she would say, "Izzy, did you ask a good question today?" That difference — asking good questions — led Rabi to science and the Nobel Prize for his work in nuclear physics.

This anecdote comes from a speech given by Robert Tuttle, Chairman and Chief Executive of SPX Corporation. He used it to make a point about innovation. But there's a much better use for it.

This is a great story for encouraging an audience to ask questions — because it might actually provoke somebody to ask one. Contrast it with the standard approach which you've heard a million times (beginning with your first-grade teacher). "There's no such thing as a dumb question." "Please ask me anything that's on your mind." "If no one asks questions, we won't learn anything." I don't know about you, but none of those will get my hand raised in the air.

There's also a problem with sincerity. Many speakers ask for questions at the conclusion of their presentations because they know they're supposed to. But they really don't want any questions. (They're nervous about looking bad. After all, the only thing dumber than a dumb question is a dumb answer.) Audiences can sense phony requests. That's why I like the story about asking good questions. Any speakers who go to the trouble of using it tell you that they really do want questions. And the story strokes your ego. (It compares people that ask questions with a Nobel Prize winner.)

A Vision, Task, and Hope

On the wall of a church in England there is a sign that reads, "A vision without a task is but a dream, a task without a vision is drudgery, a vision and a task are the hope of the world." My comments this morning concern a vision, a task, and a hope for the future of American higher education.

This gem comes from a speech given by Michael Williams, Assistant Secretary for Civil Rights, U.S. Department of Education. He used it to begin a speech about racial and ethnic relations in American higher education. It's a good opening for any speech on any subject. Just replace "American higher educa-tion" with whatever your topic happens to be speaking about.

But here's the real reason I like this piece of material: You can use it to structure your entire presentation. The vision, task, and hope become your three main points. Just give your vision for your topic, describe the task that must be done to achieve the vision, and then describe what you hope will happen. You can't get more organized than that.

Comparing Apples and Oranges

By a proper comparison, I mean one which social scientists or political scientists would say is a sustained multi-lateral comparison. It's very easy to compare apples and oranges. When you look at an apple and look at an orange, you can see the great differences. You rarely note the similarities. But if you then put on your table an apple, an orange, and a banana, you begin to see how much the apple and the orange have in common as compared with the banana or the bunch of grapes. And this is what I mean by the proper, or the larger, comparison.

This comes from a speech given by Paul Kennedy, a Professor at Yale University. He used it to compare various world powers in regard to their economic and military security. I like it because you can use it to squelch someone who dis-agrees with a previous comparison that you made.

Have you ever made a brilliant argument for or against something only to have some idiot say "that's like comparing apples and oranges"? All of a sudden the momentum shifts. Everyone who thought you were a genius suddenly wonders if you know what you're talking about. Not any more. Now you can say that your opponent is absolutely correct — you *are* comparing apples and oranges. Because apples and oranges are similar, they have a lot in common, and so on. It will swing the momentum right back to you — where it belongs.

Woodpecker Questions

Here's your chance to rebel. Take time to think . . . right now. . . .

To get started, use Banach's Woodpecker Questions. These are questions for which we have an answer, but we're not really sure it's correct. (The classic is: "Do woodpeckers get headaches?" Scientists tell us the woodpecker's brain is wrapped in a huge mucous pad, so the bird can bang away all day and never get headaches. So while the answer to the question is "no," we're not really sure.)

This concept comes from a speech given by William Banach, Executive Director of The Institute for Future Studies at Macomb Community College. He used it to set up a series of "woodpecker questions" dealing with education. (Woodpecker Question #1: Why do we use textbooks? We think we know the answer, but are we really sure? Woodpecker Question #2: Why do schools have to be places?) After each question, he presented information that would force the audience to reexamine its assumptions.

The "woodpecker question" provides a fabulous way to confront audiences inclined to disagree with you. Instead of hitting them in the face with "everything you know is wrong," you gently suggest they should be less sure about what they "know." The questions create an opening to challenge their assumptions about your topic. You just develop woodpecker questions related to the issues you want to discuss. (Woodpecker Question #1: Why do UFOs always land in deserted areas away from major cities? We think we know the answer, but are we really sure? Skeptics say a real UFO would land near the United Nations in New York, but have they ever tried to find a parking space there?)

A Yogi Berra Story You Don't Hear All the Time

I am reminded of a story about one of my hometown heroes, former Yankee manager Yogi Berra. One day in Yankee Stadium, when streaking was the fad, two people jumped out of the bleachers stark naked and rounded all the bases. When Yogi told his wife about it, she said, "Were they boys or girls?" Yogi said, "I don't know, they had bags over their heads."

Some of us have put bags over our heads when it comes to young people and sexuality.

This story comes from a speech given by Faye Wattleton when she was President of the Planned Parenthood Federation of America. She used it to make the point that many parents don't discuss sex with their children. But you can use the story anytime you want to claim that some group of people isn't facing up to an issue. Does the sales department have a bag over its head about realistically forecasting next year's revenues? Does R&D have a bag over its head about problems with a prototype? Has marketing put a bag over its head by ignoring surveys that say customers hate the new product?

I included this item because audiences like Yogi Berra stories but are tired of hearing the same ones all the time. This Yogi Berra story doesn't get told very often. It can still surprise your audience.

A Grand Opening

A medical student "dissected a cadaver completely." Then he said, "I opened every organ of the body and found no soul, so how can religious people say a soul exists?"

The medical student was asked, "When you opened the brain did you find an idea?" "No," was the answer. "When you cut open the heart, did you find love?" The medical student replied in the negative. "And when you dissected the eye, was vision seen?" Once more the answer was, "No."

I ask you on this Father's Day to understand that because some things are not seen and/or proven conclusively to exist is no reason to conclude that they do not.

This story comes from a speech given by Benjamin Alexander, President of Drew-Dawn Enterprises, Inc. He used it to encourage his audience to believe in God. But I like it because you can use it any time you want to assert that something for which you lack proof exists. ("Just because some things can't be seen doesn't mean they don't exist. Just because my efforts don't show on the bottom line doesn't mean I haven't made a great contribution to this company.") If you're like me, you'll use this story a lot.

An Amazing Story

I want to begin my remarks this afternoon with a story about a man whose parents named him Amazing in hopes he would live up to his name and achieve great things.

Well, this fellow never really did anything to merit the name. In fact, he led a rather mundane life on the family farm and stayed married to the same woman for 60 years.

Unfortunately, all his life, Amazing was the butt of countless jokes. As a result, he told his wife the only thing he wanted was that when he died, she wouldn't put his name on the gravestone; maybe then the jokes would stop.

Now, when the old fellow died, she didn't want to put him in an unmarked grave. So on his gravestone, she wrote this simple inscription: "Here lies a man who for 60 years was faithful to his wife."

And now when people walk by and read that, they point and say, "That's amazing!"

In many respects, this story reminds me of the amazing challenges many of us have as we go about globalizing our companies.

This story comes from a speech given by Jim Giggey, Sr. VP, Eastman Chemical Co. He used it to make a point about amazing challenges facing businesspeople. You can use it to talk about *anything* you find amazing — the latest medical breakthrough, the end of the Cold War, the election of Congressman Sonny Bono.

Are you uncomfortable that the joke makes fun of being faithful to one's spouse? No problem. Switch it. Make it a story about a man who worked for the same company for 60 years. ("Here lies a man who worked for the same company for 60 years." That's amazing.) Or make it someone who never complained to his boss for 60 years. Or a salesperson who accurately reported her expenses for 60 years. Or a consultant who didn't claim to have the answer to all of your problems. You can adapt the story to reflect whatever it is that you consider amazing.

DiNucci's Teeth to Butt Ratio

When we talk about leadership in the business world, we have to talk about economic Darwinism. When companies are young, small, and aggressive, they have a very low teeth to butt ratio. [See Figure 24-1.] So they're wolves. They're very carnivorous. And over a period of time, they get more successful: They take more territory; they grow bigger and more statuesque; and their bodies and their butts grow faster than their teeth. But they still have a very respectable teeth to butt ratio. And then they're tigers, and they're still very carnivorous. Then they grow some more, and then they're lions. They're the kings of the jungle.

Silicon Graphics was a wolf when I got here. I think we're now finishing our migration to becoming a tiger. I think HP is the lion today. They're at their peak.

But unfortunately, evolution doesn't stop there. The animal continues to get bigger and more and more massive. And the teeth don't really grow very much. Later, the teeth become decorative. Soon you have an elephant, and it's kind of a sad thing. Now elephants are still very smart. After all, they know as much as lions, and they get a lot of respect, but not because people are afraid of getting eaten up. An elephant won't eat you; it'll try to step on you —if it can catch you.

And the situation gets even more pitiful because it doesn't stop there. The body gets even bigger, the butt gets even bigger, and the teeth stop being even decorative. And what you have is a hippo with those little marshmellow teeth. In fact, hippos spend most of their time underwater with just their eyes out so that they don't become the ultimate lunch for the wolves, lions, and tigers.

That's the teeth to butt ratio. Nature forces you down in this direction. (Bigger butt and less teeth.) And you need to consciously try to drive yourself back up. So ask yourself these questions: Is this process reversible? Where are _you_ in the process? And what did you work on today or what do you plan to work on — is it teeth or butt? Because it's either one or the other.

This ratio comes from Joe DiNucci, Vice President of Manufacturing Industries at Silicon Graphics. He uses it when he speaks to salespeople, engineers, and anyone else he wants to motivate into being more productive. Why do I like it? The ratio speaks for itself. It's a brilliant piece of motivational material that can be applied to any audience regarding any topic. It can put some teeth into your message. So get off your butt and use it.

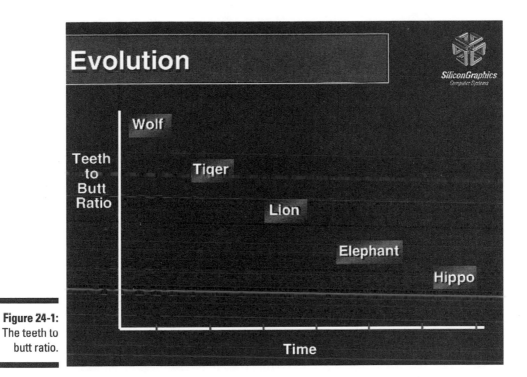

Figure 24-1:
The teeth to
butt ratio.

More Great Material

Need more great material for your next presentation? Get some from the "Great Communicator." That's right, nearly every quip, joke, and anecdote told by Ronald Reagan during his first administration is now on a CD-ROM: *Well...There You Go Again!* It's packed full of funny openers, closers, quotes, analogies, one-liners, definitions, and much, much more. You'll learn timing and delivery from the master as you see and hear Ronald Reagan tell the jokes. And here's the best part: As a *Dummies* reader, you get a special discount. For full details, see the ad in the back of this book or call 800-278-3245 and tell them that you're a *Dummies* reader.

And here are two more good sources for material:

✔ **Vital Speeches:** This biweekly publication offers the full text of speeches delivered by major figures in the arts, education, business, government, health, politics, industry, economics, and law. It's a great resource for quotes, and because you can see how other public speakers structure their speeches, you can develop ideas for organizing your own presentations. For more information, call 803-881-8733.

✔ **The Executive Speaker:** This monthly newsletter extracts good material from a wide variety of speeches and presents it in useful categories, such as openings, closings, pointmakers, and so on. This newsletter also identifies many additional sources of material and gives excellent advice about writing speeches. For more information, call 513-294-8493.

Chapter 25

Ten Simple Magic Tricks Anyone Can Perform

● ●

In This Chapter

▶ Tips on buying magic tricks

▶ Easy to perform magic tricks that you can use in your presentations

● ●

*T*he president of Mead Data Central wanted to make a lasting impression on his sales force at a company meeting. He could tell them to work harder and make more money. Yawn. They'd heard that a million times. That wouldn't do the trick. He needed a real trick. Something that would dazzle the audience. Something magical. He turned to my friend Loyd Auerbach for suggestions.

Loyd, a corporate trainer for Lexis/Nexis (then part of Mead Data Central) and a professional magician, knew just what to do. He recommended a dove pan. A dove pan is a classic magic prop. You've probably seen one if you've ever gone to a magic show. The magician puts all kinds of junk into an empty pan, lights it on fire, and covers the pan. When the cover is lifted, presto changeo . . . a dove is in the pan.

Loyd made one small change. Instead of a dove, he wanted money to appear in the pan. The effect was easy to create with another traditional magic prop called "spring money" — fake money made of compressed paper that *springs* up when it's released.

The day of the presentation arrived and the president strode on stage. He talked about how you can take a little money and turn it into a lot, and then he gave a demonstration. He took a dollar bill and put it in a pan. He lit the bill on fire and covered the pan. When he removed the cover, money began overflowing onto the stage. The president talked about how the company had to take its money and make it go for the distance. The trick was a big hit, and the salesforce got the message.

The president had been nervous about learning the trick. He was a typical executive. He could work magic with a balance sheet, but real magic? Loyd assured him the trick was foolproof and taught it to him in ten seconds. That's the kind of uncommon knowledge you find in this chapter. *You don't have to be a professional magician to use magic tricks effectively in a presentation.* The trick is knowing which ones are easy to do.

How to Buy Magic Tricks

Most people think magic tricks are difficult to learn and perform because most of them are. That's why Loyd Auerbach says forget about any trick involving sleight of hand. It takes a lot of skill and practice to learn. He also advises against walking into a magic shop and buying anything that looks good. Too often, you get home and find the trick is much more complicated than you thought.

Loyd's solution: use the magic shop salespeople as a resource. Talk to them. Tell them you're looking for a trick to use in a presentation. Tell them what you'll be talking about. If your topic is finance, you can probably find some money tricks. If you're speaking about computers, you might find a trick with electronic lights and noises. Ask the salespeople. They'll have recommendations for you.

And here's Loyd's secret: He says that you will find a good trick if you remember to always tell the magic shop salespeople that you want a "self-working trick." The phrase means just what you think it means — that the trick works by itself; there's not much to learn; it's a no-brainer. The dove pan used by the Mead Data Central president in the story that begins this chapter is an example of a self-working trick.

One more thing to keep in mind: Make sure the trick will be visible by your entire audience. Some tricks that work well for a small audience in a conference room would never work for a large group in an auditorium.

Ten Amazing Magic Tricks That Anyone Can Do

The following ten tricks are simple to do. To use them effectively, however, you must tie them into a point in your presentation. Otherwise, they're just a distraction. Fortunately, it's not very difficult to use these tricks to make a point. In this section, I suggest how you can use these tricks to help you get your point across. These tricks are only a beginning. You are limited only by your imagination.

Think also about the "patter" a magician gives as he or she performs a trick. You know, the story that explains why the magician is throwing eggs into a hat and pulling out rabbits. Make up your own patter. Just make sure it's tied into your talk.

The dove pan

You show the audience an empty pan. You put an object or objects into the pan and then cover the pan. When you remove the cover, different objects are in the pan. The original objects have been transformed.

If you want to be dramatic, you can abuse the first set of objects that you put into the pan — burn them, cut them, whatever. Then you cover the pan. When you remove the cover, the objects have been restored to their original condition. There are lots of variations.

Time to learn: 10 seconds

Price: $42.50 – $57.50 (Depending on size)

Points to make: This is a great trick for introducing anything new — a new policy, a new product, a new procedure. "I'm holding page 12 of our personnel manual — the policy about vacation days. As you know, we've been conducting a review of this policy." Put the personnel manual page into the pan. "We hired a consultant." Put the consultant's business card in the pan. "Who did a survey." Put the survey results in the pan. "And we took a hard look at the results." Put a pair of reading glasses in the pan. "And we felt we'd covered everything." Put the cover on the pan. "Then we let the issue sit awhile to see what developed." Remove the cover. "What's this? A pair of sunglasses." Take sunglasses out of the pan and look at them. "Oh, I see. It's our new policy. Hourly employees will now be eligible for two weeks paid vacation after only one year on the job instead of after two years." (Wild applause from the audience.)

You can also use this trick to contrast before and after results or show the results of combining different objects. (Drop the business cards of the people in your department into the pan. Stir up the business cards and cover the pan. Then remove the cover and pull out a chart showing the departmental reorganization plan.)

The magic coloring book (or three-way coloring book)

This trick involves what appears to be an ordinary children's coloring book. You hold it toward the audience and flip the pages so that they can view the contents. The pages all look blank. When you flip through the pages again, each page contains the outline of a picture (like a coloring book). The third time you flip through the pages, the pictures are colored-in. You can then flip the pages a fourth time to make them blank or just outlines again. You can keep flipping the pages to make them appear in any of the three choices — blank, outlines, or colored-in. (If you're speaking to a large group, you can walk around the room as you flip the pages so that the entire audience can see the pages change.)

Time to learn: 20 seconds

Price: $8.95

Points to make: This is a great trick for showing how different people perceive things differently. You flip through the colored-in pages. "That's how our company views the services we provide. We offer a full spectrum of services." Then you flip through the blank pages. "Unfortunately, this is how our customers see it. But it's not all that bad." Flip through the outlined pages. "A few of them see a dim outline of our efforts." Then talk about what your company needs to do improve perceptions of its services.

You can also use this trick to talk about "seeing the big picture" versus a dim outline or drawing a blank.

The professor's nightmare

You show the audience three unequal lengths of rope. Then you turn them into three equal lengths.

Time to learn: Ten minutes and a little practice. (You need to learn a little sleight of hand, but not much. It's worth the effort.)

Price: $3.98 purchases a bunch of rope and directions for doing the trick. Once you learn the trick, you can do it with any rope or string.

Points to make: You can talk about how things are never what they appear to be. Or that even though the budget looks like it's divided unevenly, everyone benefits equally. Or that any problems can be overcome if we all pull together. Or that you're at the end of your rope.

The split deck

This trick employs a deck of playing cards that are split in half diagonally. An audience volunteer picks a card from one half of the deck, and a second volunteer picks a card from the other half. When you turn over both halves of the chosen cards, they go together. (For example, they form the queen of hearts.)

Time to learn: 5 minutes

Price: $9.95 for regular size cards; $29.95 for oversized cards (about 6 inches by 3^1/$_2$ inches).

Points to make: You can use this trick to talk about solving the puzzle. So you can use it for any upbeat message. "It's taken some time. We've had to make some hard choices. But we now know how to (make the company profitable, improve sales, fix the defect in our product, get our new product launched on time). We've solved the puzzle."

You can also talk about how all the pieces of a plan are falling into place or that there's a good strategic fit (between any two items you choose — corporate goals, key people, various products).

The rising deck

An audience volunteer picks a card out of a deck of playing cards. You put the card back in the deck. You place the deck vertically into a cup. The cards are now standing with the back of the top card facing the audience. You put the cup aside. After a few seconds a card starts to rise by itself. After it rises a bit, you pluck it from the deck. Then you turn it so the audience can see its face. It's the card that the audience volunteer had picked.

Time to learn: 1 minute

Price: $42.00 (Jumbo); $20.00 (Regular)

Points to make: You can talk about the power of positive thinking. Or that things are looking up. Or that with hard work you'll rise to the top. Or that talent stands out in the crowd.

Perfect monte (or find the lady)

You show the audience a three-card spread that you're holding in your hand. The middle card is a queen. You put the cards together and place them face down on a table. A volunteer from the audience is asked to pick out the queen. The volunteer makes a choice. The card selected is turned over. And it's not the queen. It's not even one of the other cards. It's just blank.

Time to learn: 30 seconds

Price: $10.00

Points to make: This trick can make any point you desire. How? Just write your business message or the name of your company or product on the blank card. When the card is chosen, you can say things like, "We're the pick of the litter" or "We're always first choice."

The milk pitcher

You show the audience a crystal pitcher that appears to be full of milk. Then you take a piece of paper and roll it into a cone shape. You hold the point of the cone in your fist and then use your other hand to pour the milk from the pitcher into the mouth of the cone. When you finish pouring the milk, you unroll the cone of paper. It's not wet. Not one drop of milk has touched it. The milk has vanished into thin air.

Time to learn: 3 seconds

Price: $30.00

Points to make: You can talk about not milking your customers. Or appearances can be deceiving. Or maybe some project has been a wasted effort — like pouring resources into a hole. One of Loyd Auerbach's favorites: put a picture of a competitor in the paper cone and say that he's milking your business dry. (Or drinking up your business.)

The dream bag

You hold up a paper bag — the type you use to go shopping — and show the audience that it's empty. Then you reach into the bag and pull out a clear plastic box with a red rim. There are two red paper flowers in the box. (It looks like a box with a corsage.) You show the audience the inside of the bag again. Once again it's empty. Then you pull another box out of the bag. This time it has a blue rim and blue flowers. You repeat the procedure again. This time you pull out a box with a yellow rim and yellow flowers.

Time to learn: 7 minutes

Price: $62.00 – $72.00

Points to make: One way to use this trick is to base your patter on the color of the boxes. Show the empty bag. "We started our new product development effort from scratch. We assembled a team, materials, and ideas. Then we put together our first product." Pull out the red box. "And it didn't work. Boy, was my face red. . . . So we went back to work. Put in a lot more effort and tried again " Pull out the blue box. "This time it worked but it didn't sell. Boy, was I blue. . . . So we went back to work and tried again." Pull out yellow box. "This time it worked and it's selling. That's what the yellow means — we've come into the sunshine, but we still need to be cautious."

The change bag

A cloth bag hangs from a circular wooden frame that includes a handle. You hold the handle with one hand. You use your other hand to drop an object into the bag. (The object should be lightweight and nonbulky — a magician's scarf, a business card, a dollar bill.) Then you turn the bag inside out. Lo and behold — the bag is empty. The object you dropped into the bag has disappeared.

Or you drop an object into the bag, and when you turn the bag inside out, a *different* object falls out of the bag.

Time to learn: 10 seconds

Price: $39.00 – $87.00 (Depending on the size)

Points to make: You can drop a hundred dollar bill into the bag and talk about making money disappear. Or do it in reverse: how you started with nothing — just sheer determination — and turned it into money.

Want to criticize an old plan? Review the plan (sales, investment, research, whatever) with the audience. As you do so, write down the key points of the old plan on a small piece of paper. "So we had this plan that was supposed to solve all our problems." Throw paper into the bag. "And it's produced nothing." Show that the bag is empty — the paper has disappeared.

Inner/outer box

You hold up a red metal box. You take off the lid, and inside is a blue metal box. You remove the blue box and replace the lid on the red box. You hold the boxes next to each other. They appear to be the same size. Then you take the lid off the blue box, put the red box into it, and place the lid back onto the blue box. You're now holding the blue metal box with the red box inside.

Time to learn: 15 minutes. (Most of the 15 minutes involves practicing handling the boxes. You have to know which sides fit into each other and which sides to show to the audience.)

Price: $34.00

Points to make: This is the perfect trick when you want to talk about new combinations. Is your company reorganizing so that two different departments or divisions will be combined into one? Is your company merging with another company? Is your organization forming an alliance with another organization? In any of these situations, you can use this trick to assuage the fears of the people involved. "This blue box represents department A. When we take the lid off, we see there's a red box inside — that's department B." Remove the red box from the blue box. "Now it's true that department A is bigger than department B. But when we put them together, they're really not so different from each other." Hold the boxes next to each other. They now look like they're the same size. "In fact, I don't think there will be any problem fitting everyone together." You put the blue box into the red box.

This trick is also good for talking about creativity — combining ideas, thinking outside the box, not limiting yourself to preconceived notions. Or use it to talk about perspective — how things look depends upon where you sit.

Fresh fish

You hold up a large paper banner that reads, "Fresh Fish Sold Here Today." You rip the banner into several pieces. You fold the pieces into a small pile in your hand. Then you unfold the pieces. But they're no longer pieces; they've recombined into one large banner again.

Once you learn the trick, you can make your own banners. That opens up a lot of possibilities. You can use a banner that contains your business message. Then you can rip it up and restore it.

Or you can start with your business message on a banner. Rip it up. And when you unfold the pile of pieces, your new banner has a different business message.

Time to learn: 10 minutes

Price: $8.63 (This gets you ten paper banners and directions for doing the trick.)

Points to make: This is always a great trick for talking about teamwork. You rip up a paper banner that bears the name of your company. As you do so, you describe the forces working against your company — competitors, lack of enthusiasm, absenteeism, whatever. "These things are tearing our company apart. But we can overcome our problems if we all work together." Then you unfold the pile of paper revealing the restored banner.

You can make almost any point you want with this one. It just depends what messages you write on the banners.

The zippered gag bag

You show the audience a cloth bag that is colored in a distinctive pattern. You throw it up in the air. You catch it and then pull it inside out. The bag now has a different distinctive pattern. No big deal yet. The inside was just a different pattern than the outside. Everyone knows that. So you throw the bag in the air again, catch it, and pull it inside out. The bag should now have the same pattern as when you started, but it doesn't. It's a third distinctively colored pattern. Now throw the bag in the air again. Catch it again and pull it inside out. It's now a fourth distinctively colored pattern. Let's try all the steps again. It's now a fifth distinctively colored pattern. And when you flip it over, there's a zipper on the side. Where did that come from? There wasn't any zipper before. You open the zipper and pull out an object. (Perhaps an object that disappeared earlier in your presentation.)

Time to learn: 1 minute

Price: $24.95

Points to make: This is a great trick for showing how something changes over time. You can talk about the various stages of development for a product (each bag pattern is a different stage in development). Or the history of your company (each bag pattern is a different year or decade). Or you can talk about the changes that an individual has gone through over time.

You can also use this trick to jazz up announcements by putting the item you're announcing in the zippered pouch. "As you know, our company has changed its image several times over the years." Each bag pattern change corresponds to an image change. Then you get to the zippered pouch. "And we're changing again. May I introduce our new logo." Pull a paper out of the pouch and unfold it to reveal the new logo.

What else can be in the zippered pouch? You can put the name of the winner of a sales contest, a paper detailing someone's promotion and new job title, or a picture of your fiercest competitor. ("We started this company to give our customers the best products in the industry. As we've grown, we've gone through a lot of changes, but we mustn't lose sight of our mission to be the best. Because if we're not careful, we'll turn into — this!" Pull out a picture of a competitor.)

There you have it. I promised to give you ten easy tricks to perform in a presentation. If you've been counting, you'll notice there are twelve. Now that's real magic.

Chapter 26

Ten Fantastic Web Sites

● ●

In This Chapter

▶ Finding great material on the Web

● ●

*O*h what a tangled web we weave when first we practice to use the Internet. I'm talking about the World Wide Web — that constantly expanding mass of information that constitutes the fastest growing and most popular part of the Net. This chapter lists some sites you'll want to check out the next time you put together a presentation.

Yahoo!: http://www.yahoo.com/

Yahoo! is a collection of links organized into 14 major subject categories and numerous subcategories. If you know what you're looking for, you can go right to the relevant category. Otherwise, you can enter key words in the Yahoo! search form. Yahoo! then searches all its categories and gives you a list of relevant links.

Lycos: http://lycos-tmpl.psc.edu/lycos-form.html

Lycos claims to be the largest catalog of documents on the Net, including about 98 percent of the entire Web. Unlike Yahoo, Lycos doesn't categorize sites by subject categories. Instead, it searches its entire catalog for you. It provides a simple search form in which you enter key words.

WebCrawler: http://webcrawler.html

The WebCrawler, like Lycos, is based around a search form. You enter your key words and see what turns up. Again, like Lycos, the WebCrawler search will produce a list of links related to your query.

Quotation Search: http://www.xmission.com/~mgm/quotes/search.html

This site gets my vote as one of the absolutely best sites on the Web — at least if you're looking for quotations. Here's why: It's the only quote site I've found that allows you to search it by key words.

Bartlett's Familiar Quotations (1901): http://www.cc.columbia.edu/acis/bartleby/bartlett/

This is an electronic version of the famous book.

Cute Kids Stories: http://www.prgone.com/cutekids/stories.html

This site contains just what the name suggests — files of cute kids stories.

Murphy's Laws: http://www.Misty.com/laughweb/murphy/murphys.laws.html

No matter what the topic of your talk, you can almost always find an appropriate Murphy's Law. This site has a collection of them.

Computer Almanac: http://www.cs.cmu.edu/afs/cs.cmu.edu/user/bam/www/numbers.html

This site contains a wealth of statistics and numerical data related to computers. Brad Myers, who compiled the numbers, specifically suggests that the data is useful for speeches, and he has thoughtfully included references citing the source of each statistic.

U.S. Congress Thomas Legislative Service: http://thomas.loc.gov/

This site includes the full text of all versions of House and Senate bills for the 103rd and 104th Congress, as well as the Congressional Record for the 103rd and 104th Congress. And the best part is that all this stuff is searchable by key words.

FedWorld: http://www.fedworld.gov/

This is the motherlode, a goldmine of information compiled by the federal government about . . . everything!

Index

(continued)

IDG BOOKS WORLDWIDE REGISTRATION CARD

RETURN THIS REGISTRATION CARD FOR FREE CATALOG

Title of this book: Successful Presentations For Dummies

My overall rating of this book: ❑ Very good [1]   ❑ Good [2]   ❑ Satisfactory [3]   ❑ Fair [4]   ❑ Poor [5]

How I first heard about this book:

❑ Found in bookstore; name: [6]

❑ Advertisement: [8]

❑ Word of mouth; heard about book from friend, co-worker, etc.: [10]

❑ Book review: [7]

❑ Catalog: [9]

❑ Other: [11]

What I liked most about this book:

What I would change, add, delete, etc., in future editions of this book:

Other comments:

Number of computer books I purchase in a year: ❑ 1 [12]   ❑ 2-5 [13]   ❑ 6-10 [14]   ❑ More than 10 [15]

I would characterize my computer skills as: ❑ Beginner [16]   ❑ Intermediate [17]   ❑ Advanced [18]   ❑ Professional [19]

I use ❑ DOS [20]   ❑ Windows [21]   ❑ OS/2 [22]   ❑ Unix [23]   ❑ Macintosh [24]   ❑ Other: [25]_____
(please specify)

I would be interested in new books on the following subjects:
(please check all that apply, and use the spaces provided to identify specific software)

❑ Word processing: [26]

❑ Data bases: [28]

❑ File Utilities: [30]

❑ Networking: [32]

❑ Other: [34]

❑ Spreadsheets: [27]

❑ Desktop publishing: [29]

❑ Money management: [31]

❑ Programming languages: [33]

I use a PC at (please check all that apply): ❑ home [35]   ❑ work [36]   ❑ school [37]   ❑ other: [38] _____

The disks I prefer to use are ❑ 5.25 [39]   ❑ 3.5 [40]   ❑ other: [41]_____

I have a CD ROM: ❑ yes [42]   ❑ no [43]

I plan to buy or upgrade computer hardware this year: ❑ yes [44]   ❑ no [45]

I plan to buy or upgrade computer software this year: ❑ yes [46]   ❑ no [47]

Name: _____ Business title: [48] _____ Type of Business: [49] _____

Address (❑ home [50] ❑ work [51]/Company name: _____)

Street/Suite# _____

City [52]/State [53]/Zipcode [54]: _____ Country [55] _____

❑ **I liked this book!** You may quote me by name in future
IDG Books Worldwide promotional materials.

My daytime phone number is _____

IDG BOOKS

THE WORLD OF COMPUTER KNOWLEDGE

☐ **YES!**

Please keep me informed about IDG's World of Computer Knowledge.
Send me the latest IDG Books catalog.